REGULATING ENTERPRISE

Regulating Enterprise
Law and Business Organisations in the UK

Edited by
DAVID MILMAN
Herbert Smith Professor of Corporate and Commercial Law,
University of Manchester

·HART·
PUBLISHING
OXFORD AND PORTLAND, OREGON
1999

Hart Publishing
Oxford
UK

Published in the United States by
Hart Publishing c/o
International Specialized Book Services
5804 NE Hassalo Street
Portland, Oregon
97213-3644
USA

Distributed in Australia and New Zealand by
Federation Press Pty Ltd
PO Box 45
Annandale, NSW 2038
Australia

Distributed in the Netherlands, Belgium and Luxembourg by
Intersentia, Churchillaan 108
B2900 Schoten
Antwerpen
Belgium

Hart Publishing Ltd is a specialist legal publisher based in Oxford, England.
To order further copies of this book or to request a list of other
publications please write to:

Hart Publishing Ltd, 19 Whitehouse Road, Oxford, OX1 4PA
Telephone: +44 (0)1865 434459 or Fax: +44 (0)1865 794882
e-mail: mail@hartpub.co.uk

British Library Cataloguing in Publication Data
Data Available
ISBN 1 901362 56–6

Typeset by Hope Services (Abingdon) Ltd.
Printed in Great Britain on acid-free paper

Contents

Preface

This collection of essays seeks to analyse the diversity of regulatory structures available for the pursuit of business enterprise in the UK. There is a tendency to think solely in terms of the partnership and limited company as being the only options for collaborative business operations. Without wishing to deny the importance of these well known options the contributors illustrate that there are other possibilities which are both worthy of academic study and relevant in the practice of general commerce and in more specific spheres of commercial activity.

One aim of this work is to attempt to identify common themes in business regulation and to examine how political and economic influences have impacted upon the law governing individual enterprise systems. The current legal structures are placed in their appropriate historical context and the commentators seek to offer expert insights into likely future developments. As we approach the new millennium there is a feeling that significant changes may be on the horizon which may transform the regulatory topography of business enterprise law in the century to come.

I am grateful to the contributors for their co-operation in this venture. The technical assistance available from Hart Publishing has also been greatly appreciated.

The law is stated as at 31 July 1998.

DAVID MILMAN,
Herbert Smith Professor of Corporate and Commercial Law,
University of Manchester.

List of Contributors

Anu Arora is a Professor of Law at the University of Liverpool. She has written widely in the field of Banking Law and Regulation. Her other works include *Practical Banking* and *Building Society Law; Cases and Materials in Banking Law;* and *Electronic Banking and the Law*.

Janet Dine is a Professor of Law at Essex University and Senior Visiting Fellow at the Institute of Advanced Legal Studies, London University. She has interests in Company Law, Criminal Law, Discrimination Law and Economic, Social and Cultural Human Rights. Underlying theories of regulation in these fields are a particular focus of her work.

Cosmo Graham was the H K Bevan Professor of Law at the University of Hull from 1993–1999. From August 1999 he has been Professor of Law at the University of Leicester. He is the co-editor of *Utilities Law Review*, Director of the Centre for Utility Consumer Law and has written widely in the area of Utility Law and Regulation.

Andrew Griffiths MA (Oxon) qualified as a Solicitor and worked in commercial practice in London and Bristol. He lectures in Law at the University of Manchester. Teaching and research interests include Company Law and Corporate Governance. He has published widely in this area.

Michael Lower, LL.B., M.Phil., Solicitor, is Senior Lecturer in Law, Liverpool John Moores University. His principle teaching and research interests are in the areas of company law and UK and EC competition law with particular empasis on the legal issues arising out of joint ventures.

Andrew McGee, Barrister, is Professor of Business Law and Director of the Centre for Business Law and Practice, Leeds University. He is specialist in Insurance Law, Company Law, Limitation of Actions and Business Regulation and is author of *Limitation Periods* (3rd ed., 1998), *The Law and Practice of Life Assurance Contracts* (1995), *The Business of Company Law* (1995), and *Share Capital* (1999).

David Milman, LL.B., Ph.D., F.R.S.A., is Herbert Smith Professor of Corporate and Commercial Law at the University of Manchester. Formerly Director of the Centre for Law and Business, and Dean of the Faculty of Law 1995–1997, he has written extensively on Partnership Law, Company Law and Insolvency Law.

Terence Prime has been a Professor of Law at the University of East Anglia since 1995. He qualified as a Solicitor, and lectured on Company Law for many years at the University of Liverpool. He is a specialist on Private Companies, Partnerships and Joint Ventures.

Christopher A. Riley lectures in Company Law and Corporate Governance at Newcastle Law School, and is co-director of its Centre for Corporate Governance and Financial Market Regulation. He previously practised as a solicitor in a commercial practice, and has written widely on Company Law.

Ian Snaith, B.A., M.A., F.S.A.L.S., Solicitor, is Senior Lecturer and Ironsides Fellow in Law at Leicester University. He is the author of the *Handbook of Industrial and Provident Society Law* (1993 with updates), published by Holyoake Books, Manchester. He has published extensively in Co-operative Law, Company Law, and Insolvency, and is a consultant with Cobbetts Solicitors, Mancheser, and legal advisor to the United Kingdom Co-operative Council.

Francis Tansinda, LL.B (Hons), Maitrise en Droit (Yaounde); LL.M (International Business Law), Ph.D (The University of Manchester), is a Senior Lecturer in the Law School at theManchester Metropolitan University. He writes and supervises postgraduate students on Company Law in general but his main research area is the regulation of overseas companies and foreign investors. He is presently working on a paper on the effects of non-compliance with regulation formalities by oversea companies.

John Vaughan began his career in the building society industry and has undertaken research in this area and other aspects of the financial services sector. He is currently MBA Director at Liverpool Business School, Liverpool John Moores University where he also teaches Finance.

Table of Cases

Table of Statutes

Table of Statutory Instruments

Table of EC Legislation

Table of International Legislation

1

Regulation of Business Organisations: into the Millennium

DAVID MILMAN

PRELIMINARY OBSERVATIONS

It is a mark of a developed economy and legal system that entrepreneurs are afforded a range[1] of options with regard to the organisational vehicles available for business activity. English law typifies this truism.

The aim of this collection of essays is to plot the emergence of such organisational structures and to evaluate the manner in which they are regulated. The contributors are all expertly qualified to comment upon their chosen topic. It is felt that it is an opportune time to conduct such a review; a new government in office and the approach of the millennium combine to make this a timely exercise.[2] It would be difficult to consider every possible variant available for the pursuit of business; some organisations are therefore not covered in any depth. Thus the sole tradership, although still a popular choice for small businesses,[3] will not detain us for long because it is a misnomer to describe it as an "organisation".[4] We will also not consider commercial structures which are designed solely for investment purposes, rather than for the more active pursuit of a trade, business or profession.[5] Unit trusts[6] and their European successor, the

---

[1] An excess of options may involve social cost in delaying the establishment of businesses, whilst options are evaluated: see Chesterman, *Small Businesses* (2nd edn., London, Sweet & Maxwell, 1982), at 261.

[2] An indication of the fact that now is the time for a rethink of business organisations law is provided by the DTI announcement of a fundamental review of company law: see *Modern Company Law for a Competitive Economy* (DTI, Mar. 1998). This review, which will lead to a White Paper in 2001, will not, however, cover organisations other than companies: see p. 17.

[3] The Bolton Committee in 1971 (Cmnd. 4811, HMSO, London, 1971) suggested that some 10% of small firms in the manufacturing sector (i.e. businesses employing fewer than 200 persons) were sole traderships—see Table 2.I. The comparable figure for the non-manufacturing sector was 45.8% (see Table II in the Bolton Report).

[4] The concept of organisation implies the existence of a multiplicity of stakeholders with rules being set down to regulate respective rights and liabilities.

[5] In *Smith* v. *Anderson* (1880) 15 Ch. D 247 the CA held that an investment trust was not carrying on a business, therefore it did not have to register a company if it had more than 20 members.

[6] Unit trusts first made their appearance in the UK in the 1930s. See Vaughan, *The Regulation of Unit Trusts* (Lloyds of London Press, 1990) and Sin, *The Legal Nature of the Unit Trust* (Oxford University Press, 1997)

Open Ended Investment Company (OEIC),[7] fall within this excluded genre. Organisational systems that are regarded as illegal, such as unlawful lotteries,[8] will not be covered by this study. Finally, it should be emphasised that we are intending to review only those structures capable of being subjected to legal analysis. Amorphous business concepts, such as the syndicate, which cannot be legally defined, are outside the scope of this study.

If we can extend the metaphor coined by Roberta Romano,[9] business organisations law should be viewed as a *product* on offer to potential customers (i.e. the business comunity). One question we must resolve is whether that product in UK law is of satisfactory standard to meet the needs of that market.

The emergence of business forms in the UK can be explained by reference to various factors. Two of these stand out:

1. *Deliberate facilitation by legislature.* By "legislature" here we include supranational law making institutions (e.g. the EC Council) so as to encompass structures established at international level. The EEIG (European Economic Interest Group) affords a useful example of this scenario.[10] This structure was derived originally from the French GIE (introduced in France in 1967) and given a European-wide status by the EEIG Regulation.[11] It was introduced into English law in 1989 by the EEIG Regulations[12] which sought to implement the aforementioned European measure. Essentially an EEIG is a parasitic structure designed to facilitate subsidiary activities, like marketing and research/development. There is no limited liability associated with this structure, though the nature of its business operations means that this is not a major disadvantage. Conversely, there is no minimum capital requirement. However the size of an EEIG is limited by virtue of an upper limit of 500 employees being specified. The EEIG has a limited impact on the pattern of business organisations in this country. Official figures for 1996–7 show that there were a total of 116 registered here.[13] This category of European-wide business

---

[7] See the Open-Ended Investment Companies (Investment Companies with Variable Capital) Regulations 1996 (SI 1996/2827).

[8] See the Lotteries and Amusements Act 1976. For recent discussion of the issue of illegal lotteries, see *Re Senator Hanseatische Verwaltungsgesellschaft mbH* [1997] 1 WLR 515 and *Re Vanilla Accumulation Ltd, The Times*, 24 Feb. 1998. There is also the related problem of pyramid schemes—see the Trading Schemes Act 1996 and the background discussion by Sarker in (1995) 16 *Co. Law* 278. For criticism of this legislation, and its potential costs for legitimate businesses, see Rice in *Financial Times*, 29 Apr. 1997.

[9] This theory was expounded by Romano in her articles in (1985) 1 *J of Law, Economics and Organisations* 225 and in (1989) 89 *Columbia Law Rev.* 1599.

[10] Another illustration is afforded by the Single Member Private Company which was transported to these shores (to little or no effect) by the Private Company Single Member Regulations (SI 1992/1699)), which implemented the 12th Company Law Harmonisation Dir. (Council Dir. 89/667). See Edwards (1998) 19 *Co. Law* 211.

[11] EC Reg. 2137/85. For general discussion, see Israel (1988) 9 *Co. Law* 14.

[12] SI 1989/638.

[13] *Companies in 1996–97* (HMSO, London), 42.

organisation is likely to expand in the future, with the European company being a possibility.[14]

2. *Organic development through evolving business practice.* This category includes the importation of foreign business structures through imitation or as the necessary result of the conduct of transnational commerce. Local commercial innovations also fall under this heading.

Any attempt to rationalise the development of business organisations in the UK must first concede that they have evolved in a piecemeal fashion. At no time in our history has there been a concerted attempt by the policymakers to survey what is on offer. This lack of an overview is a serious failing. New organisational structures have been introduced with only cursory consideration given to the overall perspective. The availability of a new medium may seriously affect the viability of an existing structure, yet all too often this consequence is ignored. The arrival of the private company at the same time as the limited partnership did much to destroy the *raison d'être* of the latter. Where the new entity is the product of organic development, this may be regarded as part of a process of natural evolution, but more often than not the situation has arisen because policymakers have failed to research fully the implications of their actions.

REGULATORY REGIMES: GENERAL PRINCIPLES

Before mapping out our topography of UK business forms, some comment about regulatory principles in general will prove helpful.[15]

The degree to which business organisations should be regulated is a sophisticated issue. All jurisdictions regulate business structures, though the form and degree of that regulation do vary. That pattern of regulation may change over the passage of time. During certain periods the role of the regulators may seem to be a containing one. On other occasions regulation may be introduced to assist business organisations. We have witnessed a good example of this latter phenomenon in recent years with the adoption, on a global basis, of corporate rescue procedures designed to protect businesses from the pressing demands of their creditors, by offering a moratorium on full and scheduled repayment.[16]

---

[14] For a review of the European company and prospects for its introduction, see Dine (1990) 11 *Co. Law*, 208 and Whelan (1992) 29 CML Rev 475.

[15] For general discussion see Ogus, *Regulation: Legal Form and Economic Theory* (Oxford University Press, 1994) and Black, *Rules and Regulators* (Oxford University Press, 1997). Regulation requires regulators and the actions of regulators in the commercial arena may be subject to judicial review—for analysis see Black, Muchlinski and Walker, *Commercial Regulation and Judicial Review* (Oxford, Hart Publishing, 1998).

[16] This corporate rescue bandwagon has become a global rescue phenomenon in recent years, as many jurisdictions search for the Holy Grail in the form of the optimum model. It seems as if Australia is now leading this particular quest with its highly successful voluntary administration mechanism: see Harmer (1998) 22 *Insolvency Lawyer* 18.

In terms of the purpose of regulation, two conflicting tensions have to be managed. A system of business organisation regulation must seek to facilitate managers/entrepreneurs because that is deemed to be in the economic interests of society in a capitalist system. Equally it must accept that the pursuit of profit requires the protection of interest groups such as passive investors, creditors, employees and the public at large. It is generally recognised that there is a need to offer facilities to business,[17] but equally there is a concern about the potential for abuse, and the variation in terms of weight attached to each of these considerations cannot be doubted. That variation may be due to a dominant political philosophy, prevailing economic conditions or the degree of economic advantage afforded to entrepreneurs by a particular business structure being made available.

The aim of the regulatory regime may differ. Some forms of regulation will focus primarily on achieving equity between the participators in the business. Other mechanisms will concentrate on the external conduct of the particular business medium, examining, for example, its effect on consumers and competitors. To cater for the latter aspect a system of licensing may be introduced to establish a degree of state control over certain sensitive business activities. To engage in business without proper authorisation could lead to prosecution and the business beng closed down. Even where no licensing system is in operation anti competitive activities may merit state intervention, particularly in cases where abusive monopolies are suspected. In the following essays both aspects of regulatory control will be considered where appropriate. A unifying factor in all effective legal systems of business organisation is the need to control risk. Risk may emanate from the danger of the participants incurring personal liability to external parties for business obligations, or from the possibility of misconduct by fellow participators in the same enterprise. Many legal rules governing business organisations can be traced back to this overriding factor. A mechanism protecting a participator from risk may expose another party to danger; the law therefore needs to maintain a balance that is both economically efficient but also just. Disputes will inevitably occur between policymakers as to where to pitch the balance in particular enterprise systems.

Looking at the UK enterprise organisations profile, political philosophy has entered the equation on occasions. Certainly there was much political debate in the nineteenth century as the protagonists for and against limited liability fought their corners. Subsequently, a consensus existed in the political mainstream for many years on the benefits of limited liability and the need to regulate its abuses. However, during the 1980s and early 1990s, a policy of *deregulation*, originating in the economic theories propounded by the Chicago school of economics, became the favoured approach. That policy manifested itself particularly in attempts to reduce the regulatory burden upon small busi-

---

[17] This idea of corporate law as a facilitator was best expounded by Ballantine in (1925) 14 *Calif. Law Rev.* 12. A more recent rendering is found in the piece by Procaccia in (1987) 35 *Am. J. of Compar. Law* 581.

nesses,[18] and especially in the area of *private* company accounts.[19] The company audit, one of the shibboleths of the dominant disclosure philosophy, was challenged.[20] Although some deregulation was possible in the realm of *public* companies (*viz.*, summary financial statements[21]) the room for manœuvre here was limited by the constraints of EC law, which traditionally was more inclined towards a pro-regulatory stance. The deregulatory approach reached its zenith in the Deregulation and Contracting Out Act 1994, which permitted Ministers to repeal primary legislation deemed to be counterproductive.[22] Another strand of this right wing political credo surfaced in the desire to remove many large and monopolistic enterprises from state control. The progeny of this privatisation process are themselves a distinct form of business organisation to be studied in this work.[23]

We will see shortly that the need for economic expansion induced policy-makers in the mid-nineteenth century to make available limited liability companies. Certainly the efforts of political figures like Gladstone, who, in his capacity as President of the Board of Trade, did much to promote limited liability, must be noted. More recently, the perceived economic significance of small businesses did much to encourage the deregulatory measures in the 1980s. Clearly, where a business organisation allows participators to engage in commerce with a degree of immunity from the consequences of their mistakes, the state needs to be more alert. There is little need to impose regulatory constraints upon partnerships, because at the end of the day, the partners are all fully responsible for the firm's debts. In the case of a limited liability company,[24] neither the shareholders nor the directors suffer this fate as a rule, and so restrictions must be imposed to protect the interests of creditors and the public at large. The classic example of this is protective strategy provided by the share capital maintenance rules, which place curbs on the freedom of incorporators to use the capital contributed by shareholders for purposes other than the shared business objects. Thus capital cannot be used to fund a dividend or pay directors' salaries. In modern revisions of companies legislation, this archaic concept

---

[18] See *Lifting the Burden* (Cmnd. 9571, HMSO, London, 1985) and *Building Businesses . . . not Barriers* (Cmnd. 9794, HMSO, London, 1986).

[19] In effect we have seen a move back towards the exempt status private company, some 20 years after the exemption was abolished.

[20] The audit was introduced by the Companies Act 1900. On the disclosure philosophy, see Sealy (1981) 2 *Co. Law* 51.

[21] Introduced by the Companies Act 1989, s. 15 (see now Companies Act 1985, s. 251) and subsequently extended by SI 1992/3075.

[22] The use of these so-called "Henry VIII clauses" is controversial in constitutional terms. Under the 1994 Act, a number of deregulatory measures have been introduced, including a simpler procedure for dissolving hopelessly insolvent companies.

[23] For reading on this privatisation process, see Graham and Prosser (1987) 50 *MLR* 16.

[24] The term "limited liability company" is, in many senses, a misnomer, but it is one that is too firmly embedded in the psyche of commentators to be casually disregarded. A company is fully liable for its debts but that liability can only be met to the extent that there are available assets. Shareholders' liability is limited to the extent that they must pay fully for their shares.

is often discarded in favour of controls based upon the more pragmatic yard-stick of solvency.

In terms of the methodology of regulation, the choice here is apparently between public and private regulation. Most forms of business organisation allow a combination of these regulatory mechanisms, though usually with one influence dominant. For example, the partnership is essentially regulated by private contract,[25] whereas the company is primarily a creature of statute.[26] The picture is further complicated by the role played by self-regulatory codes. Although these rarely operate to define business structures, they do play a vital role in defining the parameters of legitimate commerce for such organisations, and in determining authority to engage in certain forms of business.[27] The problem with these codes (such as the *Yellow Book* or the *Takeover Code*) is that they can be viewed as essentially derived from contract, in that they bind only those who choose to participate in certain business markets. Other codes have the additional characteristic of ultimately being authorised by Parliament or at least being recognised by the courts.[28] Well-established private self regulatory codes can eventually receive the imprimatur of legislative recognition.

The extent to which a particular business organisation is regulated may vary according to its evolutionary progress. Some forms of business organisation are the product of conscious regulation and hence are heavily regulated *ab initio*. Others, and here we are talking about organisations based in contract, the regulation may develop in a more gradual way as the courts are left to grapple with issues not covered by the original contract. The legislature may also step in to control certain aspects of the business operation.

A general issue to be addressed in this collection of papers is the relationship between regulatory/economic theories and resulting legal frameworks for business organisations. Janet Dine focuses attention upon this particular matter in the context of companies regulation in our concluding Chapter 13.

PARTNERSHIPS

Historically, the partnership is the first of the modern business structures to emerge in English law. It is a form of business organisation that is well known in many jurisdictions and societies; in Roman law it operated under the name *societas*.[29] Partnership has been a feature of the UK business scene at least since the thirteenth century where it was familiar to merchants. Italian mercantile concepts were adopted from the sixteenth century onwards, but it was in the

---

[25] *Moss* v. *Elphick* [1910] 1 KB 846.

[26] *British Eagle* v. *Air France* [1975] 1 WLR 758.

[27] Financial Services Act 1986, s. 61.

[28] See, e.g., *R.* v. *Takeover Panel, ex parte Datafin plc* [1987] 2 WLR 699 where the *Takeover Code* received formal judicial recognition.

[29] For the characteristics of the *societas*, see Bordowski, A., *Textbook on Roman Law* (Blackstone Press, 1994), 272–276.

eighteenth century that what are now familiar principles began to feature in cases coming before the courts. The first recorded treatise on the English law of partnership was apparently produced in 1794. However, it was in the nineteenth century that the present regime took shape. Partnership is a relatively simple organisational structure based upon a natural need to combine for mutual advantage. Initially the regulation of this relationship was left to the partners themselves, and over the course of years a set of optimum partnership principles were developed by draftsmen and the courts. So, for example, the rules governing the fiduciary status of partners were prescribed.[30] These framework rules[31] were then codified by Parliament in the celebrated Partnership Act 1890, one of the more successful pieces of domestic commercial legislation. The aim of this legislation was to provide a basic structure for partnership which would operate in default of express provision between the partners. It did not seek to impose a straitjacket, but rather a modicum of certainty which would be of use in the event of disputes. Contracting out was therefore possible.[32]

At present it is estimated that there are at least 600,000 partnerships in existence in the UK.[33] The fact that there is no requirement to record the entry into partnership at a public register (one of the attractions of this model[34]) makes statistical assessment more difficult. The Partnership Act 1890 has been a successful experiment requiring little in the way of modification. Regulatory developments since 1890 have been minimal. There was an attempt, in the early part of this century, to introduce a variant, the limited partnership, which was based upon the old established concept of *commenda* which operated in this country in the Middle Ages, but this offering did not prove popular in the UK,[35] particularly when compared with the attractions of the private limited company, which came on the scene at the same time. The main problem with the Limited Partnership Act 1907 was the fact that the limited partners were prohibited from undertaking any active role in the venture; by definition they were forced to remain as dormant partners. The resulting unpopularity of the limited partnership in English law is in marked contrast to its adoption in Europe and the USA. There are 2,786 limited partnerships[36] registered at the Companies Registry.

[30] For key decisions on the fiduciary relationship subsisting within a partnership, see *Baird's Case* (1870) LR 5 Ch. App. 725; *Dean* v. *MacDowell* (1878) 8 Ch. D 345.

[31] Prior to the 1890 Act, there was legislation in 1865 (Bovill's Act), which sought unsuccessfully to facilitate the identification of partnerships.

[32] *Moss* v. *Elphick*, n. 25 above.

[33] See Pettet (1995) 48 *CLP* 125 at 132. A survey carried out for the Bolton Committee in 1971, n. 3 above, estimated that partnerships made up some 6.2% of small firms involved in manufacturing (i.e. businesses having fewer than 200 employees)—see Table 2.I in the Bolton Report. The estimate for the non-manufacturing sector was 20.3%—see Table 2.II in the Bolton Report.

[34] The downside of this informality is seen when one considers the problem of the "accidental" partnership: see Milman (1983) 4 Co. *Law* 199.

[35] For comment, see Pettet, n. 33 above, at 129. See Hahlo [1982] *Jurid. Review* 139 at 141 for an illuminating acount of the differences between the unlimited partnership (*societas*) and the limited counterpart (*commenda*). The commenda had been introduced into Ireland by statute in 1781.

[36] *Companies in 1996–97*, n. 13 above, 42.

One disadvantage with the standard partnership structure, the upper limit of 20 partners, was progressively waived over the next 100 years for most professional partnerships.[37] This capping of membership was never a problem for non-professional trading partnerships, which effectively became unwieldy once the number of partners grew beyond double figures. In terms of the "customers" using this form of business structure, it has to be conceded that partnership owes its continued popularity to professional culture, where incorporation has traditionally been frowned upon as a vehicle for chancers and not reputable professionals regulated by strict ethical codes.[38] It may also be the case that partnership has special appeal to the ethnic minority business community, an increasingly important enterprise constituency where the closely-held family business thrives.

Attempts have been made in the past to remodel partnership law. As far back as 1837, the Bellenden Ker Report on the Law of Partnerships floated the idea of accompanying limited liability.[39] More recently, in 1981, Gower produced a draft for an incorporated partnership[40] that would confer a modified form of limited liability on its members. Under this model, the maximum membership was specified at ten, and the partnership had to be registered. Neither of these proposals, separated by 150 years of commercial history, attracted legislative support, and the basic format for partnership has remained in the doldrums.

The position today is that partnership law in the UK is relatively unsophisticated, having developed little during the past century. It is therefore appropriate that the current system of partnership law in the UK is under review by the Law Commission.[41] This review has been triggered by a complex chain of events. Essentially, a critical constituency within the profession (ie, the accountants) has become dissatisfied with the key feature of partnership law, namely, joint and several liability for partnership debts (Partnership Act 1890, section 9). When one considers the size of awards (and settlements) in professional negligence claims that have had to be met by accountants in the past decade, their concern is understandable.[42] Insurance against such liability is increasingly difficult to obtain because of the expense of the premiums. As a result of these economic pressures, accountants have begun to agitate for reform. Their representatives have suggested either the abolition of the joint and

---

[37] The limit is contained in s. 716 of the Companies Act 1985, but is waived by the Unrestricted Size Regulations, the latest addition to which is found in the No. 11 Regulations (SI 1996/262). A similar rule with concessions is applied to limited partnerships.

[38] Solicitors used to be denied the opportunity to incorporate, but see now Administration of Justice Act 1985, s. 9, and the Solicitors Incorporated Practices Order 1991 (SI 1991/2684).

[39] (1837) 530 Parliamentary Papers XLIV 339.

[40] *A New Form of Incorporation for Small Firms* (Cmnd. 8121, HMSO, London, 1981).

[41] The review was announced in Feb. 1997. The terms of reference for this review were announced in November 1997. For current progress see Law Commission *32nd Annual Report* (No. 250) (HMSO, London, 1997), paras. 3.6 and 3.7.

[42] For an example of litigation causing these concerns, see *ADT* v. *BDO Binder Hamlyn* [1996] BCC 808 (subsequently settled).

several liability rule[43] (or perhaps the introduction of a cap on liability), or the introduction of a modified limited liability partnership form. This latter option has been further highlighted with the advent of such a structure in Jersey, and other jurisdictions, which has led some of the major firms of accountants to threaten to "go offshore".[44] In return, the UK revenue authorities have pointed out that this may have negative tax consequences for the firms concerned. An uneasy peace has settled on this debate whilst the Law Commission reviews the matter. Andrew Griffiths draws together these issues in his review in Chapter 2.

THE CORPORATE OPTION

The most radical addition to the menu of available business organisations came with the introduction of the freely available limited liability company in the mid nineteenth century. Prior to that date, the conduct of business through companies was obstructed. The paranoia generated by the South Sea Bubble Affair, which manifested itself in the so-called Bubble Act of 1720[45] had not subsided, even by the dawn of the nineteenth century. Companies were only available for those entrepreneurs who were fortunate enough to secure a Royal Charter, which started to be used from the sixteenth century onwards.[46] Indeed, the grant of a charter did not guarantee the facility of limited liability; that feature had to be implicitly incorporated, as the court made clear in *Salmon* v. *Hamborough*[47] in 1671. On the other hand, a charter carried commercial prestige and offered other technical benefits.[48] It is estimated that there are still some 751 chartered companies operating in the jurisdiction.[49] Another option was to secure the passage of a Private Act of Parliament,[50] though this could be an expensive process.

---

[43] In 1996 the Law Commission issued a Consultative Document reviewing this subject: see A. Griffiths, Ch. 2, this vol., for discussion.

[44] For comment, see *Financial Times*, 26 Sept. 1996: *Financial Times*, 4 Mar. 1997; [1997] *Simon's Tax Intelligence* 701.

[45] The so-called Bubble Act (6 Geo I c.18). For a review of the circumstances leading up to the collapse of the bubble companies, see Gower (1952) 68 *LQR* 214. It is a matter of considerable dispute whether the Bubble Act was the result or the cause of the bubble crash. The chronology seems to favour the latter view: see Patterson and Reiffen (1990) 50 *Jo. of Econ. Hist.* 163 where it is argued that the Bubble Act had more to do with the Crown seeking to reassert its monopoly rights over the creation of new corporations by the issue of profit generating charters than with any desire to protect investors at large. There were very few prosecutions under the Bubble Act—for rare examples, see *R.* v. *Cawood* (1724) 2 Lord Raym. 1361 and *R.* v. *Dodd* (1808) 9 East 516. In an article in (1993) 14 *Jo. of Leg. Hist.* 39 Santuari indicates (at 41) that although the Bubble Act remained on the statute book in the early 19th century there was little judicial relish for prosecutions thereunder.

[46] Early examples include the Russia Company (1555) and the East India Company (1600).

[47] (1671) 1 Ch. Cas. 204.

[48] It seems that chartered corporations were not subject to the *ultra vires* rule which used to restrict the business activities of registered companies: *Ashbury Carriage Co* v. *Riche* (1875) 7 HL 653, but this restrictive rule has largely been removed by the Companies Act 1989, s. 108 (introducing a new s. 35 into the Companies Act 1985).

[49] *Companies in 1996–97*, n. 13 above, 42.

[50] See *Palmer's Company Law* (25th edn., Sweet & Maxwell) para. 1.219.

Further advances were made with the advent of statutory companies, which were facilitated by general legislation, this latter option being widely used by railway and canal companies.[51] For the more mundane business, attempts were made to develop the so-called deed of settlement company, though the resulting organisation was far from ideal and prone to legal uncertainty.[52]

The policymakers, by the early 1800s, recognised that this restrictive approach was unsuited to satisfy the needs of capitalist expansion fuelled by the Industrial Revolution. The Bubble Act was repealed in 1825,[53] and the grant of charters (conferring limited liability) was facilitated by the Trading Companies Act 1837 (which enabled a charter to be granted by letters patent). Subsequently, in 1844, Parliament, with the passage of the Companies Regulation and Registration Act, decided to permit companies to be formed by the relatively simple process of registration. More radically, in 1855, the prize economic facility of limited liability was extended to such businesses, provided there were at least 25 shareholders involved.[54] Shareholders would, in future, be able to cap their liability for business debts by restricting their exposure to the maximum of their capital contributions. The years after 1844 saw the numbers of registered companies grow at a fast (but not consistent) rate.[55]

The primary regulatory structure for such businesses became the Companies Act (a nomenclature established by the celebrated 1862 Act), though this was supplemented by the development of judicial rules (e.g. the *ultra vires* rule[56] and the share capital maintenance doctrine,[57] which, for the most part, were restrictive and betrayed a concern with potential abuse of limited liability. By the end of the century these concerns had abated, and the leading judges in the land "signed up" to this new business organisation in the celebrated *Salomon* deci-

---

[51] Companies Clauses Consolidation Act 1845, which laid down standard terms for statutory companies.

[52] It was doubtful whether limited liability was available to such firms.

[53] Bubble Repeal Act 1825 (6 Geo IV c.91).

[54] Limited Liability Act 1855. For contemporary criticism, see (1854) 24 *Law Times*. 142. This curious requirement was dropped by the Joint Stock Companies Act 1856 in favour of a minimum membership of 7. This Act also removed the cumbersome provisional registration procedures in favour of a single registration process. An excellent review of the arrival of limited liability in England is provided by Lobban in (1996) 25 *Anglo Am. L Rev*. 397 where the relative positions in England and France are compared. Lobban's more general article on 19th century developments in (1996) 112 *LQR* 287 is also to be commended. See also the fine article by Ireland in (1984) 12 *Int Jo. of the Socio. of Law* 239. For the debate in England amongst politicians and reformers in the period immediately before 1855 see Bryer (1997) 50 *Econ. Hist. Rev*. 37. It is significant to note that limited liability was accepted by the key American states much earlier in the 19th century, with New York admitting it as early as 1811—a convincing explanation for this is to be found in Forbes (1986) 2 *Jo. of Law, Econ. and Orgs*. 163.

[55] For economic reviews of this development in capitalism and relevant data see Todd (1932) 4 *Econ. Hist. Rev*. 46; Shannon (1932) 4 *Econ. Hist. Rev*. 290. For similar research on the growth of larger companies during the latter part of the 19th century and early 20th century see Payne (1967) 20 *Econ. Hist. Rev*. 519.

[56] *Ashbury Carriage Co v. Riche*, n. 48 above.

[57] *Trevor v. Whitworth* (1887) 12 App. Cas. 409.

sion.[58] This judicial support was timely, in that companies with limited liability were seen as increasingly attractive in the late Victorian and Edwardian period, which saw many businesses fail in an economic recession which only abated with the outbreak of World War I.

This corporate option has always suffered from the disadvantage that it was essentially one-dimensional, in the sense of containing a corpus of regulation made applicable to all companies irrespective of size. Although there is evidence[59] that the concept of the closely held private company was familiar to lawyers by the late nineteenth century it was not until the enactment of section 37 of the Companies Act 1907 that private companies formally emerged. Once again formal regulation is seen to lag behind events on the ground. In the odyssey leading to the parting of the ways, the watershed event was the introduction, in 1907, of the disclosure requirement in the form of public filing of accounts.[60] Originally, this was applicable only to public companies, but this was later extended to those private companies which did not qualify as "exempt".[61] The Jenkins Committee[62] was critical of this alleviation of the disclosure requirement and recommended the abolition of the category of exempt private companies. This recommendation was carried into effect by section 2 of the Companies Act 1967. One other significant change in the law of private companies was the abolition of the maximum number of shareholders (fixed at 50) in 1980.[63]

For the first 100 years after 1855, the dominant trend in companies legislation was one of increased regulation. This is true of the Companies Acts of 1907, 1928 and 1947, and the consolidating legislation that followed in their wake (in 1908, 1929 and 1948). Although the courts may have become more comfortable with the notion of the limited liability company, the policymakers were ever alert to plug loopholes. So we had new curbs on financial assistance in share purchases[64] and on fraudulent trading[65] introduced in 1926. Very often there was an element of "shutting the stable door" about these changes, particularly as scant regard was had to their incremental effect. Little thought was given to

---

[58] [1897] AC 22. Lord Cooke in *Turning Points of the Common Law* (Sweet & Maxwell, 1997) would categorise this case as one of 4 critical common law authorities worthy of inclusion within the rubric of his Hamlyn series of lectures. Few would disagree with this assessment. For the historical context underpinning the *Salomon* ruling see Ireland, above n. 54, and (1996) 17 *Jo. of Leg. Hist.* 41 where the creeping recognition of the concept of separate personality in a number of 19th century cases is analysed.

[59] See e.g. Cotton LJ in *Re British Seamless Paper Box Co Ltd* (1881) 17 Ch. D 467 at 479.

[60] Companies Act 1907, s. 21. For the concessions for private companies see s. 21.

[61] Companies Act 1948, s. 129 (exempt private companies need not have accounts audited). The Jenkins Committee (Cmnd. 1749, HMSO, London, 1962) para 57 estimated that some 70% of private companies were claiming exempt status.

[62] *Ibid.*, para. 63.

[63] Companies Act 1980, s. 88(2) and Sched. 4.

[64] This extension of the common law capital maintenance concept was introduced in 1929 as a result of the recommendations of the Greene Committee (Cmd. 2657, HMSO, London, 1926), para. 30.

[65] Companies Act 1929, also proposed by the Greene Committee, *ibid.*

taking a broad overview of the subject; this was last undertaken by the Jenkins Committee in 1962[66]! In marketing jargon, the product was never "repackaged".

The pattern of companies regulation changed substantially as a result of the entry of the UK into the Common Market in 1972. From that date onwards, European considerations became key factors behind the reform of company law, as the harmonisation programme, based upon Article 54 of the Treaty, kicked in.[67] Indeed, the legislation enacting the EEC Treaty sought to implement the First Company Law Harmonisation Directive, in so far as it dealt with the rules on company contracts.[68] The focus of the European harmonisation policy fixed upon *public* companies, as is apparent from the critical Second Directive on company capital.[69] In implementing this Directive by section 1 of the 1980 Companies Act, Parliament introduced a formal distinction between private companies ("Ltd") and public companies ("plc"). Since that date, the two regulatory regimes have moved further apart, and there are major differences of emphasis in many substantive areas of law, differences reflected both in the minutiae of the legislation and in the judicial application of common provisions. Thus we now have formally embedded the concept of the quasi partnership,[70] a sub-species of the private company genus. If the proposals of the Law Commission[71] come to fruition, the divergence which already exists in the area of shareholder remedies will be formalised. Contemporary debates on the future of reform also reinforce that divergence; the controversy over corporate governance is essentially a matter of interest solely in the context of public companies, where the separation of ownership and control of a company is more pronounced. We have now reached the stage where separate legislation for these two different corporate models would be welcome. This is considered apposite by many commentators, when one considers that nearly 99 per cent of all limited companies are classified as private. Other jurisdictions have recognised this dichotomy in formal regulatory regimes.[72] Terry Prime will consider the regulation of private companies in Chapter 3, whilst the treatment of public companies will be covered by Chris Riley in Chapter 4.

---

[66]   Cmnd. 1749, n. 61 above.

[67]   For a review of the harmonisation programme, see Dine (1989) 14 *ELR* 322; F. Jacobs (1992) 11 *Co. Law* 4; and Andenas (1994) 15 *Co. Law* 121.

[68]   European Communities Act 1972, s. 9.

[69]   Dir. 72/91/EEC.

[70]   The leading authority is *Ebrahimi* v. *Westbourne Galleries* [1973] AC 360.

[71]   Report No. 246, *Shareholder Remedies* (Cm 3769, HMSO, London, 1997).

[72]   Thus in Germany there are separate codes for the AG (public company) and the GmbH (private company). In 1994 a formal division was introduced in South Africa with the advent of close corporations, which quickly took over the clientele of private companies: Close Corporations Act 1994. For discussion, see Henning in Patfield (ed.), *Perspectives on Company Law: 1* (Kluwer, 1995), ch. 10 and Henning in (1998) 9 *Amicus Curiae* 30.

VARIANTS ON THE CORPORATE THEME

This collection of essays will also consider peculiar forms of business structure which have emerged from the basic corporate model. We will not consider charitable companies, for the simple reason that such organisations, which usually adopt the form of companies limited by guarantee (a category introduced in 1862), are not primarily designed for the pursuit of commerce.[73]

In terms of economic significance, the group structure is of major importance. However, as far as regulation is concerned, it attracts little attention. It has been the subject of incidental statutory recognition, but at least in this jurisdiction it has not been the target of express prohibition.[74] One reason for this regulatory blind spot is the fact that the group is a more recent variant of the basic corporate structure, having emerged in the UK in the mid part of the twentieth century. There is also the fact that orthodox company law denies the group a distinct identity by adhering to the orthodoxy that each constituent member is a separate entity in itself.[75] Departures have occurred from this policy of denial, most notably in the area of accounts.[76] The group conundrum will be evaluated in Chapter 10.

Companies operating in certain sensitive spheres of business have, for many years, been subject to more intense regulation. This genre is typified by banking[77] and insurance[78] companies. The regulation of banking businesses (largely contained in the Banking Act 1987, though with some revision by the Banking Act 1998) is reviewed by Anu Arora in Chapter 6. Andrew McGee will, in Chapter 7, review the issue of the legal framework of insurance business. This regulation is mainly founded in the Insurance Companies Act 1982 but, as with banking businesses, the regulatory hand of Europe is now the dominant influence.

Another type of company deserving of special attention is the privatised company formerly run as a state enterprise.[79] Such businesses have a colourful history, featuring bouts of nationalisation and privatisation. Although formally treated as public companies, idiosyncratic factors applicable to their regulation (such as the existence of substantial monopoly rights) do merit more detailed consideration. Cosmo Graham will undertake this study in Chapter 9.

---

[73] The Charities Act 1993 is a key regulatory mechanism here. For general background, see Rice (1964) 28 *Conv.* NS 214, Warburton [1984] *Conv.* 112, Luxton, *Palmer's In Company* (Mar. 1997).

[74] Groups based upon pure holding companies were prohibited in Japan for many years: see Ch. 10 below. This prohibitive approach has been relaxed in recent times.

[75] *Adams v. Cape Industries* [1990] 2 WLR 657.

[76] See Companies Act 1985, s. 227 and Sched. 4A.

[77] Thus the statutory audit for banking companies was introduced in 1879. It was not made mandatory for companies in general until 1900. More recently, this more draconian approach is typified by the fact that the statutory obligation for auditors to "blow the whistle" on their clients (see SI 1994/524) applies to banking companies but does not apply generally in the corporate sector.

[78] For discussion, see *Palmer's Company Law* n. 50 above, para. 1.242.

[79] For the legal problems associated with privatisation, see Ch. 9, this vol.

In an age of increased transnational commerce, it is essential to bear in mind that there are businesses operating in the UK which have been created in foreign jurisdictions and whose primary regulation (e.g. in terms of constitution and powers) is a matter for such jurisdictions.[80] English law has a proud record of granting recognition to such entities, and generally it is welcoming in its attitude towards foreign entrepreneurs.[81] Having said that, the UK, as a host jurisdiction, is naturally entitled to impose its own regulatory requirements.[82] The special rules on overseas companies (of which there are 6,080 registered[83]) are to be noted here. These obligations are mapped out in Part XXIII of the Companies Act 1985, and Francis Tansinda considers these in Chapter 12.

COMMUNITY-BASED BUSINESS ORGANISATIONS

A number of current business models owe their inspiration to initiatives undertaken at local level.

The regulation of building societies will also be covered in Chapter 5 of this text by John Vaughan. The origins of these lie, as their title suggests, in local community building finance schemes. They can be traced back to 1775, and first attracted the attention of the legislature in 1836.[84] Although, in recent times, they have evolved to become close cousins of banks, they have been subject to a distinct (and more restrictive) regulatory regime, most recently expressed in the Building Societies Act 1986. That structure has been loosened somewhat by the Building Societies Act 1997, which possesses a number of deregulatory features. In essence, the 1997 Act effects a significant change by putting the regulation of building societies almost on a par with the treatment of companies. Building societies can now undertake activities unless they are expressly prohibited from doing so; under the former regime, a restrictive policy of only permitting those activities which were expressly authorised was pursued. Nevertheless, the fact that building societies' regulation is still comparatively restrictive is borne out by the desire of leading building societies to convert to public companies, and thereby become subject to the Banking Act scheme of regulation.[85]

This category might also be deemed to include bodies such as credit unions, friendly societies, industrial and provident societies and co-operatives. The first legislation on industrial and provident societies appeared on the statute book in

---

[80] This is accepted under private international law.

[81] Xenophobia does occasionally surface. The best example is provided by the Registration of Business Names Act 1916, which was enacted to stop foreigners disguising their origins by use of a business name. The public register of business names was scrapped and replaced by a more informal system of disclosure, now found in the Business Names Act 1985.

[82] See *Re FH Lloyd Holdings plc* (1985) 1 BCC 99,402.

[83] *Companies in 1996–97*, n. 13 above, 41.

[84] Benefit Building Societies Act 1836(6 and 7 Will IV c. 32).

[85] The Abbey National was the first building society to pursue this route in the mid-1980s. Several others have followed, including the Halifax (in 1997), at that time the largest building society.

1852,[86] and latest statistics indicate that there are some 10,688 registered in this country.[87] Although these bodies are incorporated, they are not companies subject to the Companies Acts.[88] A number of interesting regulatory developments have occurred in this area in recent years, and the government is presently conducting a review of the regulatory structure.[89] Ian Snaith will cover these in Chapter 8.

ORGANIC BUSINESS STRUCTURES

It must not be assumed that business models are invariably the gift of the state and regulated by legislation. Many successful structures have developed through contract and business practice, and, as a result, have been the subject of little or no foundational regulation. It would be misleading to omit these from our account of business structures. A good example of this category is provided by the franchise agreement, an increasingly popular form of business organisation. It is estimated that some 568 franchise systems are in operation at present, encompassing no fewer than 29,100 franchised units, and the volume of business conducted through franchisees is calculated as being worth some £7 billion.[90] Under a franchise agreement, a franchisor permits a franchisee to use a well-known trade name and to benefit from the exploitation of its goodwill, on condition that strict standards are maintained and a percentage of the profits is repatriated to the franchisor. A statutory definition is now available.[91] These agreements, in modern times, appear to have originated out of North American business practices, but they have been part of the UK commercial scene for much longer in the form of tied public houses. The precise legal implications of such arrangements are unclear, particularly with regard to the critical issue of whether they create a partnership nexus between franchisor and franchisee.[92]

---

[86] Industrial and Provident Societies Act 1852—see Snaith (infra) Chapter 8.

[87] Companies in 1996–97, n. 13 above, 42.

[88] *Re Devon and Somerset Farmers Ltd* [1993] BCC 410.

[89] See [1998] 4 CL 81 for details.

[90] This estimate is made by NatWest Bank in a report for the British Franchise Association in 1998: see *The Times*, 24 Mar. 1998. For general treatment of this form of business organisation see Mendelsohn, *Franchising Law and Practice* (Sweet & Maxwell, 1995). For recent judicial discussion in the House of Lords of franchise agreements see *Williams* v. *Natural Life Health Foods* [1998] 1 WLR 880. This authority is also of interest for the strong judicial support offered by the Law Lords to the integrity of the small one man company by refusing to allow the privilege of limited liability to be undermined by the imposition of liability in tort on the controller for acts committed during the course of the business operations of the company .

[91] Restrictive Trade Practices (Non Notifiable Agreements)(Sale and Purchase, Share Subscription and Franchise Agreements) Order 1997 (SI 1997/2945), para. 2. In this particular context for background discussion see Singleton [1992] *Trading Law* 194.

[92] *Jirna* v. *Master Donut* (1973) 40 DLR (3d) 303. Another interesting but unresolved issue is whether the franchisor could be viewed as a shadow director of the franchisee if the later adopts a corporate form: see Yelland (1987) *Jo. of Franch. and Distrib. Law* 118. For a consideration of some of the other potential legal pitfalls with franchise agreements see Adams [1994] *JBL* 566 and the article in *The Times*, 16 June 1998. See generally Adams and Mendelsohn [1986] *JBL* 206.

Issues of competition regulation arise (particularly in the context of major franchise networks) and the enforceability of the various types of restrictive covenant often included in franchise agreements frequently comes before the courts.[93] Apart from discrete regulation at European level,[94] English law has until recently maintained a position of lofty indifference. In 1997, franchise agreements were specifically excluded from the notification obligations imposed by the Restrictive Trade Practices Act 1976 by SI 1997/2945.

The joint venture[95] might also be regarded as falling within this heading, and it is this form of organic structure that we intend to concentrate upon. This is a loose arrangement designed to permit co-operation between businesses with regard to a particular enterprise where a full merger is deemed not appropriate. They are often used for cross border collaborative business projects and may be embarked upon as a matter of necessity because of the demands of the host country in which the business is undertaken. The problem here is one of legal definition, as is clear from Chapter 11 by Michael Lower. Joint ventures may be structured along either partnership or corporate lines. Although the UK legislature refuses to accord formal recognition to joint ventures, the courts are increasingly affording them status by a willingness to develop discrete rules of business and organisational practice for them.[96] Recognition (and regulation) at the European Union level is more explicit, a fact reinforced by the extension of the 1989 Merger Regulation to joint ventures in 1998.[97]

HYBRID OPTIONS

It would be a mistake to view the aforementioned business structures as mutually exclusive. Combinations of models can be put to profitable use. Thus, two companies may decide to combine together in a partnership for a particular project, in other words, form a joint venture.[98] A group of companies may include a partnership.[99] A company may feature in a franchise agreement.

---

[93] See e.g. *Harrods* v. *Schwartz-Sackin* [1991] FSR 209 and *Dyno Rod plc* v. *Reeve* (1998, unreported decision of Neuberger J which is noted in [1998] 6 CL 74).

[94] As a result of the decision of the ECJ in *Pronuptia* [1986] 1 CMLR 414 franchise agreements were the beneficiaries of a Block Exemption Regulation, no. 4087/88, protecting them from challenge under Art. 85 of the EEC Treaty. As it happened the Pronuptia franchise format was eventually given specific clearance by the Commission under Art. 85: see [1989] 4 CMLR 355.

[95] For general analysis, see Herzfeld and Wilson, *Joint Ventures* (Jordan, 1996) and Prime, Gale and Scanlan, *The Law and Practice of Joint Ventures* (Butterworths, 1997). A more specific issue is addressed in Bean, *Fiduciary Obligations and Joint Ventures: the Collaborative Fiduciary Relationship* (Oxford University Press, 1995).

[96] See e.g. *Elliott* v. *Wheeldon* [1992] BCC 489; *Dawnay Day & Co* v. *D'Alphen*, *The Times*, 24 June 1997.

[97] See Reg. 1310/97 which amends Reg. 4064/89.

[98] The fact that a company can be a partner was confirmed in *Newstead* v. *Frost* [1980] 1 WLR 135.

[99] Companies Act 1989, s. 22 (Companies Act 1985, s. 259)—a partnership can be regarded as an undertaking for group purposes.

Notwithstanding the existence of these options English law may not appear as diverse as other systems. For example, in Australia, the trading trust is a major player. On the continent, the variants on the partnership theme are more exotic and the foundation can play a significant role on the periphery of commerce

FACTORS AFFECTING CHOICE

In many scenarios, there is no choice about which business structure to adopt. The decision may be imposed by the law,[100] or by another contracting party. Where options exist, the basic decision is between corporate and partnership models. The former has the attractions of corporate personality, perpetual succession,[101] limited liability, ease of securing finance[102] and other technical advantages.[103] whilst the partnership offers flexibility, security and privacy. Tax can often be the critical decision mover, though the trend in recent years has been towards fiscal neutrality. Other technical considerations, involving regulatory costs, may tilt the balance.

FUTURE DEVELOPMENTS

Drawing upon this preliminary review of the evolution of business organisations in the UK, one can point to certain future developments as likely. The situation is fluid. Relative popularity can change. Thus, the partnership was the preferred choice of many businesses in the first part of the nineteenth century, but it quickly waned once the limited liability company appeared on the scene. Changes in tax law can be pivotal in this respect. First, it is a good bet that changes will be made in partnership law to open up a wider variety of options, by allowing the partnership structure to continue to be used by professional partnerships, but without the growing risk of financial calamity. The trend in recent years is to extend to partnerships the attributes of a company,

---

[100] It should be noted here that an individual who has been disqualified as a company director for unfitness is free to engage in commerce as a sole trader.

[101] Although this is a potential advantage of a company, it has to be placed in perspective. If one takes into account all of the companies registered at the Companies Registry, the average life expectancy is 11.6 years! (Source: *Companies in 1996–97*, n. 13 above, 28).

[102] By converting a business to a company the floating charge device becomes available as security. This is not available to a partnership—for discussion of this curious dichotomy see Fitzpatrick [1971] *JBL* 18.

[103] The corporate option allows the entrepreneur to become an employee of the business, and so take advantage of employment protection rights: see *Lee* v. *Lees Air Farming Ltd* [1961] AC 12, and compare with *Ellis* v. *Ellis & Co* [1905] 1 KB 324. However, some courts are showing concern about the potential for abuse: see *Buchan* v. *Secretary of State for Employment* [1997] BCC 145, but compare the more orthodox view taken in *Fleming* v. *Secretary of State* [1997] IRLR 682 and *Bottrill* v. *Secretary of State for Industry* [1999] BCC 177.

and to make available to them regulatory regimes specifically designed for companies.[104]

As far as limited liability companies are concerned, their popularity seems assured. There are now over 1,091,900 limited companies registered in Great Britain, and the number of incorporations rose by 16 per cent in 1996–7.[105] Some limitation on access to limited liability may be on the agenda (for example, by placing further restrictions on rogue directors, or imposing a minimum capital requirement for private companies) but the basic concept is as attractive as ever, as attested to by the reaction to the Lloyds affair,[106] and the demands of the accountancy profession for protection from ruinous litigation.[107] The bifurcation between private and public companies will grow and may be formalised in separate statutory regimes. The present government is embarked upon a fundamental review of companies' regulation,[108] and when that review comes to fruition, significant changes to core regulation are likely.

The issue of group companies cannot be dodged for much longer. Increasingly, English law appears out of step here with trends in related jurisdictions, whether they be of common law background or of European pedigree. Groups are increasingly recognised in various statutes; the time has come to regulate them in a more coherent fashion.

Statutory recognition will increasingly become the norm for arrangements such as joint ventures and franchise agreements. New business structures will continue to emerge. It is important that the system permits such organic growth. Organisations which have sprung up in the past 20 years will attract more explicit statutory recognition.

These are merely preliminary observations. These issues deserve fuller consideration and that analysis will be undertaken in the essays that follow.

---

[104] See here the Insolvent Partnerships Order 1994 (SI 1994/2421).

[105] *Companies in 1996–97*, n. 13 above, 18.

[106] In 1993, the Lloyds Names voted to admit corporate members, thereby indicating that the idea of unlimited liability had passed its prime in this particular business sector. For discussion, see Pettet, n. 33, at 137 ff.

[107] See Griffiths, Ch. 2, this vol.

[108] See the DTI paper, *Modern Company Law for a Competitive Economy* (Mar. 1998) for an outline of this review (see fn 2 above). For comment see Dine (1998) 19 *Co. Law* 82. The second stage of this review process was manifested by the publication of a *Strategic Framework* in February 1999. Sadly this was too late to permit full consideration in the following essays. This *Strategic Framework* is a more substantial consultative document which considers broad policy issues and contains a valuable comparative analysis of common regulatory problems in companies legislation. Matters dealt with in the *Strategic Framework* include corporate governance and directors' responsibilities, the needs of small companies, enforcement strategies, substantive regulatory controls (e.g. on share capital), implications of technological development in information systems for companies regulation, financial reporting and international issues (including the operation of Part XXIII of the Companies Act 1985 with regard to oversea companies).

2

The Future of the Partnership: Does the Unincorporated Firm with Unlimited Liability have a Role to Play in the New Millennium?

ANDREW GRIFFITHS

Businesses in the United Kingdom do not have much choice of legal structure. The registered company limited by shares is the dominant form of organisation and, although there are specialist forms for certain kinds of business such as financial institutions and workers' co-operatives, most businesses have to choose between incorporation and the traditional common law structures of sole proprietorship or partnership. Sole proprietorship is a straightforward structure, not complicated by inter-member relationships.[1] A partnership, on the other hand, is a more complex arrangement since there are two or more members who may incur liabilities on each other's behalf, and this kind of firm therefore requires a greater degree of legal regulation.[2] However, in contrast to the great swathe of legislative reform which has affected the company, partnership law has survived the twentieth century largely unscathed and is still governed by Sir Frederick Pollock's codification of the common law rules in the Partnership Act 1890 ("the 1890 Act").[3]

As a business structure, the partnership suffers from some obvious deficiencies compared to the company. Partners face the risk of unlimited personal liability for their firm's debts and other obligations whatever their own particular knowledge or involvement. Also, the firm's legal relationships with others may be cumbersome because of its lack of a separate legal personality. Nonetheless,

---

[1] A sole trader can incorporate to obtain the benefits of separate legal personality and limited liability. Single member companies are now permitted by the Companies (Single Member Private Limited Companies) Regulations (S.I. 1992 No. 1699).

[2] The word "firm" is commonly used as a general term for a business association whatever its precise legal form. The Partnership Act 1890, however, uses the term to refer to a partnership: s. 4(1). In this ch., the word will be used in the former sense unless the context requires otherwise.

[3] This Act was largely a declaration of the common law rules, although it did not provide a complete code: s. 46 preserves those rules of common law and equity which are not inconsistent with any provision in the Act. See generally Milman and Flanagan, *Modern Partnership Law* (London, Croom Helm, 1983).

it does have some advantages and is still chosen as a legal structure by relatively small businesses and professional firms. This does not mean, however, that partnership is an ideal structure for such businesses, and its use may reflect other factors such as regulatory requirements or particular difficulties in using the company. There has in fact been a recurrent interest in the question whether the choice of legal structures for businesses in the United Kingdom needs improving by the introduction of a new one which combines features of both the partnership and the company. Thus, in 1981, a Green Paper included proposals for such a hybrid structure for the benefit of small firms,[4] and in 1997, the Department of Trade and Industry published a consultation paper, setting out proposals for a special hybrid structure for professional firms.[5] These proposals also raise the question whether choice would be better improved by a new structure or by reforming the company to make it more flexible and therefore more readily adaptable for use by small businesses and professional firms.[6] This chapter will examine the shortcomings of the partnership as a legal structure for business and the deficiencies of the company as an alternative structure. It will go on to analyse the factors behind the calls for change and consider whether there is a case for extending the existing choice of legal structures.

THE PARTNERSHIP AS A LEGAL STRUCTURE FOR BUSINESS

The partnership provides a simple legal structure for a firm. The firm has no separate legal existence of its own and instead is identified with its membership[7]:

> "Persons who have entered into partnership with one another are for the purposes of this Act called collectively a firm, and the name under which their business is carried on is called the firm-name."

A partnership exists when two or more persons are "carrying on a business in common with a view of profit".[8] The 1890 Act provides some elaboration of this definition. A business can include "every trade, occupation, or profession"[9] and can be an ongoing venture or a single project.[10] The essence of partnership is the sharing of profits as opposed to gross receipts or the like,[11] although the 1890

---

[4] Department of Trade, *A New Form of Incorporation for Small Firms* (Cmnd. 8171, HMSO, London, 1981). See also DTI, *Company Law Review: The Law Applicable to Private Companies: A Consultative Document* (1994).

[5] DTI, *Limited Liability Partnership: A New Form of Business Association for Professions* (1997). See generally A. Griffiths, "Professional Firms and Limited Liability: An Analysis of the Proposed Limited Liability Partnership" [1998] *CfiLR* 157.

[6] See Freedman, "Small Businesses and the Corporate Form: Burden or Privilege?" (1994) 57 *MLR* 555.

[7] Partnership Act (PA) 1890, s. 4(1).

[8] PA 1890, s. 1(1).

[9] PA 1890, s. 45.

[10] *Re Abenheim* (1913) 109 LT 219.

[11] "The sharing of gross returns does not of itself create a partnership, whether the persons sharing such returns have or have not a joint or common right or interest in any property from which or

Act expressly excludes the relationship between the members of a company.[12] The creation and existence of a partnership do not therefore depend on registration or any special legal formality, but on the fact of profit-sharing or of an agreement to share the profits of a business, and it is even possible for parties to create a partnership without being aware of the legal impact of what they have done.[13] Equally parties who wish to share the profits of a business, but not to do so through a company, cannot escape the burdens and liabilities of partnership simply by stating that they are not partners. The courts will judge the nature of their relationship on the objective facts and not on the label which the parties choose to apply to it. Thus a creditor of a firm might agree that the repayments and interest should come out of the profits of the business, but would not thereby become a partner in the firm unless the substance of their relationship amounted to the sharing of profits rather than that of a creditor and debtor.

The crux of a partnership is therefore the relationship among the members of the firm. Although this relationship stems from their intention of sharing in the profits of the firm, the legal consequence is that each partner is also personally responsible for its debts and other liabilities, and therefore shares in its losses as well.[14] This exposure to unlimited personal liability stems from the firm's lack of legal personality and the partners' mutual agency[15]:

> "Ordinary partnerships are by the law assumed and presumed to be based on the mutual trust and confidence of each partner in the skill, knowledge, and integrity of every other partner. As between the partners and the outside world (whatever may be their private arrangements between themselves), each partner is the unlimited agent of every other in every matter connected with the partnership business, or which he represents as partnership business, and not being in its nature beyond the scope of the partnership. A partner who may not have a farthing of capital left may take moneys or assets of this partnership to the value of millions, may bind the partnership by contracts to any amount, may give the partnership acceptances for any amount, and may even—as has been shewn in many painful instances in this Court—involve his innocent partners in unlimited amounts for frauds which he has craftily concealed from them."

Partners therefore face the risk of liability generated by their fellow partners regardless of whether they actually knew or approved of the relevant behaviour, provided it occurred in the ordinary course of the firm's business. The only way in which a partner can avoid general liability for the debts of the firm's business is by registering the partnership as a limited one in accordance with the Limited

---

from the use of which the returns are derived": PA 1890, s. 2(2). See also *Lyon* v. *Knowles* (1864) 5 B & S 751; *Burnard* v. *Aaron & Sharpley* (1862) 31 LJCP 334; and *Cox* v. *Coulson* [1916] 2 KB 177.

[12] PA 1890, s. 1(2).

[13] See generally Milman and Flanagan, n. 3 above, 11–16.

[14] PA 1890, s. 9. Among themselves, however, partners are free to agree how they are to bear losses and liabilities, but otherwise must contribute equally to any losses sustained by their firm: PA 1890, s. 24(1).

[15] *In re Agriculturalist Cattle Insurance Company (Baird's Case)* (1870) LR 5 Ch. App. 725, 733, *per* James LJ. See also *ITC* v. *Gibbs* [1942] AC 402.

Partnership Act 1907. This, however, requires registration with the Registrar of Companies and there must be at least one general partner who remains fully liable for the firm's debts. The liability of the limited partners is limited to their capital contribution to the firm, but they are not permitted to play an active role in the management of the firm and lose their limited liability if they do so. The limited partnership is therefore only of use to partners who are merely investors, and for them it does not offer much advantage, if any, over the company as a means of limiting their liability.[16] In particular, limited partners face the constant danger that they would lose their limited liability if they were ever to interfere in the management of its affairs. In practice, the limited partnership does not provide a significant alternative to the traditional partnership.[17]

Partners in a professional firm face the particular risk of joint and several liability for the negligence of their colleagues. Once the firm's liability is established, then each member is personally liable whatever his or her own degree of fault or responsibility, if any.[18] Moreover, each member faces the additional risk that the ambit of the firm's potential liability for negligence may be extended without his or her knowledge by a colleague. Whilst a professional firm's liability for negligence is normally founded on a contractual relationship with the plaintiff, it can also be based on an express assumption of responsibility to a third party, and any partner in the firm is likely to have the necessary authority to assume responsibility in this way,[19] thereby extending the potential liability of the firm and all its members. This in fact occurred in *ADT Ltd* v. *BDO Binder Hamlyn*,[20] which concerned negligent audit work by a leading firm of accountants. ADT was not a client of BDO, but had agreed to buy the company in question in reliance on the accounts which had been audited. A member of BDO was found to have vouched for these accounts after being made aware of ADT's specific interest in their reliability, thereby creating the necessary special relationship and exposing every member of the firm to unlimited personal liability.[21]

---

[16] The limited partnership was eclipsed by the recognition in *Salomon* v. *A Salomon & Co Ltd* [1897] AC 22 that closely-controlled companies, even those dominated by one individual, could enjoy the benefit of limited liability through incorporation and by the favourable treatment accorded to private companies by the Companies Acts of 1900 and 1907. See Davies, *Gower's Principles of Modern Company Law* (London: Sweet & Maxwell, 1997), 47–8.

[17] It does, however, have value in the structuring of joint ventures or other profit-sharing arrangements between companies. Partnership here may have tax advantages and the normal risk of liability can be contained by the use of "clean" subsidiaries.

[18] PA 1890, s. 9.

[19] PA 1890, s. 5.

[20] [1996] BCC 808.

[21] ADT was awarded £65 million damages, but later agreed to accept around £50 million in return for BDO's agreement to drop a proposed appeal. This was still almost £20 million more than BDO's available indemnity insurance cover and led to widespread fears that a leading professional firm might soon be brought down by such a "doomsday claim". See generally Freedman and Finch, "Limited Liability Partnerships: Have Accountants Sewn up the 'Deep Pockets' Debate?" [1997] *JBL* 387.

The risk of unlimited personal liability is the major cost of using the partnership as the legal structure for a firm. This means that the creditors of the firm can look to the personal assets of the firm's members as recourse capital available for their payment. The absence of any difference in vulnerability between the firm's assets and the members' personal assets means that members have no incentive to deplete the firm's assets to shield them from creditors. Creditors do not need any special protection in this respect, unlike those of a company, and this is reflected in the absence of any special regulation for partnerships on the raising and maintenance of a firm's capital. The much lighter burden of regulation on a partnership is one advantage that it enjoys over a company to offset the burden of unlimited liability. However, whereas company law has to counter the danger which limited liability would otherwise pose to a company's creditors, partnership law has to mitigate the vulnerability of firm members to each other. This is achieved by the fact that partnership is a relationship of the utmost good faith and is therefore subject to the fiduciary rules and duties which the common law and equity evolved to provide a general framework for such relationships.[22] The 1890 Act expressly restates the duty of partners to make full disclosure in their dealings with each other and their liability to account for any secret profits.[23] Partners are also subject to the overriding fiduciary duty to exercise their powers *bona fide* and a common law duty of care.[24]

The mutual vulnerability of partners is also balanced by their right to take part in the management of the firm's business and their right of veto over the appointment of new members, although these rights, like most provisions in the 1890 Act, may be overridden by express agreement.[25] Furthermore, a partnership is automatically dissolved by the death or bankruptcy of any of its members unless there is express provision to the contrary,[26] which again can be related to the importance of mutual reliability.[27] Other legal features of the partnership stem from its lack of a separate legal personality. Although this means that the firm's legal relationships are not complicated by the interpolation of a fictitious legal personality, it can make the creation and adjustment of contractual relationships with outside parties cumbersome, especially if the firm is liable to dissolve upon the death or departure of any of the partners.[28] Another consequence is that partners, unlike the members and directors of a company, cannot be party to any contractual relationship with the firm itself and thus, for example, cannot be employees or creditors of their firm. Lack of separate personality can

---

[22] *Baird's Case* (1870) LR 5 Ch. App. 725; *Dean* v. *MacDowell* (1878) 8 Ch. D 345; and *Green* v. *Howell* [1910] 1 Ch. 495.

[23] PA 1890, ss. 28 and 29. The Act also provides that a partner must account for any profits made from a business which competes with the firm's business: PA 1890, s. 30.

[24] *Green* v. *Howell* [1910] 1 Ch. 495 and *Winsor* v. *Schroeder* (1979) 129 NLJ 1266.

[25] PA 1890, s. 24.

[26] PA 1890, s. 33.

[27] *Baird's Case* (1870) LR 5 Ch. App. 725.

[28] This can be especially problematic for the employees of partnerships: see Milman and Flanagan, n. 3 above, 28–9.

therefore make the partnership an unwieldy structuring device for a business, and the impact of this deficiency is likely to increase in accordance with the number of partners and the complexity of the business. The statutory limitation on the size of partnerships to a maximum of 20 partners, except for professional firms,[29] therefore reflects an inherent limitation on the potential for growth of a firm using this structure.

Partnership therefore offers the benefit of a simple and flexible legal structure for a business combined with a relative lack of regulation, but at the cost of exposing its members to the risk of unlimited personal liability. Further, its lack of a separate legal personality makes it an awkward basis on which to structure a complex set of legal relationships. Its value as a legal structure for business therefore depends on how the balance of these costs and benefits compares with those offered by the company.

THE COMPANY AS AN ALTERNATIVE LEGAL STRUCTURE TO THE PARTNERSHIP

In practice, the partnership tends to be used by small firms and firms of professional practitioners where the firm's members or owners are actively involved and, in the latter case, are also the key income-earning employees of the business. This raises the question whether the company provides a realistic alternative structure for firms of this kind. Of course, firms cannot simply be divided into those which are owned by active participants and those which are owned by passive investors, but they are nonetheless archetypes. In reality, there is a wide spectrum of firms ranging from those listed on the Stock Exchange, whose members are largely investors, to those owned by a single person or small group of persons who dominates its affairs. Partnership is not a realistic proposition for much of this spectrum, especially given the shortcomings of the limited partnership. The company, however, can be used across the whole range.

Unlike a partnership, a company exists as a legal person in its own right, separate from its members. A company is party to its own contracts and obligations and thereby shields its members from liability for these. The members (or "shareholders") of a company[30] cannot be held responsible for its liabilities unless there is a distinct legal basis for this other than their membership. Thus, they could be liable through agency, under a guarantee or as a result of an express statutory provision to that effect.[31] Membership of itself, however, is not sufficient to establish agency or any other basis of liability even though

[29] The standard maximum is 20 partners, but solicitors, accountants and members of a recognised stock exchange are exempted: see Companies Act (CA) 1985, s. 719(2). Other professions have been exempted by special regulations. Many firms now have hundreds of members.

[30] In relation to a company limited by shares, the terms "members" and "shareholders" are synonymous.

[31] As is the case with the Scottish partnership, which does have a separate legal personality, but whose members are deemed by statute to have the same personal liability as if it did not: PA 1890, s. 4(2).

shareholders can use their powers to control and dominate the firm.[32] The only liability faced by the members of a company by virtue of their membership is to pay any unpaid capital due on their shares, and this liability is owed to the company itself and not to the company's creditors.[33] The company's separate legal personality and the consequent limited liability of its members are its key advantages over the partnership. However, limited liability poses an obvious danger to its creditors and this danger is reflected in the fact that the company is subject to a far greater degree of regulation. There are, for example, strict rules governing the raising and maintenance of capital by a company and restricting the repayment of capital and the distibution of profits to members through dividends.[34] Companies are also subject to a detailed regime of insolvency law, now set out in the Insolvency Act 1986. This burden of regulation can be regarded as a legitimate price to pay for obtaining the benefits of limited liability.

However, the company's separate legal personality is not its only distinguishing feature as a business structure. It is also characterised by a formal separation of management from membership. Unlike partners, shareholders have no right to participate in its management. Instead, they merely have the right to appoint and remove the board of directors, and it is this body which has formal responsibility for management.[35] The members of a company may also be directors, and in this way can influence or control the running of their company, but they have no guaranteed right to do so. Since decisions of the membership on the appointment and removal of directors are determined by a simple majority of votes through an ordinary resolution, a majority shareholder can exercise effective control over the management of the company.[36] Equally, a minority shareholder has no such right and runs the risk of exclusion from management. This formal separation of management from membership in a company is ideally suited for those firms whose members are largely passive investors with little inclination to be involved in the management of its business and are content for this function to be delegated to specialist managers. Firms at this end of the spectrum accordingly tend to be structured as public companies whose shares can be listed and traded on the Stock Exchange or a similar market.[37] Here, the firm's legal structure has to accommodate and reconcile the conflicting interests of three distinct groupings, namely its members, its management and its creditors. In the absence of institutional safeguards or corrective regulation, the company's basic legal structure presents a potential for danger not only to its

---

[32] *Salomon* v. *A Salomon & Co Ltd* [1897] AC 22 and *Rayner (J.H.) (Mincing Lane) Ltd* v. *DTI* [1990] 2 AC 418.

[33] The amount payable to a company in respect of its share capital is the nominal value of the share plus any premium: see generally Gower, n. 16 above, 234–47.

[34] See generally *ibid.*, chs. 11 and 12.

[35] *Automatic Self-Cleansing Filter Syndicate Co Ltd* v. *Cunninghame* [1906] 2 Ch. 34; *Gramophone & Typewriter Ltd* v. *Stanley* [1908] 2 KB 89; *Quin & Axtens Ltd* v. *Salmon* [1909] AC 442; and *Breckland Group Holdings Ltd* v. *London & Suffolk Properties Ltd* [1989] BCLC 100.

[36] CA 1985, s. 303.

[37] See generally Gower, n. 16 above, ch. 16.

creditors, but also to its members, who face the risk that management may not maximise their return from the company. Accordingly, much of the law regulating companies can be regarded as a necessary response to the latter danger. However, where a company is used by a firm which is largely owned by its participants, this regulation can prove more of a hindrance than a help to the members and especially to members who are only minority shareholders. Before examining the nature of this hindrance in more detail, it will be useful to consider the underlying factors which influence the organisation and ownership of a firm and which must therefore influence the choice of legal structure.

THE ORGANISATION OF A FIRM:

OWNERSHIP BY ACTIVE PARTICIPANTS OR PASSIVE INVESTORS?

At first glance, it might seem curious that any firm should be owned by investors from outside and that its active participants, who might include its founders and driving force, should forego ultimate control of the firm. However, the need of such firms to be financed or refinanced by equity capital provides an economic explanation for this.[38] If the personal assets of a firm's active participants are not sufficient to finance its activities, they will have to obtain capital from outsiders. Capital could be obtained by credit or a loan, but if it is required for firm-specific investment which cannot be easily realised on the open market, then loan capital is unlikely to be available on acceptable terms. This is because firm-specific investment tends not to produce attractive security for a loan, leaving the creditor vulnerable in the event of an insolvency, especially if the business itself faces a significant risk of failure. In this scenario, the firm is likely to find finance on better terms if it is raised as equity capital from investors who are prepared to give capital to the firm in return for a share of its profits. Equity capital may also be required from outsiders if an existing financier or owner of a firm wishes to realise their investment.[39] However, equity investors face the obvious risk that the firm's management can behave opportunistically and run its affairs for their own benefit rather than to maximise its profits and the return on the equity investors' investment. They therefore require safeguards to ensure that the firm's management does not do this. Detailed contractual undertakings are unlikely to be a cost-effective means of solving this problem, given the variety of contingencies that the arrangements would have to cover, and instead it is likely to be more efficient to establish a flexible relationship which contains broad safeguards to protect the investors.[40] Ownership rights provide an ideal basis

---

[38] See Hansmann, "Ownership of the Firm" (1988) 4 *Jo. Law, Econ. & Org.* 267.

[39] This is in effect what happened when the major public utilities were privatised by the government.

[40] For an analysis of how "relational" contracting can be a more efficient way of governing dealings between parties than the classical fully-contingent contract, see Macneil, "Contracts: Adjustment of Long-Term Economic Relations under Classical, Neo-Classical and Relational Contract Law" (1978) 72 *NW Univ. LR* 854 and Williamson, *The Economic Institutions Of Capitalism: Firms, Markets, Relational Contracting* (New York, The Free Press, 1985).

for structuring such a relationship between a firm and its investors and combatting the danger of managerial opportunism. Assigning these rights to the investors also has a negative value, in that no other interest-group can have a superior or competing claim on management's attention.[41] However, the investors' ownership rights over the firm have to be adjusted if they are to perform this task efficiently. If the investors were to have the usual burdens of ownership and thus to be personally liable for the firm's debts and other obligations, there would be a substantial cost attached to their investment which would make it unviable in many instances. Limited liability therefore, either through a limited partnership or a company, forms an essential element in the relationship.[42] The company, by combining ownership rights with limited liability, can therefore be viewed as an efficient basis on which to structure equity investment.[43] Limited liability in fact contributes to the efficiency of this solution in a number of ways. First of all, it limits the downside risk of shareholding and thus the potential costs facing equity investors. Secondly, it reduces the need for shareholders to be involved in or pay close attention to the management of the company since their maximum potential loss is already established. They no longer face the risk of losing all their personal assets. Limited liability thereby enables the functions of management and shareholding to be separated so that each can be performed more efficiently by specialists. Thirdly, limited liability improves the quality of shares as an investment by making the attached risk an objective one, related to the performance and prospects of the company and independent of the relative personal wealth of the shareholders. This objectifying of the attached risk also enables shares to be traded more easily, since their value will not be affected by the relative personal wealth of their holders and has thereby facilitated the development of specialist share markets like the Stock Exchange and risk-bearing practices such as diversification.

The formal separation of management from shareholding in the company's legal structure also contributes to its value as a basis for equity investment. It

---

[41] See Hansmann, n. 38 above. This reasoning can also be used to justify the unlimited term of the shareholders' claim on their company's resources since, although an indefinite claim on the company's resources is probably not necessary to induce the provision of equity capital, the existence of a residual claim elsewhere would expose the shareholders to a risk which might be difficult to counter-balance efficiently.

[42] The costs of limited partnership are, however, likely to be higher because of the greater danger of losing limited liability. Before the company became readily available as a device for obtaining limited liability in the 19th century, creditors were often required to accept terms in their contractual arrangements which limited the liability of equity investors. The company thus had value as a transaction cost-saving device. See Butler, "General Incorporation in Nineteenth Century England: Interaction of Common Law and Legislative Processes" (1986) 6 *Int. Rev. Law & Econ.* 169.

[43] See, e.g., Easterbrook and Fischel, "The Corporate Contract" (1989) 89 *Colum. LR* 1416; Jensen and Meckling, "Theory of the Firm: Managerial Behaviour, Agency Costs and Ownership Structure" (1976) 3 *Jo. Fin. Econ.* 305; and Manne, "Our Two Corporation Systems: Law and Economics" (1967) 53 *Virg. LR* 259. On the use of efficiency as a basis of legal analysis, see Ogus and Veljanovski, *Readings in the Economics of Law and Regulation* (Oxford, Clarendon Press, 1984), 19–23, and Ogus, *Regulation: Legal Form and Economic Theory* (Oxford, Clarendon Press, 1994), 23–8.

reflects the fact that dividing these functions enables each one to be performed more efficiently. The total number of shareholders does not have to be limited to what is suitable for a managerial body and can expand to a size that is conducive to efficient and diversified risk-bearing. The shareholders' ownership rights act as a curb on management's scope for opportunism, although these rights are now dispersed and represented in their voting rights. The board of directors has to take account of the risk that these votes could be aggregated and used to cut down its discretion or even to remove it from office altogether.[44] The potential power comprised in the shareholders' voting rights is the basis of the so-called "market in corporate control", which has been presented as an important counter-balance to the discretionary power of the management of a public company.[45] According to this theory, shareholders can exert influence over their company's directors and management through their ability to sell their shares, which can affect the company's share price. If directors do not ensure that shareholders receive the maximum possible financial return from the company, they risk provoking a sub-optimal share price, with the consequent adverse publicity that that would entail, and an increased vulnerability to a take-over bid. After a takeover, the shareholders' voting rights and powers are concentrated in the hands of an effective controller and can be used decisively. The shareholders' ownership rights are also protected by other safeguards such the detailed regulation provided by companies legislation and sources such as the Stock Exchange's rules and the City Code on Takeovers and Mergers, which, for example, require a company's management to disclose detailed information to shareholders through statutory accounts and the like and thereby account for their stewardship of the company.

What Kinds of Frm are Likely to be Owned by Active Participants?

The above analysis has shown that firms whose members are largely equity investors from outside need a legal structure that affords them limited liability. The increased risk of non-payment faced by the firm's creditors, in so far as it is not mitigated by ancillary regulation such as insolvency law, can be justified as serving a wider public interest by facilitating equity investment and the efficient development of such firms. The next task is to consider what kinds of firms are likely to be owned by active participants so that their requirements in terms of legal structure can be reviewed. A crucial factor that has been identified as explaining why ownership by employees is a relatively uncommon style of organisation is the need for a firm to have an efficient means of governance or

---

[44] For this reason, shareholders' voting rights have been portrayed as equivalent to a set of unspecified promises by management to the company's shareholders: see Easterbrook and Fischel, n. 43 above.

[45] See Manne, "Mergers and the Market for Corporate Control" (1965) 73 *Jo. Pol. Econ.* 110 and Manne, n. 43 above.

collective decision-making by its members.[46] Efficient governance requires either that the members of a firm are few in number and can all actively engage in decision-making or that they all have broadly similar interests in the firm so that strong disagreement is unlikely. Once the interests of a firm's members start to diverge, then the costs of collective decision-making rapidly escalate. Members with heterogenous interests are likely to find it more satisfactory to settle their relationship with the firm through a discrete contractual arrangement rather than having to rely on a collective mechanism that may operate against their interests. It has been argued that this explains the prevalence of investor ownership through the company for firms of any size.[47] Unlike most contributors to a firm's activities, investors as a class usually have a strong homogeneity of interest, namely that their financial return be maximised. Divergences are likely to occur only where equity investors have a dual interest in the firm, say as an employee, manager or creditor. Ownership by active participants is therefore unlikely to be viable unless the cost of collective decision-making is relatively low. That is likely to be the case in a small firm or where there is substantial homogeneity among the participants, as in a firm providing professional services. It is firms of this type which have tended to use the partnership as their legal structure and for which the quality of the choice provided by the partnership and the company is a germane issue.

THE DEFICIENCIES OF THE COMPANY AS A LEGAL STRUCTURE FOR FIRMS OWNED BY ACTIVE PARTICIPANTS

The main deficiency of the company is that it is only available as a standard package with an internal legal framework which does not differentiate between the different kinds of firm which might wish to make use of it as a legal structure. In particular, whilst it has proved an efficient basic framework for firms owned by passive investors, it is much less suitable for firms at the other end of the spectrum. Thus, while the public company can be regarded as a structure modelled on the needs of the investor-owned archetype, the private company has the same basic characteristics as the public company and makes few concessions to the special needs of participant-ownership.[48] This problem also affects companies where ownership is in effect shared between active participants and investors.

The key deficiency in the company's internal framework is the formal separation of management from shareholding, with shareholders having no automatic right to participate in management, and the fact that decision-making is

[46] See Hansmann, "When Does Worker Ownership Work? ESOPs, Law Firms, Codetermination, and Economic Democracy" (1990) 99 *Yale LJ* 1749.

[47] *Ibid.* See also Hansmann, n. 38 above.

[48] Private companies are subject to a less onerous burden of regulation than public companies and the "elective regime" established by the CA 1989 enables them to dispense with some repetitive requirements if the members unanimously consent.

based on the principle of majority rule.[49] Thus, the constitution of a company has the same legal effect regardless of the size and nature of its membership and, although it is given the force of a statutory contract among the members,[50] the usual principles of contract law do not apply in some important respects. It has been confirmed in cases such as *Southern Foundries (1926) Ltd* v. *Shirlaw*[51] that members have a collective right to alter a company's articles of association by special resolution which overrides any provision to the contrary in the constitution itself or in any contract to which the company is a party.[52] This rule also applies to other statutory powers of the company's members such as their ability to remove directors by ordinary resolution and to increase the company's share capital.[53] Whilst this displacement of the law of contract in respect of a company's constitution provides a convenient level of protection to shareholders in a company whose membership consists largely of outside investors with relatively small shareholdings, it is an inconvenient obstacle for a smaller membership including active participants. Minority shareholders in such a company are vulnerable to the statutory powers of the majority, especially if their shareholding is not large enough to block a special resolution, and thus face the risk of being excluded from management. Such members would be better served by rules which recognise any mutually agreed checks and balances rather than allowing such arrangements to be disrupted by an *ad hoc* voting majority. For these companies, there is little, if any, need to provide overriding devices for the protection of shareholders on the assumption that they are a homogeneous class apart from the company's management. It is hard to justify the principle of majority rule and the sanctity of shareholders' statutory powers as a necessary protection for the firm's creditors or as serving some wider public interest. Company law has provided some redress for minority shareholders who are also active participants in their company in the form of the statutory right to petition the court for relief on the ground that "the company's affairs are being or have been conducted in a manner which is unfairly prejudicial to the interests of its members generally or of some part of its members".[54] However, this remedy provides limited reassurance to shareholders who wish to be certain of their position in advance because the protection is discretionary, hard to predict in advance and depends on the ability and willingness of a discontented shareholder to instigate litigation. Moreover, the existence of this remedy means that even a majority shareholder has to accept an element of uncertainty. There is always the danger that

---

[49] N 35 above and the relevant text.

[50] CA 1985, s. 14.

[51] [1940] AC 701.

[52] CA 1985, s. 9. In *Bratton Seymour Service Co Ltd* v. *Oxborough*, it was held that a company's constitution cannot be rectified to reflect the true intention of the subscribers. The wording can only be altered by a special resolution: [1992] BCC 471.

[53] CA 1985, ss. 303 and 121.

[54] CA 1985, ss. 459–461. See Riley, "Contracting Out of Company Law: Section 459 of the Companies Act 1985 and the Role of the Courts" (1992) 55 *MLR* 782.

a discontented colleague may resort to litigation regardless of what arrangements may have been agreed by everyone in advance.[55]

There are some drafting devices which can be used to combat the problem presented by shareholders' powers and the principle of majority rule, although this is likely to be expensive in time and money and beyond the means of many participants in smaller companies. The devices include dividing the shares into classes and attaching special rights to these classes,[56] giving certain shares enhanced voting rights in prescribed circumstances[57] and giving undertakings on how the shareholders exercise their powers in ancillary contracts such as a shareholders' agreement. In *Russell* v. *Northern Bank Development Corporation Ltd*,[58] the House of Lords considered the effectiveness of a shareholders' agreement which provided that the share capital of a company could only be increased if all its shareholders consented in writing. The agreement had been signed by all the current shareholders, comprising four working shareholders and an investor, and by the company itself, which under the normal rules of contract would have been enough to ensure that each shareholder had a power of veto over future increases in share capital. However, the validity of this provision was later challenged on the basis that it fettered the shareholders' statutory power to increase the company's capital by ordinary resolution. The House of Lords held that the agreement was partially effective since shareholders could give binding undertakings on how they exercise their statutory powers, and such undertakings can therefore be enforced against them. The company itself, however, could not give any such undertaking, and to that extent the agreement was invalid. Thus, whilst shareholders in companies like the one in *Russell* can make binding contractual arrangements among themselves, they still face a residual risk that the company itself is either not bound or not entitled to act in breach of the agreement.[59] In practice, this means that a shareholders' agreement which is intended to give shareholders a power of veto should be backed by special voting rights to ensure that no resolution to exercise any statutory power can be passed without the minority shareholder's approval. Making special arrangements of this kind would require legal expertise and add significantly to the cost of using the company as a legal structure for the firm. However, if a company is used without such arrangements being made, the firm's members face the potential costs presented by a legal structure which does not necessarily reflect their

---

[55] The members of a partnership in contrast only have a "sledgehammer" remedy of being entitled to petition the court for the dissolution of the partnership on the ground that it is just and equitable to do so: PA 1890, s. 35(f). This remedy is subject to the discretion of the court: see *Re Yenidje Tobacco Co Ltd* [1916] 2 Ch. 426. The members of a company also have a similar right to petition for its winding-up: Insolvency Act 1986, s. 122(g). See *Ebrahimi* v. *Westbourne Galleries* [1973] AC 360.

[56] *Cumbrian Newspapers Group Ltd* v. *Cumberland & Westmorland Herald Newspapers & Printing Co Ltd* [1987] Ch. 1.

[57] *Bushell* v. *Faith* [1970] AC 1099.

[58] [1992] BCC 578.

[59] If a majority do exercise their powers in breach of the agreement, the minority shareholder would have remedies against the majority personally, but no direct remedy against the company itself.

expectations. In either case, there are costs attached to the use of the company which must further diminish its appeal as a practical alternative to the partnership, although this does not of course mean that the partnership is an ideal structure.

The nature of the choice presented by the partnership and the company as potential structures for a business is clear. The company offers the great advantages of separate legal personality and limited liability, but at a cost both in terms of onerous regulation and disclosure requirements and because of the unsuitability of its internal legal framework for certain kinds of firm. The businesses for which the choice is likely to be most difficult are those where the costs of unlimited liability and lack of separate personality on the one hand, and the costs of using the company as a legal structure on the other, are both high. These costs therefore need to be analysed in more detail.

What Factors Mitigate the Costs of Using the Partnership as a Legal Structure?

Those factors which tend to make ownership by the active participants in a firm a viable basis of organisation also tend to reduce the cost of unlimited liability. Thus, the number of members is important since the risk would increase in accordance with the number of parties who could trigger a liability that might bankrupt the firm, although there would also be an increase in the potential pool of assets. There would nevertheless be an increase in the degree of uncertainty. Also, the willingness on the part of firm members to accept the risk of unlimited personal liability should depend on their degree of trust in their fellow members. Members of a small firm are likely to have much greater knowledge about each other and thus are more likely to know that they can trust and rely on each other. Mutual trust is also more probable among people who are bound by other relationships, such as family or friendship or by sharing a code of ethics, as with those working for a cause or members of a profession. Again, if a firm's members have a common skill or expertise, they are in a better position to judge each other's competence and reliability.

Such factors explain why partnership has tended to be confined to small businesses, especially family businesses or ventures among friends, and why the only businesses of any size which use it as a structure are professional firms. A firm with a large number of members without any special factors to counter the cost of unlimited liability has good reason to choose the company as its legal structure, especially if its business is likely to require establishing a complex set of arrangements which would be better facilitated by a structure affording a separate legal personality. Such firms are also more likely to be owned by outside investors, which reinforces the suitability of the company. Firms owned by active participants, however, face additional costs in using the company, but this may be offset by a lower cost of unlimited liability, making the partnership a realistic alternative. There may be other reasons for preferring partnership.

Professional regulations may prohibit the ownership of firms by anyone other than members of the relevant profession and may negate the practical advantages of incorporation.[60] Also, it is arguable that the mutual liability of partnership underpins the rationale of ownership by active participants by enhancing the homogeneity of interest among the firm's members. This does not, however, mean that the common exposure to the firm's liabilities has to be unlimited in extent and that the partnership is an ideal structure. The simple choice between the company and the partnership may not be satisfactory for firms with active participants and there does appear to be a case for improving their choice.

IS AN ALTERNATIVE LEGAL STRUCTURE NEEDED FOR FIRMS WHICH ARE OWNED BY ACTIVE PARTICIPANTS?

The main costs of the partnership for firms of this kind stem from its lack of a separate legal personality and the unlimited liability of its members. The main costs of the company are the additional burden of regulation and the unsuitability of its basic legal framework. This suggests that there is room for improvement in the choice of structure available for such firms by introducing a new hybrid structure which provides separate personality and limited liability, but with a more flexible internal framework that they can more easily adapt to suit their own requirements. Alternatively, the same goal could be achieved by making the internal framework of the company flexible or more easily adjustable so that it can be adapted to suit the requirements of a firm owned by active participants at a much lower cost. It has been argued that the latter proposition has a significant advantage over the former, because a firm which for some reason wishes to move to ownership by investors would not have to change its legal structure, but could merely adapt its internal framework to the new situation.[61] This would avoid the significant transaction costs, including potential liabilities for taxation, of changing legal structure and thus remove a potential barrier to growth.[62] In order to consider whether an improved choice for such firms can be justified, it is first necessary to recognise that they fall into two broad categories. First, there are firms with few participants. These firms may remain small or may develop into investor-owned firms. Secondly, there are those firms whose business consists of the provision of specialist services by their participants, the most important of these being professional firms. For these firms, progression to investor-ownership may not be feasible. The

---

[60] Incorporated firms of solicitors, e.g., are required to enter into a compensation fund covenant with the Law Society which exposes their members to the same potential personal liability as the members of a partnership.

[61] Freedman, n. 6 above.

[62] *Ibid.*, 559: the formalities which would probably be required to effect a change of structure "would set up a psychological and practical barrier to change".

partnership has already been adapted to suit the needs of such firms by disapplying the statutory maximum size, and they raise a distinct set of issues from firms that are merely small.

The Position of Small Firms

Empirical evidence suggests that unlimited liability is not regarded as a major handicap by small firms and that limited liability is not the major reason for incorporation.[63] One reason for this is that the use of a limited liability structure is unlikely to give such firms much of a strategic advantage in their dealings with their major creditors. Whilst it does achieve a *prima facie* shift of risk from the firm's members as a class onto its creditors as a class, the apparent shift may be wholly or partially reversed by other factors. The impact of limited liability on the creditors of a company is modified by insolvency law and by the willingness of the courts in some circumstances to pierce the corporate veil.[64] For example, members of a company who are also directors or shadow directors may be required to make a contribution to its assets in the event of an insolvency, if they have engaged in wrongful trading as defined in the Insolvency Act.[65] Also, the duties which company directors owe to their company can operate as a mitigation of limited liability in the event of an insolvency.[66] Since these modifying devices tend to affect those who are actively involved in the affairs of a company, they are likely to have a much greater impact on the members of small firms. The balance of risk established by a limited liability business structure can also be adjusted in the specific contractual arrangements with the firm's creditors. Creditors can, for example, seek guarantees from a company's members and reverse the impact of limited liability. They can also counter the increased risk of non-payment by taking additional security or charging a premium for their credit. One advantage that the company does have over the partnership in this respect is that it can give a floating charge over its assets to secure its liabilities.[67] The members of a small firm with limited liability are liable to be required to give personal guarantees to its major creditors, and using a company as a legal structure is therefore unlikely to achieve much advantage over partnership in practice.

Nevertheless, limited liability may be of benefit to a small firm, and it is worth considering at this stage whether enabling a small firm to trade with limited lia-

---

[63] Freedman, n. 6 above, 560–6.

[64] For a discussion of the way in which doctrines of company law can be viewed as adjusting the *prima facie* balance established by limited liability, see Bahls, "Application of Corporate Common Law Doctrines to Limited Liability Companies" (1994) 55 *Mont. LR* 43, 72–7.

[65] Insolvency Act 1986, s. 214.

[66] The liability of the directors to the company for breach of duty in effect constitutes an asset of the company that can be recovered for the benefit of its creditors: see, e.g., *Bishopsgate Investment Management Ltd* v. *Maxwell* [1993] BCC 120 and *Re D'Jan of London Ltd* [1993] BCC 646.

[67] See Milman and Flanagan, n. 3 above, 9–10.

bility can be justified before evaluating the means open to it to achieve this end. Limited liability has been defended on the ground of economic efficiency,[68] but the arguments are most convincing in relation to the public company, where limited liability can be regarded as essential to protect shareholders who are passive investors and therefore to secure equity capital.[69] Limited liability has, however, also been justified as serving the public interest by stimulating entrepreneurship, innovation and diversification,[70] although it is questionable whether these activities are sufficiently beneficial to society to merit an incentive. A further justification is that limited liability provides a better default position than unlimited liability.[71] This view takes account of the fact that the initial balance of risk established by a particular legal structure can be adjusted by the affected parties and holds that creditors are better placed to do this than shareholders.[72] This argument again is more convincing where the shareholders are passive investors and has also been challenged on the basis that negotiating special terms is likely to be inconvenient or too costly for many creditors and that some, like tort victims, have no opportunity to do so.[73]

Limited liability could only provide a better default position if accompanied by general safeguards to deter the firm's members from unreasonably exploiting their position. In the case of a company, extensive safeguards are already in place, although they could be strengthened by a specific minimum capitalisation requirement.[74] Once such safeguards are in place, it is arguable that any further benefit to creditors or the wider public interest afforded by unlimited liability is outweighed by the additional costs to the firm and its members.[75] The disadvantage of unlimited liability as a safeguard for creditors is that it presents members with an automatic risk of loss which varies solely in accordance with their

[68] See Booth, "Limited Liability and the Efficient Allocation of Resources" (1994) 89 *Northwestern Univ. LR* 140; Cheffins, *Company Law: Theory, Structure and Operation* (Oxford, Clarendon Press, 1997), 499–508; Easterbrook and Fischel, "Limited Liability and the Corporation" (1985) 89 *Univ. Chic. LR* 89 and Halpern, Trebilcock and Turnbull, "An Economic Analysis of Limited Liability in Corporation Law" (1980) 30 *Univ. Toro. LJ* 117.

[69] See n. 43 above, and the relevant text.

[70] See, e.g., Posner, "The Rights of Creditors of Affiliated Corporations" (1976) 43 *Univ. Chic. LR* 499; Macey, "The Limited Liability Company: Lessons for Corporate Law" (1995) 73 *Wash. Univ. LQ* 450–2; and Ribstein "The Deregulation of Limited Liability and the Death of Partnership" (1992) 70 *Wash. Univ. LQ* 417, 447–8.

[71] See generally Ribstein, n. 70 above.

[72] See Cheffins, n. 68 above, 75–82; Macey, n. 70 above, 433, 450; and Posner, n. 70 above.

[73] See Easterbrook and Fischel (1989) 89 *Colum LR* 1416; Landers, "A Unified Approach to Parent, Subsidiary and Affiliate Questions in Bankruptcy" (1975) 42 *Univ. Chic. LR* 589 and "Another Word . . ." (1976) 43 *Univ. Chic. LR* 527; and Prentice, "Groups of Companies: The English Experience" in Hopt (ed.), *Groups of Companies in European Laws* (Berlin, de Gruyter, 1982).

[74] A public company must have a minimum share capital of £50,000, at least 25% of which must be paid up along with the whole of any premium payable: CA 1985, s. 118. A private company is subject to neither requirement.

[75] It is therefore inefficient in accordance with a standard which has been termed "Kaldor-Hicks efficiency", which requires that the net surplus of benefits over costs be maximised: those who gain should be able to compensate the losers and still be better of than otherwise, although this is left as a theoretical possibility rather than being a requirement of the standard: see generally n. 43 above.

relative personal wealth, and in many cases this is likely to be excessive. It may therefore deter some people from membership of a firm without limited liability and may induce those who do become members to devote too much of their time and other resources to controlling the activities of their colleagues and other defensive practices.[76] Unlimited liability may therefore have a stultifying effect on some small firms and inhibit their efficient development and organisation.

It is therefore arguable that there is a good case for enabling small firms to use a limited liability legal structure, subject to suitable safeguards, for the protection of their creditors. It is also arguable that the costs which such firms have to incur in adapting the unsuitable legal framework of the company cannot be justified as protection for creditors, and instead constitute an unnecessary barrier to such firms' access to limited liability. There is also a case, therefore, for providing small firms with an alternative means of obtaining limited liability. One possible model for reform here is the limited liability company (or "LLC") which has proved a popular innovation in the United States.[77] This was first introduced in Wyoming in 1977, modelled on the German *GmbH* and the Latin American *limitada*, to attract inward investment from Latin America by providing a familiar structure. It has a flexible governance structure and members are free to decide whether management powers should be retained by them or delegated to a separate body. The main source of the LLC's popularity in the United States, however, was a ruling that it would normally be treated as a partnership for federal taxation purposes and therefore avoid the usual danger of double taxation. However, in the United Kingdom, a similar effect could be achieved by reforming the internal legal framework of the company to make it more flexible, which arguably would be more efficient than presenting small firms with a different structure of their own.[78]

The Position of Professional Frms

Unlimited liability is placing an increasing burden on the members of professional firms because of a surge in the number and size of claims made against them for negligence.[79] The increased cost of professional negligence is reflected in a deterioration in the terms on which they can obtain indemnity insurance

[76] See generally Ribstein, n. 70 above, 427–33.

[77] See generally Bahls, n. 64 above; Macey, "The Limited Liability Company: Lessons for Corporate Law" (1995) 73 *Wash. Univ. LQ* 433; Lobenhofer, "Limited Liability Entities in Ohio: A Primer on the Limited Liability Company and Partnership with Limited liability" (1994) 21 *Ohio NULR* 39; Ribstein, n. 70 above; and Spudis, "Limited Liability Companies: An Introduction" in Wood (ed.), *Limited Liability Companies: Formation, Operation and Conversion* (New York, John Wiley, 1993).

[78] Nn. 61–2 above, and the relevant text.

[79] See generally Freedman and Finch, n. 21 above, and Payne, "Reaching their Limit: The Liability of Professional Partnerships in England" in Rider (ed.), *The Realm of Company Law* (London, Kluwer Law, 1998).

and an increase in the fees charged to clients.[80] For these firms, the impact of unlimited liability is also exacerbated by their size, since they are not subject to the normal statutory maximum.[81] Furthermore, it is not easy for professional firms to control the cost of negligence. The standards used to determine liability are far from clear,[82] and there are legal obstacles to limiting the firm's liability in advance in their contractual arrangements with their clients. Members of some professions are prohibited from attempting to do this,[83] and in any event any such arrangement must be consistent with fiduciary principles and reasonable under the Unfair Contract Terms Act 1977. There are no clear guidelines as to what would be effective in practice in this respect.[84]

Partnership has been regarded as more in keeping with the fiduciary nature of professional services, in which a personal bond between practitioner and client has traditionally been regarded as of great importance,[85] but the escalating cost of unlimited liability because of negligence claims has led professional firms to seek a limited liability structure. Whilst professional firms are now permitted to incorporate,[86] and some have chosen to do so,[87] there has been much greater interest in the idea of providing them with a hybrid structure, culminating in the DTI's proposals for a Limited Liability Partnership (or "LLP").[88] Apart from the unsuitability of the company's internal legal framework, professionals may also face significant tax disadvantages if they incorporate. These could result both from the alteration in the legal nature of their relationship with their firms and from the transfer of the firm's business to a company.[89]

---

[80] See, e.g., Morris, "Limiting Auditors' Exposure to Risk" in *Palmer's In-Company*, May 1996, and Turnor, "The Professional Liability Crisis" [1996] *Commercial Lawyer* 58.

[81] N. 29 above.

[82] See Freedman and Finch, n. 21 above, 391–5.

[83] Accountants are prohibited by the CA 1985, s. 310(1), from any attempt to limit or exclude their liability for auditing work. The Solicitors' Act 1974, s. 60(5), renders void any provision in any agreement relating to proceedings before a court or tribunal which purports to exempt a solicitor from liability for professional negligence. Solicitors are also restricted by their professional conduct rules, which regard any attempt to exclude liability through a contractual provision as unacceptable, although a limitation of liability is acceptable provided it is not set below the minimum level of cover required under the Solicitors' Indemnity Rules: see *The Guide to the Professional Conduct of Solicitors 1993*.

[84] See Common Law Team of the Law Commission *Feasibility Investigation of Joint and Several Liability*(London, HMSO, 1996), paras. 5.10–5.26.

[85] See generally Director General of Fair Trading, *Restrictions on the Kind of Organisation Through Which Members of Professions may Offer Their Services: A Report by the Director General of Fair Trading* (London, OFT, 1986).

[86] Solicitors were permitted to practise through limited companies by the Solicitors Incorporated Practice Rules 1988, which came into force on 1 Jan. 1992. Auditors were permitted to incorporate by the CA 1989. However, the benefit of limited liability may be negated by professional regulations: n. 60 above.

[87] See, e.g., "KPMG partners embrace plc status to avoid liability", *Financial Times*, 1 Oct. 1995, and "Law partners go to the legal limit", *Sunday Times*, 28 Apr. 1996.

[88] N. 5 above.

[89] These disadvantages stem from partners becoming employees of their firm for purposes of taxation and National Insurance and the alteration in the nature of their interest in the firm. It has, however, been argued that changes in the taxation of partnerships make this advantage somewhat illusory: see Simmons, "The Decline and Fall of Partnership" [1994] *Professional Practice Management* 97.

In terms of the cost of unlimited liability, there appears to be a much stronger case for providing professional firms with an additional legal structure than small firms. However, the question whether limited liability can be justified in this context raises more difficult issues. Clients are not creditors in the sense that they extend credit on pre-arranged terms, but only become creditors if they suffer loss from a sub-standard service or some other malpractice. Their expectation is not to become creditors of the firm at all. The members of professional firms also have the advantage of sharing a common expertise, and are likely to be far better placed than clients to judge the risk of negligence occurring and to take action to remove or contain this risk. Their mutual liability therefore performs the important function of giving these members a clear incentive to use their superior skill to minimise the risk faced by their firm's clients.[90] The question is whether the efficient performance of this function requires the members' mutual liability to be automatic and unlimited. As noted already in relation to small firms, the impact of automatic unlimited personal liability is crude and the incentive which it provides may therefore be excessive.[91] This is especially likely to be the case in large professional firms. It is arguable therefore that whilst more stringent safeguards are required in this situation, a limited liability structure would nevertheless provide a better basis for professional firms as well. The interests of clients would have to be protected by alternative regulatory devices to ensure that members did use their superiority of expertise to minimise the risk of negligence and that firms had a satisfactory level of resources to meet any claims for negligence and other liabilities. In this respect, it is worth noting that the members of a professional firm using a limited liability legal structure would in any event have some incentive to prevent negligence by their colleagues, since they risk the loss of their financial stake in the firm and damage to their professional standing and reputation.

A case can therefore be made for introducing a limited liability structure for professional firms along the lines of the LLP proposed by the DTI.[92] Removing the ubiquitous and unremitting threat of unlimited personal liability and replacing it with limited and more carefully targeted safeguards could facilitate a more efficient organisation and management of professional firms and expedite their growth and restructuring.[93] However, one consequence of this development would be a decrease in the homogeneity of the firm's members, since they might no longer face an equal level of risk for the firm's liabilities. This would depend on members being personally liable for their own negligence and on the extent of their personal liability for the management of the firm and

---

[90] See DeMott, "Our Partners' Keepers? Agency Dimensions of Partnership Relationships" (1995) 58 *Law and Contemporary Problems* 109.

[91] See also Kalish, "Lawyer Liability and Incorporation of the Law Firm: A Compromise Model Providing Lawyer-Owners with Limited Liability and Imposing Broad Vicarious Liability on Some Lawyer-Employees" (1987) 29 *Ariz. LR* 563.

[92] N. 5 above.

[93] See Kalish, n. 91 above, and Ribstein, n. 70 above.

the supervision of others,[94] in which case their individual exposure would differ according to the riskiness of their particular field of expertise and their level of personal responsibility for matters of management and supervision. Members would then be more likely to have conflicting views on such matters as the proper basis for sharing profits, the size of the firm's indemnity insurance cover and the settlement of claims.[95] This would tend to make the firm's internal arrangements more controversial and more complex than in the case of a partnership, and increase the costs of settling the firm's internal arrangements. It would also counteract a major reason for these firms being owned by their active participants.[96] The extent of this problem in practice would depend on how great a degree of divergence is actually permitted by the ancillary safeguards, including the regulations of each profession,[97] and these factors would also determine how far a move towards ownership by passive investors would be feasible. For this reason, professional firms might be better served by a more direct response to the problem of burgeoning negligence claims, as has occured in Germany and Australia.[98] Such a response would focus on the legal difficulty which they face in limiting their liability in advance and would, subject to suitable safeguards, improve their ability to do this. However, a special legal structure for professional firms could provide a useful basis for a move in both directions. In the United States, for example, this has been achieved through a form of LLP (or "RLLP") that is available to professional firms through registration.[99] The RLLP was first introduced in Texas in 1991 in response to a surge of professional negligence claims against law firms which followed the widespread failure of banks and savings and loans institutions, and versions have since been introduced in most other states. However, RLLPs remain partnerships in legal nature and the members are shielded from personal liability by the terms of the relevant enabling statute. The earliest RLLP statutes provided members with only a limited shield, protecting them from personal liability for professional negligence except for their

---

[94] The DTI's proposals are based on the assumption that firm members would be personally liable for their own negligence. For an analysis of the legal basis of this personal liability and its potential scope, see Griffiths, n. 5 above.

[95] See Hamilton, "Registered Limited Liability Partnerships: Present at the Birth (Nearly)" (1995) 66 *Univ. Col. LR* 1065.

[96] See Hansmann, n. 46 above.

[97] Nn. 60 and 86 above.

[98] In Germany, a new form of organisation has been introduced for professional firms which is permitted to make contractual arrangements to limit liability: see Pilny, "Germany Offers Lawyers New Partnership Vehicle", *International Financial Law Rev.* Feb. 1996, 14–16; Rotthege, "Practising Law in Germany: New Organisational Forms", *Global Law & Business*, Nov. 1995, 21–5, and Weber Rey and Marlow, "The Law Affecting Professional Partnerships in Germany" (1995) 10 *ICCLR* at 340–3. In New South Wales, the Professional Standards Act provides two schemes whereby professional firms can limit their liability in advance, subject to various safeguards for the protection of their clients: see Whalley, "Limiting the Liability of Professional Partnerships: Searching for the Holy Grail Down Under" (1998) 19 *Co. Law* 125.

[99] See generally Bergman, "Covering your Assets: Missouri's New Limited Liability Partnership Law" (1995) 63 *UMKC LR* 679; Hamilton, n. 95 above; and Lobenhofer, n. 77 above.

own or that of someone under their supervision and control, but subsequent RLLP legislation has tended to provide a much wider shield.[100]

CONCLUSION

Partnership therefore faces an uncertain future in the new millennium. Whilst it has the advantage of providing a simple legal framework that is readily obtainable, it does not offer the organisational advantage of separate legal personality, and the members of a partnership face the onerous burden of unlimited mutual liability. It is arguable that the extent of its continuing use is due more to the deficiencies of the company as an alternative legal structure than to the intrinsic qualities of the partnership. The key defect of the company in this respect is its rigid adherence to an internal legal framework that suits the requirements of a firm which is largely owned by passive investors and is costly to adapt for a firm largely owned by its active participants. The partnership has therefore tended to be used mostly by small firms and professional firms, where ownership by active participants tends to be more viable as a style of organisation.

However, there is a case for making the benefits of limited liability available at a lower cost to both small firms and professional firms, provided that this is accompanied by safeguards to protect the legitimate interests of creditors and clients. Thus, whilst the case for a limited liability structure is much stronger for firms owned by passive investors, it can also be justified more generally as an efficient basis or default position for establishing the overall set of arrangements between a firm's members, its creditors and other interested parties. The unlimited mutual liability of partners, on the other hand, provides a safeguard for clients which may prove excessive and stultify the efficient development and organisation of some of those firms which use this structure. The pressure for reform has been more intense in relation to professional firms because trends in liability for negligence have sharply increased the burden of partnership liability. Whilst the mutual liability of partners in a professional firm can be defended as a valuable safeguard for its clients and also as reinforcing the members convergence of interest which ensures the effficiency of ownership by active participants as a style of organisation, this reasoning does not mean that their liability has to be unlimited. The pressure for reform has resulted in proposals for the LLP and, although this structure is likely to be confined to professional firms, it could mark the eclipse of the traditional partnership. Thus, whilst the unincorporated firm with unlimited liability will no doubt have a role to play in the new millennium, it may prove to be narrower than before.

---

[100] See Hamilton, n. 95 above, 1066. The State of Delaware, where the leading firms of accountants have registered as RLLPs, has amended its legislation to provide a much wider shield for members.

3

Structuring the Law of Private Limited Companies Through the Next Millennium

TERRY PRIME*

"Some topics in company law become briefly fashionable, others are rightly debated time and again. One of the latter is the appropriate legal regime for smaller businesses".[1]

1. INTRODUCTION

Since many of the problems of the law affecting private limited companies arise from the very nature of company law and the use to which it has been put, a historical perspective is essential when deliberating on issues of reform. The majority of businesses operating as private limited companies would undoubtedly be classified as small, whether the measure of smallness be turnover, number of employees employed or number of participants within the venture.[2] This in itself indicates an appropriate perspective from which to approach evaluation of the modern law of private companies.

A hundred years ago a writer attempting to consider what needed to be done to reform company law to confront the problems of the twentieth century would also have been likely to put emphasis on the needs of small business.[3] The

---

* Terry Prime BA PhD, Solicitor, Professor of Law University of East Anglia.

[1] Editorial (1988) in *Company Lawyer*, Vol. 9, 118.

[2] The definition of small in this connection varies with the perspective of the individual or body attempting the definition. See e.g. J. Freedman and M. Godwin, "The Statutory Audit and the Micro Company—an Empirical Investigation" [1993] *JBL* 105.

[3] Indeed writing in 1882 Pollock recommended the introduction of the limited partnership firm precisely because of the perceived need for such form: "Essays on Jurisprudence and Ethics" (London, MacMillan and Co., 1882), 100. The need had in fact been recognised in two government reports earlier in the century but remain unremedied at its close: the *Departmental Report on the Law of Partnership to the President of the Board of Trade*, made 1 Mar. 1837, and the *Report of the Select Committee of the House of Commons* 1851 No 509. The Report of the Select Committee recommended the appointment of a commission of adequate legal and commercial knowledge to consider the matter and make recommendations for change!

available choices for a small business, in which two or more people wished to come together to venture capital, were simple and stark. On the one hand, there was simple partnership, the great business form which had dominated national commercial expansion in the eighteenth and nineteenth centuries so far as businesses of small and medium size were concerned, which taken together represented the power house which generated British commercial and industrial dominance. On the other was the limited company essentially developed and devised as a means by which large sums of capital could be raised for major strategic industrial and commercial developments such as canals and railways. Only the latter offered limited liability, and the formation of such a company had traditionally been complex and expensive, and thus ill-suited to the needs of small and medium sized business.[4] It is true that during the nineteenth century changes had been made to company law which had made the adaptation of the form to small businesses both possible and practicable, as was demonstrated by the House of Lords decision in *Salomon* v. *Salomon*,[5] but this decision had demonstrated ample differences of judicial approach and remained extremely controversial. The prevailing uncertainty arising from the *Salomon* decision was emphasised by the fact that the closely held company had been recognised, if the decision stood, in a system of company law which did not distinguish between public and private companies. The unresolved tensions arising from the decision of the House of Lords were there for all to see. Equally, the unlimited liability which attached to all participants in a partnership was certainly ill-suited to any small or medium sized business in which only some of the partners intended to participate actively in its management, others simply being prepared to venture capital for the return that it might bring them. Here, the liability of the inactive partners being unlimited meant that they could be ruined by the commercial mismanagement of those who managed the business, their liability not being restricted to the capital ventured. The need for some rethinking of the law affecting small and medium sized business organisations was clear and obvious.

In undertaking reform, three fundamental alternatives were available. First, it would have been possible, at least theoretically, to devise some new form of business organisation, simple and inexpensive to set up and run, to meet the needs of small and medium sized businesses, while taking into account the social and economic needs of society in general.[6] A second alternative would be to set

---

[4] The best succinct account of the development of company law and partnership remains that contained in P. Davies (ed.), *Gower's Principles of Company Law* (6th edn., Sweet & Maxwell, 1997) chs. 2 and 3. See also Prime and Scanlan, *The Law of Private Limited Companies* (London, Butterworths, 1996) 10 ff.

[5] [1897] AC 22.

[6] Such forms are widely recognised elsewhere. In civil law countries the Gesellschaft mit beschränkter Haltung (GmbH) of Germany and the société à responsabilité limitée (SARL) of France, which is based on the German model, could be said to be of this type. In the USA there is specific Close Corporation legislation in most states, albeit conforming to one of two separate models. A most interesting recent example elsewhere is the close corporation legislation of South Africa.

up a modification to partnership law enabling partnerships to be established in which a combination of entrepreneurs and passive capitalists could come together, with the former carrying on the management of the business and having unlimited liability, and the latter having their liability restricted to the capital that they chose to risk in the business. Thirdly, company law could be modified to consolidate the position supported by the House of Lords that small and medium sized companies could be set up simply, quickly and cheaply, conferring limited liability on all participants with no or only limited publicity about their operations.

In the event, in 1907 the legislature, with more energy than reflection, accomplished both the second[7] and third solutions simultaneously.[8] In the event, as is well known, it is the second solution which commerce has taken up as the option that it prefers to use, with the result that, for better or worse, the small limited liability company has become the norm as the instrument of twentieth-century economic activity.

The experience of this century, however, has demonstrated strongly the weaknesses of the model solution. Simply making available to small and medium sized business the possibility of speedy and cheap incorporation does not mean that the resultant structure is well suited to meet the aspirations of those who employ it. True, it gives them limited liability. However, the participants are absorbed into a structure designed to regulate the operations of a large business, having very many owners (the shareholders) who do not know one another, and who necessarily delegate the management of the company to a small number of specialists, the directors. In the majority of small businesses most or all of those who entrust capital will participate in the operation of the business, will know each other well, will be capable of making their decisions relatively informally and quickly since they are in day-to-day contact, and will wish to keep the overall financial position of their business as secret as possible since, in the majority of cases, it will be their only or major source of income and wealth. Much of the development of company law in this century, in so far as it impacts on private limited companies, has been directed at trying to meet these particular deficiencies in spite of the statutory form which the legislature has created. To understand the degree of need for, and direction of, reform a consideration of these issues is necessary. The analysis can be divided into two main headings. First, the attempt to create the intimate personal commercial shareholder relationships necessary for small and medium sized business, and, secondly, general issues of over-formality, which can be brought together under the general topic of deregulation.

---

[7] The Limited Partnerships Act 1907, on which see Prime and Scanlan, *The Law of Partnership* (London, Butterworths, 1995), ch. 14.

[8] The Companies Act 1907 exempted small private companies from certain of the requirements of publicity, thereby giving them much of the advantage of partnership in this connection. Developments in the latter half of the 19th century had meant that it was possible to form such small companies, but the publicity requirements prior to 1907 were a significant disadvantage.

2. QUASI-PARTNERSHIP

It is a feature of small businesses in the UK that those who put capital into them are usually the same people who are involved in their management. As the Bolton Report[9] clearly stated nearly 30 years ago "virtually all small firms are managed by people with a stake in the firm, and the majority are managed by those having a controlling interest, usually the founder or member of his family". The clear link between ownership and management indicates a small group of people operating closely together in a situation of close interdependence. As such, the relationship is necessarily very personal. In France the personal nature of the relationship is conveyed by the term *intuitus personae*. However, in legal terms this form of relationship, whilst characteristic of partnership, is certainly not characteristic of company law. As has been well stated in relation to both English and French law:

> "The whole spectrum of individual participation in business organisation runs from a close and active personal involvement in the running of an enterprise, to a detached and impersonal investment in a profit making machine. The first typifies the situation in many partnerships, while the latter describes a situation of most shareholders in large public companies or SAs".[10]

As such, there has been a great need to adapt the impersonal structure of the company to meet the needs of a style of operation which in practice, but not in law, has been of a partnership nature. The basic structure of Anglo-American company law has been built around the concept of the public company with freely transferable shares, and managed by a small body of directors who are accountable to and removable by a large body of shareholders. The expectation, however, in the small business is that all or most of the participants will participate in the business, that they will not be removed from management except for specific cause and that their shares should not be freely transferable so that the participants may control who becomes a member of the "firm". While these expectations are fully recognised by basic partnership law,[11] they are ignored by company law. As such, it is highly necessary that the basic structures of company law be adapted to meet these requirements, thereby creating a "partnership" nestling within the limited liability structure. The ingenuity of lawyers and the flexibility of the courts have allowed this process to be undertaken with some degree of success, and, indeed, the resultant creation has even been given a technical name, that of Quasi-Partnership.

---

[9] Report of the Committee of Inquiry on Small Firms (Cmnd 4811, HMSO, London), para. 1:3, 6.

[10] R. R. Drury, "Legal Structures of Small Businesses in France and England Compared: (1978) 27 *ICLQ* 510 at 524.

[11] See generally Prime and Scanlan, n. 7 above.

3. THE QUASI-PARTNERSHIP UNDER ENGLISH COMPANY LAW

Brenda Hannigan has identified the characteristics of the quasi-partnership type company with clarity:

"As a quasi-partnership it will usually have been formed or continued on the basis of a personal relationship involving mutual confidence. There may be an agreement or understanding that all or some of the shareholders are to participate in the conduct of the business. Restrictions on the transfer of shares will be the rule rather than the exception. The individuals involved may also have made relatively substantial capital contributions to the company. Shareholders in such companies will be a small, close-knit group, involved in the day-to-day operation of the business, and financially and personally committed to the company".[12]

These identifying features suggest that shareholder interests in such companies lie in four main areas:

1. in employment and participation, given their close involvement with the company;
2. in maintaining the *status quo*, in order to protect the basis on which the business has been set up;
3. in the proper conduct of the company's affairs, in order to ensure continued good will among the parties and the prosperity of the business;
4. in their financial position, given the commitment of their personal resources to the company.

4. THE EVOLUTION OF THE QUASI-PARTNERSHIP CONCEPT

The recognition of such diverse interests and expectations within a single legal structure has not been easy for English company law. It was not until the 1960s and 1970s that the term "quasi-partnership" was coined as a name for such organisations as are now under consideration.[13] The adoption of such a form may arise from the variety of antecedents and reasons. A business set up initially as a partnership may subsequently incorporate and become a quasi-partnership. Equally, two entrepreneurs about to set up a business may incorporate it as a quasi-partnership from its very inception. Alternatively, a "one-man" company with an expanding business may develop into a quasi-partnership when the one man takes on a partner within the corporate structure which he already enjoys. Also, two separate but complementary businesses with separate proprietors may be brought together into a new corporate structure in which the proprietors

---

[12] "Section 459 of the Companies Act 1985—a Code of Conduct for the Quasi-partnership?" [1988] *LMCLQ* 60 at 62–3. An alternative title for the phenomenon is that of closely-held company.
[13] See *Re K/9 Meat Supplies (Guildford) Ltd* [1966] 3 All ER 320, [1966] 1 WLR 1112; *Re Expanded Plugs Ltd* [1966] 1 All ER 877, [1966] 1 WLR 514; *Re Filder Bros. Ltd* [1970] 1 All ER 923, [1970] 1 WLR 592; *Ebrahimi v. Westbourne Galleries Ltd* [1973] AC 360, [1972] 2 All ER 492.

assume quasi-partnership responsibilities to each other. Finally, the quasi-partnership form is the natural structure for the corporate joint venture.

All these different uses have in common the desire to obtain the protection of limited liability while modifying the constitutional structures of the company so that the participants enjoy internally the sort of rights and protections characteristic of partners. However, while the "partners" may enjoy equality of shareholding, management and voting rights, this is not essential for a quasi-partnership to be established.[14] At the heart of the concept is a relationship between the participants operating a business together on the basis of trust and confidence so that the constitutional arrangements do not express the full understanding achieved by the parties, and hence the legitimate expectations of each participant. It follows from this that the mere fact that the participants came together to form a small company does not create a quasi-partnership in the absence of the additional factors. In the words of Peter Gibson J in *Re a Company (No 003096 of 1987)*,[15] "there must be averments that something equivalent to partnership obligations were created". By the same token, as he went on to point out, a quasi-partnership can be created without there having been a pre-existing partnership, but where such a partnership pre-exists the obligations arising from that form of business organisation "might be taken to continue".[16]

5. THE COURTS' JURISDICTION TO INTERVENE

Whilst it might be common for companies to be formed by a small number of participants with mutual and legitimate expectations that they will all participate in the business and generally conduct their relationships with one another as thought they were partners, it does not follow that a remedy will be provided for them where the expectations are not met. While the actual term "quasi-partnership" seems to have been a judicial invention of the past 30 years or so, the phenomenon goes back at least as far as the simplification introduced by the companies legislation in the latter half of the nineteenth century and beyond, which, by allowing the speedy and inexpensive incorporation of businesses, made them a natural vehicle for small and medium sized businesses.[17] The provision of a judicial remedy when a breakdown between the participant occurred proved to be a matter of some difficulty for English law.[18] The present basis was

---

[14] *Per* Nourse J in *Re Bird Precision Bellous Ltd* [1984] Ch. 419 at 433.

[15] (1987) 4 BCC 80.

[16] *Ibid.*, at 84.

[17] The company at the heart of litigation in the famous case of *Salomon* v. *Salomon* was a small closely held company. *Broderip* v. *Salomon* [1895] 2 Ch. 323, 64 LJ Ch. 689, 2 Mans. 449, 12 R 395, 43 WR 612, 39 Sol. Jo. 522, 72 LT 755, 11 TLR 439, (CA): revised *sub nom. Salomon* v. *A Salomon & Co* [1897] AC 22, 66 LJ Ch. 35, 4 Mans. 89, 45 WR 193, [1895–9] All ER Rep. 33, 41 Sol. Jo. 63, 75 LT 426, 13 TLR 46 (HL).

[18] See Prime, Gale and Scanlon, *The Law and Practice of Joint Ventures* (Butterworths, London, 1997), 63. The problem has been general throughout the common law world: see for instance

introduced by the Companies Act 1980, section 75, which adopted the recommended reform under which the spotlight is no longer on the nature of the conduct of the majority, but on the impact of the conduct on the complainants interests. The current incarnation of the reform is the Companies Act 1985, section 459,[19] which provides that a member of a company may apply for relief on the ground that the company's affairs have been, or are being conducted in a manner unfairly prejudicial to some part of its membership including himself.

Undoubtedly in its most recent incarnation the unfair prejudice provision enables minority shareholders to obtain an order that the majority buy out their interests in circumstances in which they would not previously have been successful. In general, however, a remedy will not be provided for mismanagement of the company,[20] although it has been judicially stated that an application under section 459 might be successful "where the majority shareholders, for reasons on their own, persisted in retaining in charge of the management of the companies business, a member of their family who was demonstrably incompetent".[21] Further, a failure to pay reasonable dividends where there is no good reason for retaining profits, at least, if coupled with the payment of excessive directors fees,[22] may ground a successful application, as might, in appropriate circumstances, activities which will dilute a minority shareholding.[23]

Whilst a variety of remedies are available at the discretion of the court where an application under section 459 is successful, the remedy most commonly sought and given is that the majority buy out at a fair price the shares of the dissentient minority. This has given rise to difficult issues of valuation, in particular whether the shares of the minority should be valued on a discounted basis to recognise their lack of market value given the minority position which they

---

Michael Carnahan, "Relief to Oppressed Minorities in Close Corporations: Partnership Precepts and Related Considerations" (1974) *Arizona State Law Journal* 409. The difference, however, has been the different nature of the response. The US vigorously adopted a body of law for close corporation leading Prof. Barry Rider to write in 1979 that "having regard to the history of corporate development in Britain and the United States of America it is surprising that the concept of the close corporation or domestic company has achieved such a degree of recognition in the latter, but has been almost ignored in the former": "Partnership Law and its Impact on Domestic Companies" (1979) 38 *CLJ* 148.

[19] As amended by the Companies Act 1989, Sched. 19, para. 11. On the subject of s.459 see S. H. Goo, *Minorities Shareholders Protection* (Cavendish, 1994). The effect has been as predicted by M. R. Chesterman; "the only justification for keeping alive the sledgehammer remedy of winding up on the just and equitable ground in this particular context is that frequently nothing else is available. When the other more flexible remedies are subjected to appropriate reform, the sledgehammer need only be used where euthanasia is utterly essential:" "The 'Just and Equitable' Winding Up of Small Private Companies" (1973) 36 *MLR* 129.

[20] *Re Sam Weller and Sons Ltd* [1990] Ch. 602, *Re Elgindata* [1991] BCLC 959

[21] [1991] BCLC 994; *Re Macro (Ipswich) Ltd* [1994] 2 BCLC 354 as discussed in Prime, Gale and Scanlan, n. 17 above, 74.

[22] *Re Sam Weller and Sons Ltd* [1990] Ch. 682; *Re Cumana Ltd* [1986] BCLC 430; *Re a Company (No 004415 of 1996)* [1997] BCLC 479.

[23] *Re a Company* [1985] BCLC 80 (the decision of the CA is reported as *Re Cumana Ltd* [1986] BCLC 430); *Re a Company* [1986] BCLC 362.

represent. The alternative is to apply a *pro rata* asset valuation based upon the proportion of the holding of the shares in relation to the total asset value of the company. The issue has enjoyed a somewhat complex life before the courts, and the issue of valuation has certainly proved to be an additional arguable matter in litigation, thereby adding to its costs and complexity.[24]

6. REFORMING THE LAW

The recasting of sections 459 and 460 has certainly meant that oppressed minorities have a remedy which they can exploit in court. Unfortunately litigation under section 459 has often tended to be extremely expensive.[25] This has proved to be a problem in other jurisdictions.

In this country the issue has recently been considered by the Law Commission in its report *Shareholder Remedies.*[26] It would amend sections 459 and 461 by the introduction of certain presumptions to aid a petition. These presumptions are selected on the basis that the Law Commission identified by statistical survey that petitions brought by minority shareholders in small private companies under section 459 were mostly *primarily based on the grounds of exclusion of the minority from the management of the company, and sought the remedy of an order that the petitioner minority's shares be purchased to allow the minority to escape on fair terms.* To assist such petitioners, and to enable them more easily to obtain the remedy which they seek, the Law Commission would amend sections 459 and 461 by the introduction of two presumptions. The first presumption will arise where four conditions are satisfied, namely:

(a) that the company in respect of which the remedy is sought is a private company limited by shares;

(b) that the member has been removed as a director or prevented from carrying out all (or substantially all) of his functions as a director;

(c) that immediately before the removal, the member held shares in his sole name, giving him 10 per cent of the voting rights in the company; and

(d) that immediately before the removal, all, or substantially all, of the members were directors of the company. Where these conditions are satisfied the onus passes to the respondent of the proceedings to show that the removal of the petitioner as a director, or the prevention of his carrying out his functions as a director, was not unfairly prejudicial to the petitioner's interests.

---

[24] For a discussion see Prime, Gale and Scanlan, n. 17 above, 101 ff.; Prentice "The Theory of the Firm—Majority Shareholders' Oppression: Section 459–461 of the Companies Act 1985" (1988) 8 *OJLS* 55 at 83–4.

[25] See Law Commission Report, *Shareholder Remedies*, Law Com. No 246 (Cm 3769) (1997), 3.

[26] *Ibid.*

If this presumption arises and is not rebutted and, as a result, the court is satisfied that an order ought to be made for the purchase of the petitioner's shares, a second presumption arises, namely that the share purchase order ought to be on a *pro rata* basis. However, the court may in particular circumstances be persuaded to order that the second presumption should not apply, and in any event, since it is a presumption, it may, presumably, be rebutted if the respondent can show that a valuation on such a basis would in all the circumstances be unfair, and cause unjust enrichment to the petitioner.

It remains to be seen whether or not, if the law is amended in the light of these presumptions, litigation under section 459 will be simplified and expense avoided. Indeed, perhaps the acid test for the legislation to be regarded as fundamentally successful in meeting its object will be whether the petitioner's route to an order for the purchase of their shares on a *pro rata* basis is so clear and obvious that respondents will automatically settle on those terms on the mere threat from a disgruntled minority shareholder of the threat of proceedings if his shareholding is not bought out.[27]

7. SHAREHOLDER AGREEMENTS

The whole jurisdiction of the court developed to deal with quasi-partnership form, whether by use of the owner to wind up under the just and equitable basis or to make an order under section 459, is founded on the clear basis that the constitutional documents do not contain the full understanding and agreement between the parties. As a result the courts have been able to reason that to allow the parties to rely on the company's constitutional documents alone would permit the legitimate expectations of some at least of the parties to be defeated. This has been the basis of the intervention that the courts have effected. Inevitably the creativity of the judiciary in this respect has been fully matched by the ingenuity of commercial legal advisers in exploiting this thinking. Commercial lawyers have quickly realised that the best way of expressing the totality of the understanding between the participants in the business is not by adapting the constitutional documents, which would require filing and would become available to the public, and the subsequent amendment of which would be a matter of some complexity and slowness, but rather by preparing extensive shareholder agreements[28] containing the detail of the understanding between the parties, existing outside the constitutional documents, but representing an agreement on how the parties will operate the constitution which has been publicly filed. The shareholder agreements are not public documents,[29] but

---

[27] The Law Commission also suggests provisions in the articles conferring exit rights on minority shareholders in certain situations.

[28] On shareholder agreements generally see Andrew Marsden, "Shareholder Agreements in Corporate Joint Ventures and the Law" (1996) 17 *The Co. Lawyer* 194.

[29] See however the discussion by Andrew Marsden, "Does a Shareholders' Agreement require filing with the Registrar of Companies?" (1994) 15 *The Co. Lawyer* 19.

nevertheless are absolutely central to the running of a company structured with their use, so that it is true to say that in such cases, in the event of query or dispute, the first point of reference for shareholders and their advisers will be the shareholder agreement, rather than the constitutional documents themselves, a clear parallel to the situation of a partnership, where queries and disputes are resolved initially, at least, by reference to the terms of the partnership agreement.

Of course, it cannot be pretended that all quasi-partnership type closely held companies will have the benefit of shareholder agreements. Many are set up as cheaply as possible and without legal advice. Some lawyers, if their advice is sought, may not advise their use. However, in the case of many quasi-partnerships formed with the benefit of legal advice the adviser will recommend their use. Sometimes their use is dictated by outside requirements, for instance a bank or other financial institution, may demand their use in the case of a company seeking to borrow substantial sums. The use of shareholder agreements is now practically universal in the case of corporate joint ventures.

The form of a shareholder agreement has many similarities to that assumed by a partnership agreement, and this is hardly surprising, since they are used as a deliberate choice by the shareholders so as to formalise a partnership-type agreement within the shelter of a limited liability company. Such an agreement is likely to have clauses covering *inter alia* the following four matters:[30]

1. Nature of the business—a precise definition of the scope and purposes of the quasi-partnership company will be included, so that its business activities cannot be extended without the agreement of all the participants.
2. Rights and duties of the shareholders—under this each participant is given a right to participate fully in the management of the company, both at board meetings and shareholder meetings. It is likely that less important decisions will fall to be taken by majority vote, but fundamental decisions, including almost certainly all those which require unity in the case of a partnership, fall to be decided either by some qualified majority or unanimously. This is likely to be supported by entrenched voting rights in the shareholder agreement.
3. Restriction on transfer of shares—this is a common feature of all private companies, but in the case of a quasi-partnership the restrictions are likely to be particularly closely drawn and the issue dealt with in the shareholder agreement.
4. Restriction on competition—shareholder agreements, very probably, will contain provisions restricting the right of participants to compete with the business of the company, thereby creating an obligation of good faith in this respect, similar to that achieved in a partnership.

---

[30] For a full discussion of the contents of corporate shareholder agreements see Prime, Gale and Scanlan, n. 17 above, ch. 3.

The advantages of the use of a shareholder agreement over inserting provisions in the constitution of the company can be listed as follows:

1. The agreement enables parties to agree on matters which cannot be easily included in the constitution of the company, for instance, provisions with regard to future contribution of capital, how deadlock in the operation of the company is to be dealt with to avoid applications to the court under the just and equitable ground or section 459, and for arbitration between the parties can be included.
2. The shareholder agreement is flexible, with the result that it can be modified by the parties simply and easily, and without the requirement of further registration with the registrar of companies.
3. The agreement is freely negotiated by the parties and the very process of negotiation, like the process of creating a partnership, causes the parties to have to consider issues and reach agreement in relation to them. The agreement, when finalised, is relatively comprehensive, but at the same time private and not available to the public at large.[31]
4. The copy agreement, which participants will possess, operates similarly to a partnership agreement, in the sense that the parties are likely to consult it much more readily on a day-to-day basis in undertaking their activities than they are likely to consult the formal constitutional documents of a company.

The effect of shareholder agreements has now been the subject of consideration by the House of Lords in *Russell* v. *Northern Bank Development Corporation Ltd*.[32] The litigation concerned a shareholder agreement entered into as part of a bank's efforts to aid a brick making company in financial difficulties which contained, in clause 3, a provision that no new capital should be issued without the written consent of all the parties. The shareholder agreement was entered into by the individual shareholders and the company itself. It was argued that the agreement was ineffective since the provision breached the statutory power of the company to increase its share capital.

In fact, the precise ratio of the case and the propositions for which it is authority have been the subject of vigorous debate. However, taking the view which is both the most straightforward explanation of the case and which is the most orthodox,[33] it appears that the House of Lords has decided that such agreements are binding upon the shareholders but, where there is a mandatory provision of company law preventing the company from entering into such an arrangement, not upon the company itself, which would otherwise prejudice future shareholders. In the words of Lord Jauncey, delivering the judgment of the House:

[31] See, however, the discussion by Marsden referred to in n. 28 above.
[32] [1992] 3 All ER 161 at 166–7.
[33] For a fuller discussion of the issues raised by the decision in the *Russell Case* see Prime, Gale and Scanlan, n. 17 above, 78–81; Brian Davenport QC, "What Did *Russell* v. *Northern Bank Development Corpn. Ltd* Decide?" (1993) 109 *LQR* 553; Eilis Ferran, "The Decision of the House of Lords in *Russell* v *Northern Bank Development Corporation Limited*" (1994) 53 *CLJ* 343.

"While a provision in the company's articles which restricts its statutory power to alter those articles is invalid as an agreement dehors the articles between shareholders as to how they shall exercise their voting rights on a resolution to alter the articles is not necessarily so . . . [i]t is only fetters on the power to alter articles of association imposed by the statutory framework of a company which are obnoxious."[34]

8. CONSTITUTIONAL ADAPTATION

In addition to the use of shareholder agreement the closely held quasi-partnership company will meet its needs by calling in aid both general contract law and the potential to modify its constitutional documents to try to achieve a form which fully meets the aspirations of its participants. Two major areas where this will be undertaken are of particular significance, namely the incorporation of provisions (i) restricting the transfer of shares, and (ii) preventing the removal of directors.

9. RESTRICTIONS ON TRANSFERS OF SHARES

As partnership guarantees the partners the right to take part in the management of the partnership, it also provides that, in the absence of agreement to the contrary in the partnership agreement, the admission of anyone to the partnership requires the agreement of all partners.[35] This, therefore, prevents a participant from disposing of his partnership interest to an incoming partner without the consent of each of the continuing partners. In so doing, partnership recognises the close and intimate relationship which exists in this close form of business arrangement, which is also of course characteristic of the quasi-partnership form of company.

On the other hand, the traditional concept of company law has been that company shares should be freely transferable, since share ownership in a public company is an impersonal matter, the share merely being a property investment. This has given rise to the issue of what constitutional steps can be taken to modify the traditional approach of company law. There have been two such approaches, namely, by the use of provisions in a shareholder agreement, and by constitutional provision in the articles of the company.

The constitutional amendment may take one of two basic forms. One way of proceeding is to give to the company a right of pre-emption in respect of any shares of which a member wishes to dispose.[36] In such a case the shareholder

---

[34] [1992] 3 All ER 161 at 166.

[35] Partnership Act 1890, s. 24(7).

[36] There are numerous examples in the reported cases: see e.g. *Tett* v. *Phoenix Property and Investment Co Ltd* [1986] BCLC 149. If the remaining members wish to exercise the power of pre-emption they must do so in respect of all the shares to be sold; they cannot do so in respect of some only: *Ocean Coal Co Ltd* v. *Powell Duffryn Steam Coal Co Ltd* [1932] 1 Ch. 654.

concerned must give first refusal on the shares to the company, and there is usually a provision to cover the basis of the valuation on which the price is to be ascertained.[37] Of course, if the company does not exercise its pre-emption rights, the shareholder is free to dispose of the shares elsewhere.

Alternatively, the articles may provide for a total prohibition on the transfer of shares outside the company by empowering the directors to refuse to register any share transfers, thereby making the continuing shareholders, who control the company, the only possible market for the shares to the shareholder wishing to dispose.[38] In such a case the restriction is effective provided that the directors, in exercising the discretion to refuse registration, do so in good faith, in pursuance of what they consider to be the interests of the company and not for a collateral purpose. If, however, the exercise of the directors' discretion is undertaken in bad faith, for instance, so as to force a sale to themselves at an undervalue, the court will not enforce the constitutional restriction.[39] The placing of a duty of good faith on the continuing participants in this connection is interesting, since it may be said to closely parallel the duty of faith owed between partners in their financial dealings with each other and with the company's property.[40] Similarly whilst a company has the power to issue shares, if the directors seek to issue shares primarily in order to alter the balance of power within the company, the exercise of the power is for a collateral purpose, not *bona fide*, and the court will intervene.[41]

10. REMOVAL OF DIRECTORS

A major constitutional consequence follows naturally, under company law, from the separation of management and company ownership in public companies, the needs of which have dictated the evolution of the law. With the ownership of the public company being vested in a vast number of shareholders whose interest is in capital investment, management can only be undertaken by a small group of managers, the directors, dedicated to that purpose. It is in the hands of the directors that the day-to-day management of the company lies,[42] and the position of the shareholder owners is protected by making the directors constitutionally accountable to them. If a director does not maintain the

[37] For a discussion of valuation issues see Prime and Scanlan, n. 3 above, 261.
[38] See the discussion in *ibid.*, 323.
[39] *Re Smith and Fawcett Ltd* [1942] Ch. 304, [1942] 1 All ER 542; *Re Cuthbert Cooper and Son Ltd* [1937] Ch. 392, [1937] 2 All ER 466.
[40] *Bissett* v. *Daniel* (1853) 10 Hare 493 and the discussion in Prime and Scanlan, n. 6 above, 181.
[41] *Howard Smith Ltd* v. *Ampol Petroleum Ltd* [1974] AC 821, [1974] 1 All ER 1126; *Punt* v. *Symons & Co Ltd* [1903] 2 Ch. 506; *Piercy* v. *S. Mills & Co Ltd* [1920] 1 Ch. 77; *Hogg* v. *Cramphorne Ltd* [1967] Ch. 254, [1966] 3 All ER 420.
[42] See the authoritative statement of Lord Wilberforce in the HL in *Howard Smith* v. *Ampol Petroleum Ltd* [1974] AC 821 at 837; see also *Automatic Self-Cleansing Filter Syndicate Co Ltd* v. *Cunninghame* [1906] 2 Ch. 34; *Scott* v. *Scott* [1943] 1 All ER 582 and the discussion in Prime and Scanlan, n. 3 above, ch. 6.

confidence of the shareholders their remedy is to remove him from office by an ordinary resolution passed at general meeting, a constitutional equilibrium achieved by the provisions of the company's legislation.

However, in the case of a quasi-partnership, where the shares are closely held by a small group of people all of whom are intended to take part in the management of the company, the traditional constitutional position does not accord with the expectations of the participants. Inevitably, therefore, special provision must be made to protect the interests of the individual participants against the background of the common expectation in which the quasi-partnership was established. Three means may be used in pursuant of the attempt. Each shareholder may be given a contract of service as a director, so that there is a contractual protection; the right of each participant to take part in the management may be set out in the shareholder agreement; or the company constitution may be varied by a *Bushell* v. *Faith* clause. The effect of provisions in shareholder agreements is considered elsewhere.[43]

Contract of Service

If a director is given a contract of service, he has a contract on which he may rely. However, this has no impact upon the constitutional position, since he may be removed from office irrespective of a service contract or, indeed, any provision in the articles of association.[44] However, the removal of a director from his office does not deprive him from receiving compensation or damages payable in respect of the termination of his contract of service.[45] The director may, in these circumstances, thus receive substantial damages from the company for its breach of contract. As a consequence the court will not prevent the use of the constitutional power vested in the shareholders as a whole, simply because the result will be a breach of the contract of service. On occasion, the potential financial penalties of this course of action may render the use of the constitutional power prohibitive for the shareholders.

Constitutional Protection

While the position of a director cannot be protected by the simple expedient of adopting articles of association which, as a matter of direct constitutional provision, provide that no director may be removed, the ingenuity of lawyers and the compliance of the judiciary have provided a means whereby this may be

[43] See p. 49 et seq. above.
[44] Companies Act (CA) 1985, 303.
[45] *Southern Foundries Ltd* v. *Shirlaw* [1940] AC 701, [1950] 2 All ER 445. note that the copy of a director's service contract or a memorandum must therefore be lodged at the company's registered office, and must be available for inspection: CA 1985, s. 318.

accomplished. This is through the incorporation in the articles of a clause which, since its effect was litigated before the House of Lords in the case of *Bushell* v. *Faith*,[46] has come to be called a *Bushell* v. *Faith* clause. The litigation concerned a family company: these are often typical quasi-partnerships. The position of individual directors was secured, not by a provision prohibiting a director's removal, but by a more sophisticated provision in the company's articles,[47] which provided that in the event of a resolution being proposed at any general meeting of the company *for the removal from office of any director*, any shares held by that director should, on a poll in respect of such a resolution, carry the right to three votes per share. Thus, on a resolution to remove a director from office his shares would be weighted at a ratio of three to one, in effect making him irremovable. The plaintiff contended that this provision was invalid as being contrary to the company's legislation. The House of Lords upheld the defendant's contention, taking the view that, whilst the company's legislation guarantees that a director is removable by ordinary resolution, it does not prevent the weighting of votes to make such a resolution impossible to obtain, since it does not expressly deal with that situation. In actual fact it appears that the House was anxious to permit a constitutional mechanism to guarantee the right of a shareholder in a closely held company to participate in the management, Lord Donovan expressly saying: "there are many small companies which are conducted in practice as though they were little more than partnership, particularly family companies running family businesses; and it is, unfortunately, sometimes necessary to provide some safeguard against family quarrels having their repercussions in the Board Room".[48]

The General Duty of Good Faith

In general, however, there is a fundamental difference between the relationship of the participants (partners) in a partnership and that of the participants (shareholders) in a quasi-partnership. Fundamentally shareholders are seen as holding property rights represented by the share which they are, in general, free to exercise solely with reference to their own individual advantage and with no duty of good faith owed to their fellow shareholders.[49] This represents the essentially

---

[46] [1970] AC 1099, [1970] 1 All ER 53.

[47] Emphasis added.

[48] [1970] AC 1099 at 1110–1. An alternative method supported by the courts of protecting a director of a closely held quasi-company from removal is by the creation of separate classes of shares: see the discussion in Prime, Gale and Scanlan, n. 17 above, 92 and 93.

[49] Per Walton J in *Northern Counties Securities Ltd* v. *Jackson and Steeple Ltd* [1974] 1 WLR 1133 at 1144. For an interesting comparative discussion, bringing out the differences in US and English Law, see Zupora Cohen, "Fiduciary Duties of Controlling Shareholders: A Comparative View" (1991) 12 *U PA.J Int.L* 380. Of course all general fiduciary relationships in commercial law are achieved by a process of historical evolution over a period of time in response to commercial need, with the result that "an examination of the differences and similiarities among fiduciaries is complicated by the fact that the various types of fiduciaries have evolved over the centuries": Tamar

anonymous character of the shareholding of a public company. By contrast, partners owe a general duty of good faith to each other, which the courts will enforce. This is because of the close relationship that they have with one another, under which each is the agent for the others for the course of the partnership businesses.[50] Whilst it is true that directors (which in the case of a true quasi-partnership will include all of the participants shareholders) each owe a duty of good faith to the company (each, as director, is agent of the company)[51] that duty is owed to the company itself, and not to each other. Nevertheless, despite the legal analysis, the factual situation will almost certainly be one of close relationship and the utmost reliance.

The only major general exception to this principle is contained in the derivative action conferred upon the minority, enabling them to seek a remedy from the court where there has been a "fraud on the minority". The exception is created to cover the situation in which the majority have behaved improperly, and would otherwise use their control of the company to prevent the matter coming before the court.[52] However, the improper behaviour has to be of a particular variety, resulting in the acquisition of the property rights or opportunities properly belonging to the company by the majority instead. As such, the central example of this type of action is the situation where there has been a breach of fiduciary duty by directors resulting in advantage to them, and the wrongdoers are in control of the company,[53] or where the majority are seeking to expropriate the shares of the minority by simply making amendments to the articles of the association.[54] While the "fraud on the minority" exception can be of some use to protect minorities, it cannot be argued that it represents the creation of a broad principle that fiduciary responsibilities are owed by one venture shareholder to another in the case of a quasi-partnership.[55] The fact that there is no great independent body of case law in support of the principle suggests that, in general, such a duty is not owed.

Frankel, "Fiduciary Law" (1983) 71 *California LR* 795. It may be that English law is in such a process of evolution: see 54 below. Israel recently adopted the US position, having modelled itself previously on English law in this respect: see Cohen, *op. cit.*

   [50] See in particular Partnership Act 1890, ss. 28–30 and Prime and Scanlan, n. 7 above, 170 ff. and the case law discussed therein.
   [51] See Prime and Scanlan, n. 4 above, 116 ff. and the case law discussed therein.
   [52] See *ibid.*, 225 ff. and the case law discussed therein.
   [53] E.g. as in *Daniels* v. *Daniels* [1978] Ch. 406.
   [54] E.g. as in *Estmanco (Kilner House) Ltd* v. *Greater London Council* [1982] 1 WLR 2.
   [55] There appears to be an evolution in the particular area of the corporate joint venture towards implying duties of good faith among the participants: see *Elliott* v. *Wheeldon* [1993] BCLC 53, discussed by Mike Lower, "Towards an Emerging Law of Joint Ventures—*Elliott* v. *Wheeldon*" [1994] *JBL* 507; Gerard Bean, "The Operator as Manager: A New Fiduciary Duty" [1993] *JBL* 24.

Meetings

A further characteristic of traditional company law that arises from the anonymous nature of the shareholders in the public company is the complex set of formal requirements with regard to meetings. In the case of partnership, with its
close association of a limited number of people working together, all that is
required for a decision is unanimous agreement, depending on the requirements
for the particular matter to be decided. The agreement can be achieved entirely
informally, and without any formal meeting. Indeed, one of the criticisms which
can be made in this respect is that the lack of formality with regard to partnerships can lead to decisions being made by agreement which are subsequently difficult to prove, through that very lack of formality. By contrast, in the case of
companies, decisions fall to be made by either directors or shareholders, and
many formalities traditionally attach to both, with regard to the notice that has
to be given at meetings, the procedure at meetings and the requirements for
recording decisions which are made.[56] Decisions with regard to the everyday
management of the business are made by directors in directors' meetings,[57] and
more fundamental decisions by shareholders in shareholders' meetings,[58] with
the most fundamental decisions of all, those requiring fundamental constitutional change, usually requiring a special resolution and an overall majority of
75 per cent.[59] The whole scheme presupposes the necessity of assembling the relevant group together in one place at one time for discussion and the formal taking of the decision, perhaps a serviceable arrangement for the annual general
meeting of a large public company, but hopelessly complex for the operations
of a small group of people working closely together in a quasi-partnership.
Indeed, traditionally it seems likely that in the case of quasi-partnership, decisions are probably being made informally, with scant regard for the statutory
formal requirements.[60]

Because of the unsatisfactory nature of such a formal requirement in the case
of small private company, it has been quite normal for the articles of the company to provide for decisions to be achieved by unanimous informal agreement.
The Companies Act 1985, Table A, Article 53, provides that a resolution in writing executed by or on behalf of each member, who would have been entitled to
vote if it had been proposed at an annual general meeting, is as effective as if it
had been passed at a general meeting duly convened and held, and further that
it does not have to be in a single document but can consist of several written
instruments each executed by and on behalf of one or more members.

---

[56] See generally Prime and Scanlan, n. 4 above, ch. 5.
[57] See the discussion in *ibid.*, 98 ff.
[58] CA 1985, s. 369(1)(b).
[59] CA 1985, s.378.
[60] See Judith Freedman, "Small Businesses and the Corporate Form: Burden or Privilege" (1994)
57 *MLR* 555.

As part of its deregulation policy to remove unnecessary formality and paperwork from businesses, the Conservative Government in office in 1989 introduced a simpler statutory written resolution for all private companies, regardless of the provisions of their articles, in the Companies Act 1989. In broad effect, the provisions with regard to the formalities are the same as those with regard to Article 53 and the Companies legislation specifically states that the procedure can be used to pass resolutions which would otherwise be required to be passed at special, extraordinary or elective meetings. The procedure requires that a copy of the resolution be sent to the company's auditors, who are viewed as being protective of the creditors, and who may insist on the resolution being considered in general meeting or, as the case may be, by a meeting of the relevant class of members of the company. The auditors are entitled to attend and speak at such a meeting on any part of the business which affects them as auditors.

Further, the written resolution procedure does not apply to a resolution for removing a director from office, nor to the removal of an auditor, so that in both these cases the threatened director or auditor has the right to a formal meeting, and to attend and to speak in his own defence. As has been well observed; "hence dispensing with meetings presupposes continued harmony between the members. All too often this breaks down at some stage in the lives of private companies, and the meeting, which will then have to be held to attempt to resolve the disagreement, is likely to be particularly bitter. The observance of the rules will then be just as important as in relation to public companies".[61] This however, would appear to be fair enough. Informality will be the order of the day so long as the participants in the business are in agreement and the business is operating without difficulties. Where this situation no longer obtains, greater formality necessarily in practice tends to follow, even in the case of partnership, where there are no formal requirements with regard to meetings.

DEREGULATION AND CREDITOR PROTECTION

Deregulation has proved to be a generic title under which government has sought to deal with all aspects of law which seem to bear adversely and unnecessarily upon small companies. As such it extends from such things as unnecessary form filling[62] right the way through to legal issues affecting company law itself, including the issue of company meetings, already discussed, and the keeping of company accounts. From the point of view of politics the existence of a buzzword, whether deregulation or better regulation, is no doubt convenient,

---

[61] Davies (ed.), n. 3 above, 582.

[62] Cambridge University Small Business Research Centre's report, "The State of British Enterprise, Growth, Innovation and Competitive Advantage in Small and Medium Sized Firms" (1991); DTI Consultative Document, "The Company Law Review: The Law Applicable to Private Companies" (DTI, London, 1994) URN 94/529.

and enables the politician to market his grubby product. From the point of view of analytical thought it is anything but helpful. Clearly, pure external administrative matters such as form filling, planning and environmental controls and employee protection measures, whilst impacting upon small businesses carried on in companies, have nothing to do with company law and the law of business organisations as such, and lie outside the scope of this essay. However, at the heart of the everyday concept of regulation is the idea of external control of an organisation in the interests of those who are not part of it, and in relation to this there is one important area impacting upon company law itself, namely the issue of creditor protection which has, at its heart, three separate issues for company law, namely, minimum capital, the rules with regard to the keeping and publication of accounts and directors' liability.

Minimum Capital

A further characteristic of English company law, which derives from its theoretical base having evolved from public companies, is the position of company capital and the protection of trade creditors. A company has separate legal personality, and as a result those who give credit to the company must look to repayment of their loan from the company to the extent that the credit is unsecured or not covered by guarantees.[63] It is usual for financial institutions making deliberate loans to obtain security and/or guarantees; the position is otherwise in the case of most trade creditors extending credit to the company.[64] As a result, if the company to which credit has been extended runs into cashflow problems, the extent to which the unsecured creditors will obtain payment will depend on the capital resources of the company itself. Recognising this, English company law has complex provisions to protect the capital of the company and to prevent its repayment to the shareholders,[65] the theory being that the public company raises capital by share issue in the market for the purpose of its business, which must then be retained in the company to fund its business activities. There is, however, a fundamental flaw in its approach in the case of private companies, since private companies can be established with no capital at all, merely borrowing the resources needed for them to function.[66] A regime which carefully protects capital once in the hands of the company is patently flawed when there is no requirement that any capital should come into the hands of the company in the first place. The writer has pointed out elsewhere the

---

[63] *Salomon v. Salomon and Co* [1897] AC 22 and O. Kahn-Freund, "Some Reflections on Company Law Reform" (1944) 7 *MLR* 54.

[64] See e.g. Judith Freedman and Michael Godwin, "Incorporating the Micro-business; Perceptions and Misperceptions" in A. Hughes and D. Storey (eds.), *Finance and the Small Firm* (Routledge, London, 1994).

[65] CA 1985, ss. 143(3), 135, 159–181, discussed Prime and Scanlan, n. 4 above, 186 ff.

[66] Davies, n. 3 above, 236 ff.

general destabilising commercial effect of this, particularly in times of economic downturn.[67]

The Keeping and Publication of Accounts[68]

Traditional English company law, geared to the needs of public companies, does offer a justification for this. Recognising that those who deal with the company are likely to extend it credit, the law insists that financial records of its transactions are kept and annual accounts prepared. The general requirements to keep records is contained in the Companies Act 1985, section 221(1), which requires every company to keep accounting records, which are sufficient to show and explain the company's transactions, and, in particular, are such as both to disclose with reasonable accuracy at any time the financial position of the company at that time, and to enable the directors to ensure that the annual accounts comply with the requirements of the company's legislation. The accounting records are detailed records showing the day-to-day financial position of the company. The annual accounts, by contrast, are meant to show the overall financial position of the company at the end of each financial year, have to be signed by the directors and laid before the annual meetings of shareholders so that the shareholders can see the position and call the directors to account, if necessary, at the annual general meeting.[69] The responsibility of the company's directors in this connection is emphasised, not merely by requiring the directors to prepare the accounts, but also to accept responsibility for the accounts which are prepared, by approving them as a board and signing them.[70] As has been noted judicially, "the responsibility for the preparation of accounts giving a true and fair view of the company's financial state is placed fairly and squarely on the shoulders of the directors".[71]

The annual accounts, however, have a second function under company law theory in addition to that of showing the company's financial position to the shareholders. The annual accounts and accompanying reports have to be filed with the Registrar of Companies[72] and, once filed, become available to anyone who cares to search the file of the company concerned at Companies House. As a result it is possible to argue that creditors have the means of knowing the financial position of companies with which they deal, and, accordingly, if they choose to extend trade credit without drawing on the information at Companies House, they must be taken to accept the risk involved.

This argument is, however, unconvincing. It is a fact that many companies, particularly small companies, are often slow in filing details of their annual

---

[67] Prime and Scanlan, n. 4 above, 174–5.
[68] See generally *ibid.*, ch. 15.
[69] CA 1985, ss. 223–226.
[70] S. 223.
[71] *Caparo Industries plc* v. *Dickman* [1990] 2 AC 605 at 660.
[72] S. 242.

accounts, so that the information available to creditors may well be out of date. However, of even more fundamental significance is the fact that commercial life usually has to operate speedily, and it is not the practice for trade creditors to make investigations at Companies House, nor on occasion would there be time for this to be done if a particular commercial transaction is to be finalised. As a result, the protection given to creditors is illusory,[73] but the complex and demanding accounting requirements are troublesome and expensive. The trouble and expense are no doubt justified in the case of public companies, given the size of assets that they have, the profits that they generate, and the necessity to inform fully their changing and impersonal shareholder base of the evolving financial position of the companies on an annual basis. This justification however, derived from the internal advantage of the company, is hardly convincing in the case of the small private company, in which the members participate in the day-to-day running of the company and are all likely to be equally informed of the company's financial position, or at least have equal access to the information from which the financial position can be understood. Such companies are likely to generate modest profits, and the extensive and cumbersome annual accounting requirements fall heavily upon them.

The lack of practicality of the insistence on formal audited annual accounts in the case of such companies has come to be increasingly recognised by government. Special provisions were made for the accounts of small companies by the Companies Act 1985 (Audit Exemption) Regulations.[74] Under these regulations, a company which qualifies as a small company, having a balance sheet total of no more than £1,400,000 and an annual turnover of not more than £90,000, is totally exempt from the formal requirements, unless members holding at least 10 per cent of any class of shares require an audit of the accounts for the year, by written notice. Where the exemption applies and is used, the directors are obliged to confirm in a statement attached to the balance sheet that the company is entitled to the exemption, that no effective notice has been delivered requiring an audit and that the directors acknowledge their responsibilities for ensuring that the company keeps accounting records and for preparing accounts which give a true and fair view of the company's affairs. This therefore does not remove the company's obligation to file accounts showing a true and fair view of the company's affairs, but does remove the need for formal audit. Although there is an obligation to the accounts reported on by an accountant, this essential difference between the modified procedure for small companies and the full audit is that the accountant's report can be prepared by simply accepting the company's accounting records and taking no steps independently to verify them. Unfortunately the savings in costs thus achieved are likely to be very limited. However, with both the European Commission and the Department of

---

[73] See Judith Freedman and Michael Godwin, "The Statutory Audit and the Micro Company—an Empirical Investigation" [1993] *JBL* 105.

[74] (SI 1994 No 1935). The exemption is created under the reg. by the insertion of new ss. 249A, 249B, 249C, 249D, 249E and 388A into the CA 1985.

Trade and Industry[75] taking increasing interest in small and medium sized enterprises as dynamic contributors to the economy and the creation of wealth and employment within it, it is extremely likely that more steps will be taken to limit further the impact of the accounting requirements on small and medium sized businesses.

Directors' Liability to Creditors

An issue which necessarily follows from this situation is that of the potential liability of the directors and shareholders, which in the case of a small company will be largely one and the same thing, to the creditors. In principle the fundamental position of English company law is that there is no such liability. The company is a separate legal person with its own property and assets, and it is with the separate company that the creditor has transacted his business, and to which, therefore, he must look for payment. It is true that in certain narrow situations, statute and the common law have evolved specific exceptions to this principle, and in these very specific and limited situations the corporate veil can be pierced and remedies sought against the individuals trading through the corporate entity.[76] However, in general, the very narrowness of these exceptions make them totally inadequate as a means of providing an overall solution to the problem.

However, there is one exception to this of potential general value, which is worth examination. This is the concept of wrongful trading contained in the Insolvency Act 1986, section 214.

The concept comes into play on the insolvent liquidation of a company. In such circumstances the liquidator may apply for a declaration that a director or shadow director of a company has undertaken wrongful trading through the company. For the court to have power to make such a declaration, the company must have gone into insolvent liquidation, and it must be shown that at some time before the commencement of the winding up of the company, the director or shadow director knew or ought to have concluded that there was no reasonable prospect that the company would avoid going into insolvent liquidation. The wrongful trading is the trading which the company is allowed to undertake after that time and prior to winding up. The consequence of wrongful trading is that the director may be ordered to make such personal contribution to the company's assets as may seem appropriate to the courts and may also be disqualified from acting as a director in the future.[77]

---

[75] See particularly the DTI consultative document, "Accounting Simplifications: Re Arrangements to Small Company Accounts" URN 96/755.

[76] See Prime and Scanlan, n. 4 above, 25 ff. for a discussion of these narrow exceptions to the general principle of corporate personality.

[77] Company Directors Disqualification Act 1986, s. 10.

As the writer has argued elsewhere,[78] the courts have made use of the power to order a contribution under s.214 to take the old subjective standard of care generally applied at common law, and increase its impact by introducing an objective standard where a company becomes insolvent.

The fundamental purpose of the Insolvency Act 1986, section 214 is that it allows a court to order contributions from a director where a company is put into insolvent liquidation and it can be shown that before the commencement of the winding up the director knew, or ought to have concluded, that there was no reasonable prospect that the company would avoid going into insolvent liquidation. The level of skill required of him for this purpose is set out in section 214(4) and (5) in terms which make it clear that there is both an objective and a subjective aspect of the test. In addition to showing the general knowledge, skill and experience that a director has, he is also expected to show the knowledge, skill and experience that may reasonably be expected of a person carrying out the same functions as are carried out by that director in relation to the company. To avoid all ambiguity it is expressly provided that the reference to the functions carried out in relation to a company by a director includes any functions which he does not carry out but which have been entrusted to him.

Whilst it is to be recognised that the general knowledge, skill and experience required will be much less extensive in a small company operating a modest business with simple book-keeping and accountancy procedures than in a large and sophisticated organisation, certain minimum standards are assumed, in particular that the directors will keep accounting records which disclose with reasonable accuracy at any time the financial position of the company pursuant to their requirements under the Companies Act 1985, section 221.

In assessing the information which is thus available the subjective and objective parts of the test will be applied to each individual director. However, it must be borne in mind that the effects of the legislation still leave a large discretion with the directors whether or not to continue trading with a loss-making company.[79]

The need for careful monitoring of the company's financial position, and, where it is loss-making, for a careful evaluation of whether it should continue trading if directors are to avoid liability under section 214 is well shown in the careful judgment of Knox J in the first case reported on the impact of the legislation, *Re Produce Marketing Consortium Ltd (No 2)*.[80]

There seems to be every indication that the introduction of section 214 has encouraged liquidators to carry out much more detailed investigations into the previous activities of directors, since wrongful trading proceedings are much easier to establish that fraudulent trading, given the wording of section 214 and the fact that wrongful trading carries far less stigma than fraudulent trading claims or disqualification orders. Even where directors take a reasoned view

---

[78] Butterworths Company Law Service, June 1998.
[79] See the remarks of Chadwick J in *Secretary of State for Industry* v. *Taylor* [1997] 1 WLR 407.
[80] [1989] BCLC 520.

that the difficulties of a company are temporary and there is a reasonable prospect that the company will be able to trade out of them, the manner in which they conduct themselves in relation to what they put into, and perhaps more significantly take out of, the business, is likely to come under detailed surveillance. Thus in *Re Produce Marketing Consortium Ltd (No 2)* the court was *inter alia* concerned with the part played by the level of remuneration of the directors in the company's decline, and in *Re Purpoint Ltd*[81] the appropriateness of the motor car provided by the company for its director came under scrutiny. It is likely that if the case law under section 214 develops such scrutiny will intensify and not lessen.

To an extent the approach of the courts on this is reinforced by their attitude in matters of disqualification. The making of a contribution order against a director for wrongful trading may indeed, be the basis for an order for disqualification. But there are other developments with regard to disqualification which are worthy of note since, whilst the Company Directors Disqualification Act 1986 is something of a patchy document, giving rise to a number of specific grounds under which a company director may be ordered to be disqualified, there is one more general one which may be fitted into some general concept of directors' responsibility of skill and judgement. The general provision is contained in section 6 of that Act, which allows a disqualification order to be made against a director of a company which has, at any time during or after that person's directorship, become insolvent if the director's conduct makes that person unfit to be concerned in the management of a company.[82] As the writer has argued elsewhere, the effect of the court's approach to this closely parallels their approach to the Insolvency Act section 214.[83]

The limitations on this evolution of a duty of care as a practical remedy for the problem of creditor protection, are however so overwhelming as to make the well-meaning attempts of the court in effect of little value. A disqualification order does not in itself give a remedy to creditors who are out of pocket, although it does prevent company directors being involved in the activities of any other company for the period of disqualification, thereby preventing them incurring other credit by such means. The wrongful trading provision does not

---

[81] [1991] BCC 121.

[82] In deciding whether or not the person's conduct makes him or her unfit to be concerned in the management of the company, and therefore amenable to a disqualification order, the court is required by s. 9 to have regard to five specific considerations:
1. any misfeasance or breach of fiduciary or other duty by the director in relation to the company;
2. any misapplication or retention by the director of, or any conduct of the director giving rise to an obligation to account for, any money or other property of the company;
3. the extent of the director's responsibility for any failure by the company to comply with accounting and publicity requirements of CA 1985;
4. the extent of the director's responsibility for the causes of the company becoming insolvent;
5. the extent of the director's responsibilities for any failure by the company to supply any goods or services which have been paid for (in whole or in part).

[83] Butterworths Company Law Service, Aug. 1998.

suffer from the disadvantage that it does not swell the assets available to the creditors, but other practical problems come into play. In the case of many under-capitalised companies, the directors have borrowed heavily on the security of their personal assets, and necessarily the secured creditors thus obtain prior access to their wealth, leaving the directors with little against which a contribution order can be made effective. With regard to the downright unethical, the availability of any wealth or assets which would make a contribution order worth obtaining can be obscured through the use of other companies and hidden bank accounts, so as to make the position indistinct and the possibilities of obtaining funds, if an order is made, unlikely. Inevitably, where funds are apparently in short supply, liquidators tend to take the view that it is not in the interest of creditors to waste what few assets may be available to the unsecured creditors in a pursuit which is unlikely to be cost-effective.[84] The wrongful trading and disqualification provisions may therefore be clearly seen as failing to provide an effective solution to the central problem.[85]

COMPANY LAW

Conclusion

The phenomenon of a small closely held company can be seen to give rise to considerable difficulties for English law. This has been mirrored in the United States.[86] There are parallels between the two jurisdictions in their general reactions to the phenomenon, and the comments of Mark von Sternberg are as true of England as they are of the United States:

> "the recent evolution of the closely held corporation in the United States has been accompanied by parallel development in legislative and judicial attitudes. In particular, there has emerged a gradual awakening to the inadequacies of the 'concession' theory of corporation law, which maintains that corporate owners are powerless to depart from 'statutory norms' in organising the corporation, in a corresponding predisposition in favour of the contractual approach which stresses that the corporate structures should reflect the wishes of the company's shareholders. In short, a growing perception is developed that the constraining principles of corporation law may be inappropriate for a firm of corporate organisation that limits the number of its participants, and the search for a body of law to govern such an entity has resulted in an increasing reliance on partnership principles."[87]

---

[84] See A. McGee and C. Williams, "A Company Director's Liability for Wrongful Trading", Research Report 30 of the Chartered Association of Certified Accountants.

[85] There is, however, perhaps some encouragement for the future in the willingness of the DTI to bear itself the responsibility of obtaining a disqualification order with the result that increasing numbers, very properly, are being made.

[86] James Cox, Thomas Lee Hazen and F. Hodge O'Neal, *Corporations* (Aspen Law and Business 1997), ch. 14.

[87] "The Close Corporation's Counterparts in France, Germany and the United Kingdom: A Comparative Study" (1982) 5 *Hastings International and Comparative LR* 291.

Indeed, writing in 1982 Mr von Sternberg clearly categorised English law as one of the systems of law of whose company law it was true to say that "contractual norms and partnership principles have provided the underlying theory of organisation".[88] The express recognition and implied support for the use of shareholder agreements by the House of Lords has merely confirmed this view. Further the adaptability of national laws of business organisations seems to be a Europe-wide phenomenon. In 1969 in its influential report on the possibility of harmonising Member States' legislation on private limited companies, the Council of Europe took the view that there would be unlikely to be a great deal of support for a harmonising measure built around the model of a GmbH because of the adaptability of the various national systems of law, including European common law systems, to cover the situation of the closely held company.[89]

Nevertheless, the emphasis on the contractual principle of small company regulation can only extend to the approach of company law to the relations of shareholders *inter se*. The approach to the relations between the company and its shareholders on the one hand and third parties, particularly creditors, on the other is essentially a matter for regulation and therefore for concession. Even if no protection is conferred upon third parties this in itself is a regulatory statement, namely that the state takes the view that there is no reason to provide protection to those who deal with its limited companies. Thus, it seems that, with regard to the majority of areas looked at in this article, where the relations of shareholders amongst themselves and with the company are under consideration these matters can be left to the parties to work out amongst themselves using the freedom bestowed upon them by the legislature and the judiciary. However, the problem of creditor protection can only be resolved either by tolerating the present situation on the ground that, despite its patent injustice, it is commercially preferable to do so, or by direct intervention. For reasons already advanced the present situation is undesirable in its broad commercial and economic effect.

In relation to this particular issue there is much which can be learnt from German law. As is well known, the law governing the GmbH requires the provision of a minimum of 50,000 DM as capital.[90] There are rigorous provisions to ensure full payment of the share capital contributions,[91] and further restrictions preventing repayment of capital once contributed. In particular any payment to shareholders that reduces the net assets of the company below the stated amount of its share capital is deemed to constitute a repayment of share capital. If distributions are made to a shareholder in violation of the prohibition against

---

[88] "The Close Corporation's Counterparts in France, Germany and the United Kingdom: A Comparative Study" (1982) 5 *Hastings International and Comparative LR* 291.

[89] "Report on the Possibility of Harmonising Member States Legislation on Private Limited Companies (or similar bodies)" (Strasbourg, Council of Europe, 1969).

[90] S. 5(1) GmbH Act.

[91] S. 5 and para. 9.

reducing share capital, the shareholder can be made to refund the payment made by him although, if he acted in good faith, the refund will be limited to the amount required to satisfy the company's creditors if this is less than the amount returned.[92] Further, if either a refund for such a distribution cannot be obtained from a particular shareholder or his original contribution cannot be recovered from him who received it, the other shareholders are proportionately liable to satisfy the amount due.[93] They therefore have an individual incentive to ensure that capital is retained and that their co-shareholders are financially solvent.

These provisions are supported by the capital replacement rules governing shareholder loans. When the shareholders have made their share capital contribution they are no longer obliged to provide additional capital. They are, therefore, as under English law free to provide any additional finance to the company in the form of loans. However, the shareholder will not enjoy the priority of a third party creditor if the company is in financial difficulties, *and the loan is classified as a capital replacement loan.*[94] A capital replacement loan is one which is "made by a shareholder at a time when shareholders acting as prudent business men would instead have provided capital to the company". The critical test is whether the company would have been able to obtain the loan in question at market conditions from an unrelated third party. If the company could not have obtained such a loan from a third party at arm's length, then the shareholder loan is considered as capital replacement, and will be treated as capital on insolvency.[95]

These provisions could be usefully adopted into English law. They would concentrate shareholders' minds on whether the company does or does not have a good realistic future if further financial support becomes necessary. If the shareholders take the view that the company has such a future when the money market takes the contrary view, there seems to be every reason to require them to support their view with their own resources at full risk.

However, the approach of German law can, and should, be further refined. As well as a requirement of a minimum amount of capital which cannot be withdrawn without the shareholders putting themselves at risk, the minimum capital requirement can be used in another way to induce the shareholders to ensure that the operations of the company are commercially prudent. Whilst capital may not be withdrawn once provided, there is nothing to prevent it being lost through commercial activity. On the other hand, once a minimum capital requirement is seen as desirable there is every policy reason to demand that the company should retain its capital if it is to be allowed to continue trading. Directors of companies should be aware of the trading position of the commercial vehicle of which they have charge, and, consequently, be aware of the position of its assets against liabilities.[96] In commercial terms, this is no different

---

[92] S. 5 and para. 31.
[93] Ss. 31 and 24 respectively.
[94] Ss. 32a and 32b.
[95] S. 32a(2).
[96] A view beginning to find some acceptance among the judiciary: see pp. 63 and 64 above.

from requiring a driver to know where his vehicle is on the road. Both motor cars and companies have the capacity to injure others if they are not properly managed. If through its trading activities a company's capital is reduced to less than the minimum capital requirement the directors should be made to confront a choice of one of three alternatives within 21 days of such a situation being reached, namely:

1. the company should cease trading;
2. the shareholders should provide further capital so that the minimum is re-established; or
3. the trading of the company should be continued on the terms that the shareholders are jointly and severally individually responsible for any losses suffered by third parties.

To make such demands is not to argue against a risk-rewarding capitalist society. Rather it is to ask the entirely legitimate question on behalf of such a society, where has the capital risk been taken which is being rewarded?

4

Public Companies

C. A. RILEY[1]

INTRODUCTION

Numerically, public companies are exceptional. Of the nearly one million registered companies in the UK, only just over 1 per cent are public.[2] Moreover, those on which I shall focus in this essay—the very largest of these—are an even rarer breed.[3] Despite all this, however, large public companies are anything but marginal. Their absolute size, the scale of their operations and their monopolisation of some industries give them enormous influence over the quality of the lives most of us lead.[4] Given this pervasive influence, the proper regulation of public companies should be a matter of obvious public concern. Whether as shareholders, employees, consumers, creditors, neighbours, and so on, we are all significantly affected by, and therefore have a real interest in, the regulatory landscape.

In a single essay, it would clearly be impossible to detail all the contours or noteworthy features of this landscape. Rather, having briefly described, in section I, the principal regulatory strategies which company law currently employs, I shall explore *three* fundamental tensions which, I shall try to show, currently beset UK corporate regulation. The first is a *strategic* one, and concerns the best way of ensuring that a company's executives serve the interests of its shareholders. The UK's system of corporate regulation or "corporate governance" (we shall use the terms interchangeably in this essay) has, historically, been characterised as a market-based system, with the take-over and capital markets the most significant disciplinary forces on managerial behaviour. More recently, however, there has been increased pressure to place greater reliance on "internal

[1] Lecturer in Law, Centre for Corporate Governance and Financial Market Regulation, University of Newcastle. Thanks to Ian Dawson and Clare McGlynn for helpful comments on an earlier draft of this essay. The usual disclaimer applies.

[2] See J. H. Farrar and B. M. Hannigan, *Farrar's Company Law* (4th.edn., London, Butterworths, 1998), 44.

[3] These will usually be listed on the London Stock Exchange. These account for about one fifth of public companies: *ibid.*, 40.

[4] See generally J. E.Parkinson, *Corporate Power and Responsibility* (Oxford, Clarendon Press, 1993), ch. 1. More recent trends may point towards a lessening both in the scope of the operations of large companies, and in the degree of concentration in product markets. On the former, see C. Handy, *The Empty Raincoat* (London, Hutchison, 1994); on the latter, see M. W.Kirby, "The Corporate Economy in Britain" in M. W. Kirby and M. B. Rose (eds.), *Business Enterprise in Modern Britain* (London, Routledge, 1994).

monitoring" within the company. Section II explores this tension between markets and monitoring, with particular emphasis on, first, the European Community's harmonisation programme and, secondly, a number of domestic corporate governance initiatives.

In fact, pressure for governance reform has borne rather less fruit than some might have hoped. Part of the reason for that is that the debate over the relative merits of markets and internal monitoring remains unresolved. But another reason relates to the second of our three tensions, explored in section III. This goes to the heart of *law's role* in regulating companies (and, indeed, in regulating economic life more generally). That tension is between proponents and critics of deregulation. I shall argue that the deregulatory cause, whilst certainly not cutting great swathes through existing regulation, has succeeded in hindering the adoption of further regulation, a point richly illustrated by the corporate governance initiatives discussed in section II.

The third tension is also the most fundamental. It concerns the very purposes of companies and company law. The orthodox position—that companies should be run in the interests of their shareholders—has been the subject of a long-standing, but recently intensified, debate, conducted under a variety of rubrics: corporate responsibility, stakeholding, worker participation, industrial democracy, and so on. Section IV addresses these debates, and considers some of the alternatives to the shareholder-centred approach and the related justificatory arguments which their proponents advance.

I PROTECTING SHAREHOLDERS

We begin, however, in orthodox fashion, by considering the way in which companies are regulated to protect their shareholders' interests. To understand and evaluate such regulation, we need some sense of the shareholders' position within the modern, large, public company. In such companies, share ownership will typically be widely dispersed amongst many shareholders, each of whom will own only a small fraction of the company's total capital. In consequence, it has been said, ownership of the company has become divorced from its control,[5] with the latter in the hands of a relatively small group of executive managers owning only a tiny proportion of the company's shares.

There are, however, costs for shareholders in leaving others to run the company in this way. These so-called "agency costs" include the risk that managers will prove incompetent or disloyal to shareholders, together with the costs of monitoring managers, evaluating their performance, and so on.[6] The main axis of potential conflict in large public companies in the UK, then, is typically

---

[5] The seminal reference here is usually given as A. A. Berle and G. C. Means, *The Modern Corporation and Private Property* (New York, Harcourt, Brace & World, Inc., 1932) (revised edn., 1967).

[6] For a more formal treatment, see M. Jensen and W. Meckling, "Theory of the Firm: Managerial Behavior, Agency Costs and Ownership Structure" (1976) 3 *J. of Financial Economics* 305.

understood to be between the general body of shareholders and executive managers. And the regulation of public companies is centrally concerned with controlling this shareholder–management conflict. Conflict *within* the shareholder body—say between majority and minority shareholders—is certainly not unknown, but is less common than within, say, smaller companies in the UK[7] or within larger companies in some continental jurisdictions.[8]

The regulation itself is a mix of both statutory and common law provisions, the latter being most evident in the directors' fiduciary and common law duties which have thus far defied codification.[8a] The leading statute is the Companies Act 1985, although this has been subsequently amended on a number of occasions,[9] and is also supplemented by a number of additional statutes dealing with specific regulatory issues.[10] Although there is some differentiation within this body of law between public and private companies (and, in some cases, according to the size of the company,[11] or the relationships between its participants),[12] many of the rules apply without distinction to all private and public companies alike. This degree of uniformity has been subject to criticism. Given the practical differences between private and public companies, and indeed, given the differences within the "public category" itself between the largest and smallest such companies, it seems doubtful that "one size" of corporate regulation can fit all. The dissatisfaction has probably been greatest in relation to the smaller, private company, and various proposals have been advanced for producing a "legal vehicle" more tailored to their needs.[13] But, as we shall see, neither is the regulatory framework wholly suited to the really large companies with which we are principally concerned. Here, however, changes have occurred on the margins of the law, say through self-regulation.

Three Regulatory Strategies

One point which should by now be becoming apparent is the complexity of the regulatory framework. Common law exists alongside statute. Both civil and criminal norms are used.[14] Some norms are indistinctly applicable to all

[7] As starkly illustrated by the extensive case law under s. 459 of the Companies Act (CA), 1985.

[8] See E. Berglöf, "Reforming Corporate Governance: Redirecting the European Agenda" (1997) 24. *Economic Policy* 93 at 96–7.

[8a] The Law Commision is, however, currently considering the case for a statutory statement of the duties of directors; see Law Commission Consultation Paper No. 153, *Company Directors: Regulating Conflicts of Interests and Formulationg a Statement of Duties* (London: The Stationery Office, 1998).

[9] Most notably by the CA 1989.

[10] These include, e.g., the Company Directors' Disqualification Act 1986, the Insolvency Act 1986, and the Criminal Justice Act 1993 (the latter addressing, *inter alia*, insider dealing).

[11] See, e.g., the rules on accounts and audit in Part VII of the CA 1985.

[12] See, e.g., the singling out of the "quasi partnership" in the judicial development of ss.459–61 of the CA 1985 (relief against unfair prejudice).

[13] See, e.g., J. Freedman, "Small Business and the Corporate Form: Burden or Privilege?" (1994) 57 *MLR* 555.

[14] On the use of criminal provisions within company law, see J. Dine, *Criminal Law in the Company Context* (Aldershot, Dartmouth Publishing, 1995).

companies, whilst others operate more sensitively. Legal regulation is supplemented by self-regulation, whilst market forces and liability rules co-exist. This
complexity renders problematic any simple typology of rules, and also threatens
to swamp the reader beneath a mass of detail. To avoid these dangers here, we
shall organise our discussion around *three broad regulatory strategies* which,
taken together, capture much of the regulatory detail.[15] These strategies are
fiduciary duties, markets and internal monitoring.

Let us begin with the first of these: the imposition on directors of fiduciary
duties (and the common law duty of care and skill).[16] Perhaps the greatest
strength of these duties is their compensatory function. Not only do they, like our
other two strategies, provide an incentive for good managerial behaviour, but
they also provide a mechanism by which the company can, in theory at least, be
"made whole" via compensation for loss suffered through its directors' misbehaviour. That said, however, cases brought by companies against their directors
are a rarity. This does not, of course, prove the redundancy of these duties, but
it does suggest some shortcomings.[17] For one thing, given directors' control over
the disclosure of relevant information, shareholders may never discover a breach
of duty. Even if they do, they may conclude that the director lacks sufficient
resources to be worth suing. And, if those hurdles are overcome, there remain
further legal and practical barriers to a suit. Legally, the rule in *Foss* v.
Harbottle[18] precludes action by an individual shareholder against an errant
director, and there are doubts whether even a simple majority of shareholders is
free to resolve that the company can sue.[19] The derivative action offers a possible
way around this problem, permitting a suit by individual shareholders where
there has been "fraud on the minority", but the extent of this exception remains
uncertain.[20] Nor is it obvious why any one shareholder should rush to court
when any damages recovered go to the company. Some of these difficulties lie
behind the Law Commission's recent proposals on "Shareholder Remedies"[21]
although, at the moment, the likely fate of these proposals is unclear.[22]

[15] To be sure, there are some significant elements in the regulatory scheme which cannot com-
fortably be squeezed into these 3 strategies. So, some rules (such as the prohibition on loans to directors and their spouses, in s.330 of the CA, 1985) independently outlaw certain undesired behaviour
without obviously linking in to the 3 strategies.

[16] For an account of these, see P. L. Davies, *Gower's Principles of Modern Company Law*
(6th.edn., London, Sweet & Maxwell, 1997), ch. 22.

[17] These are dealt with comprehensively in V. Finch, "Company Directors: Who Cares about
Skill and Care?" (1992) 41 *MLR* 179 at 179–200.

[18] (1843) 2 Hare 461.

[19] See *Breckland Group Holdings Ltd* v. *London & Suffolk Properties Ltd* [1989] BCLC 100.

[20] For an excellent account of the complexity and uncertainty here, see Law Commission
Consultation Paper No 142, *Shareholder Remedies: A Consultation Paper* (London: The Stationery
Office, 1996), at 27–40.

[21] The principal reform of relevance here is a new statutory derivative action. See Law
Commission, *Shareholder Remedies* (Law Com No 246) (London, The Stationery Office, 1997), Cm
3769. For a discussion of the Law Commission's Consultation Paper, see the essays collected in
(1997) 18 *The Co.Lawyer* 225–68.

[22] One uncertainty is whether these proposals will be pursued independently of the current
Government's wholesale review of company law, discussed in n. 73 below and the text therewith.

The second regulatory strategy relies on "market forces" to discipline managers and to protect shareholders. We shall note three relevant markets here, but before doing so should pause to emphasise a point too often ignored. Each of these various markets depends for its effectiveness upon a supporting infrastructure of legal and self-regulatory norms. One of the central contemporary debates in company law is often couched in terms of a choice between "legal regulation" and "market forces". This stark opposition rather understates the complexity of the situation. Effective markets ought not to be seen as some "natural" alternative to humanly-constructed state regulation, but as themselves presupposing such regulation.

The first example of market forces arises from the market for managerial labour. Executives have some incentive to run companies as profitably as possible just in order to improve their own rewards and future employment prospects. This pressure is certainly increased to the extent that the executive's remuneration is directly tied to her contribution towards corporate profitability. There has been much recent concern, however, that remuneration is not in fact adequately tied in this way, but rather constitutes one of the more serious instances of managerial abuse.[23] And although such concerns led the Greenbury Group to recommend a number of measures to improve the process by which the remuneration of executive directors' is determined,[24] doubts remain about the likely effectiveness of these reforms.[25]

The second market is the capital market. In the UK, the market for shares in listed companies is comparatively[26] liquid. Shareholders can fairly easily choose to leave a company with whose performance they are dissatisfied. Onerous disclosure requirements, imposed both by statute and by the London Stock Exchange, together with restrictions on insider dealing and market manipulation,[27] aim to ensure that share prices approximate closely to the underlying value of the company. So shareholders are able to protect themselves to some extent by choosing not to enter, or remain in, an under-performing company. There are, however, doubts about just how effective this protection might be. One doubt is whether all shareholders are really as free to leave as the above account suggests. Some institutional shareholders in particular may find that their comparatively large holdings render them locked-in to their companies.

---

[23] See C. A. Riley and D. Ryland, "Directors' Remuneration: Towards Some Principles of Procedural and Substantive Review" in S. Sheikh and W. Rees (eds.), *Corporate Governance & Corporate Control* (London, Cavendish Publishing Ltd., 1995).

[24] The Study Group on Directors' Remuneration, *Directors' Remuneration* (the Greenbury Report) (London, Gee Publishing Ltd., 1995). Essentially, these measures included independent remuneration committees, composed of non-executive directors, and an improved disclosure regime.

[25] For a good overview of the arguments, see B. R. Cheffins, *Company Law: Theory, Structure and Operation* (Oxford, Clarendon Press, 1997), ch. 14.

[26] The comparison is with some continental European share markets; see E. Berglöf, n. 8 above at 99–104.

[27] See, e.g., the rules on financial assistance for the purchase of a company's shares, and on share buy-backs, in chs. VI and VII respectively of the CA 1985.

Further, there are doubts about the effectiveness of the disclosure, insider dealing and anti-market manipulation regimes. Finally, even if a company's share price did accurately reflect that company's value, and even if a shareholder could easily sell her shares at that price, this would still do little either to prevent, or to remedy, managerial misbehaviour or under-performance.

The take-over market—the so-called "market for corporate control"—promises to address at least this last deficiency. A predator, the theory runs, identifies a badly run target company, whose low share price reflects its management's under-performance. Going "over the heads" of those managers, the predator is able to offer a sufficiently attractive price to the target company's shareholders to enable it to acquire a controlling stake in the target (and thereafter to use that control to remove incumbent managers). Such a process allows existing shareholders to escape at a better price and provides an ongoing discipline for managers. The vitality of the take-over market, like the capital market, depends upon a number of factors. One is the existence of a pattern of share ownership which permits predators to make "hostile" take-overs, against the wishes of incumbent managers. A second factor is the existence of a sufficient body of regulation to support the take-over process. Two particular concerns here are that managers, fearful of losing their own jobs, be stopped from frustrating bids and that there be equality of treatment between shareholders. Both the directors' fiduciary duties and some statutory provisions are relevant here, but the main body of rules is found in a self-regulatory scheme based on the City Code on Takeovers and Mergers, published and administered by the Takeover Panel.

Although the takeover market is absolutely central to the UK's system of corporate governance, its effectiveness has again been called into question. Some of these criticisms relate to the costs which takeovers may impose on non-shareholder groups, especially employees, and are therefore properly the subject of section IV. But even in relation to the protection of shareholders, it has been argued that takeovers represent an unsystematic and expensive mechanism for controlling managers.[28]

Our third regulatory strategy—internal monitoring—has at least two components. The first involves the exercise of shareholder voice within the company. Although the management of large public companies is typically delegated to executive directors, shareholders retain a number of opportunities to speak on company matters. Perhaps the most significant of these is the power which shareholders enjoy, entrenched in section 303 of the Companies Act 1985, to remove directors by ordinary resolution. The second component of internal monitoring involves shareholder reliance on other actors within the company to monitor the performance of executive managers. Two groups might play this role. One is the company's auditors. The second potential monitors are independent, non-executive directors, acting both within the board as a whole, and

---

[28] C. Bradley, "Corporate Control: Markets and Rules" (1990) 53 *MLR* 170.

within specialised "sub-committees" charged with responsibility for those tasks which raise the greatest potential conflicts between managers and shareholders, such as the audit process itself, and the nomination and remuneration of directors.

II MARKETS VERSUS MONITORING

Historically, the monitoring strategy has played a comparatively small role in the UK, which has been characterised as heavily reliant on market controls, with "arm's-length" relationships between managers and shareholders. By contrast, the governance systems of some continental countries—and Germany is often cited as the leading example—are built on more concentrated share ownership, more active control by institutional investors and less reliance on the impersonal force of the market.[29] A number of reasons can be offered for the UK's position.[30] One is that its dispersed share ownership frustrates the collective action which shareholder voice requires. The benefits any one shareholder will gain by becoming active and voting for, say, some change in managerial policy will be as small as the percentage of shares in the company she owns. Moreover, each shareholder might calculate that her action will likely make very little difference to the outcome, and she will receive the benefits from any successful display of shareholder activism whether or not she participates. In consequence, it becomes rational for her to remain inactive and free-ride on others' efforts. Added to this, shareholders may feel that they lack the expertise to second-guess management. Finally, the legal regime itself, by making "exit" from companies relatively easy, makes markets more attractive, and thereby encourages the very share dispersion which renders monitoring so difficult. By contrast, that same legal regime has, historically, done rather little to facilitate or require greater internal monitoring.

More recently, however, there has been a renewed interest in, and increased pressure for, a greater reliance on internal monitoring. A number of spectacular corporate failures, for example, have been interpreted as revealing the deficiencies in the existing, market dominated, system. Supporting such an interpretation, commentators have explored the theoretical shortcomings of market controls and, more positively, have sought to identify the merits and the potential of monitoring as a strategy. Finally, attention has been directed towards those other states whose governance systems have relied more on internal monitoring, and whose corporate performance was, until recently at least, seen as

---

[29] See J. Charkham, *Keeping Good Company* (Oxford, Clarendon Press, 1994), esp. chs. 2–4; the essays collected in Part II of N. Dimsdale and M. Prevezer (eds.), *Capital Markets and Corporate Governance* (Oxford, Clarendon Press, 1994); C. Clarke and R. Bostock, "Governance in Germany: The Foundations of Corporate Structure?" in K. Keasey, S. Thompson and M. Wright (eds.), *Corporate Governance* (Oxford, Oxford U.Press, 1997).

[30] See G. P. Stapledon, *Institutional Shareholders and Corporate Governance* (Oxford, Clarendon Press, 1996), ch. 10.

rather more successful than our own.[31] However, proponents of greater monitoring have not had the debate all their own way. Their critics have challenged both their empirical and theoretical claims, arguing that there is simply insufficient evidence to warrant strong conclusions in favour of monitoring and against markets. The tension between these competing positions is well illustrated by two areas within which the impetus for governance reform is currently being experienced: first, the EC's harmonisation programme and, secondly, a number of domestic projects addressing aspects of UK corporate governance. It is to these we now turn.

The European Community's Harmonisation Programme

Community involvement in the Member States' company law regimes is purportedly justified by reference to its economic objectives, and in particular, its project of establishing a "single" or "internal market", defined as "an area without internal frontiers in which the free movement of goods, persons, services and capital is ensured . . .".[32] Creating such a market, the analysis runs, requires some degree of harmonisation of Member States' company law regimes, and for a number of reasons: to equalise investor protection and corporate regulation throughout the community, to prevent states undercutting the stricter regulation of their neighbours,[33] and to facilitate the formation of pan-European companies, large enough to take on the corporate giants of, say, the US or Japan.[34]

Some of the necessary harmonisation has involved only relatively technical changes to Member States' company law regimes. However, in so far as there are general, systemic differences between states' governance regimes, then achieving substantive harmonisation will require more radical surgery. And, as we have already seen, one essential systemic difference is precisely the clash between "internal" and "external" systems—between the relative weight accorded to markets and internal monitoring—in the UK and some continental states. This explains why our membership of the Community provides one impetus for reconsideration of the balance between markets and monitoring in the UK. But what, in fact, has been achieved here? The Treaty of Rome con-

---

[31] See the Commission on Public Policy and British Business, *Promoting Prosperity* (London, Vintage, 1997), esp. ch. 4; W. Hutton, *The State We're In* (London, Vintage, 1996). For more sober and cautious assessments, see C. Mayer, "Corporate Governance, Competition, and Performance" (1997) 24 *J. of Law and Society* 152 at 171, and E.Berglöf, n. 8 above.

[32] See EC Treaty 1957, Art.7a.

[33] In the USA, this has been termed the "race to the bottom". For an attempt to chart a middle course between descriptions of the US scene as a race to the bottom and as a "race to the top", see W. W.Bratton, "Corporate Law's Race to Nowhere in Particular" (1994) 44 *U of Toronto LJ* 401.

[34] *Fiscal* problems might also undermine cross-border co-operation (and investment more generally): see F. Beveridge and C. A. Riley, "The Tax Agenda of the European Community" in G. G. Howells (ed.), *European Business Law* (Aldershot, Dartmouth Publishing Co., 1996).

tained certain provisions of direct relevance to companies,[35] but the major impact of the Community's harmonisation programme has been seen in the introduction of a number of directives.[36] Although these have primarily addressed public companies, they have been concerned predominantly with technical issues,[37] and there is a widespread perception that progress has been both limited and piecemeal.[38] What has not been achieved is a resolution of the fundamental systemic question: what governance system, with what relative weight accorded to markets and monitoring, should form the basis for a "European model" of governance?

These problems can best be illustrated by considering those proposed measures where progress has been slowest. These include the draft Ninth Directive (dealing with corporate groups), the draft Thirteenth Directive (on takeovers), and, perhaps most pertinently, the draft Fifth Directive (company structure and worker participation) and the Regulation for a European Company Statute.[39] For each of these directives raises precisely the broader, systemic questions which have proved so much more problematic than tinkering with technical detail. To be sure, some of the difficulties here arise from the proposals on worker participation, which we shall consider in section IV. But, that aside, one of the major blocks to progress has been the concern that too much harmonisation between states will result in a homogenised, European-wide body of company law. What might be preferable, critics argue, is that we have a plurality of states offering alternative packages of regulatory norms, and companies "voting with their feet" by choosing the most appropriate regulatory package.[40] Colin Mayer, for example, claims that the interrelation of corporate governance and corporate performance "is a subject which is in its infancy and it is unquestionably premature to believe that policy should be directed towards the selection of optimal governance arrangements. Indeed one of the most widely accepted views is that, in the light of our ignorance, competition between rather than harmonization of financial systems is desirable".[41] And, to some extent, this has

---

[35] Principally, Art.52 (freedom of establishment) and Art.58 (equality of treatment between companies and natural persons).

[36] See generally C.Villiers, "Harmonisation of Company Laws in Europe—With an Introduction to Some Comparative Issues" in G. G. Howells (ed.), n. 34 above, at 180. Note also the Merger Reg., Council Reg. (EEC) No 4064/89, [1989] OJ L395/1—and the Reg. providing for the European Economic Interest Grouping, Council Reg. (EEC) No 2137/85, [1985] OJ L199/1.

[37] They have dealt with, *inter alia*, *ultra vires* and directors' authority, the formation and the share capital of public companies, corporate mergers within a Member State, financial disclosure and accounting requirements, divisions, group accounts, qualifications of auditors, disclosure regarding branch companies, single-member companies and prospectuses.

[38] See, e.g., C. Villiers, n. 36 above, at 194. Even the Commission itself, in its "Consultation Paper on Company Law" accepted that "most of the proposals aimed at creating uniform legal instruments of cooperation and integration have run into difficulties . . .".

[39] [1991] OJ C138. There has, recently, been some attempt to kick-start this project: see, e.g., the Department of Trade and Industry's Consultative Document, *The European Company Statute* (July, 1997).

[40] See, e.g., Cheffins, n. 25 above, ch. 9.

[41] C. Mayer, "Corporate Governance, Competition, and Performance" (1997) 24 *J of Law and Society* 152, at 171. For similar conclusions, see E.Berglöf, n. 8 above.

been recognised by the EC. Its most recent version of the draft Fifth Directive and its revised proposals for a European Company Statute both attempt to harmonise less and to defer more to each Member State's domestic regime. Further, each allows greater flexibility to states by offering more options from which they may choose.[42]

UK Governance Initiatives

The second impetus for reform arises domestically. During the 1990s, a number of projects addressing corporate governance have been undertaken in the UK. Three in particular have received much attention,[43] namely those conducted by the Committee on the Financial Aspects of Corporate Governance ("Cadbury"),[44] the Study Group on Directors' Remuneration ("Greenbury")[45] and the Committee on Corporate Governance ("Hampel").[46]

Each of these groups/committees was a non-governmental body,[47] with a membership dominated by business interests. Each promulgated a Code of Best Practice[48] containing a variety of norms of good governance. And for each such Code, the emphasis was primarily (if not exclusively) on improving internal monitoring. So, both Cadbury and Hampel sought to revitalise the board as a more effective monitor of managerial behaviour, through the appointment of non-executive directors, the separation of the roles of chairman and chief executive, and the creation of board sub-committees to deal with the audit process and the remuneration and nomination of directors. Further, each called for greater activism by institutional shareholders, whilst Hampel made a number of recommendations designed to improve the role of the AGM as an arena for shareholder participation. Finally, all three required companies to make

---

[42] See J. J. Du Plessis and J. Dine, "The Fate of the Fifth Directive on Company Law: Accomodation Instead of Harmonisation" [1997] *JBL* 23.

[43] In addition, other projects have included: The Institutional Shareholders' Committee, *The Role and Duties of Directors: A Statement of Best Practice* (1991) The Institutional Shareholders' Committee, *The Responsibilities of Institutional Shareholders in the UK* (1991); the CBI, *Good Investor Relations—A Requirement for Success* (1992); Association of British Insurers and the National Association of Pension Funds, *Share Scheme Guidance* (1993); The City/Industry Working Group (Chair: Paul Myners,) *Developing a Winning Partnership* (1995); Royal Society for the Encouragement of Arts, Manufactures and Commerce, *Tomorrow's Company: The Role of Business in a Changing World* (London, RSA, 1995); Commission on Public Policy and British Business, n. 31 above.

[44] The Committee on the Financial Aspects of Corporate Governance, *Report and Code of Best Practice* (London, Gee and Co. Ltd., 1992).

[45] The Study Group on Directors' Remuneration, *Directors' Remuneration* (the Greenbury Report) (London, Gee Publishing Ltd., 1995).

[46] The Committee on Corporate Governance, *Report of the Committee on Corporate Governance* (London, Gee Publishing Ltd., 1998).

[47] But note that the Cadbury Committee was set up by, amongst others, the (partly government-funded) Financial Reporting Council.

[48] See nn. 44–6 above. Note that Hampel has now produced a "Consolidated Code", which combines its own proposals with those of Cadbury and Greenbury.

increased disclosure, in Greenbury's case as to the remuneration of directors, and in all three cases as to compliance with the obligations of their respective Codes of Practice.

Although these projects clearly do push for a greater emphasis on internal monitoring, the modesty of their proposals has met with a good deal of criticism from many commentators.[49] Part of that modesty lies in their substantive content. So, for example, none of these Codes really addresses the fundamental problem of conflict within the role of a non-executive director, who is expected to act both as part of a collegial board and, simultaneously, as a monitor of her executive colleagues.[50] Similarly, they do too little to ensure that non-executives are sufficiently independent and enjoy the requisite resources to fulfil their roles. Finally, real doubts remain about the likelihood of institutional shareholders responding to the exhortations of these Codes to become more active. PIRC, for example, has claimed that "voting levels have only risen by 2 per cent since the publication of the Cadbury report, and still hover at below 40 per cent".[51] And Short and Keasey conclude, following their overview of existing empirical evidence, that whilst institutional monitoring of management may be greater than commonly supposed, "such monitoring tends to be carried out in private",[52] and, citing Black and Coffee,[53] is described as "crisis driven".[54]

Beyond these substantive issues, however, the modesty of these Codes is also seen in the formal status of their recommendations. As we have noted, they propose not legal, mandatory, norms but merely suggestions for "best practice".[55] If their recommended norms are to be enforced, it will be predominantly through shareholders employing their *existing* rights—say, by choosing to exit, or not to enter, non-compliant companies, or by using their existing "voice"

[49] V. Finch, "Corporate Governance and Cadbury: Self-regulation and Alternatives" [1994] *JBL* 51; C. A. Riley, "Controlling Corporate Management: UK and US Initiatives" (1994) 14 *Legal Studies* 244, 252–6 (comparing Cadbury's proposals to those of the American Law Institute's Principles of Corporate Governance); J. E. Parkinson, n. 4 above, at 191–9. On the work of the Hampel Committee specifically, see A. Dignam, "A Principled Approach to Self-regulation? The Report of the Hampel Committee on Corporate Governance" (1998) 19 *The Co. Lawyer* 140, and J. W. Barnard, "The Hampel Committee Report: A Transatlantic Critique" (1998) 19 *The Co. Lawyer* 110.

[50] M. Ezzamel and R. Watson, "Wearing Two Hats: The Conflicting Control and Management Role of Non-executive Directors" in Keasey, Thompson and Wright (eds.), n. 29 above.

[51] "PIRC welcomes government review of company law", PIRC Press Release, 4 Mar. 1998, http://www.pirc.co.uk/release02.htm.

[52] H. Short and K. Keasey, "Institutional Shareholders and Corporate Governance in the United Kingdom" in Keasey, Thompson and Wright (eds.), n. 29 above, at 49.

[53] B. S. Black and J. C. Coffee, "Hail Britannia?: Institutional Investor Behavior under Limited Regulation" (1994) 92 *Mich. ULRev.* 1997.

[54] See also Stapledon, n. 30 above, ch.4, and P. L. Davies, "Institutional Investors in the United Kingdom" in D. D. Prentice and P. R. J. Holland (eds.), *Contemporary Issues in Corporate Governance* (Oxford, Clarendon Press, 1993). Both authors suggest that a large part of such activism as currently exists covers a fairly narrow "core" of general structural (rather than company specific) issues: shareholder rights, board composition, executive remuneration, and so on.

[55] Note, however, that certain changes to the disclosure requirements regarding directors' remuneration were made consequent upon the Greenbury Report: see the Company Accounts (Disclosure of Directors' Emoluments) Regs. 1997 (S.I. 1997 No.570).

within companies to demand change. Further, in the case of Hampel this commitment to non-legal norms is buttressed by a related commitment to *flexibility*. It is to be seen in the way Hampel qualifies many of its specific guidelines, making clear that companies may have good reasons for departing from them. And it is also evident in Hampel's desire to achieve a better balance between specific rules and "general principles" of good governance, which can be applied "flexibly and with common sense to the varying circumstances of individual companies".[56] Companies are then encouraged to include in their annual reports a narrative account of how they apply these principles.[57] How effective such voluntary Codes will prove to be in achieving even their own modest substantive reforms remains to be seen. The evidence to date seems to be that most companies report high levels of formal compliance.[58] That is, however, rather different from full compliance with their spirit, and of that many commentators remain more sceptical.[59] Moreover, and with specific regard to institutional shareholders, we have already noted their apparent continuing passivity, leading some commentators to propose moving beyond ever greater exhortations[60] and instead to legislate for greater activism.[61]

III DEREGULATION AND CONTRACTUAL FREEDOM

Several justifications have been offered for the modesty of these Codes. One echoes the earlier observation regarding the EC's harmonisation programme. Given a lack of knowledge about the comparative merits of alternative governance systems, we should be cautious in making major systemic changes of unproven value to shareholders.[62] And a series of further points link in to the wider debate about the role of law in corporate regulation, and the drive for greater "deregulation". As Ogus has noted, the concept of "deregulation" is not without difficulties,[63] and its meaning may vary in different contexts. In company law, it includes the familiar idea of reducing regulatory obligations where the benefits of those obligations do not outweigh the burdens they impose. It is

[56] See para.1.11.

[57] See ch. 7, rec.1.

[58] See, e.g., A. Belcher, "Compliance with the Cadbury Code and the Reporting of Corporate Governance" (1996) 17 *The Co. Lawyer* 11.

[59] See Finch, n. 49 above. For an account of some of the barriers to full enforcement, see C. A. Riley, n. 49 above, at 256–64. For a more positive account, see Cheffins, n. 25 above, at 647–52.

[60] See Stapledon, n. 30 above, who concludes (at 250) that "in the absence of positive regulatory changes, it is probable that there will be no significant increase on current levels [of shareholder activism] in the UK".

[61] See Davies, n. 54 above, and Stapledon, n. 30 above, ch.11 (both of whom remain fairly pessimistic about the ability even of regulation to effect substantial improvements in institutional activism).

[62] See n. 41 above, and the text thereto; O. Green, "Corporate Governance: Great Expectations" in S. Sheikh and W. Rees (eds.), *Corporate Governance and Corporate Control* (London, Cavendish Publishing, 1995).

[63] A. I. Ogus, *Regulation: Legal Form and Economic Theory* (Oxford, Clarendon Press, 1994) 10.

also bound up with a particular theoretical vision of the company, usually labelled contractarianism, which promotes "freedom of contract" between those involved in companies. This championing of contractual freedom stems in part from the conceptualisation of the company as a "nexus" of contractual relations (between managers, shareholders, employees, creditors, and so forth). But it also flows from the belief that free contracting will generally deliver a better set of rules, more conducive to the promotion of the contracting parties' welfare, than will mandatory state regulation. Part of the reason for that, it is claimed, is the legislators' own lack of knowledge about what rules work best— their ignorance of the comparative merits of governance systems. Yet even if legislators were able to identify which governance system, in general, was superior to others, there is still such a diversity of companies and of intra-corporate relationships that no one ideal set of rules could ever apply universally. Rather, the parties themselves, whose own wealth is on the line, are best able to judge which rules should apply to their relationships. Finally, it is argued that legal regulation suffers from a number of formalistic problems which self-regulation and voluntary codes avoid. In particular, codes can be more flexible and more aspirational, their content can better capture a consensus within the community to which the code applies and they are more likely to be complied with fully, in spirit as well as letter.

Although there has been a good deal of pro-deregulation government rhetoric, actual reductions in corporate regulation have been quite rare (and much of what there has been has applied only to private or smaller companies, for whom the regulatory burden is arguably disproportionately large).[64] Indeed, in a number of areas, state regulation has increased rather than diminished. Some of this was necessary to satisfy the UK's obligations to the EC. But by no means all. We have seen, for example, the overhaul of insolvency legislation, with such measures as section 214 of the Insolvency Act 1986 threatening (if not, in practice, actually achieving) a fairly substantial incursion into the principle of limited liability. And, relatedly, the vast increase in the number of actions brought for the disqualification of directors marks a further tightening of the regulatory screw.

Nevertheless, the greatest impact of the deregulatory agenda can be seen not so much in the removal of existing regulation as in the effort to minimise further regulatory interventions. One illuminating example of this deregulatory philosophy can be seen in the Law Commission's Consultation Paper on Shareholder Remedies.[65] Besides listing "sanctity of contract" as one of its "six guiding principles" and asserting that "the best protection for a shareholder is appropriate protection in the articles themselves",[66] its substantive recommendations

---

[64] So, e.g., the rules on "written resolutions" and the "elective regime" introduced by ss.113–17 CA 1989 and amended by the Deregulation (Resolutions of Private Companies) Order 1996, SI No.1471, and the exemption from audit for certain small companies pursuant to s.249A CA 1985.

[65] N. 20 above.

[66] *Ibid.*, para. 14.11.

concentrated upon a number of so-called "self-help" remedies, with new regulation tempered by contractual freedom. But, more pertinently, this deregulatory inspired resistance to further regulation is also to be seen in the fate of the initiatives discussed in section II of this essay: in the stalling of the more ambitious, "systemic", aspects of the European Community's harmonisation programme and in the readiness to leave the impetus for governance reform in the hands of non-governmental bodies like Cadbury *et al.* and their non-legal, non-mandatory, flexible Codes of Practice.

Whatever their practical success in blocking new regulation, the deregulatory arguments noted above are subject to a number of weaknesses. First, they mischaracterise some of the claims for greater monitoring, which do not depend upon the replacement of one whole system with another, but merely seek relatively small, incremental improvements in limited aspects of monitoring. Secondly, the contractarian account of the corporation, from which the deregulatory agenda draws much theoretical support, has itself been subject to a good deal of criticism, much of it compelling. Critics challenge the conceptualisation of the company as a nexus of contractual relationships, and point to a range of problems—imperfect information, transaction costs, externalities—which undermine the ability of some parties to protect themselves adequately through the contracts they make with the company. Finally, many of the claimed advantages of self-regulation and voluntary codes are also doubted. Freedman, for example, argues that the same problems can beset those making rules outside of the governmental legislative process as face lawmakers themselves.[67]

In criticising the arguments for deregulation, here, the point is not to suggest that current company law is in any sense ideal. Indeed, it is a commonplace that there is much that is wrong with the current state of affairs, quite apart from its failure to embrace any substantial move towards more effective internal monitoring. Two particular criticisms stand out. The first is the lack of *coherence* in the substantive content of that law. This is true both within the individual strategies we have considered and within the regulatory system as a whole. As one example, take the development of the directors' duty of care and skill. Not only does that duty inadequately reflect the more active role of the modern director, but statutory provisions here, in the shape of section 214 of the Insolvency Act 1986 and the Company Directors Disqualification Act 1986, have been pasted onto the common law duty without proper thought to their interrelationship.[68] And, finally, whilst the corporate governance projects considered above are promulgating a new, more active role for the non-executive director, the implications of that development for existing legal duties on directors remain unexplored. The second criticism is related to this problem of incoherence, and goes some way towards explaining its existence. The current system

---

[67] J. Freedman, "Reforming Company Law" in F. Patfield (ed.), *Perspectives on Company Law: 1* (London, Kluwer Law Int., 1995), at 204–6.

[68] For an attempt to synthesise the common law duty with the statutory provision, see *Norman v. Theodore Goddard* [1991] BCLC 1028 and *Re D'Jan of London Ltd* [1994] 1 BCLC 561.

has developed with too little overall co-ordination or guiding philosophy. The core of company law dates back to the middle of the last century; additions and refinements to that core have been made sporadically, and usually in response to some specific perceived deficiency. This is not to deny that much good work has been, and is being, done here. Both the DTI and the Law Commission have major review projects under way, generating a mass of "consultative documents" and many important and worthy proposals for reform.[69] But the bigger picture often seems to be missing.[70] Moreover, as we saw above, on the central issue of greater monitoring, the government has been ready largely to detach itself from the process of change and rely instead on private bodies to carry forward reform. Of course, there is nothing particularly unusual about private, interested bodies participating in consultation over proposed regulatory reform. And indeed, other authors have argued persuasively that, in some areas, the business community has had too *little* input into business regulation.[71] But the situation in the corporate governance field seems distinctive. For these private initiatives have not been merely supplemental to, or an input into, a governmentally constructed reform programme. Instead, they have constituted a *replacement* for state action, with the government largely adopting a "wait and see" approach. It has not, for example, offered its own detailed blueprint of desirable reform against which the private initiatives would stand to be judged.

To conclude this section, we need to ask whether the UK's new Labour Government heralds a change in philosophy. In her response to Hampel, Margaret Beckett, then President of the Board of Trade, emphasised that "company law is an area where the Government's role is paramount. We set the rules by which every company must operate—how companies are to structure themselves; the proper duties of directors; the rights and the obligations of shareholders; what rules are necessary to protect creditors; and what companies must do to communicate with their shareholders."[72] To that end, the Government is to undertake a major review of company law. Its proposals were set out in its consultation document, *Modern Company Law: For a Competitive Economy*,[73] dealing primarily with the process and timetable by which the review will be conducted.[74] And although the paper promises that "Government does not intend to replace the use of best practice by legal rules",[75] this was subject to the

---

[69] See Freedman, n. 67 above, at 211–13.

[70] *Ibid.*; B. Pettet, "The Stirring Corporate Social Conscience: From 'Cakes and Ale' to Community Programmes" (1997) 50 *Current Legal Problems*, 279 at 300–302. The Company Law Committee of the Law Society, *The Reform of Company Law* (London, The Law Society, 1991) and *Modern Company Law for a Competitive Economy* (London, The Law Society, 1998).

[71] See Cheffins, n. 25 above, esp. 178–211.

[72] See "Margaret Beckett's speech at PIRC's sixth annual corporate governance conference", 4 March 1990, at http://www.pirc.co.uk/mbspeech.htm, at 5.

[73] DTI, Mar. 1998. For a useful overview, see B. Pettet, "Towards a competitive company law" (1998) 19 *The Co. Lawyer* 134.

[74] Comments on the draft terms of reference and the review process were to be submitted by 30 June 1998. Thereafter, a series of working groups will be appointed, leading to a final report and White Paper in Mar. 2001. Any legislation, then, will not be introduced until the next Parliament.

[75] See DTI, *Modern Company Law: For a Competitive Economy* (March 1998), 10.

proviso that "best practice is seen to be working".[76] Moreover, a number of areas were specifically mentioned as potential subjects for further legislation, including the duties of directors, the conduct of AGMs and shareholder control over directors' pay.

This is certainly suggestive of a greater governmental will to oversee and steer the process of modernisation. One area where the government's thinking remains unhelpfully vague, however, is in relation to the issue with which we began this chapter, namely the interests corporate regulation is to serve. Certainly, prior to the General Election, "stakeholding" "emerged as one of 'New' Labour's principal policy slogans".[77] Whatever their intentions, having assumed office, however, this clearly remains an area of enormous importance, and it is to that we now turn in our final section.

IV CHALLENGING THE PRIMACY OF SHAREHOLDER INTERESTS

Thus far, our focus has been upon regulation designed to ensure that companies are run in the interests of shareholders. We shall call this a commitment to "shareholder primacy". This commitment has not, of course, gone unchallenged, and in recent years has been the subject of much debate, conducted under a variety of "rubrics": stakeholding,[78] industrial democracy, corporate social responsibility, and so on. Before addressing these debates, we need to say a little more about shareholder primacy itself: just what does it mean to hold that a company should be run in the interests of its shareholders? Two points are important. First, it implies a clear goal for the corporation. That goal is the maximisation of the shareholders' *wealth*, which is usually understood to require that the company's own *profits* be maximised.[79] Secondly, maximising shareholder wealth certainly does not entail that other constituencies' interests count for nothing. To maximise its profits, companies must consider what its customers want, what will best attract and motivate employees, and so on. But what is crucial is that the interests of these other groups count only in an *instrumental* or strategic way; they count only to the extent necessary to maximise profits. There is no question of the interests of, say, employees enjoying independent weight, to be set against the maximisation of profits and the interests of shareholders.

Admittedly, *within* shareholder primacy there is a debate about how well others must be treated, strategically, in the pursuit of profit maximisation. Some

[76] *Ibid.*

[77] P. Ireland, "Corporate Governance, Stakeholding, and the Company: Towards a Less Degenerate Capitalism?" (1996) 23 *J of L and Soc.* 287.

[78] See generally J. Plender, *A Stake in the Future: the Stakeholding Solution* (London, N.Brealey Publishing, 1997).

[79] On the meaning of shareholder wealth, and its relationship both to corporate profits and to the company's share price, see H. T. C. Hu, "Behind the Corporate Hedge: Information and the Limits of 'Shareholder Wealth Maximization' " (1998) 9 *J of Applied Corp. Finance* 39.

seek to argue, for example, that apparent generosity towards employees, consumers, and so on, will, over the longer term, repay itself through higher profits.[80] But whether this is true or not (and trends such as globalisation, the general weakening in the bargaining power of many workers, and the sophisticated marketing techniques of large corporations, suggest some scepticism might be warranted), nevertheless the important point is that the treatment of such constituencies remains entirely strategic, and the goal of the company remains the maximisation of shareholder wealth. We can also link this to the issue of deregulation, noted earlier, and its normative commitment to freedom of contract. For the point about shareholder primacy, as set out here, is precisely that it accords to other constituencies only the treatment for which they are themselves able to bargain.

Alternatives to Shareholder Primacy

Critics of shareholder primacy offer a number of alternative governance structures for securing what they argue to be better corporate behaviour. The first entails imposing a range of legal *constraints* upon companies which limit their pursuit of profits. So, for example, through competition policy we might try to limit the formation of corporate monopolies. Environmental regulations and civil nuisance laws might require companies to reduce, or compensate for, the harmful effects their operations have on others. In fact, a moment's thought confirms that such regulatory constraints are commonplace, and to that extent shareholder primacy is already challenged. However, although much might be achieved through the use of these constraints, it is unlikely that the state's legal norms will, at any point in time, capture all desirable profit sacrificing behaviour. One particular problem, emphasised by Stone[81] and by Parkinson,[82] is the problem of "time lags": the delay between the need for, and the introduction of, any given constraint. External regulators may know much less about a company's products or production methods than corporate insiders, with the result that those regulators learn only very late, if at all, of the need for some regulatory intervention.

One can suggest a number of ways of mitigating this problem. One is through a greater reliance on broader, open-ended regulatory standards. A second is through the development of a general duty of good faith to be implied into (at least some) contractual relationships. Requiring companies to act in good faith towards, say, their employees, their creditors or their suppliers will both limit the company's pursuit of profit maximisation and do so in ways which might not be captured by specific legal norms.

---

[80] This sort of reasoning seems to inform both the Royal Society for the Encouragement of Arts, Manufactures and Commerce and the Commission on Public Policy and British Business, both n. 43 above.

[81] See, e.g., C. D. Stone, *Where the Law Ends* (New York, Harper & Row, 1975).

[82] Parkinson, n. 4 above, at 324–33.

A third way is to permit, or require, companies to behave in socially respons-ible ways. "Corporate social responsibility" ("CSR") is in fact used in a number of different senses.[83] Sometimes, the "responsible behaviour" it enjoins is sim-ply compliance with existing legal constraints. But more ambitiously, CSR is used to refer to behaviour which goes beyond compliance with the law and which reduces the harmful impact of the company's activities on third parties (including those with whom the company might have no contractual relation-ship). CSR is, perhaps inevitably, a somewhat amorphous concept, but essen-tially it remains a *constraint* on the company: it imposes further limits on the pursuit of profit, but it does not replace profit maximisation as the company's goal.

This can be contrasted with at least one conception of "stakeholding". This replaces the goal of profit maximisation with some appropriate "balancing" of the interests of its various constituencies. Unlike shareholder primacy, then, this notion of stakeholding demands that genuine (non-strategic) weight be given to the interests of other constituencies. And unlike CSR, this seems to be a more "positive" reform, in that it requires companies actively to promote the interests of others, to leave them better off, rather than merely seeking not to harm them by its operations.

Although both CSR and stakeholding (as defined in the preceding paragraph) purport to change *what* the company should do, neither necessarily changes *who* within the company should exercise decision-making power. Both are, in a sense, elitist reforms: they depend on corporate managers deciding how other constituencies will be better treated. This can be contrasted with our final chal-lenge to shareholder primacy, which entails an extension of democracy within the corporation to other, non-shareholder, constituencies. Such democracy would give these groups a constitutional right to participate in collective deci-sion-making (rather than, say, merely a right to be consulted or informed).

Normative Arguments

The above gives, admittedly, only the most superficial account of each of these alternatives to shareholder primacy. As described here, they are little more than a set of possibilities—directions in which the governance system might move. Giving real substance to them, however, will depend upon why we think that shareholder primacy requires reform. And that requires, in turn, some account of what we think the purposes and values of our corporate governance system ought to be. In contemporary debates, much of the analysis (by both defenders and critics of shareholder primacy) assumes that the point of the governance system is to promote efficiency. Efficiency does, to be sure, carry a number of

---

[83] A useful introduction to the issues is given in J.Tolmie, "Corporate Social Responsibility" (1992) 15 *UNSW Law J* 268.

different meanings,[84] but here it is being used in an "aggregative" sense, to refer the total wealth or total welfare of society. Although shareholder primacy (and, as we noted earlier, contractual freedom and deregulation) are themselves frequently purportedly justified by their claimed efficiency, critics point to various instances of market failure which ensure that the maximisation of the company's profits will not, in fact, lead to the maximisation of society's welfare (or its wealth).

One cause of market failure arises from the market power enjoyed by monopolistic or oligopolistic companies. A second concerns "externalities".[85] Companies which, in maximising their profits, pass on some of their production costs to others may reduce social welfare by so doing. A third instance of market failure concerns the generation of trust and co-operation.[86] There is a growing awareness of the importance of these "social resources" to successful, efficient, economies.[87] Yet, it is argued, the pursuit of profit maximisation by companies, and the strategic treatment of other constituencies' interests which that requires, can undermine those constituencies' propensity to trust, and to behave co-operatively towards, the companies with which they deal. Consumers, creditors, suppliers and employees will realise that the company will promote their interests only to the extent that to do so will maximise its profits. In consequence, they will "trust" that company less, and will be more likely themselves to adopt a similarly calculatively self-interested attitude towards the company.

One way of correcting for these various instances of market failure is through the use of legal constraints on profit maximisation. However, we have already noted the limitations of such constraints, and so the pursuit of efficiency might justify more substantial reform. CSR, for example, might be construed so as to require companies to internalise all of the social costs of their operations. Similarly, proponents of stakeholding emphasise the beneficial effects on trust and co-operation, and therefore efficiency, which might follow if companies give real weight to the interests of other constituencies.[88] (Their critics, on the

---

[84] See A. Buchanan, *Equity, Efficiency and the Market* (Oxford, Clarendon Press, 1985), ch.1.

[85] This refers to costs imposed on third parties which are not compensated for through the price mechanism; the obvious example is the costs imposed on the neighbours of a polluting factory.

[86] For a useful overview, see S. Deakin and J. Michie, "The Theory and Practice of Contracting" in S. Deakin and J. Michie (eds.), *Contracts, Co-operation and Competition* (Oxford, Oxford U.Press, 1997).

[87] See, e.g., F. Fukuyama, *Trust: The Social Virtues and the Creation of Prosperity* (London, Penguin Books, 1996); R. M. Kramer and T. R. Tyler (eds.), *Trust in Organizations: Frontiers of Theory and Research* (Thousand Oaks, Cal., Sage Publications, 1996); B. A. Misztal, *Trust in Modern Societies* (Cambridge, Polity Press, 1996); C. Crouch, "Co-operation and Competition in an Institutionalised Economy. The Case of Germany" in C. Crouch and D. Marquand (eds.), *Ethics and Markets: Co-Operation and Competition within Capitalist Economies* (Oxford, Blackwell Publishers, 1993); J. Gray, "The Undoing of Conservatism" in J. Gray and D. Willetts, *Is Conservatism Dead?* (London: Profile Books, 1997).

[88] See J. E. Parkinson, "Company Law and Stakeholder Governance" and J. Kay, "The Stakeholder Corporation" both in G. Kelly, D. Kelly and A. Gamble (eds.), *Stakeholder Capitalism* (Basingstoke, Macmillan Press, 1997); S. Deakin and F. Wilkinson, "Contracts, Co-operation and

other hand, emphasise the difficulties in enforcing this "balancing of interests" formula, and the danger of a resulting breakdown in managerial unaccountability.)[89] And it has been argued that extending democracy—especially to employees—might also have efficiency benefits—say by increasing workers' commitment and productivity and reducing monitoring costs and management-labour conflict.[90]

Some Problems with Efficiency

The promotion of efficiency seems to have at least some explanatory force in accounting for many existing departures from shareholder primacy. So, for example, many of the existing constraints on profit maximisation—health and safety legislation, environmental protection, consumer regulations, and so on—might be explicable as corrections for market failure. Moreover, as we noted above, normatively efficiency arguments have dominated much of the current debate in the UK about further governance reform. This is, to some extent, understandable. For proponents of reform, and especially for governments, securing an aggregatively wealthier society has powerful attractions.

With greater space, we might try to develop this normative analysis and tie down much more firmly just what form of governance structure, with how much democracy, what form of stakeholding, and so on, would best maximise social wealth. That is not my task, here, however. Instead, I want to urge some caution in this reliance upon efficiency. Notwithstanding the preoccupation with efficiency, that value has not been accepted unequivocally. There are two strands to the argument here. One is negative, criticising the normative appeal of efficiency as a guide to governance reform. The other is positive, promoting other values either to replace, or at least to qualify, the pursuit of efficiency.

The most familiar criticism of efficiency, in the sense in which we have used that term here, concerns its aggregative quality: how we can justify focusing only on the *overall* amount of wealth—on total "prosperity"—without asking who is getting what share of the corporate cake? Take, for example, the position of shareholders themselves. Suppose that the maximisation of aggregate wealth leaves shareholders worse off than they would be under shareholder

Trust: The Role of the Institutional Framework" in D. Campbell and P. Vincent-Jones (eds.), *Contract and Economic Organisation* (Aldershot, Dartmouth Publishing, 1996).

[89] See J. G. MacIntosh, "Designing an Efficient Fiduciary Law" (1993) 43 *U of Toronto LJ* 425; L. S. Sealy, "Directors' 'Wider' Responsibilities—Problems Conceptual, Practical and Procedural" (1987) 13 *Monash UL Rev.* 164.

[90] See A. Gewirth, *The Community of Rights* (Chicago, Ill., Uni. of Chicago Press, 1996), at 282–8; J. E. Parkinson, n. 4 above, ch. 12; R. A. Dahl, *A Preface to Economic Democracy* (Berkeley, Cal., Uni. of Cal. Press, 1985); S. Bowles and H. Gintis, *Democracy and Capitalism* (New York, Basic Books, 1987). For an introduction to the efficiency issues raised by workers' co-operatives, see D. Miller, *Market, State and Community: Theoretical Foundations of Market Socialism* (Oxford, Clarendon Press, 1989), ch. 3.

primacy. It may seem a poor justification to them that the corporate cake has become much larger if their own share has become smaller in the process. Unless the argument here is that *everyone* will be left better off in virtue of the move from shareholder primacy, then we must somehow justify the loss to some occasioned by the gains to others. Moreover, even if it were felt that the increase in aggregate wealth were justification enough, proponents of reform might feel that that value provided a rather shaky foundation for the improvements in the position of other constituencies which they hope to secure. That, say, a move towards employee democracy, or the giving of real weight to the interests of others, should depend on showing that these things actually promote greater wealth seems a hostage to fortune. And, finally, it ignores what are other more pressing values justifying governance reforms. In particular, we should be concerned not simply with the total amount of wealth which the corporate economy is capable of producing, but with the *distribution* of the benefits and the burdens of corporate activity. To take one example, if we are concerned about companies polluting their neighbourhood, our concern might be not that such pollution reduces total wealth, but just that some (shareholders) gain at others' (neighbours') expense.

Now, if the design of our governance system is to be driven by some account of distributive justice, (rather than simply by the pursuit of maximum total wealth), then we shall clearly need to determine what sort of treatment the various corporate constituents or "stakeholders" are entitled to insist on from the company, and therefore what rights individuals ought, morally, to enjoy. Of course, such moral considerations are deeply controversial. One approach is to ground the rights of corporate constituents in the positive morality of the community in which the company carries on its operations. So, for example, in seeking to devise the way corporations must treat their employees—whether, for example, they are to be entitled to a minimum wage, to a working environment free from sexual harassment, and so on— we might have recourse to what we sense are the current moral standards of the relevant community. Alternatively, we might seek to ground these constituents' rights in some higher, critical morality: we may want to argue that companies should not, for example, be allowed to discriminate on grounds of sexual orientation not because the relevant community *thinks* that is wrong, but because it *is* wrong.

Whichever route is chosen—and this is not the place to attempt to arbitrate between them—their regulatory consequences may frequently not differ greatly from those outlined in relation to the efficiency approach. So, for example, much might again be achieved by imposing constraints upon the company's pursuit of profits. If we thought that employees ought, morally, to be entitled to a minimum wage, this would seem only to require giving such a right to those employees (perhaps backed up by criminal sanctions). However, we noted above the strategic limitations in relying on constraints in this way. Requiring companies to act in socially responsible ways might again be necessary to secure the treatment to which, morally, other constituencies, are entitled.

Furthermore, if we recognise a moral right to, say, participate in those decisions which impact substantially on our lives, or in the exercise of authority over us, then vindicating these rights points towards some extension of corporate democracy.[91] Clearly the end-result, in terms of specific prescriptions for governance reform, may often overlap substantially with those generated by considerations of efficiency, but the justificatory arguments in play remain distinctive.

What of shareholders? Cannot they also claim a moral right—in virtue of their property in the corporation—to have the company run in their interests alone? Perhaps the most familiar justification for answering this in the negative focuses on the empirical fact of the shareholder's position within the large company. Precisely because there is now a separation of ownership and control, so that shareholders are merely passive suppliers of capital with little control over the company's affairs, then their moral entitlements do, it is argued, fall short of insisting that the company be run in their interests alone.[92]

Current Doctrine

The final issue to address here is the extent to which UK company law already instantiates these alternatives to shareholder primacy. In broad terms, it does not. Company law remains committed to a shareholder-centred conception of the company. Having said that, however, this commitment is less than complete. There already exist, within the legal framework, elements of the alternative strategies set out above. So, for example, although company law seems to set as its purpose the protection of shareholders, the strategies it adopts are less than wholly effective, and this offers *some* space for profit-sacrificing socially responsible behaviour.[93] Of course, there is much debate about just how much room there is here. As Deakin and Slinger have argued,[94] whatever the imperfections and ambiguities in the legal framework, the City Code on Takeovers imposes rather more clearly shareholder-centred obligations on directors faced with a takeover bid, precluding their adoption of defensive tactics against takeovers which they believe adversely affect the interests of other constituencies.[95]

Going beyond voluntarism by directors, we have already observed that shareholder primacy is limited by a large range of constraints imposed upon com-

[91] See, e.g., Gewirth, n. 90 above, esp. ch. 7.

[92] See M. Stokes, "Company Law and Legal Theory" in W. L. Twining (ed.), *Legal Theory and the Common Law* (Oxford, Basil Blackwell, 1986); Parkinson, n. 4 above, at 33–41.

[93] See Parkinson, n. 88 above, at 143–4.

[94] S. Deakin and G. Slinger, "Hostile Takeovers, Corporate Law, and the Theory of the Firm" (1997) 24 *J of Law and Soc.* 124 at 134–42.

[95] Compare US practice, where many states have allowed companies to adopt "Corporate Constituency Statutes", under which the board, in evaluating a bid, is allowed to consider the impact of the takeover on the interests of a range of constituencies. See M. Lipton and M. Panner, "Takeover Bids and United States Corporate Governance" in Prentice and Holland (eds.), n. 54 above.

panies, and to that extent, "pure" shareholder primacy has long since been abandoned. Relatedly, theorising on "relational contracts" claims that in long-term contracts, contracting parties may choose not to insist on the strict legal terms of their contracts, even though doing so seems to reduce their profits. This again sounds like more voluntarism, but authors such as Collins have recently argued that we might best understand this behaviour as compliance with non-legal but still binding "distinctive normative orders".[96] Added to this, we may also be seeing a move in English law towards recognising certain obligations of good faith in the performance of contracts.[97]

So far as stakeholding is concerned, some, albeit very limited, obligations have been imposed on directors to consider the interests of non-shareholder constituencies. In relation to creditors, for example, such obligations arise under both case law and section 214 of the Insolvency Act 1986.[98] And, in relation to employees, section 309 of the Companies Act 1985 provides that "[t]he matters to which the directors of a company are to have regard in the performance of their functions include the interests of the company's employees in general, as well as the interests of its members".[99] However, it is a familiar complaint that, whilst this provision might do a little to allow a director so minded to consider the employee's interests, it does very little actually to compel such a consideration.[100]

Finally, in relation to extended corporate democracy, only the most limited progress has been made. The European Works Council Directive,[101] adopted in 1994, requires larger European companies[102] to set up company-wide committees for informing and consulting employees.[103] But the modesty of the directive—being limited to information and consultation—means that it hardly qualifies as a regime of industrial democracy.[104] And we have already noted the dilution of the worker participation provisions in the most recent version of the

[96] H. Collins, "Competing Norms of Contractual Behaviour" in Campbell and Vincent-Jones (eds.), n. 88 above.

[97] R. Brownsword, " 'Good Faith in Contracts' Revisited" [1997] *Current Legal Problems* 111. For an illustration of this in the context of employment law, and the judicial development of the implied term of trust and confidence in employment relationships, see D. Brodie, "Beyond Exchange: The New Contract of Employment" (1998) 27 *Industrial LJ* 79.

[98] See C. A. Riley, "Directors' Duties and the Interests of Creditors" (1989) 10 *The Co. Lawyer* 87.

[99] See also s.719 CA 1985, allowing companies to provide for employees on cessation or transfer of business.

[100] See B. Pettet, "Duties in Respect of Employees under the Companies Act 1980" (1981) 34 *Current Legal Problems* 199.

[101] Council Dir. 94/45/EEC [1994] OJ L254/64.

[102] I.e. those companies with over 1,000 workers and more than 150 in two or more Member States.

[103] Although the directive did not originally apply in the UK, in virtue of its opt-out from the Social Policy Agreement, many companies operating in the UK chose to include UK employees voluntarily; see C. McGlynn, "An Exercise in Futility: The Practical Effects of the Social Policy Opt-out" (1998) 49 *NILQ* 60 at 61–4.

[104] See C. McGlynn, "European Works Council: Towards Industrial Democracy" (1995) 24 *Ind. LJ* 78.

draft Fifth Directive and in the revised proposals for a European Company Statute.[105]

CONCLUSIONS

The three tensions in corporate regulation addressed in this essay—the merits of internal monitoring versus markets, deregulation, and the challenge to shareholder primacy—are hardly new. But they are central, nevertheless, to the way the largest companies in our economy are regulated, and that, as we suggested at the outset, should be of considerable public interest.

Some of these tensions might be resolved through greater empirical knowledge. As we learn more about comparative governance systems, so too we may better understand their relative merits, and overcome the ignorance which currently inhibits reform. So, too, might we better understand the economic consequences of stakeholding, of greater corporate democracy, and so on. But the tensions discussed here are not simply disputes about the way the corporate world works. Rather, they depend upon competing conceptions of the company, and different understandings of the purposes and values which company law should promote. To date, much of the debate has been concerned with efficiency. Whilst this has obvious political and rhetorical merit, we should not, it has been argued, be blind to its shortcomings. In the resolution of these tensions, the government's current programme for the modernisation of company law carries a heavy responsibility.

---

[105] See J. J. Du Plessis and J. Dine, "The Fate of the Ffth Directive on Company Law: Accomodation Instead of Harmonisation" [1997] *JBL* 23.

5

Building Societies

JOHN VAUGHAN

INTRODUCTION

One of the less edifying economic phenomena of the last decade has been the realisation that mutuality is a valuable commodity. The sight of building society members circling an institution bears more than a passing resemblance to sharks in a feeding frenzy. What price 150 years of history? Well around £1,500 if you are one of the lucky holders of an account in a demutualising society when the music stops. Fuelled by a media which regularly publishes estimated values, "carpetbaggers" have placed minimum sums into savings accounts in the expectation that this will generate tenfold, or higher, returns in the near future. Major financial institutions, such as the Nationwide Building Society, are under pressure from members whose sole object is not to further its interests but to sell it to the highest bidder. This problem is not unique to building societies. Members of mutual insurers, sports and social clubs and bodies such as the Royal Automobile Club, have all discovered that demutualisation is the key to the treasure chest of accumulated surpluses. Not all have succumbed but, arguably, if the mutual was an animal it would be placed on the list of endangered species.

Demutualisation is not the only issue facing the industry, but it is the most important, for a continuation of the process will lead to the virtual extinction of building societies as we know them. It should be emphasised here that it is the legal form under consideration and not the function of the societies. Irrespective of the form there are many financial organisations offering products in both the savings and loans markets and this competition is also an issue which societies have increasingly had to face.

It is right and proper that this somewhat jaundiced opening be balanced. Proponents of the idea of demutualisation would argue that this action is for the long term benefit of customers. Providing better service and products requires capital and this cannot easily be raised by mutuals who do not have the full resources of the City to call on as compared with banking companies. The corollary of this is that societies are not exposed to the market disciplines of their banking cousins, and so the imperative of efficiency is lacking. All these charges would be disputed by those societies remaining. Perhaps a better argument is that the industry has faced a traditionally restrictive legal framework governing its trading activities. Many quite natural and commercially rational activities were outside the scope of the industry or were subject to onerous restrictions. To all intents and purposes these no longer exist, but the development of Abbey National from its building society roots does illustrate the changes that can be made. That body, now a bank, obtains almost half its profits from "non traditional" business and has recently set a target of 65 per cent from this source within the next five years. This goal might be helped by the fact that the bank expects its share of mortgage lending to fall, as borrowers seem to prefer mutuals for this activity.[1]

The development of the trading powers of the industry will be considered shortly, but while recent changes have considerably relaxed the regulatory framework to allow more operating freedom, the pressures to demutualise, which started from the basis of commercial liberalisation, are now inflated by member expectations, managerial ambitions and institutional investment. Given this, it will be a surprise if the remaining societies, or at least those of any commercial significance, can withstand the force. This chapter will therefore emphasise the key issue of change of corporate status, dealing with matters such as control and powers in less detail. For those with any affection for the industry it is hoped that this chapter is not an obituary.

HISTORICAL DEVELOPMENT

Building societies were once numbered in the thousands,[2] but their number has fallen considerably during this century by a process which seems to be accelerating. The last report of the Building Societies Commission[3] showed that there were 77 authorised building societies which between them operated 4,613 branches. They employed just over 100,000 staff who serviced 37,768,000 shareholders, 6,889,000 depositors and 6,859,000 borrowers. It is interesting to compare these figures with those from ten years previously, which showed that there were 124 societies which ran their business from 6,982 branch offices. Numbers of shareholders fell by over four million and borrowers by around 300,000. What are the reasons for this?

While much of this essay concentrates upon demutualisation, that is only part of the answer. The conversion of the Abbey National, which at the time was the second largest society, clearly caused a fall in industry assets but the main culprit in the relative contraction is merger. The process of amalgamation has been responsible for the fall in both societies and, through rationalisation, the branch network. Multiple membership of societies by individuals will also inevitably mean that on a simple head count the membership roll of the industry will also fall.

---

[1] See *The Times*, 25 May 1998.
[2] When the 1874 Act was passed there were an estimated 2,088 societies in existence.
[3] Building Societies Commission Annual Report (London, 1996–7).

Analysis of the total number of societies authorised reveals the concentration of the industry. This has long been a feature and while the composition of the top five, or ten or 20, societies changes, their grip on the industry does not. At the end of 1996 the largest five societies controlled 70.7 per cent of industry assets as compared with 60.8 per cent ten years previously. The top ten controlled 87.4 per cent (as compared with 79.3 per cent) while the top 20 held 95.3 per cent (89.9 per cent). Discussion of the industry must therefore take into account this massive disparity. It does of course exist within the corporate sphere, and obviously not all banks are multi-national conglomerates, but the point is worth emphasising. If the process of demutualisation continues there may be a limit on how far down the pecking order it will go. While the top five societies have balance sheets which would look quite respectable on flotation, the bottom five do not possess the resources to obtain a listing on any alternative market. They may though be attractive targets for other financial institutions.

The scale of merger activity can be seen from the fact that in 1960 there were 726 societies, the last 40 years or so seeing a fall of around 650. Going back a similar period there were approximately 1,000 in existence when the Halifax Building Society came into being as the result of a merger between two societies based in that town.[4] The combined society had assets of £34.9 million out of an industry total of £198 million, evidence that concentration is not a recent phenomenon.

Despite this history, the industry had very humble beginnings. The industry was a by-product of the urban growth of the industrial revolution and the need for workers to make financial provision for themselves. The development of building societies was therefore a response to the acute housing shortage in the cities and the difficulties faced by ordinary workers in obtaining finance. The first recorded society was started in 1775 by Richard Ketley. This early organisation was a "terminating Society", so called because once it had achieved its objectives it went out of existence. The objective in this case was to house the members. On joining, each member agreed to subscribe a set amount. Once funds existed to build a house these would be allocated, usually by ballot, and the process would continue until all were housed. Those provided with a property would normally also pay rent to the society so that the process of funding each successive building would accelerate. Terminating societies had a number of flaws. The unlucky last person housed would have to wait a long time, but the big difficulty was funding. The only available funds were those obtained from the members, and the idea of matching those with surplus cash with those needing finance was impossible with this type of body. Further, new members could not join unless they had the ability to pay back subscriptions to put them in the same position as the founders. For these reasons the terminating society had no long term future as an organisation type and was replaced by the

---

[4] The Halifax Permanent and Halifax Equitable merged in 1928.

permanent societies. The Leeds Permanent Building Society, which merged with the Halifax, owes part of its title to the time when societies distinguished themselves by type.[5]

The idea for the permanent society was devised in the mid nineteenth century[6] and paved the way for the division of borrowers and lenders and the development of a professional group of managers. The growth of the industry also demanded a legislative framework, and this was finally provided in 1874 with the passing of the Building Societies Act. This Act replaced an earlier one of the same name passed in 1836. This provided for a cursory level of regulation, the most important aspect being that a society had to have its rule book certified as being in accordance with the Act. No method of incorporation was provided nor were any controls given over society activities. The 1874 Act went some way to deal with these omissions but "while it provided a reasonable framework for a well conducted society, gave little protection if a society was conducted otherwise".[7] Unfortunately it seemed that there were a large number of poorly managed bodies, a fact bemoaned by Wills J, who in one judgment commented that:

> "it is the third case which has come before myself within the last few weeks in which similar enormous losses have been shown to have fallen upon the persons interested in one way or another in building societies and in which they must chiefly fall upon persons in the humble walks of life."[8]

The learned judge had no doubt that blame fell upon incompetent managers, but his words were ignored until the collapse of the Liberator Building Society a few years later. The crash of what was then the largest society led to immediate legal reform and the passing of the Building Societies Act 1894. This introduced, *inter alia*, compulsory audits; prohibited the acceptance of commission by officers; and provided intervention powers for the Chief Registrar of Friendly Societies.

Amendments were made piecemeal during the next half century and the passing of the Building Societies Act 1962 consolidated the existing legislation. The consequence was that late into the twentieth century the industry was still being regulated by the spirit, if not the letter, of statutes passed in a totally different economic context. The main problems were in the area of trading powers, which were very restrictively framed, and further change was inevitable as the industry faced increasing competition in its main markets but lacked the ability to compete itself. The 1986 Act provided significantly enhanced powers but its provisions lasted only a short time before further relaxation was called for. This process has continued with the 1997 Act which has relaxed still further these limitations. The specific provisions of these statutes will be considered below in the discussion of the powers of building societies and their supervision.

---

[5] Only 4 societies now include the word "Permanent" in their names, and of these 3 are not authorised to accept deposits: *Building Societies Commission Annual Report 1996–7*, n. 3 above.

[6] Almost certainly by an actuary, J. H. James.

[7] E.J. Cleary, *The Building Society Movement* (Elak Books, 1965), 100.

[8] *Re Companies Acts, ex parte Watson* (1888) 21 QBD 301, 308.

COMPARISONS WITH OTHER CORPORATE BODIES

At a retail level it has over the last decade been increasingly difficult to distinguish between building societies and banks, and there are strong arguments for treating them in the same way, at least for regulatory purposes. The fact that they are legally a distinct type of legal body is due in part to a change in government in 1874[9] which saw a policy shift away from forcing societies within the framework of companies legislation.[10] This treatment was inconsistent with that applied to banks and insurance companies where, for example, the Chartered Companies Act 1837 was deemed to extend to the banking industry. Early legislation therefore enshrined the concept of mutuality as opposed to the company law model of share ownership.

It is worth considering briefly what this means in practice. Both companies and societies have shareholders but there are few similarities between the two. Lord Dunedin in 1905 in considering the two types of share commented that:

"A share in a limited company is part of the capital, and is something which cannot be got rid of. It may be transferred to someone else, but it cannot be put out of existence. Comparing it with the so-called shares of this building society, the difference is apparent. A share in this building society represented no proportionate part of this company's capital. There might be as many shares in this society as people liked to apply for. The share here represented no more than an earmarked application for a contribution of £25. The share might never come to maturity. It might be withdrawn long before it was matured. It might either be paid back, or it might be wiped out in advance. Accordingly, though the word is the same, there is nothing more than a faint analogy between it and a share in a joint stock company."[11]

Historically the quotation is interesting for other reasons. The name of the society running to eight words is a reminder of the days when names actually meant something and image consultants did not exist. The share in this example was a subscription share. The idea behind this was to allocate a value to a share, in this case £25. Once an investor had saved up £25 then a share was allotted. As many shares would be issued as £25 contributions made. An individual would therefore be able to say how many shares that he/she held in the society and the extent of liability on partly-paid shares. The point though is that the concepts of authorised and issued capital and any idea of capital maintenance are not relevant to building societies in the way in which they apply to companies. The building society share appears to be much closer to a simple bank deposit than a company share but this analogy also fails to hold.

Depositors have no legal relationship with their bank other than that provided for by their contract and by general legislation governing such instruments as

---

[9]   The election of Disraeli as Prime Minister.
[10]   The Companies Act (CA) 1862.
[11]   *Liquidator of Irvine and Fullarton Property Investment and Building Society* v. *Cuthbertson* (1905) 42 SCLR 17.

cheques. They have no formal role in the management of the bank. The building society saver though is a member of the society, a fact which carries some rights which would be recognised by a company shareholder. This includes the rights to vote at general meetings and to receive financial information. It is not only the saver who is a member. A mortgagor also falls within this category. Until the passing of the 1997 Act the rights of borrowers were fewer than those of investing members, but now there is little to distinguish the two. Typically full membership rights demand that an individual holds an investment of at least £100 in the society or is a secured borrower to the same amount, and that this has been the case since the end of the preceding financial year.[12] The building society customer therefore has a relationship which is governed by the specific product contract, the rule book of the society, building societies legislation and, where relevant, the general body of law relating to banking.

Whether membership rights are effective is a different matter. For most individuals the most important part of the relationship is found in the express terms relating to their specific product. Voting levels are typically low[13] and for many people the summary financial statement received annually will be just another piece of junk mail. "Member power" is now exerting itself as regards conversions, but this is a recent phenomenon and the industry does not have any greater history of effective accountability to its customers than say banks, that is, through the need to maintain appropriate interest rate structures, product portfolios and levels of service. Apathy is of course a major reason for the lack of shareholder accountability. That and the fact that the building society member is not subject to any greater risk than a bank customer. The last building society collapse was the Grays in 1978. Ordinary members did not suffer any loss after the industry organised a rescue fund.[14] This response is unlikely to occur again as the industry is subject to a compensation scheme similar to that covering the banking industry. The Building Societies Investor Protection Board provides compensation of 90 per cent of the first £20,000 deposited with an insolvent society.[15] As with highly publicised banking collapses such as BCCI investors will now suffer a loss in the event of an insolvency.

The obvious difference in terms of accountability is that building societies operate on the one member one vote principle. It is therefore impossible to "control" a society in the way that a company can be controlled, the idea of a majority shareholding being irrelevant. This of course has both pluses and minuses. It is argued that managers are not subject to the disciplines imposed by the stock exchange, takeovers and the muscle-flexing of institutional shareholders not

[12] Building Societies Act 1986, Sched. 3, para. 36.

[13] With the obvious exception of those relating to transfers of business to commercial companies.

[14] This received High Court approval in *Halifax Building Society* v. *Registry of Friendly Societies* [1978] 3 All ER 403.

[15] Building Societies Act 1986, ss.24–30, as amended by the Credit Institutions (Protection of Depositors) Regulations 1995, S.I. 1995/1442, which implemented the EU Directive on Deposit Guarantee Schemes.

being problems to contend with. Writing before the passing of the 1986 Act, the then Chancellor of the Exchequer, Geoffrey Howe, noted that:

> "the boards of societies have, in practice, generally not been held directly to account for the success or otherwise of their policies. No board has been voted from office as has happened to some governments and to boards of some companies. The boards of societies have not been subject to the same financial disciplines from the capital markets as exist for companies."[16]

Of course the reverse situation might arguably apply now. The rush to conversion and the windfall gains leaves societies prey to the carpetbagger mentality which is prevalent today.[17] The protection of institutional shareholders who can be relied upon to support the board might seem in retrospect the only way in which mutuality can be preserved. Perhaps not; the City does not seem to have the reputation for placing long-term developments above short-term gains. Given this it is hard to suggest that individuals should do differently. Those arguing that directors are not accountable and then objecting when members actually impose their wishes are also placed in a weak position.

MEMBERS RIGHTS

The paradox discussed above about the lack of accountability in a system which seems so obviously democratic is not one confined to the building society industry. The industry itself might argue that the system is skewed too heavily in favour of individuals and, considering the expense to which the Nationwide Building Society has gone recently to defend its mutual status, it is difficult not to feel sympathy for this. Within company law it can be crudely argued that the "interests" of the company are synonymous with those of the majority shareholders. In many instances these are easily reconciled as the majority shareholders operate as executive managers. For larger companies the constituency to which they are in practice most accountable to is that of the relatively small number of fund managers within the City.

An additional problem is faced through the sheer numbers of individuals involved. This, plus member apathy over most issues, makes it virtually impossible for anybody with a genuine interest in the management of a society to have any real influence. We need therefore to provide some mechanism for allowing individuals to have an effect on decision-making which cannot be abused in a way which is detrimental to the interests of others by imposing unreasonable costs on the society both financially and in terms of management time. The way that building society law has dealt with this is similar to that which operates

---

[16] (1984) 114 *Building Societies Gazette* 625.
[17] See e.g. the *Sunday Times* of 26 July 1998 which headlined an article, "Grab your share of £10 billion". It is also possible to purchase "carpetbagger's" guides.

within the company law sphere. That is, rights are given to, *inter alia*, receive information, vote, requisition meetings and propose resolutions.

Schedule 2 of the 1986 Act provides most of the rules governing this area of activity. Part III, headed "Meetings, Resolutions and Postal Ballots" provides for the holding of an annual general meeting and explains the different types of resolutions available.[18] This area has been amended by the 1997 Act, which interestingly has a set of provisions which appear under the heading, "Accountability to Members". These changes significantly strengthen the power of members, at least on paper. First they give the right to requisition a general meeting. Previously the power to move resolutions only was given. This right requires the support of only 100 members who may be required to provide at most a £25 deposit each. The only protection seems to be that the requisition can be ignored if the proposed meeting is mainly for the moving of a resolution which is substantially the same as one which has been defeated within the last three years.[19] Where a meeting is to be convened the requisitionists can ask the society to circulate a statement to the members, but where this is abused or would be likely to diminish confidence in the society then the request can be refused. The Commission will deal with any complaints regarding this. As with the equivalent company law provisions, rules exist for the requisitionists to convene their own meeting in the event of default, with the costs payable by the society.

The term "members" in this context has also changed as a result of the 1997 Act. Previously rights were conferred largely on shareholders. Typically they would have the power to vote at general meetings and borrowers only had rights in this area in the case of mergers or transfers of business. The new position is that borrowers and shareholders are classed equally as members in most cases. Thus ordinary and special resolutions may be voted on by both classes. The differences though still exist for mergers and transfers, for two resolutions are required in these cases, one passed by each class with different rules.[20]

The ability to call a general meeting is supported by rights to move resolutions and to nominate members to the Board. The latter provisions have also been amended now to reflect the differences in size within the industry, ranging from only ten members where the society has commercial assets not exceeding £100 million to 50 where the size exceeds £5,000 million. The Act, though, retains the previous position that the register of members is a confidential document and so anybody wanting to contact fellow members to obtain support for a proposal cannot easily do so. There has long been a power vested in the regulator of the industry to grant access to the register but requests are rare. Recently

---

[18] These are similar to those contained within the CA being special and ordinary resolutions. In some circumstances there are also shareholding and borrowing members' resolutions. These are discussed in the section on conversion.

[19] New s. 20A(9) which also allows the requisition to be ignored where a meeting is proposed to be held within the 4 months starting one month after the end of the financial year.

[20] Discussed later in the section dealing with transfers of business.

the Commission has had to deal with the problem, as individuals have sought to force the issue on demutualisation, and one such instance has been reported in detail in the Report for 1995–6. A brief discussion of this will usefully illustrate the tensions which exist in the governance of the industry and the way in which the regulator is attempting to reconcile them.

Between February and April 1996 Mr Michael Hardern made application for access to the registers of some 51 societies. The stated purpose of this was to "discuss the future of the society and its continued mutuality or possible conversion" with members.[21] The Commission noted that the papers submitted to support the application appeared to go further than this purpose. A further application was made in respect of these societies and two others in June. One of the matters to be discussed was the issue of reinstatement of membership following the fact that a number of societies had expelled him. The Commission rejected the applications citing a number of reasons. First, they objected to the general nature of the applications, believing the approaches to be more to do with the generic nature of the societies as societies rather than matters directly relating to the subjects. Specifically it was thought that the consequences of allowing access to discuss demutualisation based on industry characteristics, rather than those of a specific society, outweighed the benefit of allowing it. The applicant, although making the approach as an individual, was the co-ordinator of a campaign which had a wider canvassing remit and the Commission did not want to provide further publicity for this. There was also a fear that the applicant's unstated motive, which was to encourage demutualisation, would cause instability in the industry and also conflicted with the requirements for prudent management imposed on boards. Finally, the applicant had been a member of most of the societies for a comparatively short time such that he would not have been able personally to move resolutions or nominate board candidates. The Commission did however think that expulsion of members was inappropriate.

It seems from this ruling that an application tailored to the circumstances of a specific society would be acceptable provided that it came from a member of standing. While this might still generate the instability which the Commission is seeking to avoid it is hard to argue that the matter is not relevant to the members, and the fact that it may be at odds with the policy of the Board should not be sufficient to render the application unacceptable. The 1997 Act has made some amendments to the rules, in particular applications may now only be made by those eligible to join a members' requisition for a special meeting.

POWERS

For the period between the passing of the 1986 and 1997 Building Societies Acts the issue of the powers available to a building society was an important one.

[21] *Building Societies Commission Annual Report 1995–6* (London, 1996), App. F.

While practically, of course, it remains so, from a legal perspective the matter is now relatively settled. Prior to 1986 the legislation imposed severe constraints on the industry. Basically societies were confined to raising funds in the retail markets and using these monies to make advances fully secured on residential land. The inability of the industry to compete on anything approaching level terms with other institutions made the changes of the 1986 Act inevitable, and this piece of legislation significantly altered the trading powers of building societies.

The 1986 Act created a complex set of rules designed to ensure that even with these freedoms a building society did not stray too far from its origins. The purpose or principal purpose of a building society was that of "raising, primarily by the subscriptions of the members, a stock or fund for making to them advances secured on land for their residential use".[22] In most instances these advances would be regarded as class 1 assets where they were fully secured first charges. Other types of commercial assets were placed in classes 2 and 3, class 3 being the riskiest and including unsecured loans. Initially the total of class 2 and 3 assets could not exceed 10 per cent of all commercial assets with class 3 not exceeding 5 per cent. The legislation could hardly therefore be described as generous. These rules were relaxed over time to allow 25 per cent of commercial assets to be held in non-traditional categories.

Similarly rigid rules were imposed to ensure that societies did not become too dependent on wholesale money markets and so retained their main funding base within the retail savings sector. Finally, the 1986 Act specified in considerable detail the powers to provide services available to societies with Schedule 8 listing 15 of these along with the restrictions on their exercise. Schedule 8 lasted a comparatively short time in its original form; the 15 specific powers giving way to six more generalised ones.[23] Over the ensuing years other amendments were made but the position now has been altered significantly.

The position on trading powers is now simple. Instead of provisions which are permissive, the 1986 Act has been amended to contain restrictions. The implication therefore is that building societies may do anything they like subject to the stated exceptions. These limits prevent a society from: acting as a market-maker in securities, commodities or currencies; trading in commodities or currencies; or entering into any transaction involving derivative investments.[24] Where these transactions are undertaken for normal hedging purposes they are permitted, but the Act specifically states that they will be valid even if in contravention of the restriction. One other restriction is found in the new section 9B which prohibits the creation of floating charges by building societies and declares these to be void where they breach the restriction.

This still leaves the issues of the extent to which societies can become involved in non-traditional business and the funding of the activity. The legisla-

---

[22] Building Societies Act 1986 s.5 (original version).
[23] A new Sched. 8 was substituted by SI 1988 No 1141 and subsequently by other SIs.
[24] *Ibid.*, new s. 9A.

tion effectively still restricts societies by requiring that the bulk of commercial assets be in the form of residential mortgages. It achieves this by using as a base the total assets of the society and any subsidiary undertakings less fixed and liquid assets. From this base figure is deducted the value of loans fully secured on residential land. The difference, i.e. commercial assets not fully secured on residential land, cannot exceed 25 per cent of the base figure.[25]

A limit is also imposed on wholesale funding. The base here is all funding provided in the form of shares, deposits, bills of exchange and instruments such as certificates of deposit. From this is deducted the value of shares held by individuals. The difference, in this case monies raised from the wholesale markets or from deposits, cannot exceed 50 per cent of the base figure.[26] Note that a society can only now raise money from individuals by issuing shares; it no longer has the power to accept deposits from them.[27]

While the 1997 Act may have allowed societies considerably more freedom as to the markets they operate in, the reality is that they are still required to maintain their traditional focus on retail funding and secured lending. The purpose or principal purpose is now stated as being the "making of loans which are secured on residential property and are funded substantially by its members": hardly a major change from the 1986 position. It should finally be noted that building societies like companies have a memorandum which contains details of their powers. The position where an activity outside these powers is undertaken is dealt with by the Act in a similar way to that used by the Companies Act.[28]

PRUDENTIAL REGULATION

Although there are similarities between banks and building societies, the industry has always been subject to a separate regulatory framework. This was originally entrusted to the Chief Registrar of Friendly Societies, but the 1986 Act introduced the Building Societies Commission as the responsible body for ensuring that legislative requirements were met and, among other things, for promoting the financial stability of the industry. The link with the Registry persists however, for the Commission's staff are part of the Registry of Friendly Societies.

The primary responsibility for ensuring that a society is properly managed rests with the Board of Directors. The Commission's role is therefore one of monitoring and advising. Monitoring comes in the form of receipt of returns and regular contact with each society. Returns are required on an annual, quarterly and monthly basis, and in addition to an annual meeting there will be

---

[25] *Ibid.*, s.6 (as amended by 1997 Act). The assessment must be undertaken on a quarterly basis. The Act provides for the Treasury to increase the limit to 40%.

[26] *Ibid.*, s. 7 as amended.

[27] *Ibid.*, s. 8 as amended. Note that the section does allow for some exceptions to this rule.

[28] *Ibid.*, Sched. 1.

frequent contact between the Commission and individual societies. Advice will be given as part of the contact, but in addition the Commission publishes a range of papers on regulatory issues. These consist of: prudential notes, explaining the Commission's view on how the criteria of prudent management can be met; guidance notes, which explain statutory and administrative procedures; and dear chief executive letters which provide advice on a range of issues.[29]

The criteria of prudent management referred to above are an important feature of the 1986 Act. Section 45 lists specific requirements which have to be met by all societies, failure in respect of any of them entitles the Commission to conclude that the security of investors or depositors has been prejudiced. The importance of this is that this triggers the power to exercise a range of control powers. These range from the imposition of conditions, through ordering a merger or a transfer of business, to revocation of authorisation. In extreme cases where a society is in breach of the principal purpose rule, a winding up order can be sought.[30] These powers have been strengthened by the 1997 Act. For example the Commission can now dispense with the need to seek representations from a society in advance where this is considered urgent. It should be said that these powers are exercised infrequently. The last example being that of the New Cross Building Society in 1983.[31]

DEMUTUALISATION: THE ARGUMENTS

The point made earlier about the concentration of building society assets in a relatively small number of societies and that these are large enough for a flotation indicates that the effective demise of the industry could occur quite quickly. If the top five societies were to come within company law rather than building society law the remainder would find themselves operating within the rump of an industry. This section will review the arguments for and against demutualisation and describe the processes which must be followed by a society wishing to change its legal status.

First the arguments. The Building Societies Association commissioned Professor David Llewellyn[32] to consider the case for and against. His findings were detailed in a series of working papers but the main findings were summarised in a lecture given in June 1997.[33] The main conclusion was that there was a case in favour of mutuality. An important aspect of this is the fact that evidence indicates that mutual organisations consistently outperform others in some key financial areas. These include interest-rate structures and returns on

[29] A full list of extant papers is appended to each Annual Report.

[30] See the Building Societies Act 1986, Part VI, as amended by the 1997 Act.

[31] This case involved the exercise of powers provided for under earlier legislation which pre-dated the need for authorisation. See R. v. *Chief Registrar of Friendly Societies, ex p. New Cross Building Society* [1984] 2 All ER 27

[32] Prof. of Money and Banking at the University of Loughborough.

[33] See *Building Societies' Association Annual Report 1997*.

investment. Professor Llewellyn also argued that the existence of mutuals provided diversity within the economic system by allowing for consumer choice and diversity in governance. One example of a different approach to management, he felt, was that mutuals could take a longer-term view than major companies as they were not subject to the short-termism of the capital markets. Those markets are however unable to provide significant finance to mutuals, a factor which arguably acts as a brake on riskier ventures. The wider membership base was also seen as being positive, and the fact that members were also customers may be advantageous as there was one fewer stakeholder to deal with as compared to companies. The final point provided in the Building Societies Association summary relates to the fact that many mutuals are local or regional rather than national, and so can focus their activities on the basis of greater market knowledge.

For every argument in favour there is of course a counter, and the points made above can be considered from the opposite perspective. Some of the points made relate specifically to mutuality, while others are more to do with customer focus. The point, for example, about regional focus is right as a matter of practice, as the majority of building societies are quite small. But it would be possible to point to other sectors of corporate life where the market is dominated by a small number of major players supported by a much greater number of smaller ones. Legal status is an irrelevance here.

The issue of shareholding and membership is however much more significant. It is true to say that mutuality tends to spread membership rights more widely than other models of governance, but the question of what these rights are has to be considered. The rights of voting at AGMs and to receive copies of the accounts are tangible enough, but in practice are an irrelevance to most members. The same might be true of how individual shareholders in listed companies view their rights.

Company shareholders, though, have an opportunity to benefit from the success of their company either through dividends or capital gains. Some element of retained profits will be incorporated within the share price. This is not the case for members of mutuals. There is no direct relationship between their "reward" and their investment. There is only a theoretical interest in the assets of the organisation. Yet this is the one "right" which has excited interest despite the fact that it is only of any value on dissolution. Any argument about membership rights must therefore contend with the fact that the one right which has any significant value can only realise that value by ending the status which gave it. This line is essentially based on pragmatism rather than any theoretical position, for it is unarguable that a model which gives membership to its customers must provide for wider spread of rights.

Moving on, we can consider whether the diffusion of membership frees mutuals from short-term decision making. Many criticisms of the City have been advanced about the fact that UK institutional investors have consistently valued short-term gains over longer-term developments. This can be considered in a number of ways. Either the City is irrational in not understanding that it can make more by taking a long-term view or it is acting entirely rationally by concluding that long term it is better financially to take the gain and invest elsewhere. The issue is less to do with rationality than about the differing objectives of stakeholders. Organisations which ostensibly seek to maximise shareholder interests can hardly complain when shareholders do their arithmetic and make decisions accordingly. This behaviour is apparent among those members who prefer demutualisation on the basis that the immediate gain is worth more than the long-term benefit from lower borrowing rates or higher savings rates. This assumes that mutuals do offer better rates, a proposition put forward by Professor Llewellyn and supported by press comment. It is entirely rational to prefer £1,000 today above an additional 1 per cent *per annum* interest on the average savings balance, and on this basis it is hard to disagree with the proposition that member value is increased by demutualising.

The view that, by having shareholding customers, there is a reduction in potential conflict is also weakened once the balance in the rights of the different status changes. If membership has no obvious cost or benefit to the customer, who is generally interested only in the commercial relationship, then there is no conflict. What has to be managed is the commercial contract. Once membership has a value costs of conflict rise rapidly where the interests *qua* customer are at odds with those *qua* member.

To some extent focusing on mutuality itself is something of a red herring, as the argument is about building societies rather than some abstract concept. It has to be remembered that it was not individual members who began the process but directors, the first being the board of the then Abbey National Building Society. What reasons were advanced to justify this? At the time there were two major problems. The first has been alluded to already in this discussion, and is the problem of capital. Typically, mutuals obtain capital through retaining profits. Growth is therefore organic and self-financed. The possibility of a quantum leap in activity does not exist for a mutual. There are now sources of finance other than this for building societies but at the time of the Abbey conversion these were in their infancy. The second issue related to powers. Again the situation is different now and the reforms of the 1986 Act leading up to the 1987 Act provide societies with the powers to undertake virtually any activity they want.

Interestingly, the Woolwich Equitable Building Society, which is now demutualised, published a report in 1988 setting out the arguments in favour of mutuality.[34] This did not consider the concept of mutuality as such, but concentrated on building societies. It concluded that there were strong arguments in favour of mutuality at that time. The society argued that the competitive environment in which the industry operated imposed the same financial disciplines as the capital markets. Further, that mutuality had brought commercial advantages by foster-

---

[34] *Building Societies—a Case for Mutuality* (London, Woolwich Equitable Building Society, 1988), prepared for the society by Prima Europe.

ing a long-term view and by presenting a safe home for funds. Evidence also suggested that building societies had a much more favourable image than banks, but was this a function of status?

> "Is this view of building society as friendly organisations bound up with the principle of mutuality? There can obviously be no proof. But it is worth pointing out that the positive image of building societies has survived decades through which societies imposed queues and rationing on the availability of mortgages. They were apparently seen to play fair—not to let others jump the queue, nor give priority to customers with the deepest purse."[35]

As Llewellyn did later, though, they also pointed to the wider economic benefits of mutuality, arguing that there were public policy grounds for their encouragement. Two points were made in favour of this. The first was the development of strong regional and local links and the responsibility they had shown towards lower income customers. The second was the existence of a sector which would be immune form the shocks the major banks had been exposed to.

Perhaps events since have weakened this cosy view. Locally based societies are exposed to major changes in their economic environment although none have faced the sorts of problems which have occurred within the US savings and loans industry. The collapse of the housing market and the high level of repossessions which the industry was forced into did significant harm to its image, although it must be said that other financial organisations acted in the same way. Secondly, as regards lower income customers building societies must inevitably apply similar criteria in the granting of current accounts and credit cards as clearing banks do and the significant section of the population unable to obtain banking facilities have not found building societies the answer to their problems.

There seems therefore to be an economic argument in favour of a tier of financial organisations which operate under a different corporate structure, but this needs to be balanced alongside member expectations. One question which needs to be considered is that of the objectives of a society. The legal objects are relatively clear, but the question refers to the commercial objectives in relation to the members. It can be argued that in the case of companies the goal is to maximise shareholder wealth.[36] While companies have to consider a wider range of stakeholders this overarching objective can be used as justification for a range of decisions. In the case, for example, of a takeover bid the argument in favour of rejection typically refers to the long-term advantages as opposed to the short term gain. The gains in such cases are usually relatively small, a premium over the prevailing share price. For building society members they are considerably higher, and in many instances the windfall gain can exceed the capital invested. This point does emphasise a difficulty in this area, this is that there may be no

---

[35] *Ibid.*, 15.
[36] This point is discussed in most corporate finance textbooks. See, e.g., Samuels, Wilkes and Brayshaw, *Management of Company Finance* (6th edn., Thomson Business Press,1995), 5.

direct relationship between the gain and the investment. The position of an investor with £10,000 in an account is therefore significantly different from that of the person with £100. Different again is the situation of a borrower with a £60,000 mortgage. Assuming that one accepts the premise that mutuals can offer better interest rates, the response to a proposal to demutualise will depend much more on personal circumstances than will the response to a takeover bid.

The Building Societies Commission does support the interest rate argument.[37] The main reason for this it advances as being the fact that mutuals have no need to pay dividends, although it concedes that this has not always been historically reflected in rates. The competitive nature of the industry suggests that efficiency gains are likely to be low following conversion, so little can be gained in this area. Further, it argues the fact that no society collapse this century has caused losses to personal savers means that any risk premium paid will increase on conversion. Overall the Commission's feeling is that the demise of building societies will have detrimental effects long term.

THE CONVERSION PROCESS

While there are plainly benefits of mutuality, the fact that so many of the large societies have abandoned it presents at least a pragmatic case for the alternative being more attractive. It is now worth considering the process of demutualisation. The term is not used in the legislation which prefers "transfer of business to commercial company"[38] as being a better descriptor of what occurs. The word "conversion" is commonly used to indicate the same process. The legislation is accurate, since what happens is that a "converting" society must legally transfer its business to a company regulated by companies legislation. The society therefore disappears, its business continuing under a new identity. The company to be used for this purpose may be an existing one or one specially formed for the purpose.

Resolutions

The process described in the legislation appears quite complex and onerous, and when first created in the 1986 Act it was arguably little more than a sop to the industry with little expectation that it would ever be used, given the difficulties inherent in it. Put simply the 1986 Act requires that two resolutions must be passed by the society's members.[39] The most straightforward of these is a "borrowing members' resolution". This requires a simple majority of those members who are indebted to the society by at least £100 and whose debt is fully secured

[37] Building Societies Commission, n. 3 above, 11.
[38] Building Societies Act 1986, s.97.
[39] *Ibid.*, Sched. 2, para. 30.

on land, i.e. mortgagors.[40] The second is more complicated and is a shareholding members' resolution. This is similar to the special resolution[41] in company law and requires the support of 75 per cent of those voting, the constituency in this case being members of the society holding shares of at least £100.[42] The twist is that in addition to the 75 per cent majority there is also a minimum turnout specified. In the case of a transfer to a specially formed company this is 20 per cent. Where the successor company is an existing body the rules are even more onerous. In this case the resolution must be passed by not less than 50 per cent of the members qualified to vote on the special resolution or alternatively be approved by the holders of 90 per cent by value of the shares held in the society. The only alternative to this is where the Commission can be persuaded that it is essential for the protection of shareholders that a transfer be approved simply by means of the resolution.[43]

In order to vote effectively the members will require some information. This will be delivered to them in a transfer statement which must meet the requirements of the Act, and Regulations issued by the Commission.[44] The listed requirements are exhausting[45] but not exhaustive, as there is a duty to include any information which might be relevant. The final document will be similar to listing particulars, in that it will be long, very complex and couched in technical language. Given the number of people who will receive this document the cost of production will be high and for most it will be largely unread and for many unreadable. The move to summarise complex information evidenced by innovations such as the summary financial statement has finally reached this area as, since the 1997 Act, it has been possible to issue a summary of the statement. Interested members do however have the right to request a copy of the full version. As a final point the Commission must approve the statement before it can be sent out.

Given that building societies would normally regard a turnout of 10 per cent as a major achievement these are onerous requirements. The astute reader will of course have worked out how these have been achieved, and this point will be considered shortly following a brief comment on the other statutory procedures.

---

[40] *Ibid.*, Sched. 2, para. 29.

[41] The shareholding members' resolution was introduced by the 1997 Act. Special resolutions are used in some circumstances under the Act, but in this case all members, borrowing and shareholding, are eligible to vote.

[42] Invariably this will require holding £100 on the day of the vote and at the end of the preceding financial year: *ibid.*, Sched. 2, para. 23.

[43] *Ibid.*, Sched. 2, para. 30.

[44] Building Societies (Transfer of Business Regulations), SI 1988/1153 as amended by SI 1990/1695 and the 1997 Act.

[45] *Ibid.* Schedule to regulations at note 44 above.

Transfer Agreement

The votes described above are sandwiched between two other elements of the process. The making of an agreement between the society and the successor company, the transfer agreement, and the confirmation of the transfer by the Commission. Dealing with the agreement first, this will clearly be conditional upon the approval of both the society's members and the Commission. The Act is largely silent on what would be included within this agreement but creates the idea of "regulated terms". These are those which are governed by sections 99–102 of the 1986 Act.[46] The regulated terms deal with two main areas: compensation for loss of office; and distributions and share rights. Additionally the Commission is empowered to make regulations governing this area.[47] A third area was originally provided for. This was the priority liquidation distribution, which was a right that former society members had to priority payment in the event that the successor was wound up where it was a specially formed company. In essence the member, on becoming a depositor in the new company, had additional protection for the amount of the deposit carried forward. This did not extend to any additional deposits made and was reduced by the value of any withdrawals. Thus over time it would dwindle away, but until it did the successor was obliged to provide some security for this right. The 1997 Act has abolished this protection, the Government accepting the argument that it was unnecessary.[48]

Where an officer loses a position following a transfer of business it is in order that some compensation is paid for this. In such a case this must be approved by a separate special resolution. The payment of compensation to outgoing officers following a merger in the past excited much interest from the regulators, although it seems not to be an issue now. In making a decision about whether or not to approve a merger the amount of compensation payable, normally to outgoing directors, was a factor taken into account.[49] The 1986 Act seems to preclude this now, for it states that the Commission must give approval to a transfer of business unless one of a specified set of circumstances has arisen. There would not therefore seem to be any limit on the compensation payable other than that imposed by the need for approval.

The 1997 Act inserted a related clause governing increased remuneration.[50] This requires an ordinary resolution to give approval to a proposed increase in the remuneration for directors or other officers. This obligation covers not only salary but also other benefits such as share options. It is limited by reference to increases "in consequence of the transfer", presumably those where the inten-

[46] As amended by the 1997 Act.
[47] Building Societies (Transfer of Business Regulations) 1988 as amended.
[48] See Building Societies Act 1997, s.40, repealing s.100(2)(c) of the 1986 Act.
[49] See e.g. the comments made in the *Report of the Chief Registrar of Friendly Societies 1981–2* (HMSO, 1982) 20.
[50] New s. 99A.

tion to make them existed at the time. It is unclear whether this would cover a general desire to raise salary levels at some point in the future. It is clear that conversions have increased executive salaries by significant amounts, but also that there may now be a catching up process among the remaining mutuals. For example, Mr Brian Davis, the Chief Executive of the Nationwide Building Society which recently won its fight to remain mutual, saw his salary increased by £102,000. The society commented that "conversion would mean more remuneration and share options for the chief executive but that Mr Davis had turned his back on that".[51] The cynic might define turning one's back as being something other than having what amounted to a 25 per cent rise in salary.

The more interesting regulated terms are those which relate to bonus payments and the issue of shares. This of course also answers the problem of how to make people vote for a building society conversion when they would not normally vote in the required numbers for local government or European elections, much less for such mundane things as the election of directors or rule changes. It is the issue of shares in the successor company which are then listed and therefore highly liquid which makes the exercise worthwhile. There may be no such thing as a free lunch, but shares in a building society successor come quite close.

The statutory provisions are contained in section 100 of the 1986 Act. The easiest provision relates to those members of the society who are not qualified to vote. Such members are entitled to a bonus payment equal to the proportion of the reserves which reflects each member's shareholding as a proportion of the total shares of the society. This type of distribution is likely to provide relatively small amounts, an additional interest payment of perhaps 5 per cent. The more lucrative offering is that of shares in the successor. The statutory rules governing this fail to deal properly with the practice. The Act talks about conferring rights on members to acquire shares in priority to other subscribers being limited to those who were members for two years before the qualifying date. In the case of a transfer to a specially formed society any negotiable instrument acknowledging rights to shares cannot be issued to former members of the society for two years after the conversion unless all members of the successor company are made the same offer. Nothing about free shares. In fact the Act specifically states that as regards transfers to specially formed companies any other form of distribution is unlawful. How then do the share issues work: because as they are "free" they do not class as distributions. This point was agreed in the first of the transfers, that of the Abbey National.[52]

The situation appears to be therefore that the much-hyped share issues are provided not through some carefully thought-through scheme to facilitate transfers of business but through a loophole. The restrictive way in which the 1986 Act is couched reflects the statutory regime which building societies have always been subject to. That is there are severe restrictions upon their activities.

---

[51] See "Nationwide gives £102,00 pay rise to chief executive", *The Times*, 9 July 1998.
[52] *Abbey National Building Society* v. *Building Societies Commission* (1989) 5 BCC 259.

The Abbey case has been followed by others which have dealt with practical details while leaving the main issue standing. One of these involved the former Cheltenham and Gloucester Building Society which took a conversion route which saw it transferring its business to a wholly-owned subsidiary of Lloyds Bank plc. A scheme was proposed which would involve a distribution to a wider range of persons than covered by the Act, and payment would be by the parent of the successor. The Commission's view was that this did not comply with the Act, a view endorsed by the High Court.[53] This stated that cash distributions could only be made by the society or its successor and only to those with two years' standing. It was however also stated that the Act did not preclude a third party making distributions to anybody else. On the basis of this the proposal was amended and agreed. In a later case the High Court approved an application by the then Halifax Building Society and Leeds Permanent Building Society that their proposal to issue free shares to members following their merger on their subsequent conversion was lawful.[54]

The Halifax/Leeds case takes us into a final area under this heading, that of "protective provisions". Under the 1986 Act as originally enacted, where a transfer was to a specially created successor it had to have an article which prohibited anybody from owning 15 per cent of its shares for the first five years of its existence.[55] The Halifax/Leeds transferred its business to an existing subsidiary and so would not have had the benefit of this protection. The advantage of doing this was that the priority liquidation rights discussed above would not apply. In fact, as we saw earlier, these were abolished by the 1997 Act. The same Act has also amended the protective provisions rule by disapplying it in the case where the successor acquires as a subsidiary undertaking a financial institution.[56] This term includes a building society, insurance company, a bank or a company authorised under the Financial Services Act. Additionally the successor company itself may apply to have the protection waived by means of a special resolution, and the Bank of England may also remove it if it feels that this is in the interests of depositors or potential depositors.

Approval by the Commission

The limited nature of the Commission's power to reject a request to transfer has already been referred to. Section 98 (as amended) provides for three grounds on which any rejection can be based. These are that: the members or a proportion of then would be unreasonably prejudiced by the transfer; there is a substantial risk that the successor will not become or will not retain approval under the

---

[53] *Cheltenham & Gloucester Building Society* v. *Building Societies Commission* [1994] 3 WLR 1238.

[54] *Building Societies Commission* v. *Halifax Building Society* [1995] 3 All ER 193.

[55] S. 101.

[56] New s. 101.

Banking Act; or that some relevant provision of the Act or the society's rules was not followed.[57] The Commission's view on the commercial issues can be summarised by the stock phrase used in its reports:

> "It is for a society proposing a merger or transfer of business to formulate the particular terms and conditions relating to the proposal and then for the members to vote on the proposals. It is not the Commission's role to consider either the merits or the proposed transaction or the fairness of any proposed distribution of shares or cash to members of the society in connection with it, provided these are in conformity with the requirements of the 1986 Act and the rules of the society."[58]

To date the Commission has not rejected any application to demutualise. Given the effort that will undoubtedly be put into the activity by the society in question this is not surprising. The stakes are very high and a rejection would be commercially catastrophic. The Commission has, though, referred some issues to the courts where it has been in doubt about an issue and will be involved in discussions over the key issues from an early date in the process.

MERGERS

The process by which societies merge is similar to that used to transfer business. It is in fact a much longer established process and was used as a model for the later transfer mechanism. Basically what is required is the consent of the members following receipt of an appropriate statement and the confirmation of the Commission. In some instances the cost of this process would outweigh the benefit to the larger society. Accepting a transfer of a very small society where this would require a vote would be an unattractive proposition. Because of this the Commission is empowered to allow an accepting society to proceed by means of a Board Resolution.[59] The 1996–7 Report gave an instance of this where it allowed the Cumberland Building Society to accept a transfer of engagements from the West Cumbria Building Society simply by means of a Board Resolution. The transferring society is required to obtain the members' approval.

Unlike the transfer process the reserves of the society tend to stay locked in as the combined body retains its mutual status. It is of course possible to combine the two events, as happened with the Halifax and Leeds Permanent societies. Bonus payments may still be made but these will be quite modest. They are more likely to occur where one society has a larger reserve ratio than the other and the two are being equalised.

---

[57] In this latter case the infringement may be ignored by the Commission if it is convinced that it would not have been material to the members' decision.

[58] *Building Societies Commission Annual Report 1996–7*, n. 3 above, 7. Similar statements can be found in previous reports.

[59] Building Societies Act 1986, s.94(5).

The rate of merger activity is slowing down but as the industry is contracting in terms of the number of players this is a natural occurrence. Mergers still outweigh conversions however as this table shows.

Year	Registered Societies		Societies transferring their engagements within the sector		Societies transferring their engagements out of the sector	
	Number	Assets £bn[a]	Number	Assets £bn	Number	Assets £bn
1992	110	244	5	3.26	—	—
1993	105	263	4	1.22	—	—
1994	101	278	2	1.45	—	—
1995	96	295	1	20.97	1	19.39
1996	94	292	2	0.14	1	13.89
1997 First 3 months	88[b]	297				
1997 (April–October)	81	120	1	0.19	5[c]	176.80

(a) Assets (society only) are those at the beginning of the year.
(b) Of this number 77 were authorised to take deposits.
(c) Alliance & Leicester (April), Halifax (June), Woolwich (July), thereafter Bristol & West and Northern Rock.
Source: *Building Societies Commission Annual Report 1996–97*, 8.

CONCLUSION

This essay has discussed at length the key issue facing the building society industry, namely that of demutualisation. The obvious question to ask is whether or not building societies will have any future in the next century. The same question can be asked of any mutual organisation and it may be that this form of corporate structure has outlived its usefulness. The struggle by the Board of the Nationwide Building Society to retain its status may be seen in retrospect to be almost Canute-like in its ultimate futility. At best it may have obtained a few years' respite, but the narrowness of the vote against conversion does not augur well for the next ballot. The government has hardly helped in this matter, refusing to provide any statutory protection against further attacks.

It is not only the larger societies which might become targets. A number of smaller institutions may be seen as potential targets by other financial institutions. The list of predators may not even stop there. The acquisition of a mid-range society by a supermarket chain may provide the systems and personnel to further its ambitions as a major player in the financial services market. Despite this pessimism it is unlikely that building societies will disappear completely. Conversion, either as a flotation or transfer to an existing company, with the consequent payout to the members, is only possible if somebody else is prepared to fund this. The worst case scenario is that in a decade the only surviving building societies will be those which are too small to make the cost of acquisition worthwhile.

There are other trends, too, which must be considered. The regulation of financial institutions has been steadily converging for a number of years. Banks and building societies as a matter of reality have much in common, increasingly as societies have expanded their services. Capital adequacy requirements, for example, apply equally to all financial institutions and there are strong arguments in favour of a unified supervision of the the broader banking industry. This argument has been effectively settled, for the functions of the Commission are to be transferred to the reconstructed Securities Investment Board. The banking and building societies' investor protection schemes are also to be merged.

The constraints imposed by mutuality mean that forming a new building society is not a serious option for anybody wishing to enter the retail savings or mortgage markets. The last society to become authorised was the Ecology in the early 1980s, hardly a sign of a vibrant industry. The problems of funding and the inability to retain control on the part of the founders render this an unsuitable vehicle in today's corporate market. Obtaining a banking licence is a much easier option for new entrants.

It is difficult to avoid the conclusion that mutuality has outlived its usefulness. The circumstances which gave rise to it grew in an era where self-help was viewed as being something to be achieved collectively. In a more individualistic society this concept seems almost an anachronism. Regretfully, the writer must conclude that the same is also true for the genus building society.

6

Banking Companies

ANU ARORA

INTRODUCTION

Since the 1960s, the banking and financial systems have undergone a period of considerable change in innovation and regulation. The expression "financial revolution" has been commonly used to describe the scale of changes. Traditional methods of banking and finance have been replaced by new techniques which have seen the elimination of national frontiers.

Technology has begun to exert a bigger influence as banking and financial innovation have become the norm. As demand for new kinds of financial services has grown, so product innovation has grown rapidly; syndicated loans and Eurobonds are two such examples. Further, as world trade was freed from restrictions there was a revival in international banking. The Euromarkets grew at a remarkable pace in response to the need for lesser regulated markets. New kinds of banking emerged that challenged regulatory systems based on national boundaries. Wholesale banking developed rapidly during the 1960s and 1970s. The inflation and high interest rates also encouraged banking and financial institutions to skirt around business and monetary restrictions. Capital market products, treasury and off-balance sheet (OBS) banking became a common feature of the 1980s. The 1990s saw the development of swaps, derivatives, etc.

These economic and social pressures, combined with a growing commitment by many governments toward monetarist policies, helped to produce an environment of structural deregulation. Consequently, the barriers between the traditionally separate financial institutions were eroded in many countries and new instruments and techniques developed to integrate financial markets across the globe, for example swaps. This has been particularly apparent in the USA where the banking and financial sector has undergone a major review. Consolidation and expansion have been the subject of, at times, bitter debate.[1]

Alongside structural deregulation the European Community has achieved considerable success in national deregulation of the banking and financial sector. The reason for this is that the deregulatory process has complemented

---

[1] See Philip Corwin, "Unravelling Financial Modernization: The Politics of Glass-Steagall Gridlock" [1996] *Butterworths Journal of International Banking and Financial Law* 163; and P. Corwin, "Unanimous Barnett Decision sets united States on Path to Bank Assurance" [1996] *Butterworths Journal of International and Financial Law* 215.

another main goal: the creation of the Single European Market by 1992. With regard to financial deregulation within the scheme of the common market, two components have been particularly important namely; (a) the geographic liberalisation of banks; and (b) liberalisation of capital flows between the European Community countries.

However, national deregulation has been replaced by increased supervisory re-regulation on a European Union-wide basis, or even on a wider international basis. Thus the 1980s and 1990s have seen increased international co-operation in order to protect the resilience of the international banking and financial markets. Prudential supervision and convergence of bank capital adequacy regulations have become important policy objectives.

The purpose of this chapter is to examine the role played by bank supervision and regulation in the UK banking sector. It is then intended to examine the role and impact of the European directives on bank regulation, as well as to examine the work of the Basle Committee. The chapter will conclude by dealing with the changes in bank regulation and supervision in the UK introduced by the Bank of England Act 1998.

REGULATION AND SUPERVISION

Effective bank supervision necessitates a review of the law, policy and execution of such with a high degree of co-ordination between national regulatory bodies around the world. The problems facing regulators were highlighted, in 1995, by the collapse of Barings. The demise of that bank was largely due to a modest sized bank (with a balance sheet of approximately £4 billion) undertaking large-scale derivatives business, a business which the senior management did not fully understand. Additionally, the bank was active overseas (particularly in Singapore, Tokyo and Osaka) and there was both inadequate communication between the regulators and confusion over the scope and responsibility of consolidated supervision.

An additional problem faced by supervisors is that public awareness and expectations place certain demands on supervisors. Whilst bank regulators and supervisors cannot undertake to prevent all bank failures and depositors must accept some responsibility for their decisions on where to place their deposits, public opinion demands that bank supervisors are held subject to scrutiny and made accountable.

USING THE LAW FOR BANK SUPERVISION

A striking feature of the UK banking system has been that prior to the Banking Act 1979 bank supervision was undertaken by the Bank of England largely on a non-statutory basis. The Bank of England's role in bank supervision originally developed as an off-shoot to its more established role as the central bank.[2] The Bank had indirect control of the banking sector by its ability to influence interest rates and through the establishment of its role as lender of last resort.[3] The Bank's role as the venue for the settlement of the daily balances between the clearing banks became entrenched in the nineteenth century and contributed towards its already considerable influence.

The Bank of England therefore relied on its "moral powers of persuasion" to influence and control the behaviour of banks. This enabled the Bank of England to develop a flexible approach towards bank supervision built around informal meetings between the Bank and senior management of individual banks at which statistical returns would be discussed. The Bank also encouraged management to discuss business issues openly and any Bank of England recommendations took into consideration the individual circumstances of the bank.[4] When the Bank felt the necessity for more formal action the Governor of the Bank of England issued letters of request requiring the banks to conform to new practices and procedures which the Bank deemed appropriate. Although such letters did not have the force of law, the Bank, with its uniquely dominant position in the banking sector, could expect its views to be observed. Indeed, the Bank of England's general role and influence within the banking sector made it difficult for banks to ignore such requests and recommendations.

The informal nature of bank supervision in the UK was continued by the Bank of England Act 1946[5] which allowed the Bank, where it considered it necessary in the public interest, to request information and make recommendations to banks. The Bank was also, if authorised by the Treasury, to issue directions to any bank for the purpose of securing compliance with any such recommendation. The Bank of England was, however, not obliged to supervise all banking institutions. It considered itself responsible for only those established banks with which it had a close established relationship. This excluded from the scope of its supervisory control the many "fringe" institutions or "secondary" banks which had been established in the 1950s and 1960s. The consequence of these institutions remaining outside the supervisory net became evident in the 1970s when in order to prevent a general loss of confidence and trust in the banking sector the Bank of England and the major commercial banks launched the "lifeboat" operation to bail out a number of institutions facing liquidity problems.[6] In all 26 financial institutions were given support.

---

[2] Christos Hadjiemmanuil, *Banking Regulation and the Bank of England* (Lloyds of London Press, 1996).

[3] W. Bagehot, *Lombard Street* (London, Kegan Paul, 1873).

[4] Gardener and Molyneux, *Changes in Western Banking* (London, Unwin Hyman, 1990).

[5] Bank of England Act 1946, s.4(3).

[6] "The Secondary Banking Crisis and the Bank of England's Support Operation", Bank of England Quarterly Bulletin, June 1978, p.230; and Margaret Reid, *The Secondary Banking Crisis 1973–75* (London, Macmillan Publishing, 1982).

As a result of these events the Bank extended its supervisory functions to include the previously unregulated "fringe" institutions. Nevertheless, the informal system of bank supervision was maintained.[7]

The Bank of England therefore found itself entrusted with the role of supervisor of the banking system not as a result of careful consideration, public debate or legislation but as a result of it reacting to banking crisis to which, as the UK central bank, it was able to respond.[8] The apparent shortcomings of self-regulation were obvious by the late 1970s and pressure for formal regulation of the financial sector, UK entry to the European Community and other external factors led to a first attempt to place bank supervision on a comprehensive statutory basis.

THE BANKING ACT 1979

The Banking Act 1979 (giving effect to the First Banking Directive (77/780/EEC)) was the first attempt to codify the supervisory and regulatory powers of the Bank of England. The regulatory and supervisory powers are transferred to the Financial Services Authority under the Bank of England Act 1998. Although, the Banking Act introduced formality to the UK banking system of supervision it was more "evolutionary than revolutionary"[9] and required the Bank of England to discharge on a more formal basis functions which it had undertaken informally. Consequently, the Bank advanced the view that regulation be used merely to fill the gaps, with flexibility being maintained by the Bank. The Act, however, did not introduce a single uniform system of authorisation. It divided deposit-taking institutions into four groups, namely: (a) the Bank of England; (b) recognised banks; (c) licensed institutions; and (d) institutions listed in Schedule 1 to the Act. The Schedule 1 institutions, normally regulated under other statutory provisions, such as building societies were exempted from the scope of the Banking Act. Additionally, certain types of transactions were exempted from the scope of the Act. The Act also introduced the Deposit Protection Scheme and generally considerably increased the regulatory powers of the Bank of England. A two-tier system of bank supervision was therefore adopted under the Banking Act 1979. The first-tier institutions (those which the Bank had traditionally supervised) would continue to be supervised in the pre-1979 Act style. The second tier institutions (licensed deposit-takers) comprised all other institutions and were made principally subject to the 1979 Act, which controlled the acceptance of deposits, the use of banking names and descriptions etc. The Act also conferred statutory powers on the Bank to issue and to vary directions considered to be "desirable in the

---

[7] Norton, *Bank Regulation and Supervision in 1990's* (London, LLP, 1991).
[8] Quinn, "Supervision and Central Banking" [1990] *Bank of England Quarterly Bulletin* 380.
[9] Penn, *Banking Supervision* (London, Butterworths, 1989).

interests of depositors, whether for the purposes of safeguarding the assets of the institutions or otherwise".[10]

The 1979 Act proved insufficient against the pressures of the 1980s. The enforced rescue of Johnson Matthey Bankers (a recognised bank), the fears of the Third World debt, the impact of EC bank harmonisation and the international efforts of bank supervisors (through the Basle Committee) to establish global standards of prudential supervision led to a series of consultative papers.[11]

The Banking Act 1987 and Further Intervention by the Government

The Banking Act 1987 abolished the two-tier system of recognition and licensing of banking institutions and introduced a uniform system of regulation for all "deposit-taking institutions".

The Bank of England continued to maintain autonomy from central government. The Banking Act 1987 imposed a statutory duty on the Bank to supervise and regulate the banking sector.[12] The Bank was not merely under a duty to supervise the banking sector but the Act gave it an exclusive right to supervise banks. The Banking Act 1987 therefore imposed two duties on the Bank of England, namely:

(a) to supervise the institutions authorised by it;[13] and
(b) to keep under review the operation of the Act and developments in the field of banking which appear to the Bank to be relevant to the exercise of its powers and function.[14]

The Act imposed for the first time an express duty on the Bank to supervise authorised institutions. The additional duty on the Bank to keep under review developments in the banking sector was an admission of the rapid and increasingly sophisticated developments taking place in the banking sector, and the Bank was required to have regard to these developments in the discharge of its duties. The government White Paper published prior to the Act[15] placed considerable emphasis on the flexible nature of the UK banking system and the requirement on the Bank of England to have regard to the changing nature and structure of the banking sector.

[10] S.8(1), (2) and (4), Banking Act 1979.
[11] "The Measurement of Capital: (1980) *Bank of England Quarterly Bulletin* 324; "Foreign Currency Exposure" (1981) 21 *Bank of England Quarterly* 235; "Prudential Arrangements for Discount Markets" (1982) 22 *Bank of England Quarterly Bulletin* 209; and "The Measurement of Liquidity" (1982) 22 *Bank of England Quarterly Bulletin* 339.
[12] Banking Act 1987, s.1(1).
[13] *Ibid.*
[14] Banking Act 1987, s.1(2).
[15] *Banking Supervision* (Cmnd. 9695, HMSO, London, 1985).

The question whether a supervisory body owes a depositor a duty of care in the exercise of its regulatory functions has been considered by the courts. In *Yuen Kun Yeu* v. *Attorney-General of Hong Kong*[16] the Privy Council concluded that since the Commissioner of Banking (the supervisory body in Hong Kong) had no power to control the day-to-day activities of the deposit-taking institution whose liquidation had caused loss the plaintiff, the Commissioner owed no duty of care since there were not such close and direct relations between the Commissioner and the plaintiff as to give rise to a duty of care. It was also alleged on behalf of the plaintiff that, by allowing the registration to stand, the Commissioner made a statement about the continuing creditworthiness of that institution. The Privy Council held that the Hong Kong Banking Ordinance placed a duty on the Commissioner to supervise deposit-taking institutions in the general public interest, but there was no assumption of any special duty of care towards individual members of the public.

Yuen Kun Yew v. *Attorney-General of Hong Kong* was reviewed by Saville J in *Minories Finance Ltd* v. *Arthur Young*,[17] which arose out of the collapse of Johnson Matthey Bank (JMB). Saville J held that the Bank of England was under no duty to exercise reasonable skill and care in exercising its supervisory function in order to prevent losses which arose as a result of imprudent or careless management of JMB. The learned judge said that the principles of common sense did not indicate that this obligation existed, and therefore there was no cause of action against the Bank. The action by JMB's parent company was based on the proposition that, as a depositor, it was owed a duty to exercise reasonable care and skill by the Bank of England in its supervisory role. The Bank, relying on *Yuen Kun Yeu* v. *Attorney-General of Hong Kong*, argued that it did not owe a duty of care to depositors in the UK. Saville J accepted that the decision in the *Yuen Kun Yeu* case presented strong evidence in favour of the Bank's submission, but not so strong as to dismiss the action as unsustainable. The two cases involved two independent and separate supervisory bodies operating under different legislation. Under the Banking Act 1979 (the case was decided under the 1979 Act, although it is still relevant under the 1987 Act), it could not be argued that the Bank owed a duty of care to the parent company as depositor, because section 1(5)(d) of the 1979 Act excludes from the definition of deposit any sum paid by one company to another at a time when one is a subsidiary of the other or both are subsidiaries of another company. The statutory prohibition on accepting deposits in the course of a deposit-taking business without authorisation could not apply to money deposited by the parent company. Consequently, the Bank did not owe a duty of care to persons making deposits if they did not fall within the ambit of the Banking Act.

[16] [1988] AC 175.
[17] [1989] 2 All ER 105.

Statutory Criteria for Authorisation

The Bank of England could not grant authorisation unless it was satisfied that the minimum criteria laid down in Schedule 3 were fulfilled. However, the Bank could (subject to the right of appeal) refuse authorisation even if the applicant had satisfied the minimum requirements in Schedule 3. The importance with which the Bank viewed its discretion to refuse authorisation was emphasised in its *Statement of Principles* (1988) published in accordance with section 16 of the Act. In that statement, the Bank stressed that, notwithstanding compliance with the Schedule 3 requirements, it could still refuse authorisation if it considered for any reason that there were "any significant threats to the interests of depositors and potential depositors". Other factors which could influence the discretion of the Bank in the exercise of its power to refuse authorisation were its ability to monitor the institution in connection with the Schedule 3 requirements after authorisation, and its ability to assess any risks or threats to the interests of depositors.

The Bank's Interpretation of the Schedule 3 Criteria

The Schedule 3 criteria (which closely follow those found in the Banking Act 1979, with the exception of the minimum net assets requirements) have regard to quality, rather than quantity or type of activity. The Bank monitored their fulfilment as part of its regular supervisory functions. The minimum requirements imposed in Schedule 3 are discussed in the following paragraphs.

Directors, etc, to be Fit and Proper Persons

Paragraph 1(2) of Schedule 3 to the Act provides that every person who is, or is to be, a director, controller or manager (section 105) of an authorised bank must be a fit and proper person to hold the particular position which he holds or intends to hold. With regard to a person who is a director, executive controller or manager of the institution the Bank was required to have consideration, amongst other things, for the individual's probity and whether he has sufficient skills, knowledge, competence, soundness of judgement and experience to undertake and fulfil his particular duties and responsibilities properly. The diligence with which he is fulfilling, or the time he is likely to devote towards fulfilling, his responsibilities will also be taken into consideration. Additionally, the Bank can have regard to a person's reputation and character, including such matters as whether he has a criminal record, including certain spent convictions. Any convictions for fraud or other dishonesty or violence are relevant; any convictions with regard to contravention of any banking, insurance, investment or other financial services legislation designed to protect members of the public from financial loss due to dishonesty, incompetence or malpractice will be especially relevant. The Bank also had regard to the person's record of non-compliance with various non-statutory codes, e.g. the Take-over Code.

Once an institution had been authorised the Bank continued to monitor the individuals concerned with regard to the "fit and proper" requirement. In this respect the Bank looked for an understanding of the institution's business and future development and for evidence of sound judgement with regard to commercial and administrative matters in connection with the business.

In respect of shareholder controllers, the Bank could take into account their business interests, their financial soundness and strength and, in the case of bodies corporate, the nature and scope of their business. The Bank could have regard to the influence of the shareholder on the authorised institution and in particular to any threat which holding the position might pose to the interests of depositors, or of potential depositors. For example, a financially weak shareholder controller would not be a fit and proper person if his financial condition was likely to undermine confidence in the authorised institution.

The Bank could also make enquiries of outside sources about the person concerned and it may consult other regulatory authorities.

Business must be Directed by Two Persons

Paragraph 2 of Schedule 3 provides that at least two individuals must effectively direct the business of an authorised institution; commonly referred to as the "four eyes" principle. It will, therefore, not be sufficient for the business to be carved up so that one person deals with certain specific aspects of the business only. These provisions are intended to ensure that at least two minds are directed to the formulation and implementation of the policy of the institution. Both persons "must demonstrate the qualities and application necessary to influence strategy, day-to-day policies and their implementation".[18] In addition both persons must have sufficient experience and knowledge of the business and the necessary authority to detect and resist any imprudence, dishonesty or other irregularities in the institution. Paragraph 2 requires that such persons must "effectively direct" the business, and that was interpreted by the Bank to mean that executive authority must be vested in at least two individuals. They need not be on the board provided they report directly to it.

Composition of Board of Directors

In the case of a UK authorised institution, the directors must include such number (if any) of directors without executive responsibility for the management of its business as the Bank considers appropriate, having regard to the circumstances of the business and the nature and scale of its operations. The

---

[18] Bank's *Statement of Principles,* para. 2.

Bank attached considerable importance to the role of non-executive directors, placing some importance on their ability to bring an "outsider's independent perspective to the running of the business and in questioning the approach of the directors".[19] The Bank considered that non-executive directors have an important role as members of an institution's audit committee.

Business to be Conducted in a Prudent Manner

Paragraph 4(1) of Schedule 3 requires that an authorised institution must conduct or, in the case of one which is not yet authorised, will conduct its business in a prudent manner. Whilst the Bank could have regard to other factors, it reviewed all applications for authorisation with this paragraph in mind. The prudent manner criterion is the one which in the Bank's judgement was most relevant to the interests of depositors. It was also relevant in determining whether directors, controllers and managers were fit and proper persons to hold their respective positions. Sub-paragraphs (2) and (8) specify a number of conditions which are to be taken into account in deciding whether a particular institution is conducting its business in a fit and proper manner. However, these requirements are not exhaustive and other matters may be considered, such as the institution's management arrangement, the institution's general strategy and objectives, planning arrangements, policies on lending and other exposure, and bad debt and taxation provisions.

It is required by paragraph 4(2) and (3) that an authorised institution maintain a level of capital commensurate with the nature and scale of its operations, and sufficient to safeguard the interests of its depositors and potential depositors. In deciding whether adequate net assets are maintained the nature and scale of the institution's operations, the risks inherent in those operations and any other business undertaken by the group of companies, in so far as they may affect the deposit-taking institution, are taken into consideration.

Therefore, the lowest net asset requirement of £1 million, will operate as a minimum guide to the Regulator. In assessing the institution's risks potential, the Bank (and now the Financial Services Authority) will take into account management expertise, experience and record, its internal controls and accounting procedures and its size and position in the market.

Paragraph 4(6) requires the institutions to make adequate provision for the depreciation or diminution of the value of its assets. The Bank, therefore, expected institutions to make provision for liabilities which are, or will be, expected to be discharged and for any losses which it will or expects to incur. In examining the institution's provision for depreciation etc., the Bank was entitled look at the institution's internal system for monitoring the recoverability of loans, the frequency with which provisions are reviewed, and the institution's policy in valuing security.

[19] *Ibid.*, sched. 3, para. 3.

Business must be Conducted with Integrity and Skill

Paragraph 5 requires the business of the institution to be conducted with such integrity and professional skill as is appropriate to the nature and scale of its activities. Again the Act gives no indication of the meaning of these terms but the *Statement of Principles* emphasises that the Bank considered integrity and skill as distinct elements. The first requirement refers to the ethical standards of business, which could be called into question, e.g. contravention of statutory provisions designed to protect the public against dishonest conduct, incompetence and malpractice. The Bank judged these indiscretions against the criteria set out in Schedule 3, together with the interests of depositors and potential depositors.

Minimum net assets

The minimum net asset requirement of £1 million sterling for all institutions applies at the time of authorisation. The Treasury may, after consultation with the Bank, by order vary the minimum net asset requirement. In addition, section 67 restricts the use of a name which indicates the institution is a bank, banker or carrying on banking services to institutions with a minimum paid-up capital (or equivalent) of £5 million.

The Bank's Informal Requirements

In addition to the statutory requirements which have to be satisfied when an application is made under the Banking Act 1987, the Bank of England expects an applicant to be introduced to it by a well-known bank or professional adviser. A series of discussions may take place to clarify the applicant's business plans and a detailed feasibility study of the institution's business may be required by the Bank.

Continuous Supervision

Once authorised the deposit-taking institution is under the continuous scrutiny of the Bank of England which has considerable powers to revoke or restrict authorisation[20]; to require information and documents;[21] to order investigations and, where necessary, obtain relevant court orders relating to deposits held by the institution.[22] The Bank can revoke authorisation if, after

---

[20] Banking Act 1987, ss.11–13.
[21] Banking Act 1987, s.38.
[22] Banking Act 1987, ss.41–44.

authorisation, the Schedule 3 criteria are not continued to be satisfied, or if the authorised institution has failed to comply with an obligation under the 1987 Act; or if the institution has a "shareholder controller" in respect of whom the Bank had given notice of objection; or in any other case where the interests of depositors of the institution concerned are, or are likely to be, in any way prejudiced.[23] Alternatively, the Bank can impose restrictions or conditions on the institution, including requiring the removal of a director, or requiring a controlling shareholder institution from engaging in certain classes of transactions or impose limits on the acceptance of deposits.

The Arthur Andersen Report

The collapse of Barings led to the accounting and consultancy firm of Arthur Andersen being appointed to review "supervision and surveillance"[24] at the Bank of England. Although the Bank agreed to implement the proposals contained in the Arthur Andersen report, the Bank noted that, like Bingham LJ in his inquiry after the BCCI collapse,[25] the Andersen report did not call for a radical change to the style of bank supervision. The Bank, however, accepted the need to clarify the standards and processes of supervision, strengthen some key tools to supervision, to restructure and expand its banking supervision divisions etc.

Bank of England Accountability

The Bank of England was created by Royal Charter in 1694, and, until brought into public ownership by the Bank of England Act 1946, it existed as a corporation owned by private stockholders.[26] Whilst the Governor and the Court of Directors are appointed by the Crown (under the Bank of England Act 1946, section 2), the Treasury had the legal power to issue directions to the Bank if "national interest" so requires.[27] However, the Bank is not a Department of State or administered by a Minister, but a public corporation with rights to manage its internal affairs independently. The Bank was required under the 1987 Act to publish an annual report on its supervisory role.[28]

The full extent of the Bank of England's independence from the Treasury was evidenced by the Bank's supervision of both BCCI and Johnson Matthey

[23] Banking Act 1987, s.11.
[24] Hall, "UK Banking After the Arthur Andersen Report" [1996] *Butterworths Journal of International Banking and Financial Law* 525.
[25] *Inquiry into the Supervision of the Bank of Credit and Commerce International, 1992,* No. 198, (HMSO, London, 1992).
[26] Giuseppi, *The Bank of England: A History from its Foundations in 1694* (Evans Publishers, 1966).
[27] Bank of England Act 1946, s.4.
[28] Bank of England Act 1987, s.I (3).

Bankers. In the latter case the Bank of England mounted a rescue of Johnson Matthey and failed to inform the Chancellor of the Exchequer, with the result that he unintentionally misinformed the House of Commons about the extent of the Bank's financial commitment to Johnson Matthey.[29] Indeed, the Bank was required neither by legislation nor by convention to consult the Treasury in respect of individual banks. That autonomy was reinforced by section 84(5) of the 1987 Act which prevented the Bank from disclosing information to third parties unless "disclosure appears to the Bank to be desirable or expedient" in the interests of either the depositors or the wider public interest. Whilst some liaison between the Bank of England and the Treasury was inevitable the Bank was determined to safeguard its autonomy. The Bank expressed the view that since banking supervision had been delegated any liaison with the Treasury was confined to keeping "them informed if there is likely to be a difficult or substantial or controversial issue".[30] Bingham LJ in his report on the BCCI affair gave some explanation of what constitutes a "difficult or substantial or controversial issue". He suggested that the Bank of England should consult the Treasury in, at least, the following circumstances[31]:

(a) failure of an institution which will have implications for the financial system or the economy;
(b) where foreign or diplomatic relations may be jeopardised;
(c) where weaknesses in the legislative structure of supervision are exposed;
(d) where questions are likely to be raised in Parliament, or
(e) where the Bank of England seeks the assistance of state departments under section 84(5) and disclosure of information requires the consent of the Treasury.

The Bank of England enjoyed considerable freedom in relation to its supervisory functions. Nevertheless, the Bingham Report was extremely critical of the lack of consultation between the Treasury and the Bank prior to the BCCI collapse. The Report concluded that although the collapse of BCCI was not likely to have serious adverse effects on the UK financial system or economy the consequences of the crash would cause diplomatic and foreign relations problems, hardship and loss to a significant number of retail customers and political controversy. In such circumstances Bingham LJ concluded that the Treasury and ministers should have been consulted, not because immediate action was required, but because it was preferable for consideration to be given to "potential problems before they became emergencies". In the wake of such criticisms it was, perhaps, inevitable that the Bank of England's supervisory powers and authority were reviewed. In May 1997, the government announced its intention to reform the powers and functions of the Bank of England (see below). Further, Article 105(6) of the Maastricht Treaty (the UK has opted out

---

[29] Page, "Self-Regulation: The Constitutional Dimension" (1986), 49 *Modern Law Review* 141.
[30] Treasury and Civil Service Committee, Minutes of Evidence, H.C. 26 (1991–2), 107.
[31] N. 25 above, 151–2.

of Articles 105 (1)–(5) which relates to monetary policy) aims to confer responsibility for bank supervision to the European Central Bank.

TREASURY INPUT TO BANK SUPERVISION THROUGH THE BOARD OF BANKING SUPERVISION

The Government White Paper on Bank Supervision[32] published after the Johnson Matthey affair, proposed the establishment of the Board of Banking Supervision to assist the Governor of the Bank of England in the performance of his banking supervisory functions.[33] The Board was actually created in May 1986 and the Banking Act 1987 gave statutory recognition to it.[34] The establishment of the Board was intended to create a mechanism through which the Treasury could have greater involvement in the role of bank supervision.

The Board consists of three *ex officio* members, namely the Governor of the Bank, the Deputy Governor of the Bank and the Executive Director of the Bank, and six independent members appointed jointly by the Chancellor and the Governor of the Bank. The Act imposes a statutory duty on the independent members to advise the *ex officio* members on the exercise by the Bank of its supervisory functions and any matters arising from the exercise of such a function. The Government White Paper[35] envisaged some of the areas in which the Board might have an active role:

(a) board issues involving the supervision of institutions authorised under the Act;
(b) the development and evolution of supervisory practice;
(c) the administration of the new Act;
(d) the structure, staffing and training of the Banking Supervision Division.

Any member of the Board may raise any matter of concern in the field of banking supervision and discuss with and provide advice to the governor on such matters.

The Bank of England must make regular reports to the Board on such issues as the Board may reasonably require (section 3(4)). The *ex officio* members are not bound to follow the advice of the independent members of the Board, but they must give notice to the Chancellor of the Exchequer whenever it is decided that the advice of the independent members is not to be followed. The independent members then have a right to notify the Chancellor of their reasons for the advice.[36] The Bingham Report throws some light on the role of the Board of Banking Supervision. A paper on BCCI was prepared before the first meeting

[32] H.M. Treasury; Dec 1985; Cmnd. 9695.
[33] "Bank Supervision" (H.M. Treasury; Cmnd. 9695, HMSO, London, 1985), paras. 5.1–5.8.
[34] Banking Act 1987, s.2(1).
[35] N. 33 above.
[36] Banking Act 1987, s.2(5).

of the Board of Banking Supervision in which mention was made of "very substantial " losses, although no figure was actually mentioned. In July 1987, a further paper was presented to the Board which reported the Bank's unwillingness to undertake consolidated supervision of BCCI. The various proceedings of the Board, requests for further reports and debate demonstrate the value of the Board as a "supervisory instrument".[37]

TREASURY INPUT TO BANK SUPERVISION THROUGH ITS RIGHT OF
OBJECTION TO SHAREHOLDERS

Sections 21–26 of the Banking Act 1987 extensively increased the powers conferred on the Bank (under section 14 of the Banking Act 1979) to protect the UK banking sector from aggressive foreign control or other undesirable take-overs. Certain defined persons are required to give notice to the Bank before changes in individual shareholdings can be effected by authorised institutions. The Bank is given wide powers of objection to a proposed controller and the Bank is required to assess the suitability of a prospective controller and his intentions regarding the institution of which he proposes to acquire control.

Additionally, the Treasury are empowered to direct the Bank of England to serve notice of objection[38] to a person who has given notice of intention to become a controller or who has become a controller without giving relevant notice. The grounds for objection are not specified but are regulated by section 183 of the Financial Services Act 1986, which empowers the Treasury to disqualify or restrict the authorisation on the ground that the institution is connected to a country which does not offer equal treatment to UK persons or institutions in the investment, banking or insurance fields. The section 23 provision was introduced as an amendment to the Banking Bill and it was made plain that it was aimed specifically at Japan, as part of a concerted campaign by the UK and USA to gain access to the Tokyo market.

This power to object is given to the Treasury rather than the Bank, which indicates that political and economic reasons may dictate its usage.

THE ROLE OF AUDITORS IN BANK SUPERVISION

One of the key features of the Banking Act 1987 was the relaxation of the duty of confidentiality owed by a bank auditor to the client, ie the bank being audited. Section 47 provides that auditors (or reporting auditors) will not be in breach of their duty of confidentiality if they pass information to the Bank of England, whether or not in response to a request made by the Bank. In *Price*

---

[37] N. 25 above.
[38] Banking Act 1987, s.23.

Waterhouse v. *BCCI Holdings (Luxembourg) SA*[39] Millett J held that it was in the public interest to disclose confidential information to the Bank of England in furtherance of its supervisory functions, but it was also in the public interest to disclose information to an inquiry set up to investigate the BCCI collapse. Section 47 does not impose a statutory duty on auditors to disclose information to the Bank of England, but they may be liable in negligence if they fail to communicate with the Bank when circumstances indicate that they ought reasonably to have done so. The information communicated must be acquired either as an auditor, accountant or in some other professional capacity, in respect of an authorised institution and must have been acquired in the relevant professional capacity and be communicated to the Bank in good faith. Although, in reality the Bank expects the management of a bank to report relevant information, nevertheless the Auditing Practices Committee has issued guidance which stresses that whilst auditors are not required to change their working habits, auditors should in so far as possible, preserve their professional relationships with their client banks. Auditors are, therefore, advised to draw to the attention of their clients any concerns they have and request that these be reported to the Bank of England. Where the bank concerned fails to respond promptly, or where the interests of depositors necessitate auditors may report directly to the Bank of England. Such a change may arise where there has been an adverse occurrence, or adverse change in the auditors' or reporting accountants' perception of the institution. The BCCI affair highlights the dangers of ignoring bank audits. Audits are normally directed at a company's shareholders, but once published may be used for a number of unrelated activities: whether auditors awe a duty of care to persons relying on the published accounts clearly depends on the proximity of the relationship.[40]

The Single European Market

The financial services sector was slow in working towards a comprehensive common market and, in 1985, the Cockfield Report[41] gave priority to the freeing of international capital movements.

The Cockfield Report outlined a new strategy in the establishment of the single market. The report rejected the proposition that a commitment to a common market in financial services could not be achieved until regulatory arrangements had been harmonised between members. This had delayed the evolution of a single market in financial services as national authorities sought to impose their own regulation on other Member States. The Cockfield Report

---

[39] [1992] BCLC 583.
[40] *Caparo Industries plc* v. *Dickman* [1990] 2 AC 605; *Al-Nakib Investments (Jersey) Ltd* v. *Longcroft* [1990] 1 WLR 1290.
[41] European Communities Commission, *Completing the Internal Market*, COM(85)310 final, June 1985.

concluded that "experience has shown that relying on a strategy based totally on harmonisation would be over-regulatory, would take a long time to implement, would be inflexible, and would stifle innovation".

The new strategy proposed by Cockfield required a distinction to be drawn between what was essential to harmonise and what was to be left to mutual recognition by national regulations. This strategy represented a completely new approach to achieving the single market in financial services and was based on three main features:

(a) There would be an agreed set of minimum harmonised regulations.
(b) Operating outside this set of minimum regulations there would be mutual recognition of the regulatory arrangements of other member States.
(c) Regulation would be based on home-country requirements.

It was recognised that it would no longer be necessary to harmonise all regulatory requirements. National authorities would be left to regulate other areas, but on the basis of mutual recognition of each Member State's regulatory and supervisory systems.

The Cockfield Report was followed by the Single European Act 1986, which committed the European Community to the completion of an internal market in "goods, persons, services and capital". It was accepted that harmonising the laws of Member States was not necessarily the best way to achieve this. Only essential matters would therefore be harmonised, leaving others in the hands of national governments, but on the basis of mutual recognition. It was also agreed that regulation would be based on home-country requirements. In the banking sector, for example, common regulation relates to the authorisation criteria, minimum capital requirements, the definition of own funds (equity capital), large exposure limited, deposit protection arrangements, control of major shareholdings in banks and recognition that sound accountancy and internal control mechanisms must exist.

The EC "Passport"

The idea of mutual recognition had been firmly accepted by the mid-1980s and creating a single market in financial services meant removing regulatory barriers to EC firms operating outside their country of origin. EC Member States agreed to "mutually recognise" (accept as adequate) the regulatory standards of other Member States. Consequently, authorisation in one country in the Community would also constitute authorisation to conduct business in all Community Member States. Thus, an EC firm authorised in one Member State ("home state") can choose whether to supply services through branches or on a cross-border basis without having a physical presence in the host state.

The passport directives in the different areas of financial services have a number of aspects in common.

Each passport directive, or set of directives, defines its scope in terms of type of institution and activities carried out. This is significant because the activities covered by a specific type of authorisation may vary from state to state.

The directives require firms to be authorised and have established the conditions which must be satisfied for initial and continuing authorisation. These authorisation requirements generally relate to three main areas: the need for adequate management and controls (e.g. accounting procedures): minimum levels of capital a firm must have for initial and continuing support of its business; and the "fitness" requirements of shareholders and controllers (including directors and manager) of the institution. The Directives emphasise the division of responsibility between home and host states. In general, the home state takes responsibility for the prudential supervision of a firm and all its branches and the "fitness" of its controllers and major shareholders. The conduct of a firm's business with customers, however, is largely the responsibility of the authorities in the host state.

The directives also address relations with non-member countries. The intention is to allow firms from non-member countries access to European markets on the same terms as European firms if similar access is permitted by non-member countries to European firms.

Second Banking Co-ordination Directive

The purpose of the Directive[42] was to remove the obstacles left by the First Directive[43] to the free provision of banking services on a cross-border basis and to assist in the EC-wide establishment of credit institutions.

The Second Directive has resulted in fundamental changes in the legal framework of banking business in the Community, with the purpose of creating a single banking market with no internal barriers to the movement of banking services and the establishment of branches but not subsidiaries within the Community.[44] This has been made possible by the creation of a "single banking licence" through "mutual recognition" and the application of a minimum of Community standards on prudential supervision.

The Second Directive applies to "credit institutions" (as defined in the First Banking Directive[45]). Such an institution is defined as an "undertaking whose business is to receive deposits or other repayable funds from the public and to grant credits for its own account". The Second Directive also applies to "financial institutions" (i.e. subsidiaries 90 per cent owned by one or more credit

---

[42] 89/646/EEC, [1989] OJ L386/1; SI 1992/3218, was implemented in the UK on 1 Jan, 1993.

[43] 77/780/EEC.

[44] The distinction between a branch and subsidiary has been criticised: see W. van Gerven, "The Second Banking Co-Ordination Directive and the Case-law of the Court of Justice" (1991) 10 *YEL* 57, 59.

[45] Art.I of Dir. 77/80/EEC, n. 43 above.

institutions and complying with certain conditions, including a guarantee from a parent company.[46] Activities which are not authorised in the annex to the Directive and entities that are not authorised and supervised as credit institutions (i.e. as deposit-taking institutions) will not benefit from mutual recognition. Thus, the single banking licence is valid in other Member States only with respect to banking activities that are enumerated in the annex to the Directive. The annex therefore defines the scope of the principle of mutual recognition. Credit institutions authorised in their home Member State will be entitled in each of the other Member States:

(a) to establish branches;[47] and
(b) to offer their services freely to individuals and businesses without the need for any further authorisation by the host member State.

Mutual recognition is extended to a branch but not to a subsidiary of a credit institution. A subsidiary, being a separate legal entity, is required to obtain its own licence before it can engage in banking activities.

A host Member State may subject a credit institution from another Member State to licensing and supervision requirements if it wishes to undertake any services in addition to those specified in the annex. The requirements must satisfy the following conditions:

(a) credit institutions from the host Member State must be subject to the same requirements;
(b) the imposition of licensing and supervision requirements in the host Member State in addition to those already imposed by the home member State must be justified on grounds of public policy; and
(c) the likelihood of causing harm to the public must justify the licensing requirements or other restrictions in question.

Although mutual recognition permits a Community credit institution to provide its services anywhere in the Community the Second Directive prevents "forum shopping". It states that the principle of mutual recognition requires that the Member States do not grant an authorisation or withdraw an existing authorisation where it appears that the institution has opted for the legal system of one Member State for the purpose of evading the stricter standards of supervision in other Member States.[48] The power to refuse or withdraw an authorisation is only given to home Member States. Host Member States do not have the power either to refuse or to withdraw an authorisation to operate a branch of a credit institution from another Member State.

The annex (reproduced in Schedule I to the Second Banking Co-ordination Directive Regulations) to the Second Directive enumerates activities, which in the opinion of the Commission, are considered to be "integral to banking" and

---

[46] Arts. 1(6) and 18(2).
[47] Arts. 18 and 19.
[48] Second Banking Co-Ordination Directive, 8th recital.

which constitute the provision of traditional banking services in the Community.

The agreed list of banking activities has been drawn up on a liberal universal banking model. The most important and far-reaching aspect of the list is the inclusion of all forms of transactions in securities. The Commission recommends that the annex be updated under a flexible procedure so that it can respond to changes in banking services and practice.

Branches Establishment

A credit institution which wishes to establish a branch in another Member State is required to inform the authorities of its home Member State of its intention to establish a branch in the host Member State.[49] The notification must be accompanied by certain information concerning the credit institutions and the branch, in particular information relating to the operations and structure of the branch.[50] The home Member State authorities must communicate this information, together within information on own funds and solvency ratio of the credit institution, to the authorities in the host Member State within three months.[51] The only action open to the authorities of the home Member State is to refuse a referral to establish a branch to the authority in the host state. In such a situation the home Member State must give reasons for such a refusal, which is subject to appeal in the courts of the home Member State.[52]

Role of Supervisors

The Second Directive is based on the principle of "home country control" under which each credit institution will be supervised by the authorities of the home Member State, even in connection with activities carried out across the border in another Member State.[53] Consequently, the various supervisory functions to be exercised over a bank's activities, including the activities of it branches in other Member States, will fall to the authorities of the Member State where the bank has its head office. The Second Directive, however, provides some exceptions to this rule, for example, the host Member State will retain primary responsibility for the supervision of liquidity of the branches of credit institutions and exclusive responsibility for the implementation of monetary policy. Therefore, the authorities in the host country no longer have competence over solvency regulation; this transfer of power has been achieved by the simultaneous entry

---

[49] Arts. 19(1) and 20.
[50] Art. 19(2).
[51] Art. 19(3).
[52] Art. 19(3).
[53] Second Dir., 4th and 10th recitals, Arts. 13 and 15.

into force, along with the Second Banking Directive, of the Community directives concerning solvency ratios[54] and own funds.[55]

Foreign Banks and the Single Market

Whilst the Second Banking Directive created the single market in banking services for EC countries, it also affected the position of non-EC banks.

Community legislation makes a distinction between the establishment of a subsidiary within the Community by a foreign bank and the establishment of a branch. Subsidiaries of foreign banks incorporated in any Member State of the EC are legally independent entities subject to Community Law and to the national legislation of the country of incorporation. They are considered Community credit institutions and have the same rights and obligations as other "domestic" EC credit institutions.[56] Once authorised by the supervisory body of the country of incorporation, such subsidiaries enjoy the same freedom under the Second Banking Directive to establish branches as institutions originating from within the EC Member States. The main issue for foreign banks is the conditions for entry into the Community market, embodied in the notion of "reciprocity".

In contrast to subsidiaries, branches of non-EC banks do not qualify for the EC-wide licence, and will not benefit from mutual recognition and the privileges attached to it. The activities of a branch of a foreign bank will be limited to the territory of the Member State where it is located and will be subject to the national legislation of that country.

A number of other directives intended to create a level playing field, have been given effect to in the UK.

The Council Directive on the Supervision of Credit Institutions on a Consolidated Basis.[57] Directive 92/30/EEC requires the consolidated supervision of the financial condition of a credit institution, including credit or financial institutions in which it holds a participation. Consolidated supervision means that the authority supervising the parent credit institution will apply the financial data of the whole group in monitoring compliance by the credit institution with its supervisory standards (e.g. solvency ratio; lending limits and restrictions on investments by credit institutions in the non-trade sector). Consolidated supervision must be distinguished from the principle of home Member State supervision as provided for under the Second Banking Directive. The consolidated supervision will be the responsibility of the regulatory authorities in the home Member State where the parent credit institution has its

---

[54] 89/647/EEC [1989] OJ L386/14.
[55] 89/299/EEC [1989] OJ L124/16.
[56] Second Dir., Arts. 18(1) and 19(1).
[57] 92/30/EEC [1992] OJ L110/52 implemented in the UK in 1993 (BSD/1993/1) replaces Dir. 83/350/EEC.

head office.[58] Whenever possible supervision by the home Member State will be exercised in consultation with the regulatory authorities of the Member States of the subsidiary institutions, so that competitive distortions between the consolidated group and the domestic credit institutions of the countries in which the members of the group are established will be avoided. However, the Directive on Consolidated Supervision does not preclude supervision of a subsidiary by the authorities where the subsidiary is authorised.

The Directive on Consolidated Supervision only applies where a credit institution, i.e. a deposit-taking institution, is the parent company. Consolidated supervision extends to credit and financial institutions in which a credit institution has a participation.[59] "Financial institution" is defined as an "undertaking, not being a credit institution, whose principal activity is to grant credit facilities (including guarantees), to acquire participation or to make investments". "Participation" means ownership, directly or indirectly, of 25 per cent or more of the capital of another credit of financial institution.[60] Where ownership is between 25 and 50 per cent of the capital of another credit or financial institution, there is discretion whether and how consolidation may be effected.

Consolidated supervision is not limited to participation in credit and financial institutions located in the Community, but an exemption from credit restrictions is given to the transfer of the necessary information. An application of the principle of supervision on a consolidated basis to credit institutions whose parent companies have their head office in non-Community countries and to credit institutions situated in non-Community countries whose parent credit institutions have a head office in a Member State will be made possible by reciprocal bilateral agreements to be entered into between the competent authorities of the Member States and the non-Community countries concerned. Within the EC, and to enable the home state to perform the necessary consolidated supervision, all Member States are directed to ensure that the necessary information for consolidated supervision can be exchanged.

The Solvency Ratio Directive,[61] and the Own Funds Directive[62] apply to consolidated supervision of the whole group, even to those affiliates that are involved in market risks rather than credit risks. The dual regulation results in a competitive disadvantage for banks which have to maintain capital to cover both credit risks (under the Solvency Ratio Directive) and market risks (under the Capital Adequacy Directive).

Supervision of control of large exposures is proposed to be carried out on a consolidated basis in accordance with the Council Directive on Monitoring and Controlling Large Exposure of Credit Institutions.

---

[58] Art. 3(8).
[59] Art. 2.
[60] Art. 1, indent 6.
[61] 89/647/EEC [1989] OJ [386/14, implemented in the UK in Dec. 1990 (BSD/1990/3).
[62] 89/299/EEC [1989] OJ L124/16 implemented in the UK in Dec. 1990 (BSD/1990/2).

The Solvency Ratio Directive[63] must be read together with the Own Funds Directive.[64] The aim of the Solvency Ratio Directive (given effect to in the UK in 1990) is to ensure that every credit institution authorised under the Second Directive has sufficient and sound capitalisation to withstand losses caused by the realisation of risks inherent to the banking business. The Solvency Ratio Directive represents the Community's version of the capital adequacy rules of the Basle Committee on Banking Regulations and Supervisory Practices that were proposed by the "Basle Agreement".[65] The Solvency Ratio Directive requires the Member States to adopt the measures necessary to comply with its provisions, which in turn will satisfy the Basle Agreement.

The Solvency Ratio Directive is applicable to all credit institutions as defined by Article 1 of the First Banking Directive. If a credit institution is a parent undertaking and to be included in the consolidated supervision of a banking group, the solvency ratio is to be calculated on a consolidated basis in accordance with the provisions of the Directive on Consolidated Supervision and the Bank Accounting Directive.[66]

The Solvency Ratio Directive addresses only the credit risk incurred by a credit institution. It provides a formula for computing a credit institution's solvency ratio. The Bank of England's capital requirements will continue to be specified as target and trigger risk-asset ratios. The 8 per cent minimum standard required by Article 10(1) remains the base line for the Bank's discretion in setting the requirements at both consolidated and solo (or solo consolidated) levels.

In January 1994, the UK implemented the Council Directive on the Monitoring and Control of Large Exposures of Credit Institutions.[67] At the same time the Bank of England undertook a review of its policy on large exposures. The mandatory imposition of large exposure limits is based on the idea that the controlling of exposure is an integral part of prudential supervision, and excessive concentration of exposures to a single client or group of connected clients might result in an unacceptable danger of loss. The Directive is intended to neutralise distortions of competition arising from differing large exposure limitations in the various Member States. The Bank of England requires each bank to set out its policy on large exposures, including exposures to individual customers, banks, countries and economic sectors, in a policy statement. In the case of UK-incorporated banks, this policy should be formally adopted by the bank's board of directors. The Bank of England expects banks not to implement significant changes in these policies without prior discussion with it. Significant departures from a bank's stated policy may lead

---

[63] N. 61 above.
[64] N. 62 above.
[65] Committee on Banking Regulations and Supervisory Practices, International Convergence of Capital Measurement and Capital Standards, July 1988.
[66] 86/635/EEC [1986] OJ L372/1.
[67] 92/121/EEC]1993] OJ L29/1.

the Bank of England to reconsider whether the bank satisfies the statutory minimum criteria for authorisation.

The Large Exposures Directive contains basically the same definitions as other directives but the term "exposure" includes all risks defined in the Solvency Ratio Directive.

The Large Exposures Directive also provides for a reporting requirement of large exposures. The definition of large exposure is consistent with the definition in the Large Exposure Recommendation but a special limit will apply to exposures by a credit institution to its affiliates other than own subsidiaries which will be 30 per cent of own funds in the aggregate. The Directive also grants Member States' authorities the right to exempt certain exposures including loans to certain affiliates of credit institutions and claims against central governments, central banks and European Communities. The control of large exposures will be segregated on the basis of a consolidated supervision.

In 1986, the Council of the European Communities adopted the Directive on the Annual Accounts and the Consolidated Accounts of Banks and Other Financial Institutions.[68] In order for borrowers, creditors, shareholders and the public, from different Member States, to be able to compare the annual accounts and the consolidated accounts, this Directive provides for Community-wide harmonised accounting standards for credit and financial institutions. The provisions governing annual accounts of credit institutions are also necessary to provide a uniform basis for the co-ordination of supervisory standards for authorisation requirements and other purposes. The Directive addresses the specific problems of credit institutions and requires broader publication of their financial status than is required for other companies. The Directive is currently being revised.[69]

A Directive on Deposit Guarantee Schemes[70] was adopted by the European Community in May 1994, and it has been implemented in the Member States. Under changes proposed to the UK scheme,[71] qualifying deposits placed with the UK branch of a bank from another European Economic Area (EEA) country will be covered by the bank's home country deposit protection arrangements, rather than by the UK scheme. The cover of the UK scheme will be widened to branches of UK-incorporated institutions throughout the EEA. The other main changes introduced were the extension of the UK scheme to include deposits in other EEA currencies as well as sterling, and to increase the level of cover offered by the UK scheme from 75 per cent to 90 per cent of the first £20,000 of the deposit.

---

[68] 86/635/EEC [1986] OJ L372/1 which came into force in the UK under the Bank Accounts Directive (Miscellaneous Banks) Regs. 1991 (SI 1991/2704) and the the Companies Act 1985 (Bank Accounts) Regs. 1994 (SI 1994/233).

[69] [1997] *Journal of International and Banking Financial Law* 97.

[70] 94/19/EC [1994] OJ 5.

[71] Credit Institutions (Protection of Depositors) Regs. 1995, SI 1995/1442, implemented on 1 July 1995.

There are no changes to the structure of the Deposit Protection Scheme nor the way it is funded. However, the UK scheme will "top up" cover to UK branches of EEA banks whose home state cover is less generous than that offered here, with branches which choose to pay for this option given the same total level of cover as is offered to depositors with UK-authorised institutions.

Guarantee schemes exist in most Member States but they differ widely in their legal structure and in the scope of protection they confer.

Agreement was reached among the Member States on a directive to reinforce prudential supervision within the European Community following the collapse of BCCI.[72] It came into effect on 16 July 1996.[73] It covers not only credit institutions but also investment firms and insurance companies. The Directive has four main provisions:

(a) It requires supervisors to refuse authorisation where group and ownership links preclude effective prudential supervision.

(b) Member States must require that a financial undertaking has its head office in the same state as the registered office.

(c) It allows Member States to widen the range of disclosure gateways, to allow supervisors to provide confidential information to, amongst others, those supervising the accountancy profession, and to bodies responsible for the detection and investigation of breaches of company law (including external inspectors).

(d) Member States are required to place a duty on auditors, and experts (e.g. reporting accountants) appointed by supervisory authorities, to report material breaches of law and certain other concerns to the supervisory bodies.

Globalisation and the Regulatory Response

The biggest banking and financial banking institutions now span 50 or more countries and may have 300 or more entities within the group.[74] This has been the feature of banking since the 1970s. However, banks now tend to centralise the controls and management of their overseas entities, consolidating similar risks being run in different subsidiaries. This allows the head office to exercise stronger control over the volume of a particular type of risk being run across the group. For example, for some UK banks, the management of their global foreign exchange book will be in London during London office hours, then it will switch to the UK operation but under strict limits set by London: after the United States close it will move again, to the Far East, but still under the controls set by London.

---

[72] 95/26/EC [1995] OJ L168/7.

[73] Bank of England Notice 55/1996/9.

[74] Deputy Governor of the Bank of England, "International Regulatory Structure: a UK Perspective" (1997) 37 *Bank of England Bulletin* 214.

So for global groups, the control activities in the various scattered legal entities now depends on the adequacy of centrally located controls.

The response of the regulators to centralised controls has been an increased focus on information sharing and reaching agreement on respective responsibilities. The initial focus of the Basle Committee on Banking Supervision (set up by the central bank governors of the G10 countries) in 1974 was to define the role and responsibilities of home and host supervisors of internationally active banks. These were set out in the 1975 concordat, which has been updated on a number of occasions. Individual supervisors in both the banking and securities industries have acted to reinforce co-operation arrangements through formal bilateral agreements with their overseas counterparts.

The importance of international regulatory co-operation is now widely acknowledged as an agenda of inter-governmental meetings.

REFORM OF BANK REGULATION AND SUPERVISION

The Bank of England Act 1998

The Labour Government's decision to grant operational independence to the Bank of England is radical.[75] The Bank of England Act 1998[76] establishes a Monetary Policy Committee within the Bank and gives it statutory responsibility for the formulation of monetary policy. The Bank is therefore given the primary monetary policy objective of price stability and, subject to that objective, the objective of supporting the government's other economic policies. Allowing the Bank of England to fix interest rates enhances the credibility of UK monetary policy. The Act also makes substantial provision for openness and transparency in the conduct of monetary policy and enhances the accountability of the Bank. Moreover, such a requirement is consistent with the requirements of the European Monetary Union.

At the same time the regulation and supervision of financial and investment business has been brought within a single regulatory framework. Whilst the decisions taken should enhance the reputation of the Bank of England in issues of monetary policy, the removal of the Bank's key traditional function (eg bank supervision) will undoubtedly lead to a reduction in the Bank's status: a process that will gather greater pace if and when the UK government subscribes to the final stages of Economic and Monetary Union.

The justification for centralising all regulation within one body is the increased blurring of the distinction between institutions (e.g. banks, building societies, securities companies, insurance companies) and the products they offer. The new regulatory body will oversee the operations of banks, financial

---

[75] The Chancellor's statement to the House of Commons on the Bank of England, 20 May 1997, Parl. Doc. 49/97.

[76] S. 13, Bank of England Act 1998.

services companies, securities firms and fund managers. Under the Government's proposals, the reforms will be introduced in two stages. The first, following a new Bank of England Act 1998,[77] involves the transfer of responsibility for banking supervision from the Bank to a newly created Financial Services Authority (FSA). Section 21 of the Bank of England Act 1998 transfers to the new FSA the functions formally exercised by the Bank of England under the Banking Act 1987, the Banking Co-Ordination (Second Council Directive) Regulations 1992 and section 101(4) of the Building Societies Act 1986, together with its functions under section 43 of the Financial Services Act 1986 and the Investment Services Regulations 1995 and its functions under section 171 of the Companies Act 1989.

The new single regulator, the FSA, will not assume its full role until the proposed new financial regulatory reform act is enacted, probably in late 1999. The supervisory functions of the Bank of England will be transferred when the Bank of England Act 1998 is implemented, in Summer 1998.

Both the Board of Banking Supervision and the Deposit Protection Board are retained, but membership of both will in future be determined by the Chairman of the Financial Services Authority. The Chairman of the Authority will replace the Governor of the Bank of England where necessary.

The cost of banking supervision has, until the Banking Act 1998, been concealed. Banks have not had to pay for the costs of authorisation or supervision. However, a significant part of the costs of the running of the Bank of England have been met by requiring banks to place non-interest bearing cash ratio deposits with the Bank. The cash ratio deposit regime is put on a statutory basis under the 1998 Act. However, the Financial Services Authority needs funds to supervise banks (estimated initially at approximately £50 million *per annum*). Subject to a minimum annual tariff, the level of the FSA's annual fee will be set by reference to the "FSA fee base" which is modelled on the current structure of "eligible liabilities" used to calculate the required level of cash ratio deposits. However, the definition of eligible liabilities is extended.[78]

Under the second stage, the three existing self-regulatory organisations will be subsumed within the already enlarged regulator, thereby creating a new super-regulator.

A substantial degree of rationalisation will therefore be achieved through the emergence of the super-regulator, with the Treasury assuming ministerial responsibility for the new regime. The Bank retains its supervisory responsibilities in respect of wholesale markets (e.g. foreign exchange, gold and money markets) and it will continue with its role as "lender of the last resort".

The nationalisation of the statutory framework of investment business will undoubtedly have many potential benefits, reduction in the cost of regulation, greater consistency in approach within and across sectors, a clarification of

---

[77] The Act received Royal Assent in April 1998. It came into force on 1 June 1998 (the Bank of England Act 1998 (Commencement) Order 1998; SI No. 1120).
[78] See Sched. 2 to the Bank of England Act 1998.

accountability, a reduction in the duplication of supervisory functions and enhanced co-operation with overseas regulators. Unless, at least, some of these benefits can be retained there are dangers that the new super-regulator may become a burcaucratic nightmare.

7

The Regulation of Insurance

ANDREW McGEE[1]

The regulation of insurance business in the UK has a long history.[2] At the present day no one seriously doubts that insurance is a business which needs to be regulated.[3] A considerable edifice of statutory and other regulation has been erected.[4] Some of this regulation appears to work well, whereas other parts are much more problematic. This essay deals with the various aspects of the regulatory structure. Part I summarises the arguments for regulation in this area. Part II summarises the existing regulatory structure and identifies the problem areas. Part III analyses the problem areas in more detail and tries to relate the problems to more general theories of regulation. Part IV considers some possible approaches to the problems.

PART I: WHY REGULATE?

For present purposes it is proposed to accept Selznick's definition of regulation as

"sustained and focused control exercised by a public agency over activities that are valued by a community."[5]

For present purposes the context of a "public agency" will be quite widely interpreted. Regulatory bodies in the field of insurance include the Department of Trade and Industry and the Securities and Investments Board (soon to be replaced by the Financial Services Authority). Ombudsman schemes are also important in the insurance industry. The arguments for regarding them as part of the regulatory structure are considered in Part II, whilst the operation of the schemes is considered in Part III.

[1] Professor of Business Law and Director of the Centre for Business Law and Practice, University of Leeds. Thanks are due to Antonio Martinez-Arboleda of the Department of Law, Leeds University, for comments on an earlier draft of this essay. The author naturally remains solely responsible for the finished version.
[2] See the text to n. 15 below for a summary history of the legislation.
[3] Some of the reasons are recited below.
[4] See e.g. J. Tapp, "Regulation of the UK Insurance Industry" in J. Finsinger and M.V. Pauly (eds.), The Economics of Insurance Regulation (Basingstoke, Macmillan, 1986).
[5] Selznick, "Focusing Organizational Research on Regulation" in R. Noll (ed.), Regulatory Policy and the Social Sciences (Berkeley, University of California Press, 1985), 363.

The importance of insurance of various kinds in modern society cannot be doubted. It has been observed elsewhere[6] that if Benjamin Franklin were alive today, he would surely have to accept that there are now three things in life which are unavoidable, and that insurance is the third of them. Few people can get far into adult life without having at least one of motor insurance, household insurance (buildings and/or contents) and life assurance. The importance of the last of these grows steadily as successive governments seek to pass responsibility for pension planning[7] onto individuals. Of course, the more important an activity is within any society, the more pressing the need to ensure that it is carried on in a proper way.

The usual reason for permitting a business activity but regulating it may be said to be the view that the activity itself is valuable, but that social harm is likely to result from allowing it to be carried on unfettered. This harm usually results from either the incompetence or the dishonesty of those carrying on the activity, often coupled with the complexity of the activity and the relative ignorance of the consumers of the activity.

It is easy to see that insurance readily meets this definition. The complexity of many of the products sold by the insurance industry cannot be doubted, especially in the case of life and investment policies. At the same time the opportunities for dishonesty and the potential consequences of incompetence on the part of insurers are so great that the public interest clearly requires regulation. This in turn leads to the question of how to regulate.

The regulation of business activity is commonly further divided into social regulation and economic regulation.[8] Both types of regulation may be said in a broad sense to address problems of market failure. The former is concerned mainly with competition law issues, whereas the latter deals most commonly with information failure and externalities. As it is clear that the structure of insurance regulation in the UK is a form of social regulation, issues about economic regulation[9] will not be considered any further in this essay.

In the context of insurance, information failure[10] may be regarded as the primary justification for regulation, though it is possible to show that lack of regulation can have undesirable knock-on effects on persons other than policyholders.[11]

---

[6] A. McGee, "Insurance Law" in G.G. Howells (ed.), *European Business Law* (Aldershot, Dartmouth, 1996).

[7] Many pension policies are also life policies.

[8] D. Swann, "The Regulatory Scene: An Overview" in K. Button and D. Swann (eds.), *The Age of Regulatory Reform* (Oxford, Clarendon Press, 1989).

[9] One clear example of economic regulation of insurance business is Reg. 3932/92/EC, which deals with anti-competitive agreements in the insurance sector.

[10] Insurance may be regarded as a prime example of Akerlof's model of the way in which information deficits can lead to an equalisation of price at the expense of quality: see G.A. Akerlof, "The Market for Lemons: Quality Uncertainty and the Market Mechanism" (1970) 89 *Q.J. Econ.* 488.

[11] Such effects are commonly referred to as "externalities". The question of how to regulate for externalities generally is a matter of some complexity, which is not pursued further here. For a good introduction to the issues and the literature on the subject see A.I. Ogus, *Regulation: Legal Form and Economic Theory* (Oxford, OUP, 1994).

The information failure is of various kinds, each of which needs to be identified here. First, potential policyholders ("prospects" in the jargon of the insurance industry) may not realise their own need for insurance. Secondly, those who do have at least some awareness of their need for insurance may yet lack the sophistication to appreciate quite what kind of insurance will best suit their needs. It is fair to say that this is a problem encountered more in relation to life and investment policies than in relation to general insurance. Although most people can tell motor insurance from travel insurance, and perhaps even tell household buildings insurance from household contents insurance, the number who can accurately distinguish term assurance, endowment assurance and whole-of-life policies is probably considerably fewer. Thirdly, even those who know what sort of policy they want may have difficulty making an informed choice between different companies and different policies. To make a choice of the first kind requires a knowledge of the reputations and business practices of different companies which is hard to come by for those outside the industry. An important distinguishing feature of insurance is that purchasers must pay their premium in advance, trusting to the probity and competence of those running the business to ensure that funds will be available to pay any claims which might arise. The one-sided nature of this bargain, coupled with the lack of information available to purchasers about the probity and competence of particular insurers, may be regarded as a good reason for imposing at least some form of regulation. To make a choice of the second kind requires a detailed study of the wording of competing policies. Few people ever get to see competing policies; even fewer have the inclination to make a detailed study; and fewer still have the technical expertise to make an informed critical comparison.

The question of externalities may also be briefly dealt with. The absence of (suitable) insurance against various risks may cause those who lack it to become a financial burden on others. This is especially so in the case of pension planning and permanent health insurance, as well as in motor insurance, where the lack of cover may cause a risk to fall on the Motor Insurers Bureau, which is in effect funded by all those who do pay their premiums.[12] These externalities may result from any of the three kinds of information failure identified above, though they may also result from a wilful (and, in the case of motor insurance, criminal) refusal to take out a policy even where the need for one is clearly identified. This last type of externality is dealt with, not by regulation of the insurance industry, but by the imposition of a legal requirement to be properly insured before driving a motor vehicle on a public road.[13] This aspect of the subject is not considered further in this essay. The problems so far identified may be regarded as constituting a sufficient justification for the regulation of the insurance industry. That regulation needs to be calculated to ensure that the industry is conducted on the basis of financial solvency by individuals who are honest and competent

---

[12] For the Motor Insurers Bureau see *The Encyclopaedia of Insurance Law* (London, Sweet & Maxwell).
[13] Road Traffic Act 1988, s.143.

and who have an appropriate attitude to customer service and customer relations. The next part will describe the schemes currently in place.

The existing scheme of regulation of insurance business must be divided into a number of distinct areas:

- regulation of freedom to carry on business (prior authorisation and ongoing monitoring);
- regulation of the marketing and selling of investment products;
- regulation of brokers in general insurance;
- complaints-handling schemes.

Freedom to Carry on Business

The earliest legislation imposing control on the freedom to carry on business was the Life Assurance Companies Act 1870, which was succeeded by the Assurance Companies Act 1909. Both required the payment of deposits to the regulatory agency as a precondition of starting business, but did not create the kind of prior authorisation system which is in use today, since there was no attempt to assess the suitability of applicants—once the money was paid, permission was given. The development of EU law in the area of freedom to provide services[14] led to the Insurance Companies Act 1974, which was in turn replaced by the Insurance Companies Act 1982. This statute, as amended, is the basis of the present structure.

The Insurance Companies Act 1982 imposes a regulatory system under which prior authorisation from the Department of Trade and Industry is required before carrying on insurance business.[15] That authorisation will not be given unless the DTI is satisfied that the managers of the business are fit and proper persons for the purpose.[16] Insurance business is divided into a number of classes, and separate authorisation is required for each class. It is possible and common to be authorised for only some classes of business.

The Act imposes requirements of financial solvency[17] on insurance companies. There are also ongoing accounting and supervisory arrangements,[18] which

---

[14] For a fuller account of this aspect of the subject see A. McGee, *EC Insurance Law* (Brookfield, Ashgate, 1998).

[15] The scheme of prior authorisation is more or less laid down by the first generation of Insurance Directives (First non-Life Dir. 73/239; First Life Dir. 79/267, so that it would not be possible for the UK to make significant relaxations in the requirements, even if it were thought desirable to do so.

[16] Insurance Companies Act 1982, ss.3–9.

[17] Ss. 32–35B.

[18] Ss. 17–31.

may lead to the restricting or withdrawal of authorisation.[19] It is a criminal offence to carry on business without authorisation.[20] The Department of Trade and Industry does each year remove a small number of authorisations, either in relation to specific classes of business or for all classes of business.

It is also a requirement that those concerned in the management of an insurance company must appear to the DTI to be fit and proper persons. This rule does not affect those lower down the hierarchy of the company and therefore has nothing to do with the authorisation or monitoring of individual salespersons within the company.

These rules are clearly intended to address one part of the information deficit problems addressed above, namely the need for the purchaser to pay for the product in advance and then to trust that the insurer will still be available and solvent if a claim arises.

Conduct of Business Rules

Each of the SROs under the Financial Services Act (FSA) 1986 has its own conduct of business rules, based on the Securities and Investments Board's (SIB's) Core Conduct of Business Rules 1992.[21] As their name implies, these regulate in some detail the ways in which regulated businesses go about their affairs. They are intended to ensure that businesses show proper regard for the needs of their clients and that the financial aspects of the business are appropriately conducted. Thus, in particular, they impose strict rules on the process of dealing with and accounting for client money.

Marketing and Selling of Investment Policies

This area is governed by the provisions of the Financial Services Act 1986. This Act was intended to regulate the marketing and selling of investment products generally. A major part of this regulation covers investment insurance policies. Such policies make up the great majority of life policies sold at the present day. The Act does not in any way regulate the *content* of such policies, being restricted, at least in relation to insurance, to issues of marketing and selling. At present the administration of the statutory regime is in the hands of the Personal Investment Authority, which is a designated agency appointed for this purpose by the Secretary of State. The regulatory scheme is in the process of fundamental change, for legislation is under way which will transfer responsibility for nearly all[22] financial services regulation in the UK to a new body called the

---

[19] Ss. 11–13.
[20] S.2.
[21] See A. McGee, "The SIB Core Conduct of Business Rules" (1992) 13 *Company Lawyer* 129.
[22] But not the activities of Building Societies.

Financial Services Authority (FSA). Indeed this body already exists, though no powers have yet been transferred to it. The intention is that the new FSA will be a more effective co-ordinator and director of the regulatory system than the present conglomeration of regulatory bodies. It remains to be seen whether this hope will be fulfilled; in any event it is not at all clear that the transfer of powers to the FSA, currently expected to be completed sometime in 1999, will in the short term result in any significant changes in the rules discussed here. Indeed, it is hard to imagine how these rules could plausibly undergo further fundamental change.

The Conduct of Brokers in General Insurance

This is an area where, unusually, a system of certification rather than of licensing has been adopted. The Insurance Brokers Registration Act 1977 creates the Insurance Brokers Registration Council ((BRC), which, as its name implies, has the statutory function of providing a registration system for brokers.[23] However, registration is voluntary, since it is perfectly possible to operate as a broker in general insurance without being registered. By the standards of the late 1990s this arrangement can only be regarded as anomalous, given that the provision of broking services in life assurance is now so highly regulated. It must be remembered, however, that in 1977 even the introduction of a voluntary system of registration was a novelty in this area. It should also be said that brokers in general insurance do not have quite the same opportunities as their life assurance counterparts[24] to cause major financial loss to their clients,[25] though bad advice at the time the policy is taken out can lead to a voidable policy or to a policy which does not provide the cover which the client requires. Although a few actions against insurance brokers do appear in the Law Reports,[26] there does not appear to be a major problem with the quality of advice given by such brokers. Certainly there is not the same problem of misselling as appears to exist in relation to life policies. This is no doubt because general brokers do not market themselves in the same aggressive way as life brokers; nor are potential policyholders so easily misled into taking out polices which they do not need. Despite the anomalous character of the present regulatory system, it is not to be expected that compulsory registration and/or licensing will be introduced at any time in the near future.

---

[23] Insurance Brokers Registration Act 1977, s.2.

[24] In a fair number of cases the same office deals with both life and non-life business.

[25] For an account of the duties of brokers in general insurance see A. McGee, "The Duties of an Insurance Broker" (1991) 7 PN 162.

[26] Examples in the present decade include *Punjab National Bank* v. *de Boinville* [1992] 3 All ER 104 (CA). Of course appearance in the Law Reports is not the most reliable of guides to the volume of cases, since by no means all disputes reach even the stage of issue of proceedings, far less going to court. Of those that do go to court, not all appear in the Law Reports.

A more interesting question might be to ask what purpose the IBRC has in fact served in the 20 or so years of its existence. As a general principle it may be said that certification arrangements, if they become established and popular, can help to raise standards by raising awareness of quality issues and allowing for an informed debate about them within the industry. This in turn may lead to greater consumer awareness, to the point where membership of the certifying body becomes a general consumer expectation. In the case of the IBRC it is far from clear that any of this has happened.

Complaints-handling Schemes

It is open to debate whether complaints-handling mechanisms such as ombudsman schemes should be regarded as part of the regulatory apparatus. These schemes are clearly distinguishable from other bodies considered here in that they act only *ex post facto* and deal with specific cases rather than addressing general principles. It is not a formal part of their agenda to be involved in setting and maintaining general standards. On the other hand this formalistic account of the rules of these schemes may justly be regarded as somewhat unrealistic. First, it is clear that more traditional regulatory agencies may also have a disciplinary function which is exercised in relation to particular cases, even if that is not their primary function. Secondly, there can be no doubt that the pronouncements of the various ombudsmen active in this sector do in practice have the effect of laying down standards which are of general importance—the industries concerned take note of what the ombudsmen say and adjust their complaints-handling procedures accordingly. For these reasons the ombudsman schemes will be treated in the present context as forming part of the regulatory apparatus, though account will obviously be taken of the limitations of their regulatory role.

So far as insurance is concerned, there are at present two schemes of significance.[27] These are the Insurance Ombudsman Bureau (IOB) and the Personal Investment Authority Ombudsman Bureau (PIAOB).[28] The workings of the schemes will be described only very briefly here.[29] Both offer policyholders a service, free to them and funded by the industry, in which they can seek relatively quick and informal consideration of their complaints against their insurance companies.[30] Decisions of the ombudsmen are binding on the member companies (up to £100,000) but not on policyholders, who may reject those decisions and go to court if they prefer. The IOB, but not the PIAOB, has an

---

[27] A small number of companies are party to the Personal Injury Arbitration Service. For discussion of this see Cadogan and Lewis (1991) 1 *Ins L & P* 109; Bridges-Adams [1998] *NLJ* 755.

[28] The author is a member of the Council of this scheme, but writes in a personal capacity.

[29] For a fuller account of the IOB see A. McGee, *The Financial Services Ombudsmen* (London, Fourmat, 1992).

[30] But not complaints against a company with which they are not insured.

obligation to make a decision which is fair and reasonable in all the circumstances, even if this means departing from strict legal rules. The IOB dates from 1981, the PIAOB from 1994. Both have seen steady increases in their workloads over the years.[31] Membership of the IOB is voluntary (though nearly all major general insurers are members) but membership of PIAOB is compulsory for all PIA members. The practical impact of these schemes is difficult to assess, not least since any changes in culture which they have generated will by their nature be dispersed among product providers generally. Moreover, even those providers whose behaviour has been changed by contact with the ombudsman schemes may not always be willing to admit the fact.

The above sketch does no more than explain the general outlines of the regulatory system for insurance in the UK. Clearly the system is fragmented. Some of it depends on EC legislation, some depends on purely domestic legislation, other parts reflect the traditional UK preference for some form of self-regulation. It could not be claimed that there is any overall coherent pattern of regulation. This is no doubt partly explained by the *ad hoc* way in which the system has grown up, but it may also be relevant to observe that different parts of the regulatory structure address quite different objectives. That observation leads conveniently into an examination of the successes and failures of the present system.

PART III: AN EVALUATION OF THE SYSTEM

It is usually easy to write about the failures of any system, less so to write about its successes—good news is no news—and it is often thought that successful regulation offers no lessons. Despite that, it is important to say at the start of this part that the failures of the system appear to occur in one specific area, namely the selling of investment insurance policies and pension policies. The requirements of prior authorisation of insurers, coupled with ongoing monitoring, appear to work well. Certainly it has been some time since there has been a major insurance company failure within the UK. Where companies have got into financial difficulties, the matter has generally been resolved by encouraging them to merge with others. The provisions of the Policyholders Protection Act 1975 are also available to give policyholders some measure of relief from the consequences of failure when this cannot be avoided.

It is difficulty to judge the success or otherwise of the Insurance Brokers Registration Act 1977. Since the system it creates is a purely voluntary one, any failure, financial or otherwise, on the part of a general insurance broker cannot by itself be counted as an example of regulatory failure. In any event the aim of the 1977 Act is clearly exhortatory rather than regulatory in the strict sense.

---

[31] Though the IOB naturally suffered a decline in 1995, after investment cases were hived off to the PIAOB. Its load for the relevant years was 1993 6,344; 1994 8,500; 1995 6,438.

That leaves the Financial Services Act 1986. As explained above, this Act was intended to regulate the marketing and selling of investment policies. In particular, the relevant provisions of the Act were motivated by a desire to clean up an industry which had come to be perceived as a regulatory problem. However, since the coming into force of the Act there has been at least one major problem in relation to the selling of pension policies. The introduction in July 1988 of personal pensions was welcomed by the insurance industry as an opportunity to sell pension plans linked with life assurance policies. Unfortunately, for many prospective policyholders the taking out of a personal pension meant leaving their existing defined benefits scheme (usually an occupational scheme). This scheme would have given them guaranteed benefits, the level of which was boosted by a contribution (often substantial) from their employers. For many, perhaps most, it was unlikely that the returns from a money purchase scheme could ever hope to match the benefits in the scheme which they were induced to leave. The enormous levels of pension misselling which resulted[32] are still in the process of being resolved by the industry. The detailed issues about the pensions review lie outside the scope of this essay, but what is clear is that the episode as a whole is a serious instance of regulatory failure. Indeed, there is a widespread perception within the financial services sector as a whole that the 1986 Act has been a failure. However, there is serious disagreement about the nature of that failure and the reasons for it. The industry view at the time was that the Act was unduly prescriptive in its approach and failed to respect adequately the tradition of self-regulation in this sector. It was also said that the idea of having detailed rulebooks for each of the areas of activity was likely to prove unwieldy and unworkable. The second objection proved to have some force in it, as was recognised at a later stage when the rulebooks were greatly simplified on the adoption of a set of Core Conduct of Business Rules.[33] The first objection is more contentious, since it goes to the broader question of whether the industry was in need of tighter regulation or whether self-regulation had proved broadly effective. On the part of the consumer lobby there was a strongly-held view that the previous regulatory system had proved inadequate and that something stricter was needed. Such a clash of ideologies is hardly new; what is more surprising is that there is now general agreement that the 1986 Act has not solved the fundamental problems.[34] At present the issues are perceived as mainly lying in the structure of the regulatory system. It is for this reason that the system is now in the process of yet another overhaul. Legislation in the pipeline will create a Financial Services Authority to take over all the functions of the existing SROs in an effort to centralise the whole system under a single regulator. It appears likely that the new system will become operational some time in late 1999. Although the coherence which this promises to bring can only be

---

[32] Estimates of the scale of this problem vary, but PIA has estimated that the total cost of compensating those who have suffered loss from misselling might be as high as £5bn.

[33] See A. McGee, "The SIB Core Conduct of Business Rules" (1992) 13 *Company Lawyer* 129.

[34] For a governmental view see Alistair Darling (1996) 4 *Int ILR* 171.

welcomed, it is still open to doubt whether having a single regulator really addresses the fundamental problems in this area. The nature of these problems is well-known. The industry suffers fundamentally from over-capacity, so that there is pressure on product providers either to steal business from each other or to boost the overall size of the market by selling policies to those for whom they are not truly suitable. Moreover, the practice of paying salespeople wholly or mainly on the basis of commission creates undesirable pressures on those individuals to sell policies without regard to the needs of purchasers. At the same time the number and character of potential purchasers has changed significantly in recent years. This is a consequence of the trend of the past 20 years towards encouraging individuals to take greater responsibility for their own financial planning (especially in relation to retirement) coupled with increasing levels of affluence, which have led to more people having enough disposable income to be in a position to think seriously about buying investment-type products. Where at one time it was reasonably safe to assume that potential purchasers were reasonably sophisticated individuals of above-average intelligence and education, it must now be recognised that increasingly there are purchasers in the market who lack these characteristics. The point is of major importance because in earlier times it was reasonable to assume that purchasers were well capable of looking out for their own interests, whereas it is clear that there is now a class of purchasers who understand relatively little of what they are buying and are certainly not able to make a reasoned judgement about the suitability (absolute or relative) for their needs of any product which may be offered to them. This is a point which seems to have had relatively little attention in consideration of the problems of this area, though it is suggested that it ought to be regarded as one which has major impact. From the point of view of regulatory theory it may be said that the situation of relatively sophisticated sellers providing a highly complex product to purchasers, some of whom really need the product but for some of whom it is at best an irrelevance, is a classic case of market failure in the sense of an information deficit. The sellers are well-equipped to know what is appropriate, but the buyers are not and must therefore rely on the advice of the sellers, who have a vested interest in selling as much of the product as possible. This description of the market in investment insurance products is undeniably redolent of the market for other forms of professional services in which advice plays a large part. Indeed, the description might equally be said to apply to legal services, for example. If this point is accepted, then it is instructive to compare the way in which those services are regulated. In broad outline it may be said that in the case of legal services the underlying assumption is that there is a situation of inequality of expertise between provider and purchaser, such that providers must be subject to quite stringent regulation. First, there are strict entry barriers to the legal profession, designed to ensure a high level of competence and probity. Secondly, there are significant ongoing disciplinary arrangements. Thirdly, and perhaps most importantly of all, the rules of professional conduct make it quite clear that the relationship between provider and purchaser is a fiduciary one, in which the provider is required at all times to consider the best interests of the purchaser and to put those interests before his own. This is perhaps the most important feature which distinguishes the conduct of a profession from that of a mere business. If this analysis is then applied to the financial services sector, it can be seen that the sector falls short of professional standards of regulation in certain respects. First, the entry standards are still relatively low. There are now some minimum training requirements for those wishing to sell investment policies,[35] though the standards required fall far short of what is expected of legal practitioners. It goes without saying that entry requirements for any profession have to be set at levels appropriate to the activities of that profession, and it might of course be argued that the level of competence required in order to sell investment policies is much lower than that required to be a legal practitioner. The point is a fair one, but it does not follow that no competence is needed, and it is legitimate to ask whether the current levels of training are in fact sufficient to ensure proper professional competence. The second element of the regulation of the legal profession identified above is the existence of ongoing disciplinary requirements. These are certainly in place for those selling investment insurance policies, since there is an ongoing requirement for authorisation, and that authorisation can be withdrawn at any time if it appears that the salesperson has ceased to be a fit and proper person for the job. It is fair to say that the withdrawal of authorisation is quite a common event—this is an aspect of the disciplinary process which is invoked fairly readily. The third element of professional regulation identified above is the existence of a fiduciary relationship between provider and purchaser. This is certainly not found in the context of financial services. The rules on the duty owed by providers to purchasers are complex and need to be examined carefully.

The FSA created a new regime for the marketing and selling of investment policies. This regime was superimposed on the existing common law system, which was not declared to be inapplicable in cases involving investment policies. The logic of this rather curious arrangement appears to be that a proposer or policyholder can take advantage of whichever of the two regimes, common law or statutory, offers the best prospects of success in any given case. However, in order to understand the duties of the agent and thus the rights of the proposer, it is necessary to consider carefully the position under the FSA.

The basic concept employed in the FSA is that of *polarisation*, which means that insurance intermediaries either must be the agent of one single product provider or must be completely independent of all product providers. This concept merely embodies in its most rigorous form the distinction previously alluded to between agents and brokers, though the FSA uses the terminology of Company Representatives (commonly called tied agents) and Independent Financial Advisers ("IFAs").

---

[35] Under PIA Rules such representatives are required to have undertaken an approved training scheme, normally the Financial Planning Certificate.

The position of the IFA under the FSA is clearly a difficult one. His independent status requires him to give impartial advice to his clients about the difficult questions identified above. He needs to have a very wide-ranging knowledge of all products on the market and to be able to compare them intelligently and to relate that comparison to the particular needs of his client. There can be no doubt that his obligation is to behave in a truly professional fashion, and one of the strongest ways to demonstrate this is by considering the position of the IFA who concludes that his client's interests would be best served by not buying any investment product at all. If he gives this advice and it is accepted, the IFA will earn no commission, since commission is paid only on investment products. Nevertheless, it is abundantly clear that the IFA's duty is to give exactly that advice.

The position of the tied agent is radically different. Polarisation requires him to represent only one company (or group of companies owned by the same parent company). This is a very strict rule, for the tied agent is not allowed to recommend the products of any other company; indeed, he is not even allowed to comment on the merits or otherwise of any such products. The latter rule was introduced in an effort to prevent tied agents from making disparaging remarks about rival products, but it also has the effect of prohibiting any complimentary remarks.

Why is There a Problem?

Reference has already been made to the large number of complaints concerning alleged misselling of investment policies. Two related issues arise. The first is why there are so many complaints, and the second is why these complaints are so often difficult to resolve. Only the second of these will be considered here.

At the present time the major source of contention turns on a point which might be regarded as being one of mere detail, but which in fact goes to the heart of the issue of regulation of investment policies, namely the notion of the "suitability" or otherwise of policies. This question may be divided into two parts. The first is whether the intermediary could have recommended a more suitable policy within the same company, whilst the second is whether an investment policy of any kind was suitable.

More Suitable Policy Available

The PIA Rules say that a tied agent must not recommend a particular policy unless he is satisfied that no other product offered by his company would be more suitable to the needs of the investor. Evidently, this raises the problem of comparative evaluation of products in relation to particular investors, which is not necessarily a straightforward matter. In regard to comparisons between different life policies, the issue most commonly arising is that of the length of the policy. Most companies offer policies ranging from ten years (five in a few cases) to 25 years, and even policies which can continue throughout the lifetime of the policyholder ("whole-of-life policies"). Naturally, the longer the policy continues, the more money the company can expect to make and the greater the commission paid to the agent. This increased commission is in effect paid for by the policyholder, who will find that in a longer policy the time taken to pay off the commission and accumulate some value in the policy is greater. This means that the policyholder is locked into the policy for a considerable period if he wishes to avoid making a loss on the transaction. The tied agent naturally has an incentive to sell the longest possible policy, but this may well not be in the best interests of the investor: not all investors can legitimately make a commitment to go on paying into a savings policy every month for 25 years, since changes in their lives over that period may make it impossible to keep up the payments. Inevitably, there are more than a few cases of investors who have to allow policies to lapse and who thereupon find that they will receive poor value for their investment. Given modern changes in working patterns, which mean that fewer people will be in work constantly throughout their adult lives, it is not surprising that cases of this kind happen. Nor is it surprising to find the PIA Ombudsman increasingly reluctant to uphold sales of policies over ten years. It may be observed, however, that the problem could be largely eliminated if commission structures were redesigned to take away the incentive to sell longer-term policies.

No Investment Policy Suitable

The question here is whether there is any situation (and if so, what) in which an investor's needs would be better suited by some investment vehicle other than an investment contract, but in which an investment contract is nevertheless "suitable" for that investor within the meaning of the PIA rules?

At first sight it might seem obvious that the question must be answered in the negative, since there is an obvious and attractive argument that the policy is not suitable if there is something else which would be better. There are, however, some difficulties with this simple approach. First, at the simple level of construction it is to be observed that the requirement is not that the policy be "the most suitable", but merely that it be "suitable". Secondly, the argument effectively conflates the duties of a tied agent with those of an IFA, whereas it was apparently the intention of the FSA to draw a sharp distinction between the two groups. Thirdly, it may be said that the argument seeks to impose on the tied agents a duty which the FSA actually forbids him to perform, since under this theory it would be necessary for the tied agent to be familiar with the products of other companies and with alternative investment vehicles, even though he is not allowed to sell them, to advise the investor to buy them or even to compare their advantages and disadvantages with those of the products which he does sell. Thus, the agent would have to decline to recommend a policy (presumably this would mean declining to recommend any policy sold by his company) but would have to refuse to give any detailed explanation for that refusal, even if pressed by the investor. Fourthly, it must be observed that this theory is completely at odds with the practice of the entire insurance industry. Of course that fact does not by itself invalidate the theory, but it does show just how radical a contention it is. In effect, accepting that the policy can never be suitable in such a case involves imposing on tied agents exactly the kind of fiduciary duty which was discussed earlier in the context of legal services. It is for this reason that the question is rightly to be regarded as fundamental. So long as it is accepted that the sale of a policy in these circumstances can possibly be legitimate, it will remain clear that the selling of investment policies is a business rather than a profession. Yet, to acknowledge that such sales are always missales will have far-reaching effects on the industry. Quite apart from the need to re-conceive the role of the tied agent, there is the problem that this approach would significantly reduce the number of investment policies sold—to put it in the simplest terms, many people who currently buy investment policies would be advised by the tied agent to put the money in the building society instead.

The two types of case considered here illustrate the crux of the problem of regulating this area. The culture of the industry and its financial circumstances dictate one solution, whereas a rational consideration of the objectives of regulation dictates an alternative and totally opposite solution. Much of the ongoing difficulty in this area results from the clash between these two approaches.

PART IV: SOLUTIONS

It has been argued above that the major problem lies in the failure of the industry to adapt its notions of customer relations and customer service to the changing character of its market and to increasing consumer expectations. The question is, to what extent can regulatory mechanisms address this failure. It is important to remember that legal regulation is not the only determining factor in the way an industry works. There are also important issues about the culture of that industry. Obviously, legal regulation can contribute to changes in culture, but these changes will be greatly diluted and delayed if they go against the grain of opinion within the industry at the relevant time. Thus, changing the mindsets of those who lead opinion within the industry is also essential and must accompany (or even precede) attempts to change behaviour patterns by legislation. The history of the FSA 1986 clearly shows this. As has been explained above, that is an Act which, together with its delegated legislation, lays down quite strict rules of conduct in relation to the selling of investment policies. Yet no one could seriously claim that the years since the coming into force of the Act have seen a major improvement in the standards of conduct of insurance salespeople. A cynic might suggest that the major effect of the Act has been that the misselling which has gone on has been exposed a few years afterwards, whereas under the old law it might never have been exposed. Of course, even this might fairly be regarded as progress, and it cannot be denied that the pensions side of the financial services sector, in particular, is currently making major efforts to clean up the damage left by the misselling of pensions in the late 1980's and early 1990s. However, the continuing high level of complaints to the PIA Ombudsman[36] tends to undermine the view that general standards of behaviour have risen significantly.[37]

It would appear that either of two conclusions might be drawn from this. The first is that legislation is irrelevant in raising standards in the industry, whilst the second is that legislation can be relevant to this task, but the particular legislation was not suited to the task or was ill-timed. It is submitted that the first of these arguments should be rejected. If it is accepted that legislation is in principle capable of contributing to culture change, then there is no obvious reason why the insurance industry should be a fundamental exception to that general rule. It is much more likely that the legislation was ill-designed or ill-timed.

On the question of design, a number of problematic features may be identified. First, the FSA is undeniably complex in structure and in detail. It created a plethora of regulatory authorities, and the rules adopted for these authorities were themselves detailed and complex. A criticism made by the industry at the time was that these rules failed to see the wood for the trees and were inflexible. Given the wide range of situations which could arise, it was suggested that it would have been preferable to write the rules in more general terms, laying down principles rather than trying to cover every possible case. There is no doubt some force in these arguments, but the obvious counter-argument is that this would have involved vesting considerable discretion in the industry itself, and this appeared to be ruled out by the very problems which gave rise to the Act.

This is turn leads on to the more fundamental point that the FSA involved a departure from traditional principles of self-regulation. Historically this industry had been allowed to regulate its own affairs, including its rules of conduct, on the assumption that it could be trusted to do so effectively. The philosophy of the FSA is incompatible with this approach. This was a change in approach which caused great hostility at the time. It raises a question of the highest importance about the problems of approaches to regulation in industries which have traditionally been self-regulated. In such industries the end of self-regulation is naturally greeted with suspicion and even outright hostility. It does not follow that the change is unjustified, but it seems unlikely that the change can simply be imposed without substantial efforts at justification and explanation. It may

[36] In 1994–5 (its first year, which began on 18 July 1994) PIAOB received 330 complaints. In 1995–6 the figure was 2,717; in 1996–7 4,310 and in 1997–8 5,800 (Annual Reports for the respective years).

[37] Naturally, not all such complaints are justified, but the level of complaints is obviously rising (see previous n.), though the proportion which are upheld declined in 1997–8 to 38%, having run in the region of 45–50% in earlier years: see the successive PIAOB Reports mentioned in the previous n.

be that at the time of the FSA too little of this was done, though it may also be said that the level of hostility of the industry was such that no amount of ratiocination at the time could have done much to dilute it. That hostility led to sustained unwillingness by the industry to take on board the underlying principles of the new legislation. This can in part be blamed on the industry, but it appears that the principles were not sufficiently spelled out at the time. The saga of the pensions misselling scandal is sadly illuminating in this regard. It will be remembered that new-style personal pensions became available on 1 July 1988, whilst A-Day for the FSA was 28 April 1988. Thus, from a purely formalistic point of view there was no justification for any salesperson to sell these pensions on the basis of the old standards of conduct. Yet it is quite clear that that is exactly what happened. It is perhaps not surprising that the industry should have failed to adapt to the new regime within three months, but it is more surprising that the misselling should have continued on such a scale for so long afterwards. It is also clear that misselling was by no means limited to pensions. During the period 1990–4[38] the largest single ground of complaint to the Insurance Ombudsman was of the misselling of investment policies.[39] Although some of those cases related to events which had happened before A-Day, many did not. It was impossible at that time to observe any pattern which would have suggested that the FSA was likely to result in a fall in the volume of complaints.

The conclusion to be drawn from this is that legislation was never likely to be effective unless accompanied by a serious effort to change expectations. However, that effort might well have taken an unacceptably long time if it had to be undertaken prior to the legislation. The answer would seem to lie in legislation accompanied by education. What seems to have happened is that there was legislation as a substitute for education. The period since the coming into force of the FSA has been one of painful re-education for many major product providers. In 1998 there are at least some signs that some of the lessons have been learned. More and more providers are seeking to move away from a commission-based remuneration system to a proper professional salary system. There is also a slow reduction in the number of product providers, a necessary process if the over-capacity in the industry is to be eliminated. The training schemes in use in the industry are producing tied agents who are at least more aware of their responsibilities.

At the same time very serious problems remain. The volume of complaints to the PIA Ombudsman continues to rise,[40] whilst the pressure to sell investment policies, especially pension policies, is unabated.

A number of possible specific reforms may usefully be identified. The first is the abolition of the commission system. Some product providers have recently

---

[38] This pre-dates the introduction of PIA; during this time complaints about investment insurance policies went to the IOB. The author personally handled about 200 such cases while working as Legal consultant to the Insurance Ombudsman during that period.

[39] See the IOB Reports for the respective years.

[40] See n. 36 above.

begun to experiment with this solution. It offers the obvious advantage that individuals are no longer presented with the same incentive to sell products regardless of circumstances and of the dictates of proper professional behaviour. The other side of the equation is that the elimination of misselling will result in a reduction in the total level of sales. Since sales staff are effectively paid for out of the profits of selling (whether on a formal commission basis or not) the long-term result must be a reduction in the number of sales staff. This will be a part of the process of slimming down the industry to a level which is sustainable in the long run. From a regulatory point of view and from a consumer point of view this is a necessary and desirable process. But it must be recognised that it will result in job losses among sales staff.[41]

The second possible reform is the imposition of much stricter control on the nature of the products which may be sold. There is no realistic prospect of enabling the average purchaser of an investment policy to understand the complexities of existing products. However, if prior authorisation of investment products were required, it would be possible to take a restrictive approach, so as to ensure that there was only a small range of products on the market, and that these products were relatively simple, flexible and likely to suit the needs of at least the great majority of investors. On the face of it the major argument against this solution is that it would tend to reduce both competition and innovation. In reality, competition in this sector does not take place in any meaningful form, since that would require investors able to make an informed choice between products: the impossibility of achieving that has already been explained. Innovation would to some extent be reduced, but a critical observer of the financial services sector over the past decade might well conclude that much of the innovation has been in the development of products which are increasingly complex without necessarily being any more suited to the needs of investors. Although prior authorisation of products would go entirely against the traditions of financial services regulation in the UK, it is suggested that it merits serious consideration as a way forward. This is a situation where the need of investors for suitable and comprehensible products ought to be allowed to prevail over the wish of the providers to offer more varied and complex products.

Both the suggestions made above may justly be regarded as radical. The Financial Services Authority has certainly not as yet given any evidence of a willingness to take so radical an approach. It is of course early days (the FSA will not begin to exercise formal powers until 1999 at the earliest) but the practice of cautious, incremental regulation of the industry, conducted so as not to alarm practitioners unduly, is ingrained in financial services regulation in the UK, and it may legitimately be doubted whether the FSA will feel able to be so radical. If it does not, then the process of dragging the industry into the twenty-first century is likely to be both painful and slow.

---

[41] In practice it is likely that these can be absorbed by natural wastage, since most companies turn over about 80% of their individual tied agents each year.

8

Regulating Industrial and Provident Societies: Co-operation and Community Benefit

IAN SNAITH[1]

1. INTRODUCTORY

This essay begins by examining, in this first section, the legislative history and modern range of industrial and provident societies. Section 2 deals with their most significant features as legal structures for business; section 3 considers the role of the regulator and section 4 analyses the prospects for law reform and the direction it is likely to take. Comparisons are made throughout with the legal regime governing registered companies.

1.1. History[2]

The origin of the term "industrial and provident society" is unclear. E.W. Brabrook, a former Registrar of Friendly Societies, has said that the term indicated that the societies were intended to be "industrial as making their profits by the mutual exertion of the members and provident as distributing their profits by way of a provision for the future".[3] If this was ever true, it does not feature in the current legal definitions in any way which affects the operation of societies. The only meaningful definition of an industrial and provident society under the current law is of a society "for carrying on any industry, business or trade" (section 1(1)) which is either a *bona fide* co-operative or conducts or intends to conduct its business for the benefit of the community (section 1(2)). These matters are discussed more fully below but indicate the redundancy of the words "industrial and provident" for practical legal purposes. In addition, the

---

[1] MA, FSALS, Solicitor, Senior Lecturer and Ironsides Fellow in Law at the University of Leicester, Consultant with Cobbetts Solicitors, Manchester.
[2] See I. Snaith, *Handbook of Industrial and Provident Society Law* (Manchester, Holyoake Books, 1993) sect. 2.1. and I. Snaith, "Co-operative Principles and UK Co-operative Law Reform" 29 *Journal of Co-operative Studies* 48 at 48–51.
[3] E.W. Brabrooke, *Provident Societies and Industrial Welfare* (London, Blackie and Son 1898) 3.

concept is not generally used in discussion outside the legal field as societies will be known as co-operatives, working men's clubs, housing associations and so on. However, the history of the legislation governing these societies gives some indication of the needs of the societies for which it was designed and of a continuing, if gradual, tendency towards deregulation.

In 1852, the industrial and provident society emerged from existing friendly society legislation as a result of the efforts of the early co-operative movement in alliance with leading Christian Socialists. A series of Acts dating from 1793 acknowledged the existence of, and gave some protection to, friendly societies—the mutual insurance providers which provided contributory benefits in cases of sickness, death or bereavement. In 1834 and 1846 further Friendly Societies Acts were passed which permitted the registration of trading societies such as co-operatives operating in the retail trade, but they were not designed for them. Societies could trade only with their own members, could not own land and could own other property only through trustees. As a result, the consumer and worker co-operatives which sprang up in the 1840s required a separate legal framework and campaigned for new legislation.

In 1852 the first Industrial and Provident Societies Act (IPSA) became law. The Act provided that societies could be established for "carrying on or exercising in common any labour, trade or handicraft, except the working of mines, minerals or quarries beyond the limits of the United Kingdom and except the business of banking whether in the United Kingdom or not". However, the Act conferred neither limited liability on members nor corporate personality on the society. The 1852 Act was amended in minor respects in both 1854 and 1856 but the Industrial and Provident Societies Act 1862 remains the model for later legislation dealing with societies. It repealed the three previous Acts, re-enacted many of their features and gave societies wider powers.

For the first time societies were given corporate personality separate from their members and so could sue and be sued in their own name, own property without trustees and become members or shareholders in other societies or companies. The Act also conferred limited liability on their members on exactly the same terms as were applied to companies. Members were not to be liable for the debts of the society beyond the amount unpaid on their shares, and their liability ceased altogether a year after their withdrawal from the society.

Like a company, an industrial and provident society was required to meet disclosure requirements in return for the limited liability of its members. It had to have a registered office, to provide a copy of its rules to any person who demanded it, to permit the inspection of certain books and registers by members and persons with an interest in its funds and to make an annual return to the registrar. This took account of the fact that these trading organisations dealt with people other than their own members whether as suppliers, lenders or employees.

In 1876 and 1893 consolidating Acts were passed to give industrial and provident societies a separate legislative base. The framework of the current legislation was provided by the 1876 Act. The Act of 1893 further consolidated the legislation and stood as the principal Industrial and Provident Societies Act for 72 years.

The Prevention of Fraud (Investments) Act 1939 limited the range of organisations which could register under the Industrial and Provident Societies Act to *bona fide* co-operative societies, societies for improving the conditions and the social wellbeing of members of the working classes and societies for the benefit of the community generally. Thus the key concept that this legislation should be available only for co-operatives or societies operating for the benefit of the community was introduced as a measure to prevent their use as a vehicle for share pushing schemes.

The current legislation—the Industrial and Provident Societies Act (IPSA) 1965—brought together in one statute all the legislation from 1893 to 1965 but made very few changes to the law. It reduced the range of societies that may register under it to *bona fide* co-operative societies and societies for the benefit of the community.

Since 1965 a number of changes have been made by later legislation, but the 1965 Act remains the principal measure governing societies. The Industrial and Provident Societies Act 1967 was passed to permit societies to borrow on the security of a floating charge. Before the Act, English societies were held to be unable to give such charges because of the decision in *Great Northern Railway Company* v. *Coal Co-operative Society*[4] that the exemption in the Bills of Sale Acts for companies was inapplicable to societies. This meant that, due to the practical impossibility of registering a document creating a floating charge under the Bills of Sale Acts, a society, unlike a company, was unable to grant such a charge. In Scotland, the concept of the floating charge was not recognised at all until 1961 and consequently societies could not provide that form of security. The 1967 Act provided a system of registration for societies in both jurisdictions—in England by disapplying the Bills of Sale Acts on the basis of the registration of a document creating a floating charge, and in Scotland by incorporating the provisions of the Companies (Floating Charges) (Scotland) Act 1961.

The Friendly and Industrial and Provident Societies Act 1968 established new rules governing the accounts that societies are required to prepare (including rules concerning group accounts), the submission of annual returns and the qualifications and rights of auditors. At the time of its passage the Act brought the law on these matters broadly into line with the law applicable to companies. Since 1968 the law on company accounts has undergone major change but the law applicable to societies is still governed by this Act.

The Industrial and Provident Societies Acts 1975 and 1978 dealt respectively with limits on the size of the shareholdings individual members are allowed to

---

[4] [1896] 1 Ch. 187; and see *Re North Wales Produce and Supply Society Ltd* [1922] 2 Ch. 340; by way of contrast, see Phillimore J's obiter disapproval of the *Great Northern Railway* decision in *Clark* v. *Balm, Hill and Co* [1908] 1 KB 667 at 670 and Lloyd J's support for the latter view in *Slavenburg's Bank* v. *Intercontinental Natural Resources Ltd* [1980] 1 WLR 1076 at 1097–8.

have in a society and on the scale of deposit-taking schemes that societies can operate. In each case the current limit was raised and power was conferred to make further changes to those limits by statutory instrument.

The Credit Unions Act 1979 set up a structure for the registration of credit unions as industrial and provident societies. A society registering under this Act is subject to the 1979 Act where it differs from the 1965 Act. The differences include the minimum membership required, the nature and uses of share capital, the society's powers and objects, its rights to hold land and its lending and investment powers. Credit unions are also subject to more stringent regulation than other societies because of their nature as financial institutions.

The 1980s produced no primary legislation principally concerned with societies. However, the Insolvency Act 1986 applies on the winding up of a society— including its provisions on liability for wrongful or fraudulent trading. However, it is uncertain whether the CDDA 1986 applies to society directors and the provisions about administration orders, voluntary arrangements and administrative receivership do not apply to insolvent societies.[5]

The Friendly Societies Act 1992 introduced a new but little-used route for social clubs registered under the Friendly Societies Act 1974 to re-register as industrial and provident societies and removed the registrar's statutory duty to provide an arbitration service for societies.

In 1996, two deregulation orders made under the Deregulation and Contracting Out Act 1994[6] amended the Industrial and Provident Societies Act 1965 and the Credit Unions Act 1979 to ease the burdens on societies and credit unions while dealing with some of the disadvantages they face compared with companies.

The Deregulation (Industrial and Provident Societies) Order 1996 SI 1996/1738 from 1st September 1996 reduced the minimum membership for non-federal societies from 7 to 3 and gave societies up to seven months from the end of their accounting period to submit an annual return. It also extended the time limit for registering charges on society assets from 14 to 21 days and allowed late submission without the need for a court order—subject to third party rights. To remove and discrepancy between the treatment of societies and that of companies, it permitted societies with turnover under £90,000 to opt out of any audit and those under £350,000 to opt out of a full audit of their accounts.

The Deregulation (Credit Unions) Order 1996 (SI 1996/1189) from 1 September 1996 allowed credit union membership to be based on either living or working in a locality and increased the shareholding limit for a credit union member to the higher of £5,000 and 1.5 per cent of the credit union's total shareholding and increased the limit on borrowing by a member of a credit union approved by the Registry for the purpose to the lower of £10,000 or an amount worked out by reference to the society's total shareholding or reserves.

---

[5] *Re Devon and Somerset Farmers Ltd* [1993] BCC 410, and see sect. 2.5. below.

[6] The Deregulation. (Industrial and Provident Societies) Order 1996 SI 1996/1738 and The Deregulation. (Credit Unions) Order 1996 SI 1996/1189.

A Consultation Paper published in May 1998 foreshadowed a number of other reforms to the IPSAs, including easier (and therefore cheaper) registration of societies and rule amendments by the use of a statutory declaration procedure; the application of the rescue procedures and director disqualification orders applicable to companies to insolvent societies; reform of the system of registration of charges to bring it into line with that applicable to companies and strengthening of the regulatory powers of the Registry of Friendly Societies. The reform of the system of regulation applicable to the financial services industry will involve the transfer of the Registry's functions to the Financial Services Authority, and this will include its function of registering societies simply as business organisations as well as the supervisory role it performs in respect of credit unions.[7]

1.2. The Current Range of Societies

The Annual Report of the Chief Registrar of Friendly Societies indicates the number and variety of registered societies. In 1996 there were 10,654 societies with 9.1 million members, £12 billion of members' funds and total assets of some £41.5 billion. Over the five years to 1996 the membership figures (subject to an increase in 1994), the nominal value of members' funds and the number of societies have consistently declined but the nominal value of assets (not adjusted to take account of inflation) has increased.[8]

The nature of the societies using the Acts can be analysed in at least two ways. The IPSAs provide a business structure used by two types of organisation: *bona fide* co-operatives and businesses conducted for the benefit of the community. This legal typology is considered in detail below.[9] However, it encompasses a wide range of business or not for profit activities in various economic sectors and the statistical information provided in the annual reports of the Chief Registrar of Friendly Societies is collected and published by reference to activities. The following table (on p. 168) and accompanying text derived from the Report of the Chief Registrar[10] indicates the distribution of societies, members and assets among the eight categories used to classify societies by reference to their activities.

The activities referred to in the Table are as follows:

A *credit union* is a savings and loan co-operative with a common bond (such as employment or residence) linking its members. It is registered under the Credit Unions Act 1979 as well as IPSA 1965. Members save by buying society shares and then borrow from the society at a low rate of interest.

---

[7] See sects. 3.3. and 4.2. below.

[8] *Report of the Chief Registrar of Friendly Societies 1996–7* (London, Registry of Friendly Societies, 1997), 35.

[9] Sect. 2.1.

[10] N. 8 above, 35.

Activity	Number of Societies	Number of Members	Value of Assets
Credit Unions	550	191,000	£100,348,000
Retail	127	5,965,000	£2,595,902,000
Wholesale	127	45,000	£1,434,757,000
Agriculture	958	251,000	£744,790,000
Fishery	83	4,000	£19,819,000
Clubs	3,662	2,089,000	£552,350,000
Housing	3,985	176,000	£19,156,844,000
General Services	1,109	407,000	£16,923,606,000

Retail societies run shops, supermarkets and department stores. The Registrar uses this category to cover both those societies which form part of the co-operative movement and other retail societies. Most of the societies in this category will be consumer co-operatives operated and run on the basis of co-operative principles with a membership consisting of those who buy from the co-operative at retail level. However, some employee-controlled co-operatives are also retail businesses but have employees as members and operate for their benefit rather than the benefit of consumer members. Consumer co-operatives do not usually restrict themselves to trading with members. They often have no system of recording purchases in a way which allows them to offer a distribution of surplus in accordance with transactions. However, their membership base is intended to be their customers.

Wholesale and productive societies are societies engaged in manufacturing or wholesaling. Many are secondary co-operatives which have other societies as their members and provide wholesale goods for retail societies or operate further along the chain of production or distribution to supply goods and services to their member societies. Others have either employee members or a co-partnership structure in which membership includes both employees and users of the society's services.

Agricultural societies include marketing and requisites co-operatives. Both operate in the field of agriculture with a membership composed of businesses involved in farming. They may be sole traders, partnerships, companies or other societies. A marketing co-operative will buy up the produce of its members to improve their collective bargaining position and gain economies of scale. Any surplus will either be invested in the co-operative's business or returned to members as a dividend on sales to the society. Requisites societies are effectively specialised consumer co-operatives operating for the mutual benefit of their farmer members. They obtain seed, fertiliser or agricultural equipment or supply services such as crop spraying or seed testing for their members and any surplus distribution will be on the basis of purchases from the society. Some societies in this category operate for the benefit of the community to develop agriculture or agricultural techniques.

Fishing societies provide services for those engaged in the fishing industry and operate on a similar basis to agricultural co-operatives.

Clubs which provide social and recreational facilities for their members can register under IPSA as an alternative to operating as unincorporated associations or companies limited by guarantee.

Housing societies include co-ownership societies which own houses or flats occupied and leased from the society by individual members. Self-build societies build houses for the occupation of their members by their co-operative efforts. These categories of society are likely to be registered as co-operatives operating for the mutual benefit of their members. However, the vast majority of registered housing societies are housing associations which aim to provide housing for those in need, often within a particular geographical area or for a defined class of persons such as the elderly. Those provided with housing do not control the society. These societies register as community benefit societies as they operate for the benefit of people other than their members.

General services societies represent a miscellaneous category which includes insurance and superannuation societies, co-operative development societies and residents' service societies.

2. KEY IDENTIFYING FEATURES OF SOCIETIES

This section considers in more detail the key identifying features of industrial and provident societies. In section 2.1. those requirements for registration which serve to distinguish these societies from other forms of business organisation are explored. In sections 2.2. to 2.5. the main characteristics of the legal regime governing registered societies and their corporate governance are compared with the rules applicable to registered companies.

2.1. Registration Requirements: Co-operatives and Community Benefit Societies

Section 1 of the IPSA 1965 permits the registration of a society if it meets certain requirements. Of these the two central criteria are that:

(a) It is "a society for carrying on any industry, business or trade (including dealings of any description with land), whether wholesale or retail" and
(b) Either
    (i) it is a *bona fide* co-operative society or
    (ii) in view of the fact that its business is being or is intended to be conducted for the benefit of the community, there are special reasons

why it should be registered as a society rather than as a company under the Companies Act 1985.[11]

In addition, its registered office must be in Great Britain or the Channel Islands, its rules must deal with all the matters listed in Schedule 1 to the IPSA 1965 and it must have at least three members (or two if they are both registered societies). A society with withdrawable share capital cannot be registered with the object of carrying on the business of banking.[12]

The requirement of an object of carrying on any "industry business or trade" is sufficiently wide to impose few restrictions on the societies which may be registered. However, section 1(3) of the Act provides that a society carrying on business with a view to making profits mainly for the payment of interest, dividends or bonuses on money invested with, lent to or deposited with the society or anyone else will not be regarded as a co-operative society. This makes the criteria of being a *bona fide* co-operative or conducting business for the benefit of the community the central registration requirements.

(a) The Nature of a Co-operative

The IPSA 1965 does not define a *"bona fide* co-operative" or, apart from the restriction in section 1(3), give any guidance on the interpretation of the phrase. That matter is left to the administrative discretion of the registrar. The Registry of Friendly Societies (RFS) has published guidelines on its criteria. It requires the co-operative's business to be conducted "for the mutual benefit of the members with the benefits they receive deriving mainly from their participation in the business".[13] The more detailed guidelines are based on what are now the first three of the seven co-operative principles agreed by the International Co-operative Alliance (ICA).[14] These principles have been developed from the practices of the "Rochdale Pioneers" from whose consumer co-operative, established in 1844, the modern co-operative movement dates its origins.[15]

The first principle requires that membership on a voluntary basis and without discrimination on gender, social, racial, political or religious grounds be open to anyone able to use the co-operative's services and willing to accept the responsibilities of membership. This applies to people within the group whose needs the co-operative is established to serve—consumers for consumer co-operatives, employees for workers' co-operatives, or tenants for housing co-

[11] Ss. 1(1)(a) and 2.
[12] Ss. 1(1), 2(1) and (2) and 7(1) and the Deregulation. (Industrial and Provident Societies) Order 1996, SI 1996/1738, arts. 3 and 4. Credit unions must meet different registration requirements under the Credit Unions Act 1979.
[13] N. 8 above, 38.
[14] See n. 2 above, sect. 3.3.
[15] See W.P. Watkins, *Co-operative Principles Today and Tomorrow* (Manchester, Holyoake Books, 1986), ch. 1; D.J. Thompson, *Weavers of Dreams* (University of California, Center for Co-operatives, Davis, Cal., 1994); and J. Birchall, "Co-operative Values and Principles: A Commentary" (1997) 30 *Journal of Co-operative Studies* 42.

operatives. This principle is intended to ensure that a group of existing members cannot exclude new members in order to increase their own claim on the assets and profits of the society.

The second principle provides that co-operatives are to be democratic organisations controlled by their members with elected representatives being accountable to the membership. In "primary" co-operatives this is to take the form of "one member one vote" while in secondary (or federal) co-operative organisations a more flexible concept of democratic organisation is required. This would permit voting by reference, for example, to purchases by retail society members from a "secondary" wholesale society. The key concern of this principle is that, in a primary co-operative, voting control is in the hands of members as such, and is not related to their capital contribution as would usually be the case in a registered company limited by shares.

The third principle relates to the society's capital structure and the economic participation of its members. It emphasises the democratic control by members of the co-operative's capital and that limited compensation, if any, is to be paid on capital subscribed as a condition of membership. Any surplus not used as reserves, for the development of the co-operative or supporting other activities approved by the membership, is to benefit members in proportion to their transactions with the co-operative. Thus any dividend distributed to members must be related to their transactions with the organisation and not to the scale of their capital stake. In a consumer co-operative this would relate to members' purchases from the society, for a workers' co-operative to their work contribution, or in a marketing co-operative to their sales to the society. This is linked to the concept that the members control the society by voting rights unrelated to their capital stake and emphasises the primacy of a membership benefiting from the co-operative's activities over suppliers of capital gaining a financial reward.

The remaining four ICA principles are of less importance in determining the legal structure of co-operative organisations. The fourth underlines the autonomy of co-operatives both from government and from external suppliers of capital. Co-operatives are to remain "autonomous self help organisations controlled by their members" and the terms of agreements with other bodies should reflect this. The importance of education and training for co-operative members, elected member representatives and employees and of informing the general public about the nature of co-operatives is acknowledged in the fifth principle. The sixth principle emphasises the value of co-operation among co-operatives through local, national, regional and international structures and the seventh notes their commitment to "the sustainable development of their communities". These matters must be permitted and facilitated by the legal structure, but do not otherwise determine its form.

The RFS has stated that the requirement that a society be a *bona fide* co-operative applies not only on first registration of the society or the registration of rule amendments or on an amalgamation of societies but also throughout the society's existence. The issue is not only whether the society's rules reflect the requirement but whether its business is run in accordance with co-operative principles or community benefit objectives. There may be some doubt about how far the registry is in practice able to police this operational requirement, but the policy clearly contemplates such an approach and in 1990 two societies were investigated on this basis.[16] It is clear that the registry would consider complaints by members that a society was no longer a *"bona fide* co-operative" and it has the power under sections 16 and 17 of the IPSA 1965 to suspend or cancel a society's registration on the ground that it appears to the registrar that the society is not a *bona fide* co-operative or a community benefit society.

(b) What is Community Benefit?

The focus of this requirement is on the benefit the society provides to people other than its own members and that its business will be in the interests of the community. It is also expected to have rules prohibiting distribution of its assets among members and to be non-profit-making. In addition, the co-operative requirements of member control and limited return on capital are usually applied.[17]

A key element in the statutory definition of societies to be permitted to register on this basis is that there should be "special reasons" for registration under the IPSA rather than the Companies Act (CA) 1985. This is linked to the community benefit requirement as it is "in view" of the conduct in the business to that end that the special reasons will be found. One could interpret this provisions as a statement of the fact that in view of the community benefit purpose there are "special reasons" for registration under the IPSA rather than the CA 1985. This would mean that once "community benefit" was established the special reason was also made out. However, the registry has tended to seek some additional special reason beyond the fact of community benefit, arguing that a company limited by guarantee can be used to achieve many of the features of a non-profit-making organisation which benefits persons other than its own members and prevents asset distribution to members. The exemption from the need to register an industrial and provident society with the Charities Commissioners and the power to pay interest gross without deduction of tax are among possible reasons.[18] It is submitted that the powers of the Registry to terminate the registration of a society not fulfilling the statutory requirements, as against the need for members of a company to seek court assistance to prevent inappropriate constitutional amendments, might also amount to a "special reason".

The inclusion of requirements about the substantive structure and objectives of a society as a condition of registration distinguishes industrial and provident

---

[16] N. 2 above, sect. 3.3. and *Report of the Chief Registrar of Friendly Societies 1989–90* (Registry of Friendly Societies, London, 1990) at para. 4.9.

[17] N. 8 above, 39.

[18] See *ibid.*, at 9 to 10 for a discussion of the application of the "special reason" rule to housing associations.

societies from registered companies. It permits and, indeed, requires the RFS to satisfy itself that those conditions are satisfied at the point of registration. It also empowers the registry to terminate registration if it takes the view that the relevant requirement is not satisfied. The policy justification for this approach is that the IPSA regime provides certain benefits not available to companies. Members of an industrial and provident society can be given the right to hold withdrawable share capital in a business organisation and to pass their shares and loan stock on death by nomination outside the general rules of testate and intestate succession. Societies can reorganise themselves and/or change the ownership of assets by conversion, amalgamation or transfer of engagements by special resolution or end their existence by instrument of dissolution signed by a proportion of the membership without either court order or a formal winding up process.[19]

The regime provides a form of registration intended to ensure that the cooperative or community benefit nature of the registered society is preserved, and to permit aggrieved members to look to the regulator for assistance if that status is threatened. This would not be possible in the case of a registered company if a sufficient majority chose to alter the nature of the organisation in a formally correct manner. Only the minority shareholder protection rights conferred by sections 459 to 461 of the Companies Act 1985 and the possibility of a just and equitable winding up under section 122(1)(g) of the Insolvency Act 1986 would be available to members with such concerns. Both of these remedies require court intervention. Since a minority of members of an industrial and provident society is unlikely to have a significant financial interest in litigating to protect the co-operative or community benefit nature of the society, the legislature has provided a regime whereby those values can be protected by the regulator so long as the society does not convert itself into a company.[20]

2.2. Corporate Personality, Capacity and Limited Liability

Once a society is registered under IPSA it becomes "a body corporate by its registered name in which it may sue and be sued, with perpetual succession and a common seal and with limited liability".[21] In this sense it has the same status and legal position as a company registered under the Companies Act 1985. However, due to the particular nature of these societies and the length of time since the IPSAs have been updated, there are a number of differences between societies and companies.

A minor anomaly affecting societies in this area is the continuing requirement that they have and use a seal. The liberalisation of formalities for the execution

---

[19] IPSA 1965, ss. 50–54 and 58.
[20] IPSA 1965, s. 52 permits this transformation or the amalgamation of a society with or a transfer of its engagements to a company—in each case by a 75% majority of those voting.
[21] IPSA 1965, s. 3.

of documents introduced for companies both in England and Wales and Scotland do not apply to societies.[22]

More significantly, the IPSAs contain no provisions equivalent to sections 35 to 35B of the Companies Act 1985 as amended by Companies Act 1989. As a result the *ultra vires* doctrine applied by the courts to companies applies to societies without any statutory modification.[23] Consequently, any contract or other act by a society which is outside the provisions of the objects set out in its rules raises severe legal problems. Such an act will be a breach of duty by the society's directors but may also affect the position of the other party to a contract. It seems that the use of a power conferred by the rules, for example to make a contract or to guarantee a debt, for a purpose outside the objects of the society would be unenforceable by the other party if it were aware of the purpose for which the power had been used. Likewise, the use of a power which does not exist at all under the society's rules will make the transaction unenforceable by the other party. On the other hand, the use of a power for a purpose beyond the rules in circumstances in which the other party was unaware of the incorrect purpose will not affect the enforceability of the transaction.[24]

This contrasts with the position of a registered company since the 1989 amendments to the Companies Act 1985. In that case acts cannot be questioned on the basis of lack of capacity due to any provision in the company's memorandum of association and a third party not proved to be acting in bad faith is also protected against any limitation in the company constitution on the powers of the directors to bind the company or to authorise others to do so.[25] As a result the capacity of industrial and provident societies is limited in a way that does not apply to companies—despite the fact that, in the case of co-operatives, the organisations are commercial organisations operating in the same market and circumstances as registered companies.

The limited liability of the members of societies is modelled closely on the equivalent provisions applicable to the members of companies.[26] The shares issued by societies are, however, potentially different in nature from the shares issued by registered companies. The legislation permits the rules of a society to determine whether the share capital held by members is to be withdrawable—a facility not available to registered companies.[27] Some of the largest registered co-operatives societies take advantage of this possibility.

The historical development of consumer co-operatives in the UK was based on the withdrawability of share capital. A member was permitted to deposit

[22] CA 1985, ss. 36A and 36B inserted by the CA 1989, s. 130(2) and the Requirements of Writing (Scotland) Act 1995, s. 14(1), 15 and Sched. 51 respectively.

[23] See *Ashbury Railway Carriage and Iron Company* v. *Riche* (1875) 7 HL 653 and *Rolled Steel Products (Holdings) Ltd* v. *British Steel Corporation* [1984] BCLC 466.

[24] *Halifax Building Society* v. *Chamberlain Martin Spurgeon* [1994] EGCS 41 and (1994) 11(4) *Construction Law Digest* CA at 21–23 and LEXIS.

[25] CA 1985, ss. 35 and 35A inserted by CA 1989, s. 108.

[26] Compare IPSA 1965, s. 57 with Insolvency Act 1986, s. 74.

[27] IPSA 1965, ss. 1(1)(b), 7 and Sched. 1 para. 9.

money in his or her share account or to have credited to it interest on share capital or amounts of dividend based on transactions with the society and to withdraw amounts from the account. The rules of the society would deal with the rights and duties of members in relation to their withdrawable shares and would usually include procedures whereby the board of the society could limit, delay or suspend the right of withdrawal in the event of a run on the society's funds.

When banking regulation in the UK was placed on a statutory footing by the Banking Act 1979, the problem arose that, in the absence of any special legislative provision, withdrawable share capital and any loan capital which operated on a similar basis would fall within the definition of a deposit for the purpose of the Banking Act and, indeed, was subject to the same risks as a bank deposit in the event of default on insolvency. As a result, a regime of exemption from the Banking Act for certain co-operatives was developed on the basis of the operation of a Co-operative Deposit Protection Scheme (CDPS) established by the Co-operative Union and the Co-operative Bank PLC. The Scheme has been continued under the Banking Act 1987 and is formally incorporated in regulations made by the Treasury.[28]

Although the withdrawable share capital of societies enjoys blanket exemption from the Banking Act 1987, any other form of deposit (such as loan capital) only enjoys exemption if the society participates in the CDPS. For those who participate in the CDPS, the protection of the scheme extends to withdrawable share capital.[29]

This has a peculiar result. The members/shareholders of these trading organisations enjoy protection beyond the usual limited liability of investors in company shares and holders of non-withdrawable shares in a society. Not only do the holders of withdrawable shares covered by CDPS avoid any loss beyond the amount unpaid on their shareholding, they also recover 90 per cent of the value of their shareholding from the scheme. This compares with the plight of the unsecured creditors who may receive little or nothing in the liquidation or receivership of the society. Indeed, in the case of the one consumer co-operative society to go into liquidation in recent years, the holders of withdrawable shares received 100 per cent of the value of their shareholding as the Co-operative Wholesale Society Ltd topped up the 75 per cent then available under the CDPS. This decision was motivated by the perception in the movement's central federal society that while the consumer co-operative movement consists of some 40 separate independent societies, the general public see the movement as a single entity. Consequently, a default in the repayment of withdrawable share capital on the liquidation of one society might cause a run on the withdrawable shares of all the others.

---

[28] Banking Act 1987, s. 4(4) and the Banking Act 1987 (Exempt Transactions) Regulations 1997, SI 1997/817, regs. 5 and 7 and Sched. 1.
[29] *Ibid.*

However, the contradiction involved in this situation is clear. The members who own the society and contribute its share capital do not perform the function of risk takers. They have the status of protected depositors—albeit the protection comes from contributions made to a mutual scheme by a range of societies. While this reflects the absence of the level of reward for risk taking available to the holders of equity in a registered company, it is odd that the owners of a mutual business outside the financial services or banking sector should receive this level of protection. This position may prove impossible to sustain after the current CDPS expires on 31 March 2000. As the number of consumer co-operative societies in the scheme decreases and the size of the remaining member societies grows the exposure of the scheme in the event of the insolvency of a society with a large amount of protected loan and share capital becomes harder to sustain.

2.3. Absence of Equity and Limited Return on Capital

The problems and anomalies introduced by the existence of the CDPS for those societies with withdrawable share capital were discussed in the last section. A more fundamental problem about the availability and cost of capital for societies arises from the very principles which define them and allow their registration in the first place.

The third co-operative principle is as follows:

> "Members contribute equitably to, and democratically control, the capital of their co-operative. At least part of that capital is usually the common property of the co-operative. members usually receive limited compensation, if any, on capital subscribed as a condition of membership. Members allocate surpluses for any of the following purposes: developing their co-operative, possibly by setting up reserves, part of which at least would be indivisible; benefiting members in proportion to their transactions with the co-operative; and supporting other activities approved by the membership".[30]

The guidelines issued by the registrar of Friendly Societies about qualifying to register as a "*bona fide* co-operative" under the Industrial and Provident Societies Act express this as follows:

> "(c) interest on capital will not exceed a rate necessary to obtain and retain sufficient capital to carry out the society's objects ;
> (d) profits, if distributable amongst the members, will be distributed in relation to the extent that members have either traded with or taken part in the society's business;
> (e) membership must not be artificially restricted with the aim of increasing the value of any proprietary rights and interests."[31]

---

[30] N. 2 above, sect. 3.3.
[31] N. 8 above, 39.

For "community benefit societies", factors taken into consideration by the Registrar in deciding whether to allow registration "are whether it is non-profitmaking, and whether its rules prohibit distribution of assets among members".[32]

These concepts are quoted at length because they represent at one and the same time a central element in the definition and purpose of an industrial and provident society and a significant constraint on its ability to raise capital. Since co-operative members are primarily seen as consumers, employees, tenants, borrowers etc., depending on the type of co-operative in question, any ultimate surplus generated by the business does not belong to members as shareholder/investors but the members as user/participants. Thus any distribution of dividend is to be related to transactions with the business—purchases by consumer members, hours worked by employee members etc.

As a result equity share capital is, by definition, never directly available to a co-operative. There can never be a class of shares whose holders are entitled to whatever remains after all other claims have been paid off. The withdrawable share capital used by consumer co-operative societies is one expression of this. Since the share can always be sold back to the society for par value and is not transferable other than on death, it can never be traded or increase in capital value. The return on it will be limited to interest payments, while any dividend paid from distributable profits will be proportionate to a member's transactions as a consumer and not to shareholdings. On the solvent dissolution of the society the rules may require that any surplus is transferred to another co-operative society (which in turn has, in its rules, a similar prohibition on distributions to individuals) or they may permit distribution to members in proportion to transactions with the society during a specific period fixed by the rules. They should not permit distribution of a surplus according to the level of a member's shareholding.

These restrictions prevent societies from issuing equity or ordinary shares whether they are to be listed on the Stock Market or not. They do not prevent an issue of listed loan stock. It may be that, if the rules of a society are silent on the destination of any final surplus after a solvent liquidation of the society, a loophole in the present legislation would permit the distribution of the surplus to members in proportion to their shareholding. This flows from the effect of section 55 of the IPSA 1965 which permits societies to be dissolved by the use of a resolution or order available to a company under the Insolvency Act 1986. So a winding up order or resolution can be used to dissolve a solvent society. When the destination of the ultimate surplus after the payment of all debts and the repayment of capital invested by shareholders is considered, section 107 of the Insolvency Act 1986 appears to apply so as to require distribution "among the members according to their rights and interests in the" society.

This section might well result in a distribution according to shareholding levels unless some other indication could be found in the society's rules on the

---

[32] *Ibid.*

"rights and interests" of members. One such provision might be the rule requiring the distribution of any dividend by reference to transactions or prohibiting such a distribution. However, if that rule expressly limited itself to a surplus of that kind, it might be held to be inapplicable to a winding up. Should a society use the alternative method of dissolution by an Instrument of Dissolution signed by 75 per cent of its members under section 58 of the IPSA 1965, that section provides for distribution according to the method stated in the instrument unless the instrument leaves that matter to the Chief Registrar. In both cases it seems that the distribution can only be among those entitled by law and not to a wholly different group.[33] Despite the uncertainty that may arise in a case in which a society's rules were silent on this question and a solvent dissolution by members' voluntary winding up or the use of an Instrument of Dissolution occurred, it is clear that the use of equity share capital in a society is not practical.

This may explain the absence from the IPSA 1965 of any of the statutory capital maintenance rules to be found in the Companies Act 1985. There is no reference to a subsidiary society holding shares in its holding society, financial assistance by a society for the acquisition of its own shares, issues of shares at a premium or at a discount, the nature or value of any non-cash consideration to be provided on the allotment of society shares, or, understandably in the light of the possibility of issuing withdrawable share capital, the purchase or redemption by a society of its own shares.[34]

The inability of societies to use equity as a means of raising capital may arise from the nature of the organisations permitted to register under the IPSAs. However, the absence of any statutory provisions for the maintenance of capital cannot be justified on this basis. The central rationale for such provisions is that the creditors of a body corporate whose members enjoy limited liability for the business debts need protection from the return of value to the shareholders ahead of the payment of creditors. This applies to societies just as it applies to companies. The implications of issuing shares at a discount overtly or by inadequate valuation of non-cash consideration provided for them, the problems associated with an absence of statutory rules about the availability of a surplus for distribution to members and the threat to creditors inherent in the withdrawal of share capital by members need regulation—albeit regulation tailored to the particular needs of mutual societies.

2.4. Corporate Governance

In this area a number of interesting comparisons can be made between societies and companies. Some differences between the two forms of business organisation arise from their different nature, others from differences of legislative

---

[33] *Re Buckinghamshire Constabulary Widows and Orphans Fund Friendly Society* [1978] 1 WLR 641.

[34] CA 1985, s. 23 and Parts IV and V; and note the exemptions for societies in many cases from the Public Offer of Securities Regulations 1995, SI 1995/1537, by reg. 7(2)(q)(ii) and (iii), (r) and (u).

approach. It is assumed here that the central issue is to ensure that both directors and executive managers perform in accordance with the interests of the
owner/members of a company or a co-operative or of the community served by
a "community benefit" society to optimise business efficiency and avoid shirk-
ing and self dealing. The centrality of "democratic control" in the definition of
a co-operative or a "community benefit" society does not alter the actual or
potential conflict of interest between owners and controllers. Societies with a
small membership which is not widely dispersed geographically may succeed in
holding executives and directors to account through general meetings, the statutory audit and the election of the board But problems similar to those identified
in large listed companies[35] will arise in societies with a large and widely dispersed membership. In this section the issues of legal duties; "voice" and "exit"
as member remedies and of self-regulation are addressed.

(a) Legal Duties and their Enforcement

The option of litigation to enforce the duties of directors or executives applies in
societies and companies. The directors of societies owe their society the common
law fiduciary duties and duty of care and skill developed by the courts in the context of companies.[36] Those duties will apply to them as board members in the light
of the function to be performed by those in that position in the particular society.

Senior executives or managers will be subject to the express and implied
duties owed to the society as a result of their contractual relationship with it. In
many cases, the executives, like their equivalents in companies, will also be
directors. In others, most noticeably consumer co-operatives, they will not be
board members but will, in practice, attend board meetings and play an important role in making and discussing both general policy and particular decisions.
They will also have powers delegated to them by the board in accordance with
the society's rules or powers flowing directly from the rules.[37] In such cases the
courts are likely to impose on non-director executives fiduciary obligations
appropriate to their actual relationship with the society and the board. In an
appropriate context, for example wrongful trading,[38] a non-director manager
or executive may qualify as a shadow director because s/he is "a person in accordance with whose directions or instructions the directors" are accustomed to
act.[39] In these respects the legal duties of directors and senior managers of societies are similar to those of company directors.

---

[35] A. Berle and G.C. Means, *The Modern Corporation and Private Property* (New York,
Macmillan, 1932) and see Bradley, "Corporate Control: Markets and Rules" (1990) 53 *MLR* 170.

[36] See n. 2 above, sect. 7.2.

[37] See C. Mills and I. Snaith, "Governance of Consumer Co-operatives: Rules and Realities"
(1997) 30 *Journal of Co-operative Studies* 70, and I. Snaith and R. Amass, "Corporate Governance
in Co-operatives: Lessons and Contrasts" (1998) Vol 1–2 Part 3 *Corporate Governance
International* 4.

[38] Insolvency Act 1986, s. 214.

[39] Insolvency Act 1986, s. 251.

They are, however, subject to more acute problems of enforcement should a minority of members wish to pursue this. As the duties are owed to the society, only the society will generally be permitted to enforce them in the courts in accordance with the well known rule in *Foss* v. *Harbottle*[40] and subject to its exceptions. However, the IPSA 1965 provides no equivalent to the statutory minority protection remedy afforded by sections 459 to 461 of the Companies Act 1985. This forces society members who believe that directors or senior executives have breached their duties to the society to pursue a just and equitable winding up or to approach the RFS to request administrative intervention.[41] In cases of fraud or the misapplication of society funds or property by a person holding them, a useful summary remedy is provided by the IPSA 1965 should the society or the RFS wish to pursue the matter.[42] In addition, as with registered companies, in a case of insolvency or change of control the office holder in the insolvency or the society itself may well sue former directors or executives for breaches of duty which could have been pursued only with difficulty by a minority of members.

Another omission from the armoury of societies seeking sound corporate governance by directors and executives is the absence from the IPSAs of provisions regulating society rules indemnifying directors against the consequences of a breach of duty or specific forms of self-dealing by directors or executives. The Companies Act 1985 regulates loans to directors, substantial property transactions with them, long service contracts and a failure to disclose an interest in a contract. Such provisions are to be found in the legislation governing building societies and friendly societies as well as in the Companies Act 1985.[43] The absence of such detailed regulation of self-dealing forces societies to rely on the more open textured common law duties which suffer from problems of interpretation and enforceability. Against this background we examine the application of the concepts of "voice" and "exit" to the role of society members.

(b) "Voice" and "Exit"

A fundamental feature of the corporate governance debate as it applies to large listed companies is the contrast between voice and exit as means for the shareholders to control management.[44] Since the seminal work of Berle and Means, the division of ownership and control in the large listed company has been seen

---

[40] (1843) 2 Hare 461; and note the applicastion of the rule to any legal entity capable of suing in its own name and under whose rules a majority can bind a minority in *Cotter* v. *National Union of Seamen* [1929] Ch. 58 and P.L. Davies, *Gower's Principles of Company Law* (London, Sweet and Maxwell, 1997), ch. 23.

[41] Insolvency Act 1986, s. 122(1)(g) as applied by the IPSA, s. 55(a) and ss. 47–49 respectively.

[42] IPSA 1965, ss. 64 and 66.

[43] CA 1985, s. 310 and Part X; Building Societies Act 1986, ss. 62 to 70; and Friendly Societies Act 1992, s. 27 and Sched. 11.

[44] See J. Parkinson, "The Role of Exit and Voice in Corporate Governance" in Sheikh and Rees (eds.), *Corporate Governance and Corporate Control* (London, Cavendish Publications, 1995), 75, and Snaith and Amass, *op. cit.* n. 37 above, on which this section on corporate governance is based.

as the key factor to be taken into account. If there is an active and liquid market in the company's shares, shareholders have the option of following the "Wall Street Rule" and selling their stake if they are dissatisfied with the performance of the business. This will be a more cost-effective option for the shareholder with a small proportionate stake in the company than an attempt to use the general meeting or other mechanisms of "shareholder democracy" to ensure efficient management in the interests of the shareholders by the replacement of directors or executives or the determination of company policy. This "Anglo Saxon" governance model contrasts with the German two tier board model which depends on "voice" and the role of the supervisory board in appointing and monitoring the executive management board.[45] In recent years the possibility of the use of "voice" by institutional investors in the US and UK systems has been discussed as a remedy for the perceived failures of the market based system.[46]

In the case of an industrial and provident society the interest of the shareholder–members in the economic efficiency of the business is more complex. In a co-operative, the governing principles will ensure that if there is any distribution of dividend or other value directly to members it will take the form of a dividend on transactions with the society rather than a return related to shareholding. In practice many societies do not distribute any dividend. In those cases, benefits should come in the form of lower prices or better services for members. In market terms, it may be hard for an individual member to be aware of such economic benefits. For example, price reductions or other benefits related to purchases from a co-operative's retail business are indistinguishable from the effects of competition from other retailers as to price or quality. In addition to these factors, the rule of one member one vote detaches the size of the capital stake held by a member from their voting power. Up to £20,000 of share capital may be held by an individual member but each member must have only one vote. The shares are not usually transferable other than on death and there is no market in the shares. As a result, corporate governance in a co-operative can be usually be concerned only with "voice". "Exit" would only be possible in the event of demutualisation by conversion to a listed company and the allotment of a "windfall" free share holding in the new PLC to existing members. The low probability of such an development is discussed below.[47]

It follows from these differences that societies, not raising capital through listed share issues, are not subject to a market in corporate control, and so the Stock Exchange "Yellow Book"[48] will be applied only partially to those few societies which use the market to raise money by issuing listed loan stock. As

---

[45] J. Charkham, *Keeping Good Company: A Study of Corporate Governance in Five Countries.* (Oxford Clarendon Press, 1994).

[46] P. Davies, "Institutional Investors in the UK" in D.P. Prentice and P. Holland (eds.), *Contemporary Issues in Corporate Governance* (Oxford, Clarendon Press 1993).

[47] See the text to n. 52 and the following paragraphs.

[48] *Stock Exchange Listing Rules*, London. 1998.

noted above, the detailed statutory rules about self-dealing by company directors do not apply to societies, and even the accounting rules applicable to societies are less demanding than those imposed under company law[49] so that the information available to members would be less complete than in the case of a company if compliance were limited to the legal minimum.

The system used to elect and monitor a society's board will depend on the size and nature of the society. In smaller co-operatives a board of directors may be elected by the annual members' meeting or by postal ballot. In larger societies with a membership dispersed across a wide area, indirect election may apply. There may be one or more intermediate committees or delegate structures, each of which elects the tier above with members electing the basic regional or district committee so that the board is elected by regional committees or a delegate meeting.

Once elected, the board of directors typically has powers similar to those conferred on company directors by Article 70 of Table A of the Companies (Tables A to F) Regulations 1985,[50] which delegates all the company's managerial power to its board of directors. This allows substantial delegation of managerial responsibility and prevents the members from interfering in management. Instead, they must rely on their powers to control the society's affairs indirectly. This system is typical of the approach taken in most large registered societies, although more recent editions of some of the model rules proposed for use by societies include a more detailed treatment of the respective powers and roles of the board of directors and the full time executives of the society.[51] Unlike companies, in which the general meeting of the shareholders represents a direct forum for participation in person or by proxy, large societies may either have a tiered delegate structure, with the general meeting being a meeting of delegates of regional committees or a single meeting of members held in a number of different locations with cumulative voting over time. Directors are often elected by the weighted votes of the regions or other subdivisions or by the regional committees themselves. The pool of potential candidates for the board may be the members of the regional committees.

This indirect form of representative democracy makes a take-over or other attempt to change the control of a society difficult.[52] "Exit" by "demutualisation" and conversion into a PLC seems to be virtually impossible without board agreement because of the cost and complexity of the mechanisms and transactions to be approved and established for conversion to a listed company. These procedures would be difficult to achieve by a resolution passed at the initiative of ordinary members at a general meeting—even where the general meeting does not consist of delegates rather than individual members. In addition, apart

---

[49] Compare Friendly and Industrial and Provident Societies Act 1968 with CA 1985, Part VII.
[50] SI 1985/805.
[51] See Co-operative Union Model Rules (11th Edn. 1998).
[52] As was discovered in 1997 when an attempt was made by a group of financiers to take control of the Co-operative Wholesale Society Ltd so as to demutualise it.

from some of the members, none of those with established interests in a consumer co-operative are likely to favour this step.

The indirect election of the board makes it difficult for a group of members to obtain control by a change in board composition. Existing lay elected directors committed to co-operative ideology are unlikely to find a similar role in any new listed PLC structure and will be unenthusiastic about conversion on grounds of both principle and self interest. If the members were tempted by the possibility of a substantial "windfall" of listed shares, the indirect democratic structure of large societies limits their power to insist on a conversion or other demutualisation. Only managers, who may gain financially from share options or other benefits after conversion, are likely to have both an interest in following this route and influence to promote the idea within a co-operative. However, even their interest in demutualisation may be outweighed by the greater accountability they would experience in a PLC subject to the disciplines of the Stock Market. The legal powers of the board would also prevent them from converting a society into a company without the agreement of the directors.

The use of indirect means to elect or remove directors and the complex delegate structure applicable to general meetings in the larger societies also makes the use of "voice" by members difficult. Consequently, the corporate governance of these organisations has to be considered in the absence of the possibility of "exit" in the sense used when public companies are discussed and with limits on the availability of "voice" to shareholder/members. More precisely, the individual member at the base of a large society relies on the "voice" of the representatives elected to regional committees or other tiers to control those further representatives elected as directors of the society who, in turn, have to control the executive management. "Exit" will mean the choice of a member to resign. There is no separate market in corporate control of the kind found in the case of listed companies.

(c) Self-regulation[53]

It has long been accepted that in the case of the listed public company, effective corporate governance by the use of "voice" is problematic. However, the recommendations of the Cadbury Report emphasised the role of the non-executive director in the context of a code of best practice intended to achieve improvement by the use of audit committees, remuneration committees and a significant phalanx of non-executive directors in the board room.[54]

The boards of consumer co-operatives present an interesting mirror image of the public company, and most other industrial and provident societies will have boards dominated by elected non-executives. In the case of consumer

---

[53] See C.Riley, "Controlling Corporate Management: UK and US Initiatives" (1994) 14 *Legal Studies* 244, and Snaith and Amass, op. cit. n. 37 above.

[54] *Report of the Committee on the Financial Aspects of Corporate Governance* (the Cadbury Report) (London, Gee, 1992), paras. 4.10–4.18.

co-operatives, executives are absent from the board and the model provides for an exclusively lay and elected board which appoints, dismisses and controls senior executives. However, while non-executive directors of companies are in practice selected rather than elected and are often expected to have relevant managerial and business expertise, the elected lay directors of many industrial and provident societies will have neither. This explains many of the features of the Co-operative Union Code of Best Practice[55]—a useful example of the application of the self regulatory approach to societies.

The Report examined the governance needs of one particular group of industrial and provident societies. It deals with societies with a large membership and often an indirect form of member control where the senior executive management does not form part of the society's board. The Report focuses on improving the internal mechanisms of control of co-operatives. This is to be achieved by defining the responsibilities of the society's organs and providing an exhaustive list of information to be made available by management to the directors and subsequently to members. This would ensure that both the directors of a consumer co-operative society and its executives were fully aware of their roles. Directors were to have a supervisory role.

The Co-operative Union Report recommended that the chief executive and the financial controller should become members of the board of directors. This measure was intended to clarify the legal liability of those officials in the performance of their management duties. However, this was rejected by the co-operative movement, and other methods of tackling the anomaly might be more appropriate. Board membership for executives might jeopardise the formal independence of the executive from the board of directors. A formal separation of functions may facilitate the supervisory role of the board. The distance between the board and the executive may reduce the risk that the former will be influenced by the decisions of the latter and may encourage more detached behaviour.

For industrial and provident societies a two tier structure would strengthen the process of governance by clarifying the distinction between the functions of the executive on one hand and the role of the supervisory organs of the society on the other and by imposing clear and direct liability on the executives. The danger of recognising a management executive is that this could confer on executives excessive power flowing directly from the co-operative's rules and weaken the lay board's control. This risk could be avoided by ensuring that the rules guarantee the ultimate powers of the lay supervisory board and their overall control of management.[56]

The Cadbury Report went to considerable lengths to distinguish the role of the executive directors from that of the non-executive directors, but it did not

---

[55] Co-operative Union, *Corporate Governance Code of Best Practice* (Manchester, Co-operative Union, 1995); and see B. Harvey, "The Governance of Co-operative Societies" in Sheikh and Rees (eds.), *Corporate Governance and Corporate Control* (London, Cavendish Publications, 1995).
[56] See n. 37 above.

address the possibility of a two-tier board system—presumably because of the inconsistency of such a system with the operation of the market for corporate control. This was despite the emphasis placed on the importance that the non-executive should be 'independent of management and free from any business or other relationship which could materially interfere with the exercise of their independent judgement'.[57] The demarcation between the role of the board and the executives in the industrial and provident society is usually much clearer than it is in a company with the result that the requirement for certain duties to be delegated from the board is less apparent.

The reliance of the Co-operative Union Corporate Governance Working Party on self regulation is in line with the Cadbury approach.[58] Although the objectives of the co-operative or community benefit form of business are different from those of the investor-controlled company, there are some similarities between their systems of governance. The recommendations of the Report of the Co-operative Union Working Group on the corporate governance of consumer co-operatives will go some way to bringing standards of governance into line with those demanded of companies.

The separation of ownership and control and its implications for monitoring and disciplining management apply in principle to both companies and societies in which the owners, whether shareholders or members, have little to gain from participation. This suggests that it is naïve to rely on "shareholder" or "member" democracy as the sole guarantee of effective corporate governance for either type of organisation.

The use of a two-tier board system to provide effective corporate governance through "voice" could be applied across the co-operative/company divide. In the case of UK and American listed companies the existence of institutional investors, the availability of the "exit" option by the sale of shares, and the thriving market in corporate control provide alternatives. For co-operatives, the absence of these controls suggests that the members' "voice" requires amplification. A two tier board structure might achieve this. However, the imposition of such a system by legislative intervention would impose a rigid system on all societies, and any threshold for its operation based on the size and geographical distribution of a society's membership would be difficult to fix. This may therefore be a matter best left to voluntary action by societies with the assistance of guidance from the regulator.

(d) Balance Between Stakeholders

The question of the role of the stakeholders in industrial and provident societies raises some interesting issues. In the case of a community benefit society, the purpose of the society is to benefit people other than its own members. Hence, the members and the constitution have the role of ensuring that the managers

---

[57] Cadbury Report, n. 54 above, para. 4.12.
[58] See n. 53 above.

continue to pursue this aim. In the case of a co-operative, the key factor distinguishing the society from a registered company of the conventional kind is that the members are stakeholders other than by investment. Thus in a consumer co-operative they are the customers of the business, in a worker co-operative they are its employees and in a marketing co-operative, one group of suppliers. This group elects the board and controls the general meeting. The regulatory regime formally recognises this but the discussion in the last section indicates that problems of governance, similar to those applicable to company shareholders, are faced by the dominant stakeholder group in a society.

However, the legislation governing societies has consequences for other stakeholders. The quirks of the insolvency regime applicable to societies discussed below[59] affect the rights of creditors—for example, the holders of fixed charges know that they can never be subjected to an administration order and the administrator's power over the assets charged to them, but the preferential creditors do not have priority at the beginning of a receivership and have to wait for a winding up to begin. Employees are, theoretically at least, in a weaker position in a society which is not structured as a workers' co-operative, as the IPSA 1965 contains no equivalent to section 309 of Companies Act 1985 imposing a duty on directors to consider the interests of the company's employees. This oversight arises from a failure to keep the IPSAs in line with the Companies Acts.

Thus the main differences in the power of the various stakeholder groups in societies flows from the absence of a capital market or market in corporate control and, in many cases, the fact that managers are dealing with elected, part time, non-executive directors or committee members. The position of the formally dominant stakeholder group in a co-operative can be compared to that of the shareholders in a company, and thus will vary according to the size of the organisation and the degree of separation between ownership and control. The position of other groups is affected by legislative anomalies.

2.5. Insolvency and Asset Distribution

In the area of insolvency, the contrast between the legal rules governing societies and those governing companies is marked. The discrepancies arise from a failure at the time of the passage of the Insolvency Act 1985 to extend that legislation (which later became the Insolvency Act 1986 and Company Directors Disqualification Act 1986 (CDDA)) to industrial and provident societies. Its operation in respect of such societies depended on section 55 of the IPSA 1965 and its application of winding up procedures to societies as if they were companies. It seems that this is insufficient to apply those parts of the Insolvency Act 1986 which introduce the concept of administrative receivership, those dealing

---

[59] Sect. 2.5.

with company voluntary arrangements or those providing for an administration order. These provisions are all stated to apply only to companies and cannot easily be argued to be applied to societies by section 55 of the IPSA 1965 which appears to be limited to the dissolution of a society "on its being wound up in pursuance of an order or resolution made as is directed in regard to companies by the" Insolvency Act 1986. It appears that, for the same reasons, the CDDA 1986 does not apply to societies.[60]

Subject to those discrepancies, the transformation or dissolution of an industrial and provident society can be achieved either by methods specified in the IPSA 1965 (amalgamation, conversion, transfer of engagements, or instrument of dissolution[61]) or by methods available under the Insolvency Act 1986 as applied to societies by section 55(a) of the IPSA 1965—a members' or creditors' voluntary winding up by resolution of the society in general meeting or a winding up by order of the court on the petition of a member (if the society is solvent), a creditor or the society itself. The concepts of amalgamation, transfers of engagements and conversion provide an easy and speedy means of reorganisation providing resolutions commanding the necessary majorities are passed in a formally correct manner by two consecutive meetings of the members of the society. No conveyancing formalities or court approvals are required for such reorganisations although the rights of creditors are preserved by section 54 of the IPSA 1965. There is some uncertainty whether these procedures simply represent possible devices available to societies to achieve certain ends or whether they might be interpreted as being mandatory and a source of protection of the rights of members when fundamental reorganisations are in prospect. If the former argument is accepted, the directors might achieve the same effect without consulting the members at all if the powers conferred on them by the rules were sufficiently extensive.[62]

Receivership under a fixed and/or floating charge is possible in English law if a society has provided such security to a creditor and receivership is triggered under the terms of the charge. However, the receivership will be contractual and not an administrative receivership under the Insolvency Act 1986, with the result that none of the provisions of that Act applicable to such receiverships will apply to the society. The most important lacuna caused by this situation is the absence of priority for preferential debts in a receivership of a society due to the fact that section 40 of the Insolvency Act 1986 does not apply.[63] Thus it is only in the liquidation of a society that these creditors (mainly employees and tax authorities) achieve priority, and it is by reference to the date of that event that their priority will be fixed. This acts as an incentive to those creditors to place a

---

[60] *Re Norse Self Build Association Ltd* (1985) 1 BCC 99,436 and *Re Devon and Somerset Farmers Ltd* [1993] BCC 410; see also Snaith, n. 2 above, para. 12.9.1. and I. Snaith, "Insolvency Proceedings and Industrial and Provident Societies—a Case for Reform" (1991) 7 *Insolvency Law and Practice* 90.

[61] Ss. 50–54 of IPSA 1965.

[62] See Snaith (1993) op. cit n. 2 above, op.cit. sect. 12.3.

[63] *Re Devon and Somerset Farmers Ltd* [1993] BCC 410.

society in liquidation at the earliest possible date so as to apply section 175 of the Insolvency Act 1986 through section 55(a) of the IPSA 1965.[64]

In Scotland, it appears that, by virtue of a legislative oversight, while the ranking of a floating charge and the right of its holder to security over the society's property is the same as in the case of a company, the remedy of receivership is denied to the floating charge holder who can only resort to winding up to enforce his or her charge.[65]

In this area the main problems faced by societies are the absence of the rescue regimes of administration orders and voluntary arrangements open to companies and the risk that a minority of members representing a sufficient majority of those voting might demutualise a society by conversion into, amalgamation with, or transfer of engagements to, a company or dissolve the society and distribute its assets by means of a members' voluntary liquidation under the Insolvency Act 1986. If mutual status is regarded as sufficiently important to warrant its own business structure and statutory regime, it is surely worthy of the possibility of rescue from insolvency by the means available to companies and of a threshold for a demutualisation decision based on the whole membership rather than only those choosing to vote.

3. REGULATORY ISSUES

3.1. The Role of The Regulator: Paternalism v. Deregulation

The system developed in the IPSAs from the nineteenth century onwards has tended to be restrictive and paternalistic. This reflected the origins of the legislative framework in the Friendly Societies Acts and the origins of the organisations regulated as self-help associations for working class and lower middle class members. However, progressive deregulation occurred throughout the history of the IPSAs as the powers available to societies were widened. For example the 1871 Act clarified the power of societies to hold land after the registrar had taken a restrictive view on this point and limits on the maximum shareholding available to individual members and on the extent to which societies can operate deposit-taking schemes continue and alterations to these limits were permitted by Statutory Instrument rather than primary legislation only from the late 1970s.

The central registration requirements that a society be either a *bona fide* cooperative or a community benefit society and the administrative requirement that the society in fact operates on this basis are the most obvious examples of a regulatory and paternalistic approach. However, without such requirements the justification for the availability of a separate legal regime for these organi-

---

[64] See Snaith (1993) op. cit., n. 2 above, para 12.9.3.

[65] See Snaith (1993) op. cit., n. 2 above, para 12.9.4. for detailed reasoning in support of this proposition.

sations might be lost. A company can be structured to operate as a co-operative or a non-profit-making or charitable organisation with community benefit objects. Only the special features of easy transfers of engagements and amalgamation, the possibility of withdrawable share capital and the use of the nomination procedures for a transfer of property in the society outside the usual succession rules distinguish societies from companies. If these features were regarded as dispensable then only the need to protect the founders' intention to create a co-operative or community benefit organisation by the intervention of a regulator rather than members' applications to the courts under relevant Companies Act provisions would justify a separate regime.

The 1996 Deregulation Order[66] was primarily concerned with unnecessary administrative requirements in the registration process, the obsolete need for at least seven members (which it reduced to three), the unrealistic deadline for the submission of annual returns and the problems faced by societies as a result of the failure to apply to them the relaxation of audit requirements for companies with a low turnover. They did not represent a move to deregulation in the central context of the role of the RFS. The Consultation Document of May 1998[67] contemplates a greater degree of deregulation by the use of the statutory declaration route for registration and certain later requirements. However, the legal requirements would remain the same. It would be the means of satisfying them and the enforcement of them, by possible prosecution for perjury rather than an administrative inspection of documents, which would change.

The paradox of deregulation in the context of these societies is that its logical conclusion might be the demise of this legal business structure altogether. This is undesirable if provision for member based organisations and the encouragement of mutual self-help are policy objectives. While it is legally possible to use a company or, indeed, a partnership structure for a co-operative and a company or trust structure for a community benefit organisation, the absence of a form of association specifically geared to the needs of such organisations might discourage their growth and undermine their continued existence.

However, a measure of self-regulation has long been accepted by RFS through its practice of agreeing "model rules" with sponsoring bodies encouraging the establishment of particular societies. A reduced fee is charged if such rules are used and the registration proceeds with less scrutiny by RFS officials. Similarly, a self-regulatory approach to corporate governance issues has been developed by some of these bodies and the CDPS represents a form of self-regulation by consumer co-operatives with the backing of the statutory exemption from Banking Act regulation.[68]

The role of the regulator and of self-regulation combines with the occasional intervention of the courts. They have become involved in the interpretation of

---

[66] The Deregulation (Industrial and Provident Societies) Order 1996, SI 1996/1738.
[67] HM Treasury and The Registry of Friendly Societies, *Proposals for a New Industrial and Provident Societies Act* (London ,Registry of Friendly Societies, 1998).
[68] See sects. 2.2 and 2.4 above.

the legislation and the consideration, from time to time, of issues such as rule amendments, insolvency procedures, the capacity of societies and their powers to grant security over their assets.[69] Judicial intervention has been limited but has tended to highlight the peculiarities of societies compared with the position of companies without methodically developing a jurisprudence which acknowledges the modern rationale for the IPSA regime in preserving the co-operative or community benefit nature of the societies.[70]

3.2. Credit Unions: A Special Case

This essay is not concerned with the special position of credit unions. It is sufficient to note that the role of the regulator in that context differs from that applicable to other industrial and provident societies. Under the Credit Union Act 1979, more extensive powers are conferred on the regulator and a more restrictive regime in terms of share capital, loans, the powers and objects of societies and the size of the membership applies.[71] All of these features of credit unions reflect their position as financial institutions in respect of which the FRS adopts the role played by the Bank of England in relation to banks. There is a concern about their prudential position and the risk of failure. As a result the FRS requires regular reports from credit unions and engages in positive monitoring of their financial position as well as issuing prudential and other guidance about governance and business practice.[72]

3.3. Financial Services Authority: The New Regime

It was announced on 23 July 1997 that all the functions of RFS as well as those of the Building Societies Commission and the Friendly Societies Commission would be transferred to the Financial Services Authority (FSA), the new single regulator of financial services. This is likely to happen in late 1999 after the expected passage of the Financial Services and Markets Bill in the 1998–9 Parliamentary Session.[73]

---

[69] See respectively *Hole* v. *Garnsey* [1930] AC 472 and *Datchet Co-partnership Housing and Allotment Society Ltd* v. *Official Solicitor*, CA (Civil Division) (Transcript Association) 19 May 1990 LEXIS; and the discussion in Snaith, n. 2 above, sects. 4.5.1.(ii) and 12.7; *Re Devon and Somerset Farmers Ltd* [1993] BCC 410 and the discussion in Snaith, n. 2 above, sect. 12.9; *Halifax Building Society* v. *Chamberlain Martin Spurgeon* [1994] EGCS 41 and (A94) 11(4) *Construction Law Digest* at 21 to 23 and LEXIS; and discussion in Snaith, n. 2 above, sect. 11.2; and *Great Northern Railway Company* v. *Coal Co-operative Society* [1896] 1 Ch. 187 and discussion in Snaith, n. 2 above, sect. 11.2.

[70] The observations of Lord Atkin in *Hole* v. *Garnsey* [1930] AC 472 at 493 represent an exception to this tendency.

[71] See Snaith, n. 2 above, ch. 13.

[72] See n. 8 above, 16–22.

[73] *Ibid.*, 6, and H.M. Treasury, Financial Services and Markets Bill: A Consultation Document (3 parts) (London, July 1998).

The FSA will have wide responsibilities—taking on the banking supervision role of the Bank of England, the role of DTI in regulating the insurance industry and the role of the Securities and Investment Board and the Self-regulating Organisations under the Financial Services Act 1986. While the prudential supervision role of RFS in relation to credit unions and the roles of the Building Societies Commission and the Friendly Societies Commission as financial regulators fit this pattern well, the role of the RFS in relation to industrial and provident societies sits ill within that body. The registration and maintenance of publicly available records in respect of societies operating as trading co-operatives or housing associations does not involve financial or prudential regulation and is analogous to the function of the Companies Registry rather than that of financial regulators. It seems that the role to be performed and, *de facto*, the staff performing it are unlikely to change after the transfer, but it is clear that the transfer itself was a pragmatic decision dictated by the destination of the regulators of friendly societies and building societies rather than the needs of industrial and provident societies. However, the transfer of RFS to the FSA will preserve the special role of the regulator of these societies—a dimension which might have been lost had the registration function been transferred to Companies House with its much larger company client base and absence of the RFS tradition of vetting amendments to rules or constitutions. This question, in turn, hinges on the issue of whether a special legal regime for co-operatives and societies operating for the benefit of the community can be justified.

3.4. Demutualisation

Perhaps the central question about the desirability of a special regime for societies is the issue of demutualisation. If a group of founder members establish an organisation with a constitution which operates in a particular way and on a particular basis, how far should the law permit them to tie the hands of their successors who may wish to alter the nature of the organisation—possibly for personal gain? The conversion of a significant number of the larger UK building societies from the special mutual structure with which they were established to banks in the form of PLCs with listed shares has raised this issue acutely. On such a conversion the members would typically receive a substantial amount in the form of a "windfall" of shares in the PLC while retaining their status as depositors with the organisation.

Industrial and provident societies can be converted into companies by a majority of 75 per cent of those voting on a resolution to achieve this.[74] The legislation lays down no provision as to the constitution of the company into which the society converts itself or to which it transfers its engagements. On the face of it, this means that a large enough majority of a small proportion of total

---

[74] S. 52, IPSA 1965.

membership voting on the question could change a *bona fide* co-operative or a community benefit society into a registered company with equity shares and under the control of investor members with votes related to their level of share-holding. The procedures followed on notice of meetings, method of voting and the information provided to members are all left to the rules of the society in question under the IPSA 1965—even when a major transformation of the society is proposed. Such matters are supervised by the regulator under the legislation governing building societies and friendly societies.[75]

As a matter of policy this process is questionable even where the original members leave the matter to the general law, of which they can be presumed to be aware. However, as a mandatory provision of the Act which overrides any contrary provision of the rules of the society it amounts to a rather odd charter for demutualisation. A society set up long ago to operate as a co-operative or community benefit organisation may have accumulated substantial assets by the efforts of its members and others. It can then apparently be converted into a company operating on a profit-making basis with listed shares and a substantial windfall to current members by means of a vote meeting a special majority requirement only in respect of those actually voting without an element requiring the turnout to reach a particular level as is required in the case of a building society.[76] This lacuna appears to be particularly irrational when, as the case law suggests, the courts may restrain a rule amendment if it can be shown that this would violate the intention of the founders of the society.[77] The inadequacy of the conversion option as a possible "exit" route for those members of a large society with indirect board elections who are dissatisfied with its governance has been pointed out above.[78] However, this co-exists with the risk of ill considered demutualisation by the vote of a minority of the total membership of a smaller society.

Legislation should, as a minimum, require a proportion of total membership to participate in a fundamental decision, as the legislation governing building societies does.[79] One might argue, particularly in the case of community benefit societies that such a conversion—or indeed a *de facto* "conversion" by rule amendments from a community benefit society into a *bona fide* co-operative— should either be prohibited or subjected to some scrutiny by the regulator. The present law makes clear the inadequacy of the industrial and provident society as a means of protecting particular objectives as compared with a charitable trust.

---

[75] Building Societies Act 1986, s. 93–98 and Scheds. 16 and 17, and Friendly Societies Act 1992, s. 85 and Sched. 15.

[76] Cooperative Union 11th edn attempts to achieve this by applying a high quorum provision and threshold for calling meetings where such a conversion is proposed.

[77] *Hole* v. *Garnsey* [1930] AC 472 and *Datchet Co-partnership Housing and Allotment Society Ltd* v. *Official Solicitor*, CA (Civil Division) (Transcript Association) 19 May 1990 LEXIS, and the discussion in Snaith, n. 2 above, sects. 4.5.1.(ii) and 12.7.

[78] See the text to n. 52 and the following paras.

[79] Building Societies Act 1986, s. 97 and Sched. 2, para. 30.

4. LAW REFORM: PROPOSED AND POTENTIAL CHANGE

4.1. The Need for Reform

The analysis presented in this essay so far illustrates the case for reform of the law on industrial and provident societies. In recent years a number of developments have indicated that such measures might be in prospect.

The United Kingdom Co-operative Council, an umbrella organisation for all co-operative sectors established in 1991 as a voluntary successor to the former statutory Co-operative Development Agency, published a proposal in 1995 for a new Co-operatives Act for the United Kingdom.[80] This proposal advocated a new framework Act for co-operatives which would, subject to limited exceptions, limit the use of the word "co-operative" in the name of an organisation to those registered under the new Act. The proposal also intended to remove the main discrepancies between company law and co-operative law on matters such as insolvency, corporate capacity, capital maintenance, accounting requirements and so on. The proposed legislation would have established a Co-operatives Commissioner with specific responsibility for co-operatives and power to regulate their operation.

4.3. The 1998 Consultation Document

The UKCC Proposal and a draft Bill to implement it were the subject of discussions between the Treasury Ministers, RFS and the UKCC in 1997 and 1998.[81] This led to the publication in May 1998 of an RFS Consultation Paper on proposals for a new Industrial and Provident Societies Act. This put out for consultation proposals for the reform of the existing legislation applicable to all societies—whether co-operatives or community benefit societies. It took up many of the UKCC suggestions and added others which concerned the RFS. Comments were invited from all interested parties on the basis that the present legislation was being reviewed "with a view to updating it should a legislative slot become available".[82]

Five main issues were raised in the paper:

(a) The statutory definition of the organisations to be registered under the legislation—whether the present definitions should be retained and perhaps elaborated and whether additional definitions applicable, for example, to clubs or housing associations should be added;

---

[80] United Kingdom Co-operative Council, *A Proposal for a Co-operatives Act for the United Kingdom* (Manchester, UKCC, 1995).

[81] See n. 8 above, 8.

[82] HM Treasury and The Registry of Friendly Societies, *Proposals for a New Industrial and Provident Societies Act* (London, RFS, 1998), para. 1.

(b) Whether the legislation should be amended to permit the registration of societies by a system of statutory declarations along the lines permitted by Companies House with power for the registrar to intervene after registration if a society's rules were later found not to conform to the legislation;

(c) The alignment of areas such as accounting requirements, insolvency, corporate governance issues, the registration of charges and the powers and capacity of societies with company law; and

(d) Clearer supervisory powers for the RFS.

The tenor of the consultation document indicates that law reform in this field is likely to be applied to the whole range of industrial and provident societies rather than particular types of society such as co-operatives and that it may take the form of amending legislation—perhaps with enabling powers to permit the application by Statutory Instrument of current and future provisions of company law to societies. Greater speed and economy in the registration process by the use of statutory declarations is envisaged in the document with greater powers being conferred on the registry to deal with violations uncovered at a later stage. Such reform will retain the special nature of these societies while reducing the practical application of the paternalistic regulatory approach at the point of registration.

The tests predicated on the nature of the organisations registered as co-operatives or community benefit societies would remain in law although the "statutory declaration route" to registration would limit the practical application of those rules. It is clear that such reform would not involve the wholesale integration of these societies with the company registration system. However, the major discrepancies between the law applicable to them and the law governing companies would be eliminated. The timing of any new legislation will depend on the availability of parliamentary time although a short amending Bill stands more chance of inclusion in the government programme than a whole new legislative code for co-operatives or community benefit (or "not for profit") societies.

4.4. The European Dimension

Finally it must be noted that the direct role of the European Union in the development of UK law in this area has been minimal. The most important effect of the EC company law harmonisation programme has been to require extensive changes to UK company law from 1972 onwards so that it would comply with the directives introduced by the Community.[83] The fact that industrial and provident societies were not within the scope of those directives led the law

---

[83] See P.L. Davies, *Gower's Principles of Company Law* (London, Sweet and Maxwell, 1997), 54–61 for a summary of these developments.

governing companies to depart more and more from the rules to be found in the 1965 IPSA. The development of anomalies on matters such as the capacity of societies and their agents, accounting and audit rules and, to a degree, capital maintenance was due to the UK response to company law harmonisation. The anomalies on corporate governance and insolvency were mainly home grown.

More positively, the existence of Directorate General XXIII of the Commission of the European Community with a remit to deal with the "social economy" (co-operatives, associations and mutuals) has engendered proposals for European Co-operative, Mutual and Association Statutes along the lines of the European Company Statute.[84] However, at the time of writing, the prospects for legislative action on these regulations to permit the formation of pan-european, co-operatives, mutuals or associations along the lines of the proposed Societas Europea[85] do not appear to be good.

[84] See EC Commission, *Proposal for a Council Regulation (EEC) On The Statute for a European Co-operative Society,* (Brussels, EEC Commission, 1991; United Kingdom Co-operative Council, *Final Report of the Working Group on Proposal for a Council Regulation (EEC) On The Statute for a European Co-operative Society*, EN Rev. 3 of 16 Dec. 1991 (Manchester, UKCC, 1992) and M. Lynch and I. Snaith, *The Scope of Non-user Investor Members of a European Co-operative Society* (Manchester/Brussels, UKCC and DG XXIII of the EC Commission, 1995).

[85] COM(91)174 final [1991] OJ C176/1; and see Department of Trade and Industry, *Revised Proposal for a European Company Statute* (London, DTI, 1992).

9

The Regulation of Privatised Utilities

COSMO GRAHAM[1]

One of the central problems for company law has been the issue of the legitimacy of the private power of the corporation. Corporate law theorists who have dealt with this issue divide, roughly, into two camps: those who see companies as private enterprises, whose power is constrained by various markets and those who see companies as social enterprises, where the imperfections or absence of market constraints are rectified by regulatory action undertaken by the state, or under the threat of state action.[2] This debate has taken place on the terrain of company law in general, that is, the protagonists have given little consideration to the specific regimes which have been created for different types of companies, usually taking into account the different economic functions undertaken by those companies. This essay examines a particular statutory model, that created for British utility companies, in order to see what light it sheds upon these company law concerns.

In Britain most of the utility companies have been transformed from nationalised industries to private sector companies in about ten years (1984–93). It was accepted from the start that the market constraints on these companies were insufficient as they were, entirely or in part, natural monopolies. A regulatory system was created and some of the concerns underlying this regulatory system echo the concerns of those interested in promoting the social responsibility of companies in a wider sense. Thus, for example, Parkinson discusses a number of techniques for strengthening corporate responsibility. His discussion ranges over improving the inward flow of information, altering directors' fiduciary duties, increased disclosure, mandatory consultation, wider board representation and ensuring implementation of policies through, for example, performance targets.[3] He also goes on to discuss the issue of employee representation on the board of directors.[4] Parallels to all of these issues can be seen in the

---

[1] Professor of Law, Law School, University of Hull. My thanks to Lisa Whitehouse for her comments on this piece. This essay concentrates on electricity, gas, telecommunications and water, with occasional reference to rail.

[2] For discussion of this issue see C. Graham, "Regulating the Company" in L. Hancher and M. Moran (eds.), *Capitalism, Culture and Economic Regulation* (Oxford, Clarendon Press, 1989) and, of course, J. E. Parkinson, *Corporate Power and Responsibility* (Oxford, Clarendon Press, 1993).

[3] Parkinson, n. 1 above, ch. 11. I have omitted the possibility of re-formulating criminal and tortious liability, as I see this as in effect replaced by the oversight of the regulators.

[4] *Ibid.*, ch. 12.

arrangements for the regulation of public utilities and in debates around particular issues.

However, what makes the utilities a particularly fascinating area to examine is the changes undergone by certain of them, telecommunications and the energy industries primarily, away from naturally monopolistic industries towards competitive markets. This has been accompanied by much debate about the future of regulation in these industries, with talk about the demise of regulation, or at least reducing the regulatory task to that of being a sectoral competition authority. Such developments look like a victory for those who argue that companies are really just private enterprises, constrained by market forces. It appears that the special model of utility regulation which was created after privatisation and which addressed, albeit imperfectly, the concerns of social enterprise theorists, has been overtaken by competitive markets where technologically feasible. This view is an exaggeration, as developments are more subtle and have involved regulatory interventions into companies operating in these utility markets.

The lesson is that in terms of policy intervention the two conceptions of company law are neither polar opposites nor incompatible. In certain areas we may decide, or policy-makers may decide, that market mechanisms are the appropriate means for improving the position of society. So, for example, the argument for competition in the energy sectors has been that prices will be reduced, thus increasing the net wealth of society. At the same time regard must be had to ensuring that the benefits of competition are equally distributed and so, in rhetoric at least, the government has had to consider non-market measures. None of this may happen through devices which conventionally fall within the ambit of company law, but that raises another question of what is the desirable regime within which to pursue certain forms of regulation, that is, a generic model of company law as opposed to specialised statutory regimes? That is too wide a question to address here.

In order to pursue these issues, this essay takes the following form. After some necessary introductory discussion about the policy of privatisation and the purposes of regulation, I examine the regulatory system that was created, focusing on the institutions created, their duties, their inter-relationship with other public bodies, including consumer representatives, and issues surrounding the provision of information, both from the companies and the regulators. There is not, therefore, any detailed discussion of regulatory processes, the working of price controls, social obligations or quality of service issues.[5]

Having done this, I will then go on to look at how the industries have developed from being monopoly suppliers to competitive industries and the subsequent restructuring of certain companies into multi-utilities in order to point out just how different the utilities sector is becoming and what challenges this raises for the regulatory system. This will lead to my final section, a discussion

---

[5] On all these matters the best starting point is T. Prosser, *Law and the Regulators* (Oxford, Clarendon Press, 1997).

of the future of the regulatory system, based on the Labour Government's review of utility regulation.[6]

PRIVATISATION OF THE UTILITIES[7]

The political tensions surrounding privatisation had an important influence on the shape of the industries when they entered the private sector, and therefore the regulatory task. The policy of privatisation extended to all nationalised companies, not just the utilities, and it is now widely accepted that it was not a programme, in the sense of being planned beforehand, rather an improvised policy which developed momentum as the political and policy benefits became clear. At the heart of the policy of privatisation there was arguably a tension between the "pragmatic" aspects of the policy and the "ideological" aspects. On the pragmatic side privatisation was attractive because the sale of nationalised industries facilitated the reduction of government borrowing, which opened the way for reductions in direct taxation, as well as encouraging the creation of a class of small shareholders, who were thought to be more likely to be favourable to the Conservative Party and government. The sale of nationalised industries also had the advantage of providing a solution to the problem of how to control nationalised industries, an issue that had never been resolved satisfactorily and was threatening to be a particular problem, given that the telecommunications and water industries were both in need of large amounts of investment capital.

The ideological justification was that privatisation was an element in the rolling back of the state and a means of replacing state decisions in commercial areas with the disciplines of market forces. By opening up the utilities to competitive forces they would become more efficient and more responsive to their customers. A side effect of this, albeit one not stressed in public pronouncements, was that once the industries were subject to market forces, the power of the trade unions would be reduced, as they would no longer have the protection of being in the public sector.

The area of greatest tension between these two aspects was the issue of how much competition the utilities would be subjected to after privatisation. If the object of privatisation had been to raise the greatest amount of money for the government, then competition would have to be severely limited, as a company subject to competition is a more risky investment than a monopoly and will command a lower price. If encouraging market forces had been the primary aim, then the utilities would have been restructured to encourage competition and

---

[6] Department of Trade and Industry, *A Fair Deal for Consumers* (London, HMSO, 1998), and Department of Trade and Industry, *A Fair Deal for Consumers—Response to Consultation* (London, HMSO, 1998).

[7] This sect. is based on C. Graham and T. Prosser, *Privatising Public Enterprises* (Oxford, Clarendon Press, 1991), ch. 1; and C. Graham, "Privatization—The United Kingdom Experience" 21 *Brooklyn Journal of International Law* 185.

their markets opened to competitors. Because of the importance of the prag-matic aspects of the policy, and the need to gain the support of the incumbent management to make the privatisation run smoothly, the government was very cautious over allowing competition and conducted very little restructuring. So in gas, telecommunications and water no attempt was made to re-structure British Gas, BT nor the regional water and sewerage companies even though various proposals existed for splitting up British Gas and BT into competing regional companies. In addition, the government was very cautious about open-ing up the markets to competition. British Gas retained a monopoly over gas supply in the United Kingdom, with the exception of the large industrial and commercial sector, whilst in telecommunications a regulated duopoly was cre-ated, consisting of BT and its sole competitor, Mercury Communications. Significantly, despite external advice, simple resale of telecommunications ser-vices was not allowed.

The only sector where there was significant restructuring and added compe-tition was in electricity in England,[8] partly as a response to the severe criticism levied at the privatisation of British Gas. The Central Electricity Generating Board was broken up into three units: the companies responsible for power gen-eration, the companies responsible for the distribution and supply of electricity and a national transmission grid, owned by the distribution and supply com-panies. Power generation became a competitive market, as other companies were allowed to enter it, although the market was dominated by the two large generating companies, National Power and PowerGen, and the publicly owned nuclear power generator.[9] As in gas, supply to domestic and smaller industrial companies remained a monopoly in the hands of the regional supply and distri-bution companies whilst the market for the largest firms was opened up to com-petition.

As well as being cautious about creating competitive product markets, the government was also cautious about allowing the capital markets free rein from the day of privatisation. So all the private utility companies were equipped, before flotation, with a "golden share". The effect of this was to prevent hostile take-overs for a limited period of time, five years in the case of the electricity and water companies.[10] So for that period of time the capital market was replaced by a government power, in addition to that provided by the normal channels of competition law.

---

[8] In Scotland and Northern Ireland electricity supply remained the responsibility of three verti-cally integrated companies undertaking generation, distribution and supply.

[9] This problem was created by the government's original intention to privatise the nuclear power stations as well. When it became clear that this was not feasible, new arrangements were made which gave the two generating companies a dominant position in the market.

[10] Unless the context indicates otherwise "water companies" refers to the water and sewerage companies.

THE PURPOSES OF REGULATION

If the utility markets were, even after privatisation, not fully competitive, then, if only to reassure the public, it was necessary to set up a regulatory system in order to prevent the privatised companies from exploiting their dominant and monopolistic positions, in particular as regards pricing. I will describe this system in outline shortly, but first its aims need to be discussed. One of the difficulties in so doing is that there was little public discussion of the purposes of regulation, outside of the two reports by Professor Littlechild.[11] Littlechild argued that regulation was really only a second best surrogate for market forces and that it should, ideally, be seen as temporary, just a way of "holding the fort" until the forces of competition arrived. He was also concerned that regulation should be as non-discretionary as possible, in order to prevent the growth of large bureaucracies and so that the companies should have the maximum incentive to act as efficiently as possible. So, if the government felt it necessary to control the prices of utility companies, he recommended a system which has become known as "RPI–X", that is, that utility prices should rise no more than the Retail Price Index minus a particular number to be decided upon (the "X") and that the price control should be re-set at periodic intervals.

STATUTORY DUTIES OF REGULATORS AND UTILITY COMPANIES

Although in this ideal scheme the role of the regulator is solely to mimic market forces, without regard to any social obligations the utilities may have, as a number of commentators have pointed out, the legislation is more ambivalent.[12] Although the legislation varies somewhat in detail,[13] the basic scheme is that there are two primary duties for the regulator and the Secretary of State. They must exercise their powers to ensure that all reasonable demands for services are met and that the companies are able to finance their activities. In gas and electricity there is an additional primary duty, namely to encourage the development of competition. Alongside duties to encourage efficiency and competition, the regulators are also required to pay attention to certain social obligations of the utilities, such as taking into account the interests of the elderly and the disabled. Although the issue of social obligations has become increasingly important, initially most regulators saw their primary job as being in some sense surrogates for the competitive market and social issues as being a secondary matter. Nevertheless, the important point is that there was a fair amount of

[11] S. Littlechild, *Regulation of British Telecommunications Profitability* (London, HMSO, 1984) and *Economic Regulation of Privatised Water Authorities* (London, HMSO, 1986).

[12] See T. Prosser, n. 1 above, ch. 1 and A. McHarg, "Accountability in the Electricity Supply Industry" 6 *Utilities Law Review* 34.

[13] See Telecommunications Act 1984 (TA), s. 3; Electricity Act 1989 (EA), s. 3; Water Industry Act 1991 (WIA), s. 2; Railways Act 1993 (RA), s. 4; Gas Act 1986 (GA), s. 4.

ambiguity from the start about the obligations of the regulators. In particular, although there was a rhetorical commitment to "light touch" regulation, it soon became apparent that acting as a market surrogate would require detailed intervention on a number of issues.

In addition to the regulators being required to take into account social issues, the legislation and the licences also placed certain obligations upon the utility companies, primarily to provide service to all those who reasonably requested it[14] and also placing some limitations on their power to cease providing services to those consumers who did not pay their bills. The issue of when a utility was entitled to disconnect a consumer became highly controversial in all the industries, except telecommunications, and the regulators have been very active in trying to encourage companies to reduce the number of disconnections, something which has been quite successful, at least up to the onset of competition. So from the outset, the utility companies were not treated as ordinary companies, being under obligations to provide service and somewhat restricted in the sanctions they could impose for non-payment, and this is reflected in the ambiguity of the regulatory duties. When we look at the way that the competitive market has developed, we will see that social obligations will continue to be imposed on those companies which wish to participate in the market.

INSTITUTIONAL STRUCTURE

Utility services can only be provided under the terms and conditions of a licence, which may be granted by the regulator or the Secretary of State. The role of the regulator is to ensure that these terms and conditions are adhered to, propose changes to them, publish information about the industries, advise the Secretary of State, deal with complaints and enforce competition law in the particular sector. Although I have referred imprecisely to the "regulator", the legislation vests all the formal powers in one person, known as a Director General, who is appointed by the Secretary of State. The Director General is assisted by his or her staff, who form the regulatory office, for example, the Office of Telecommunications. The Directors General are usually described as "independent" of government, which means, crudely, that the government cannot give specific directions to the regulators on how to carry out their functions, except in certain quite limited circumstances, such as when national security is imperilled.[15] Apart from such limited circumstances the Secretary of State can only give a Director General directions on what matters he or she ought to have regard to in deciding whether or not to exercise any of their functions under the legislation or in deciding the priority of matters which ought to be reviewed. With the exception of telecommunications, any such directions have to be published in

---

[14]   EA, s. 16; GA, ss. 9 and 10; WIA, ss. 41, 45 and 98; BT Licence Condition 1.
[15]   TA Sec. 94; EA, s. 96; WIA, s. 208; RA, s. 118. But there are no such powers under the Gas Act!

the annual report of the regulator[16] and no such formal directions have ever been given. By contrast, the Rail Regulator was required to have regard to the Secretary of State's guidance until 31 December 1996, and this guidance was given and published.[17]

Although the regulators are very much central figures in the development of policy for their industries, they must work in the context of legislation which provides significant input for other public agencies. This can be illustrated by looking at their powers to alter the licences of the utilities. A utility's licence may only be altered in one of two ways: either by consent or, if consent is not forthcoming, after a reference to the Monopolies and Mergers Commission (MMC) by the regulator and an MMC report recommending the modification of the licence. The regulator has some discretion in how to implement the MMC's recommendations.[18] The Secretary of State may intervene either to prevent a reference to the MMC by the regulator or to prevent a modification being made by consent when he or she thinks that it is more appropriate to proceed by way of reference to the MMC.

In this example, which is central to the regulatory regime, we can see that the regulator must be careful to ensure that other public agencies are in agreement with his or her policies in order to carry them through to a successful conclusion. This is also true in other areas, and it is noteworthy that the government has significant decision powers in a number of matters, especially in relation to the electricity industry. The Secretary of State may require public electricity suppliers to have available generating capacity from non-fossil fuel sources, the Secretary of State sets the fossil fuel levy, may give directions about the maintenance of fuel stocks at generating stations and gives consent for the construction of generating stations and overhead power lines. In addition the Secretary of State has the power to make regulations relating to the supply and safety of electricity and may grant exemptions from the need for an electricity licence.[19]

Under the Conservative governments these powers were not exercised in a manner which would interfere with market forces. Thus consents for new gas-fired generating stations were freely given, leading to rapid development of the use of gas for generating power. This development was one of the elements in a crisis that blew up in 1992 over the issue of pit closures and the future of the coal industry. In the face of political uproar the government promised a review of the issue which, in the end, simply delayed the decision and did not change the underlying direction of policy. In the process the Director General of Electricity

---

[16] TA, s. 47(3); GA, s. 39(2); EA, s. 47(2) and 50(20)(c); WIA, s. 27(3) and 193(2)(b); RA, s. 69(2) and 74(2)(c).

[17] RA, s. 4(5). The guidance was published in Office of the Rail Regulator, *Annual Report 1993–4* (London, HMSO, HC 662, 1993–4).

[18] See *In the Matter of an application by Northern Ireland Electricity Plc for Judicial Review*, (Unreported) QB Div., 24 June 1998 and, more generally, C. Graham, "Regulatory Responses to MMC Decisions" in P. Vass (ed.), *Regulatory Review 1997* (London, Centre for the Study of Regulated Industries (CRI), 1998).

[19] EA, s. 5, 29, 32–7.

Supply was criticised for his lack of action by the Trade and Industry Select Committee even though many of the energy policy issues fell outside his remit.[20] By contrast, in 1997 the Labour government announced that it would defer decisions on applications for new power stations in order to conduct a review of how issues of security of supply and fuel diversity should be taken into account in these decisions.[21] The result has been that the government has decided to address a number of perceived problems in the market for electricity generation and, whilst that is being done, it will normally regard new gas-fired generation as being inconsistent with its energy policy concerns relating to diversity and security of supply.[22] For our purposes, the point is not that one decision is better than another, but that fundamental issues relating to the industry are not in the hands of the regulator.

Even setting aside the role of government, regulators also have to co-ordinate their policies with other agencies. This has become particularly evident with the convergence of the telecommunications, broadcasting and computer markets, but also applies in the field of energy efficiency and economic regulation of the water industry, where the major cost drivers are the environmental obligations imposed upon the water companies.[23]

A major area of interest is in competition law, specifically, the regulation of mergers, which is part of the market for corporate control.[24] Here, with one exception, the privatised utilities are subject to the normal process of merger control, which means that the Office of Fair Trading advises the Secretary of State who decides on whether or not to make a reference to the MMC. In making this decision the Secretary of State has a wide discretion and, although both Conservative and Labour governments have said that references will be made primarily on competition grounds, references have also been made for other reasons. If the MMC reports that a take-over is against the public interest the

---

[20] See Trade and Industry Committee, *British Energy Policy and the Market for Coal* (London,, HMSO, HC,237 1992–3), paras. 290–1.

[21] DTI Press Notice P/97/810, 3 Dec. 1997. For the terms of the review see DTI Press Notice P/97/868, 22 Dec. 1997, HC Debs. Written Answer.

[22] See Department of Trade and Industry, *Review of Energy Sources for Power Generation* (London, HMSO, 1998), ch. 5. Note also the power contained in Energy Act 1976, s. 14.

[23] On convergence see Culture, Media and Sport Select Committee, *The Multi-Media Revolution* (London, HMSO, HC 520, 1997–8) and European Commission, *Green Paper on the Convergence of the Telecommunications, Media and Information Technology Sectors, and the Implications for Regulation Towards an Information Society Approach* (Brussels, European Commission, COM(97)623. On energy efficiency two good summaries are S. Tierney, "Ofgas and the Energy Efficiency Debate" 7 *Utilities Law Review* 15 and G. Owen, *Energy Policy, the Government and the Energy Regulators*, GEC 95–35 (Norwich, University of Norwich Working Paper July 1996). On water and the environment see *Open Letter from the Director General of Water Services to the Secretary of State for the Environment, Transport and the Regions and the Secretary of State for Wales and Accompanying Paper: Setting the quality framework—an analysis of the main quality costings submission 2000–05* (Birmingham, Ofwat, available at http://www.open.gov.uk/ofwat/open.htm).

[24] Although there will be a new Competition Act in place by the end of 1998, there are no plans to alter the system of merger control.

Secretary of State then decides what action, if any, to take.[25] In this process the regulators are formally just one of a number of interested parties consulted by the relevant agencies. The one exception is water, because the Water Industry Act provides that references between water companies, above a certain amount, are to be automatically referred to the MMC and that the MMC is required to take into account whether or not the reduction in the number of water companies will make it more difficult for the Director General of Water Services to carry out his job.[26]

However, in addition to these provisions, the government also held a golden share in many of the privatised utilities. Without going into detail, what this share did was to prevent a take-over of the utility without the consent of the government, so that the capital market could not operate in the normal way. In some cases, the purpose of holding a golden share seemed to be to prevent any take-overs in a sector, such as electricity, whilst in others, there seemed to be no such objection, for example the take-overs of Britoil by BP and Jaguar by Ford or the failure to take a golden share in Railtrack. In another case, the flotation of the National Grid Company, the government used its golden share to obtain concessions from the owners, the regional electricity companies, in terms of providing a payback to consumers.[27] Although this discussion has been in the past tense, the government still holds golden shares in certain companies, notably the electricity generating companies, which suggests that there are still areas where it is reluctant to see normal market forces operate.

In terms of utilities, the most interesting developments have occurred after the golden shares in the English regional electricity companies (RECs) lapsed in March 1995. By the end of 1996, all 11 companies had changed hands, with seven of them having American owners, two being owned by water companies, one by Scottish Power and one (Eastern Electricity) by the Hanson Group.[28] Although it might have been thought that these take-overs raised public policy questions worthy of investigation by the MMC, especially Scottish Power's take-over of Southern Electricity and the two water and electricity mergers, no reference was made until the generating companies each made bids for RECs. Instead, any regulatory issues which arose were dealt with through the Director General negotiating licence amendments with the companies concerned. The generating companies' bids for the RECs were perceived to raise a different order of issues because they were a direct challenge to the industry structure that had been created on privatisation. The MMC duly investigated and found, by a majority, that although the bids could be expected to have effects adverse to the

[25] If the merger has a European dimension, it may fall within the jurisdiction of the European Commission. This has happened only once in relation to the takeover of Northumbrian Water by Lyonnaise des Eaux and this transaction was referred back to the British authorities: see MMC, *Northumbrian Water/Lyonnaise des Eaux*, Cm 2936.

[26] WIA 1991, ss. 32–5.

[27] For details see A. McHarg, "Government Intervention in Privatised Industries: The Potential and Limitations of the Golden Share" 9 *Utilities Law Review* 198.

[28] Eastern has subsequently been sold to Texas Utilities.

public interest, these could be cured by suitable licence amendments and so recommended that the take-overs be allowed. The government, however, did not agree with this conclusion and refused to allow the bids to proceed. Shortly after the change in government in 1997, it appeared as if a more active reference policy might be followed when the Trade and Industry Secretary referred the bid by Pacificorp for Eastern Electricity to the MMC, primarily so that the MMC could investigate the regulatory, rather than the competition, implications of the take-over. The MMC found that there were no public interest objections to the proposed merger[29] but, in the event, Pacificorp were beaten to their target by Texas Utilities, which gave similar assurances to the regulator as had been given in other cases.

These assurances were that sufficient financial and management resources were available to enable the REC to carry out its statutory and licence obligations; to ensure that the Director General is provided with relevant information from any company in the acquiring company's group; to co-operate with the regulator in ensuring appropriate financial separation and financial independence for the REC and to ensure that the REC agrees to the appropriate licence amendments. One way of viewing these assurances is to say that they are aimed at ensuring that, although ownership has changed, the REC carries on with its functions as before, which highlights how they are different from ordinary private sector companies which may often expect quite radical changes after a take-over.

One other point is that, although the government has prevented vertical integration by the generating companies, the Director General of Electricity Supply has encouraged it in the case of Eastern Electricity. The background here is the continuing concern with the domination of the market for electricity generation by the two big companies. After investigation of the situation in the early 1990s, the Director General obtained voluntary undertakings from the generators that they would dispose of a certain amount of capacity, which was bought by Eastern Electricity, thus making it the fourth largest player in the market for electricity generation. Allowing Eastern to become a vertically integrated electricity company whilst preventing the power generators from so doing is not, in itself, an inconsistent approach, given the greater market power of the generators. What it does demonstrate, however, is that electricity markets are not ordinary markets, they are in some sense being managed by public bodies.

CONSUMER REPRESENTATION[30]

One of the concerns of company law literature is whether or not companies are responsive to their various stakeholders, such as shareholders, employees and

---

[29] Cm 3816.

[30] For overviews of this subject see National Consumer Council, *Consumer Representation in the Public Utilities* (London, National Consumer Council, 1996) and Consumers' Association, *Utilities in Transition—a Consumer Perspective* (London, Consumers' Association, 1997) ch. 11.

the wider public. One group of people with an interest in company performance is the consumers of its products or services. The regime created for the regulation of privatised utilities attempted to ensure consumer concerns would be systematically taken into account by the regulators and, to a lesser extent, the companies.

In each industry there are specific institutions whose job it is to represent the consumer interest, even though the precise arrangements vary from industry to industry in significant ways. In the water and electricity industries, consumer representation is the job of regional consumer committees, with the support of a national committee, which are part of the regulator. In telecommunications there are national committees and specialised subject committees, for example representing disabled users, as well as some local committees. The national committees are part of the regulator, whilst the local committees are funded by the Department of Trade and Industry. In gas, there is a national council, with a regional presence, which is *not* part of the regulator and therefore operates independently.

A key issue for all the consumer bodies is their ability to obtain information from the companies. However, none of them have any rights to obtain information from the companies; at best they have rights to meet periodically (electricity and water),[31] or to have their representations considered (BT).[32] In addition, the electricity and water companies are required to consult the consumer committees on a variety of codes of practice. British Gas, and other gas companies, were required to give the Gas Consumers' Council information on their general policies and information relevant to complaints, regardless of whether they were carrying out transportation, shipping or supply functions.

In terms of working with the regulator, the practice has been varied. The most systematic has been the Director General of Water Services who has sought to involve the consumer committees in a wide range of issues, from disconnections to the reviews of the price control and development of companies market plans. Elsewhere the record has been more patchy, with regional electricity consumer committees not being systematically involved by the regulator and tending to concentrate on less technical issues, although this has not been true of recent work by the national umbrella group.[33] In gas most of the activity has surrounded disconnection issues and, more recently, the development of competition in domestic supply, but the regulator seems not to have paid any more attention to the Gas Consumers' Council than she has to anyone else. In telecommunications, although the regulator has consulted the national committees, he has also used a range of other devices to obtain consumer opinion, from public meetings to the creation of various *ad hoc* panels to represent the consumer interest.

---

[31] Cond. 24 of PES Licence, Condition G9 of water appointment.
[32] Cond. 29 of the BT licence.
[33] See A. McHarg "Representation of Consumers in the Electricity Industry" 4 *Consumer Policy Review* 88.

The arrangements for consumer representation in the future will be different, according to the government's Green Paper, and I will discuss this below. However the record of consumer bodies in the regulation of utilities has a number of cautionary tales for those interested in trying to ensure that companies take into account a wider spread of views than just those of the shareholders. Simply setting up an institution does not, without more, guarantee that it will have any influence on the development of policy and practice. Effectiveness is partly a question of institutional design,[34] partly a question of resources and personnel and, crucially, a question of whether such bodies have adequate access to information because, without information, they cannot make an informed contribution to any debates.

INFORMATION

Something needs to be said about the disclosure of information by utility companies, as this is an important strategy for those who argue for greater social responsibility for companies in general. The framework is that the regulators have broad powers to demand information from the companies relevant to their functions and fairly wide powers of publication, although there is some difficulty over the limits of their powers.[35] The information produced by regulators can be divided into two categories: information relating to the quality of service provided by the companies and financial information, which is provided by the companies in line with guidelines set down by the regulators.

In the first legislation, for gas and telecommunications, the regulators were given no powers in relation to the quality of service provided by the companies. It soon became apparent that this was an important omission and, after Oftel's initial efforts at dealing with quality of service, a set of specific statutory powers was brought in for all the regulators by the Competition and Service (Utilities) Act 1992. Since then, the regulators have developed a wide battery of performance measures, although the approach taken has varied considerably.[36] At one extreme, Ofwat publishes a large amount of information on the performance of the companies and has measures in place to ensure the accuracy of company data. At perhaps the other extreme, Ofgas publishes no quality of service data itself but relies on British Gas to do so, in accordance with criteria laid down in the British Gas licence originally in 1991 and now split between Centrica and Transco. Compared to the position under nationalisation, much more information about company performance is now available, as well as means to provide compensation for individual consumers in cases where stan-

---

[34] There has been much controversy in relation to consumer bodies over whether they should be independent of the regulator or part of the regulator. See J. Ernst, *Whose Utility?* (Buckingham, Open University Press, 1994), ch. 6 for discussion.

[35] See Public Accounts Committee, HC 89, 1996–7, Questions 151–7.

[36] See Consumers Association, *Utilities in Transition* (1997), ch. 6, for a discussion.

dards do not meet those set by the regulators. Similarly, in relation to financial reporting, regulatory approaches vary considerably, from the detailed approach taken by Ofwat and Oftel, to the much less directive approaches of Offer and Ofgas, although important technical differences can be found, such as over the use of current cost and historical cost accounting measures.[37] Although the regulators have been criticised on a variety of grounds about the effectiveness of these arrangements,[38] in practice Ofwat and Oftel have ensured that much more information about the companies that they regulate has found its way into the public domain.[39]

Before leaving the issue of information, there are two additional points. The first relates to the group structures within which utility businesses operate. Most utilities now operate within corporate groups, of which the regulated utility business is only one part. This has led to the regulators developing accounting guidelines, and indeed imposing certain requirements on the board of a utility business, which attempt to ring-fence the utilities activities from the rest of the group. This has become a greater problem with the development of competitive domestic markets and multi-utility companies, and more will be said in due course. The second issue relates to the recent White Paper on freedom of information.[40] As well as proposing that freedom of information legislation would apply to public bodies, the White Paper suggests that it should also apply to "privatised utilities". Although originally unclear, the government has said that it wants freedom of information obligations to cover those companies which carry out statutory functions, that is, functions and duties conferred by statute.[41] This does not clarify the matter, because the relevant statutes impose a number of duties on licence holders, as well as providing them with certain powers. The government does not wish to extend freedom of information obligations to all licence holders because this would "extend the private sector coverage far beyond that appropriate with the primary, public sector purpose of [freedom of information]".[42] This indicates that, for some purposes, utilities are not seen as purely private sector companies. The question is whether an expansive or limited view of their public functions is taken.

---

[37] See M. Board *et al.*, *Accounting Requirement for Regulated Industries* (London, CRI 1998) for a description of current practices.

[38] E.g., see National Consumer Council, *Unclear Waters: Consumer Prices and Water Company Financial Information* (London, National Consumer Council, 1997).

[39] There has, however, been criticism that much less information about the activities of the electricity companies is now in the public domain.

[40] Cabinet Office, *Your Right to Know* (London, HMSO, 1998), Cm 3818.

[41] See *Government Response to the 3rd Report from the Select Committee on Public Administration*, HC 1020 (1997–8), para. 18.

[42] *Ibid.*

DIRECTORS' REMUNERATION

As far as the regulatory system is concerned, this is the case of the dog that did not bark. The salaries of the directors of privatised utilities, and other associated means of payment, became a matter of some political controversy in the mid to late 1990s to the point where the Employment Select Committee held an inquiry into the topic.[43] Despite the wide public controversy, none of the regulators took any action on this matter and only Clare Spottiswoode, the Director General of Gas Supply, gave evidence to the committee. She argued that the entire purpose of the regulatory system was to look at prices charged, not the costs of utilities. Although this is an over-simplification, as the discussion of multi-utilities below indicates, the committee, and the government in its response, accepted that it was undesirable to involve the utility regulators in the determination of executive pay.[44]

Although the issue of directors' pay was something that the Labour Party tried to exploit in the General Election campaign, when it came to the issue of changing the regulatory system to take this issue on board, it has shied away from any changes. The Green Paper on utility regulation states that utility companies should adopt best practice in setting arrangements for determining boardroom pay. In addition, the government was attracted to a closer link between directors' remuneration and the achievement of customer service standards, particularly for companies operating in monopolistic markets. In order to achieve this, regulators are to be encouraged to write an annual open letter to the relevant remuneration committee setting out the performance of that company against its service standards.[45] The Director General of Water Services recently reiterated that this was a job for the shareholders, although the regulator could help by making it clear on what basis decisions about price controls were made. So therefore, if a director's pay was linked to meeting specific service standards and the regulator made it clear that those standards were not being reached, this would send a clear signal to the shareholders.[46]

RECENT DEVELOPMENTS—REGULATING FOR COMPETITION

This, then, is the regulatory structure created in the aftermath of privatisation. It can be characterised as being concerned with the economic problems of the regulation of monopoly, that is, product market competition, with the issue of

---

[43] Employment Select Committee, *The Remuneration of Directors and Chief Executives of Privatised Utilities* (London, HMSO, HC 159, 1994–5). See now Treasury News Release 135/98, 11 Aug. 1998, "Boardroom pay continues to rise".

[44] Spottiswoode's evidence is at HC 159–ix, Question 1829, the Committee's conclusions at paras. 63 and 64 and the government's response is HC 38 (1995–6).

[45] *A Fair Deal*, n. 7 above, paras. 3.34–3.38 and *Response*, n. 7 above, paras. 28–33.

[46] See Office of Water Services Press Notice 29/98, 7 July 1998.

social obligations as a secondary matter. A very conservative approach to capital market competition was taken, with the normal competition law powers being buttressed by golden shares. Finally, just to make sure that no unwanted developments occurred, the government retained key powers in a number of important areas.

However, the competitive environment within which these industries operate has changed significantly since privatisation, in part due to the development of government policy. With the exception of water, all the industries have been opened up to competition in the domestic as well as the industrial and commercial sectors. The key economic fact relating to all these industries is that they are "network" industries, which means that services have to be delivered over a network which is a natural monopoly, although perhaps not in telecommunications. Thus in order to introduce competition competitors must be given access to the network on fair terms and conditions. The policy problem is that the incumbent utilities operated supply businesses as well as network businesses. The regulators have been concerned to ensure both fair terms for interconnection and separation between the supply and network businesses as the information provided by competitors to the network business could be used to the advantage of the supply business, thus stifling the growth of competition.

In telecommunications the key event was the government's review of the duopoly policy in 1991 after which it was decided that the telecommunications sector would be opened up to all firms who wished to enter it. The result has been a massive expansion in competition, even though BT remains the dominant player in the market. BT's licence conditions changed significantly in this period, primarily as the regulator sought to provide protections against BT acting anti-competitively. The original licence included a prohibition on cross-subsidising certain activities, primarily apparatus supply, provided for separate accounts for the apparatus supply and systems businesses and a provided for a code of practice on the confidentiality of customer information.[47] After the duopoly review, and with the increase in competition and the development of new telecommunications services, these provisions were amended and supplemented by new licence conditions. In particular, Oftel developed sophisticated new conditions which, in essence, required BT to provide disaggregated financial information for each of its businesses in order to try and ensure that it was not cross-subsidising various activities.[48]

Whereas in telecommunications the transition to a competitive market place was relatively smooth, in gas matters it proceeded much less easily. Essentially the regulator and British Gas had a series of protracted disputes over the introduction of competition into the industrial and commercial sector.[49]

---

[47] BT Licence conds. 18, 20 and 38.

[48] BT Licence conds. 20A and 20B; see also Oftel, *Interconnection and Accounting Separation* (London, Oftel, 1994) for discussion of this issue.

[49] For a history see C. Robinson, "Regulating the British Gas Industry: The MMC, the Government and the Future of Regulation" 6 *Utilities Law Review* 43.

This culminated in two references to the MMC, one by the regulator and the other by the Secretary of State. The MMC came down, amongst other conclusions, in favour of liberalising the domestic market in gas but recommended that, in consequence, British Gas should be split into two different companies, one dealing with the pipeline business, the other with gas supply. After some hesitation, the government rejected this part of the report, believing instead that it could create an effective internal separation within the business. Although, ironically, British Gas has now voluntarily split itself into two businesses,[50] this has led to some specific licence conditions designed to keep the activities of the two halves separate.

As well as a condition in Transco's licence providing for separate accounts,[51] two other provisions need to be mentioned. First, Condition 8A deals with the managing director of Transco. This provision requires that the licensee shall appoint a managing director who will be responsible for the conduct of the transportation and storage business. The managing director will be provided with the necessary persons, equipment and finance to enable the licensee to comply with its obligations under the Gas Act 1995. The managing director is required to report to the directors if these resources are not sufficient to carry out the obligations and, in any event, is required to make an annual report on these matters to the directors. Any such reports are to be given to the Director General of Gas Supply who may arrange for them to be published. The people and equipment supplied to the managing director shall not be used in other activities of the licensee, unless approved by the Director. Certain arrangements are allowed to be managed by employees other than the managing director if they do not involved an "unjustified cross subsidy" (Condition 8A 3 (2)). Finally, the licensee is only allowed to give directions to the managing director where the statutory or contractual obligations or the directors' duties so require.

The second relevant condition is amended standard condition 25 which in essence provides that the licensee shall not dispose of any parts of the transportation or storage system without the consent of the Director or, in cases involving a significant part of the gas transportation system, the Secretary of State. This is similar to a provision that was in the Rolls Royce golden share in relation to the nuclear business before it was sold to British Aerospace minus the reference to the regulator.

We can see here very detailed provision in the licences reaching right into the internal organisation of a company unlike other plcs. The justification for this seems to be the natural monopoly elements of the transportation business or, to put it another way, the fact that Transco is carrying out a function, by virtue of its licence, which is not simply a private matter, the state has an interest in ensuring the continued working of the gas transportation pipeline.

---

[50] British Gas Transco, responsible for gas transportation, and Centrica, responsible for gas supply.
[51] Standard Cond. 2, as amended.

In relation to the electricity supply companies I have mentioned above that the industry was restructured upon privatisation, separating generation, transmission and distribution and supply. As regards the distribution and supply companies their licences provide for separate accounts for separate businesses, a prohibition on cross-subsidies, restrictions on the disposal of parts of the distribution system and requirements about arrangements for the health and safety of employees.[52] This approach has been carried further as, in the Green Paper reviewing utility regulation, it was proposed to introduce separate licences for the distribution and supply activities of the electricity supply companies.[53] Although not stated in this review, the implication would seem to be that, by analogy with gas, operations would be carried out by separate companies holding the licence, or at least separately identifiable business units.[54]

This sort of intervention into the internal structure of a company has not been restricted just to issues relating to competition. The most high profile intervention occurred in the water industry as a consequence of the severe drought in 1995 and the way that it was handled, or mishandled, by Yorkshire Water. The episode was notable for some inept public relations by Yorkshire Water, suggesting rota cuts initially without consultation with local industry and avoiding the use of standpipes by doing everything possible to deal with the problem, including the employment of a vast fleet of tanker trucks to ferry water to the afflicted areas. The events were also noticeable because Yorkshire Water was penalised heavily by the regulator, who amended the company's licence to reduce permissible price increases from RPI + 2.5 to RPI + zero for the year beginning in 1997, and to allow only lower price increases than those allowed in the existing price limits for the following two years. In addition, a number of management changes were required, including the appointment of non-executive directors with experience and understanding of the interests of consumers.[55]

MULTI-UTILITIES

The coming of competition in domestic supply, as well as the prospect of the liberalisation of European utilities markets, has led utility companies to consider a number of strategies for survival within the new markets. One strategic option has been to develop what are known as multi-utilities, that is businesses which operate more than one utility service. Currently these fall into two categories: monopoly utility network companies (water and electricity) and multi-utility

---

[52] Public Electricity Supply Licence conds. 2,4,25 and 27.

[53] *A Fair Deal*, n. 7 above, paras. 4.13–4.15 and *Response*, n. 7 above, paras. 51–4.

[54] This is made clear in Offer, *Reviews of Public Electricity Suppliers 1998 to 2000: Separation of Businesses Consultation Paper* (Birmingham, Offer, 1998).

[55] See Ofwat, *Report on Conclusions from Ofwat's Enquiry into the Performance of Yorkshire Water Services* (Birmingham, Ofwat, 1996).

supply companies (primarily providers of electricity and gas).[56] In one instance, that of Hyder, the Welsh electricity and water company, the core operational activities of the regulated businesses are combined in Hyder Operations, leaving a small amount of residual activity in the companies which actually hold the licences. In a sense, this has made the utility companies into "virtual" utilities which contract for the activities which they are obliged to provide under licence. This is a further future possibility for the development of utility companies.

The opening of the gas and electricity markets to domestic competition has given rise to what are known as "dual fuel" companies, that is companies who offer to supply the customer with both gas and electricity. If this is considered alongside the increasing use of gas for electricity generation, the existence of separate regulators for gas and electricity seems increasingly problematic. As a result, the government has proposed, in its Green Paper,[57] merging the two offices, thus creating a single regulator for the energy sector. One of the aims will be to overcome any co-ordination problems that might have existed or might develop.

For their part, the regulators see two main problems arising from the development of multi-utilities; the problem of identifying costs for the purpose of price reviews and ensuring appropriate independence for the licence holder. The problem in terms of costs is that price controls are set on the basis of a future prediction of what the costs of an efficient business would be. With a multi-utility, or any group undertaking competitive and regulated activities, there is a danger of the company loading costs onto the monopoly or regulated business, as well as a problem of double counting, for example, if two regulators allow the costs to be funded twice. In order to deal with this the regulators have put in place guidelines on cost allocation between regulated and non-regulated companies and guidance on transfer prices to associated companies. For the future they will review the working of these guidelines, seek greater co-ordination between regulators and greater transparency from the companies.

In relation to the question of independence, which has only so far been at issue in water and electricity, both regulators have put in place licence conditions which are aimed at ensuring independence of the licence holders. In relation to water this includes certain restrictions on the conduct of board members, relating in part to conflicts of interest, and requiring the Director General's consent for transfers of assets to associates and guarantees or loans to associated companies. In electricity there are also restrictions on transfer of assets and the giving of loans and guarantees, as well as restrictions on the activities the

---

[56] The distinction is drawn in *Regulatory Issues Associated with Multi-Utilities* (London; Birmingham; Belfast: Directors General of Electricity Supply, Gas Supply, Telecommunications, Water Services, and Directors General of Electrical Supply (N. Ireland) and Gas (N. Ireland), May 1998), (a joint consultation paper issued by all the regulators). App. 3 gives a list of the current multi-utilities.

[57] *A Fair Deal*, n. 7 above. paras. 4.4–4.12 and *Response*, n. 7 above, paras. 44–7.

licensee can carry out and a requirement to ensure that sufficient resources are available to carry out activities.[58]

SOCIAL OBLIGATIONS IN A COMPETITIVE MARKET

Although it might be thought that with the onset of a competitive market there would be no need to impose social obligations on utility companies, this has not been the case in practice. In the gas supply industry, gas supply companies are, amongst other duties, under an obligation to supply domestic customers, to offer new contracts to existing customers, are subject to certain limitations as regards their power to disconnect and to report on the fulfilment of their social obligations under the licence.[59] Similar provisions exist in relation to the licences of those companies which are going to supply the competitive electricity market.[60] In the telecommunications industry, the most competitive of all the utilities sectors, the increase in competition has not brought with it a lessening of interest in social obligations. The reverse has happened, because Oftel has undertaken a large amount of policy development in this area, in part inspired by developments in the European Community.[61]

THE FUTURE LEGISLATIVE STRUCTURE

At the same time that the utilities are undergoing significant and far-reaching changes within their industries, the government is also undertaking a review of the system of utility regulation, the first results of which were published in a Green Paper.[62] This promises significant changes to the regulatory system, which need some discussion, especially as they tie in with some of the themes that have already been mentioned.

The first issue is that of the stakeholder debate. One of the consistent criticisms of the privatised utilities has been that they are primarily concerned with the issue of returns to their shareholders, to the exclusion of all else, except possibly larger salary payments for the directors! This, the critics argue, is the result of a regulatory system which has, as one of its primary duties, a concern with the companies' ability to finance themselves and no inbuilt representation of other interests, rather a domination by single, often idiosyncratic individuals. They advocate instead a stakeholder approach which involves identifying the stakeholders involved in the utilities and trying to construct a remit for

[58] The Director General of Electricity Supply is currently considering tightening these requirements.

[59] Gas Suppliers' Licence Standard Conds. 2, 4, 15–21.

[60] Second Tier Electricity Supply Licence, Sect. C.

[61] See Oftel, *Universal Telecommunications Services—Statement* (London, Oftel, 1997) and *Universal Telecommunications Service—Consultative Document* (London, Oftel, 1997).

[62] *A Fair Deal* and *Response*, n. 7 above.

regulation based around an "optimal balance between their interests".[63] This proposal has a kinship with the views which see the company as a social enterprise and aim to extend board membership to include, most commonly, employees but also, at times, people representing other interests. Instead of focusing on the company's board, supporters of this approach wish to replace individual regulators with commissions, which is felt would be better at balancing the various interests involved.[64]

In so far as this approach is aimed at improving the accountability of regulators there are a number of potential problems, such as ensuring the openness of deliberations amongst the commissioners.[65] More seriously, the stakeholder approach is just a re-statement of the problem, rather than a solution. Its virtues are in pointing out that there is a wide range of interests which are affected by the decisions of regulators, and utility companies, and that these interests do not necessarily coincide. It does not, however, follow that the best approach to this issue is to try and strike a balance between the competing interests. As has been pointed out,[66] the job of regulators is to take the right decision, which may not involve balancing the various interests. To take a concrete example, one way in which the utility companies have driven down costs, and thus prices to consumers, is through shedding workers, through both compulsory and voluntary means. This process creates costs for the, by now, ex-employees, as well as benefits for the consumers, but it is an open question whether slowing down the process, in search of a balance, would have been a better option, as it would have put the costs of supporting the employees on the consumers of utility services, rather than making it a question for government policies relating to re-training and welfare benefits, that is, a question for citizens as a whole.

In any event, it is not clear that the government sees a need for any significant change on these lines. In the Green Paper[67] three proposals for changing the regulatory offices were mentioned. The first was to appoint a statutory advisory group to support the sectoral regulators, which is simply an extension of existing practice. The second was to replace individual regulators with small executive boards, which again is probably just a variant on existing practice as the regulators do not make their decisions in isolation without consulting their senior staff. Finally, they might replace individual regulators with a small commission, with a four-day-a week chair and other members working at least one day a week. In practice this looks like little change as well, as the chair would have much more time and information available than the other members. After consultation, the government concluded that, in energy and telecommunica-

---

[63]   See D. Corry *et al.*, *Regulating Our Utilities* (London, IPPR, 1994). The quotation is from 35.

[64]   *Ibid.*, 84–6.

[65]   Generally see C. Graham, *Is There a Crisis in Regulatory Accountability?* (London, CRI, 1996), 42–5.

[66]   P. Vass, "Consumer Representation Integration or Independence?" in P. Vass (ed.), *Regulatory Review 1995* (London, CRI, 1995).

[67]   *A Fair Deal*, n. 7 above, paras. 7.4–7.13.

tions, individual regulators should be replaced by full-time executive boards of three people; a chair and two others.[68]

This does, however, lead into a second issue, namely the duties placed upon the regulators. The critics of the current system have argued that it places too much weight on the ability of the companies to finance their activities and the promotion of competition, at the expense of the consumer interest. In the Green Paper the government proposed to amend the general duties of regulators into a new primary duty "to exercise their functions in the manner they consider best calculated to protect the interests of consumers . . .".[69] The paper pointed out that wherever possible and appropriate this should be done through the promotion of competition and also that regulators should not tighten price controls to the point that investment and continuity of supply by the industry are put at risk. In other words, there will be little change to the existing duties and the same problems will still exist, namely that of balancing the interests of the consumers with the ability of the companies to finance their activities, as well as balancing these interests with the promotion of competition.

Another area where change is promised is in the relationships between ministers and the regulators. As we have seen above, ministers have a number of powers of intervention in relation to the regulatory system. No change is proposed to these, but instead the government proposes that there should be statutory guidance on the social and environmental objectives for each sector and that regulators should be placed under a duty to have regard to that guidance. In addition, where government is going to take action which would have significant financial implications for the utilities, this will only be done through legislation.[70] Such guidance will be subject to full consultation and will last for a number of years, such as the length of a Parliament or a price control round.

These proposals are an explicit recognition that government may have a social and environmental agenda for the utility sector or, to put it another way, that utilities are not considered as ordinary companies. One way of interpreting this proposed system is that it assumes that, for most of their activities, utilities are just like any other company. However, in the areas where government has non-economic objectives, it will intervene in a transparent fashion, so that deviations from a strict market approach can be seen and government will be accountable for setting the policy priorities which will be implemented by the regulators. Although one might wonder about the attractiveness of such proposals to any government, the point for present purposes is the recognition of utilities as a sector raising different problems from that of other companies.

This flows through to the government's proposals for reforming the system of consumer representation. Broadly speaking, the existing system of consumer committees is to be replaced by new, independent consumer committees, organised on

---

[68] *Response*, n. 7 above, paras. 69–70. The government hopes to extend this model to water as well.

[69] *A Fair Deal*, n. 7 above, para. 3.6 confirmed in *Response*, n. 7 above, para. 16.

[70] *A Fair Deal*, n. 7 above, paras. 2.13–2.19 confirmed in *Response*, n. 7 above, paras. 10–12.

a national basis with new rights to information from the regulator and the companies, the latter courtesy of freedom of information legislation.[71] In the context of the development of utility markets, this raises a number of questions. If we assume a competitive market for energy and telecommunications services, why is there a need for a specific statutory set of consumer arrangements? Such services are critical to the quality of people's life but so is the provision of food, and statutory consumer representative bodies do not exist in this sector. Again, it is not necessary to answer this question, simply to raise it to show how, even though the utilities are moving away from monopoly to competition, they are still seen as in some sense different from other companies and hence worthy of special arrangements.

CONCLUSIONS

What I hope has been evident from this essay is how the regulation of utilities occupies a middle ground between the extremes of unfettered market forces and state control. Once market forces were recognised as having a legitimate role to play in relation to utilities, the policy question has become how to create effective markets and how to ensure that issues which markets are poor at or incapable of taking into account, such as social and environmental obligations, can be factored into the regulatory system. This will remain a live issue, even in the new world of multi-utilities and competitive markets. However, the move away from nationalisation, via privatisation, towards competitive domestic markets has meant that governments have had to be more open about such interventions, something reflected, to an extent, in the Green Paper. This is not to say that these policies or interventions have always been successful, merely to point out the terms of the policy agenda which will continue into the future.

I also hope there are at least two lessons for those interested in developing the social responsibility of companies. One is to caution enthusiasts for new institutional forms and regulation that the creation of these new institutions is merely the beginning of a story, not the end of it. How a regulatory system works in practice is just as, if not more important, than the hopes initially vested in it. Secondly, there may be an argument for tailoring specific regimes for corporate responsibility, rather than trying to produce some general schema based in company law as a whole. There is something to be said for trying to think what social obligations a specific group of companies should deliver as opposed to concentrating on social responsibility in the abstract.

[71] *A Fair Deal*, n. 7 above, paras. 3.10–3.18 confirmed in *Response*, n. 7 above, paras. 17–19.

10

Groups of Companies: The Path towards Discrete Regulation

DAVID MILMAN

INTRODUCTION

Historical Perspective

If I can start this paper with a confession, I must admit that when constructing the series of essays for this collection I did not immediately contemplate a separate discussion of groups. The legal tradition in which I was raised merely treated groups as an interesting side issue within the broad subject of company law, a sub-plot within the fascinating saga of lifting the veil of corporate personality. That tradition (which was founded upon strict legal analysis and largely disregarded any economic perspective) has waned in the academic community[1] in the past two decades, and for the purposes of any constructive discussion of groups that change in perspective must be welcome. It is now universally recognised that groups deserve to be recognised as a form of business organisation *sui generis*, and indeed that they represent the preferred choice for the conduct of large scale commerce.

Having resolved to give groups the attention they deserved I was faced with an immediate dichotomy. The academic literature on groups of companies is extensive[2] and of high quality; the actual and formal legal regulation of groups

---

[1] For the most part UK legislators and many judges in the English law seem reluctant to see the light in this respect: see e.g. the comment of Robert Goff LJ in *Bank of Tokyo* v. *Karoon* [1987] AC 45 at 64.

[2] For general treatment of the subject see Wooldridge, *Groups of Companies:The Law and Practice in Britain, France and Germany* (London, IALS, 1981); Hopt (ed.), *Groups of Companies in European Laws* (Berlin, de Gruyter, 1982); Hadden, *The Control of Corporate Groups* (London, IALS, 1983); Sugarman and Teubner (eds.), *Regulating Corporate Groups in Europe* (Baden-Baden, NOMOS, 1990); Schmitthoff and Wooldridge (eds.), *Groups of Companies* (London, Sweet & Maxwell, 1991), McCahery, Picciotto and Scott, *Corporate Control and Accountability* (Oxford, OUP Clarendon, 1993), chs. 16–20; Dine, *Models of Companies and the Regulation of Groups in The Corporate Dimension*, ed. Rider (Bristol, Jordans, 1997), ch. 15 . Further comparative perspectives are offered by Blumberg (1986) 11 Jo of Corporation Law 611 and (1990) 15 Del J of Corp Law 283; Gillooly (ed.), *The Law Relating to Corporate Groups* (Sydney, Butterworths, 1993) and Austin in Grantham and Rickett (ed.), *Corporate Personality in the 20th Century* (Oxford, Hart, 1998), ch. 4.

on the other hand is patchy and seems, for the most part, to betray a reluctance to grasp the nettle posed by the critical issues. Why this might be so will be one question to consider in this latest academic contribution to the debate.

English law offers no formal definition of a group, though strangely it does seek to define the key players within a group, namely parent and subsidiary undertakings (Companies Act 1985, section 736). However, a group is a well understood concept in the commercial world. A group may be defined as a family of related companies or businesses in which one company (the parent or holding company) maintains effective control over the other members through share ownership. Commonality of shareholding, coupled with unified managerial control, is the distinctive characteristic of a group. Co-operative arrangements between companies based upon friendly cross holdings will not be regarded as forming a group structure for the purposes of this essay. In the evolutionary process groups represent an advanced stage of development building upon the now established concept of the limited liability company enjoying its own distinct personality which is separate from the identity of its shareholding members . It is well recognised that there is a time lag between developments in business and resulting legal regulation and this is one reason why the law in the UK (and in many other jurisdictions) has been so tardy in addressing some of the related problems. As Hadden has indicated, however, there may be special factors at work here, adding to that dilatory approach, namely a concern not to upset the international business community which depends so heavily upon legal stability in this area.

Groups first made their appearance in the USA. The critical event seems to have been the abolition (in 1888) in the key state of New Jersey of the rule prohibiting companies from owning shares in other companies.[3] It is more difficult to track their entry onto the English scene. There was no formal rule banning holdings in shares of other companies and therefore no statutory repeal on which to focus attention. What is clear is that groups were beginning to feature in litigation from the turn of the twentieth century (though in these early days the concept of a group does not appear to have been fully appreciated by the courts) and the first attempt at statutory regulation came in the 1928 Companies Act, in which section 40 stated that the balance sheet of a holding company had to provide financial details on subsidiaries. Hadden has researched this subject in depth,[4] and by way of confirmation he points to the period of the 1920s and

---

[3] See Blumberg (1990) 15 *Delaware Jo. of Corp. Law* 283 at 325. In Japan prohibitions on group formation existed in Japan for many years after 1945: a ban operated on "pure" holding companies (i.e. parents which themselves did not conduct any business) in the form of Art. 9 of the Anti-Monopoly Law (see Oda, *Japanese Law* (1992) at 347–8). This hostile approach was partly due to concerns about large industrial combines and their role in the rise of Japanese militarism and also due to a policy of protecting against monopolies. A more permissive stance was adopted in 1996. In the USA there are still restrictions in the banking sector, but these are on the point of being relaxed. In South Africa it is not possible for a close corporation to be a subsidiary of another company for the reason that corporate membership is prohibited.

[4] See e.g. his piece in (1984) 12 *Int Jo. of Sociology of Law* 271 (a rare empirical study of group structures). Hadden has undertaken similar research in Australia: see his article in (1992) 15 *Univ. of NSW Law Jo.* 61.

1930s as an appropriate point of entry for groups into the conscious jurisprudence of UK company law. The potential problems posed by groups preoccupied the Greene Commitee[5] which reviewed company law in the 1920s. On publication of this report in 1926 proposals were tabled for consolidation of financial information within a group. These proposals manifested themselves in the Companies Act 1928 and were consolidated in the 1929 legislation.[6] The issue was revisited by the Cohen Committee[7] which suggested in 1945 further enhancement of the statutory mechanisms for the disclosure of group financial data. The Companies Act 1947, sections 14–18, duly obliged by providing for group accounts, and this reform was then consolidated within sections 150–154 of the 1948 Act. This period also saw the ban on financial assistance in share purchases being extended to financial assistance being provided by a subsidiary of the company whose shares were being acquired (see Companies Act 1948, section 54). The Jenkins Committee, which reviewed companies regulation in the early 1960s, did consider certain aspects in the law relating to groups and did suggest minor changes in the test for determining whether a company was a subsidiary of another.[8]

Groups have been the focus of media attention in recent years in the wake of a number of spectacular collapses; the reverberations of Maxwell, BCCI and Polly Peck are rarely out of the public spotlight. These cases show the great significance of groups in the UK (and international) business scene and the difficulties posed for effective regulation.

Reasons for the Emergence of Groups

There are essentially two reasons why a group structure develops. First, it may arise in piecemeal fashion through the process of corporate acquisition. Thus, an acquisitive company acquires a controlling shareholding in another company, and in the process a parent/subsidiary nexus is created.[9] More interestingly, groups have developed on a strategic basis to take advantage of loopholes/opportunities created because of the legal fiction that a company is distinct from its shareholders (which translates into the position that a subsidiary is separate from the holding company that owns its shares). For example, there may be considerable tax advantages in fragmenting a single business enterprise into a collection of distinct entities.[10] With the growth of transnational commerce the

---

[5] Cmd. 2657.
[6] See Companies Act (CA) 1928, s. 40 and the consolidating (and more sophisticated) CA 1929, ss 125–7.
[7] Cmd. 6659.
[8] Cmnd. 1749, para. 156.
[9] In the UK the usual practice is to acquire 100% control of the company which becomes the subsidiary.
[10] See Morse, ch. 4 in Feldman and Meisel (eds.), *Corporate and Commercial Law: Modern Developments* (1996) for a discussion of the VAT treatment of groups.

group is the ideal vehicle for the effective and profitable conduct of business in several jurisdictions. Potential liabilities can be isolated[11] and profits can be moved around within the group to maximum advantage, particularly through the practice of transfer pricing.[12] The creation of a local subsidiary may also be necessary both for diplomatic and technical legal reasons in the context of the inward investment policies pursued by the host jurisdiction. This stategic usage of a group, particularly an international group, may be taken to extremes by entrepreneurs wishing to exploit this structure for fraudulent purposes.[13]

LEGAL PROBLEMS IN REGULATING GROUPS

Identifying Constituent Members and Consequences of Being a Group Member

A basic issue to determine is whether a particular firm forms part of a group. Unfortunately this is not an easy matter to resolve and has caused difficulty for legislators throughout Europe.[14] This conundrum was most recently addressed in English law in the Companies Act 1989. Prior to this legislation the test for whether a company was a subsidiary of another was based upon strict notions of control.[15] The 1989 provision (which sought to implement the Seventh EC Company Law Harmonisation Directive[16]) adopted a more flexible/realistic approach[17] and also included partnerships within the broad definition of subsidiary undertaking. Basically under section 736 of the Companies Act 1985 a company is regarded as a subsidiary of another if the other company holds (or controls) a majority of its voting rights, or if the other company controls its board of directors. Further amplification of questions of voting rights and board control is provided by section 736A.

By virtue of the combined effect of sections 227 and 258 of the Companies Act 1985 a subsidiary undertaking is to be consolidated within the group accounts regime if one of four alternative tests is satisfied. These tests focus on control of a majority of voting rights or control of a majority of the board or the fact of a dominant influence exercised by virtue of provisions in the constitution or by

---

[11] The growth of ruinous tort litigation is often cited as a reason for the proliferation of subsidiaries in the USA: see Hansmann and Kraakman (1991) 100 *Yale L.J.* 1879 at 1881.

[12] For a review of the transfer pricing issue see Picciotto, ch. 20 in McCahery, Picciotto and Scott, n. 2 above.

[13] In such a case the English courts will not hesitate to ignore the separate identities of the respective group members: *Re A Company* [1985] BCLC 333.

[14] See Wooldridge in ch. 6 of Drury and Xuereb, *European Company Laws: A Comparative Approach* (1991). For group accounts in Commonwealth jurisdictions see e.g. Corporations Law, s. 294A (Australia) and Financial Reporting Act 1993, ss. 10–13 (New Zealand).

[15] CA 1948, ss. 150–4 dealt with group accounts. The test for control found in s. 154 was based on control of the board or of more than 50% of the voting rights.

[16] EEC/83/349. For discussion see Turley (1986) 7 *Co. Law* 10.

[17] A similar change in approach is reflected in non-EU jurisdictions such as Australia.

contract. The concept of undertaking is defined under section 259 as being sufficiently wide to encompass a company, partnership or other unincorporated association.

Once the membership of a group has been determined one consequence is that the question of access to financial information by stakeholders in the group needs to be addressed. The basic rule here is that shareholders in the parent company are entitled receive full information about financial health of the whole conglomerate, and the published accounts must be group accounts. Shareholders in subsidiaries do not enjoy this right of access, and indeed under existing law their right to seek disclosure of details of intra-group transactions is somewhat limited.[18] Although there is an obligation to submit consolidated accounts to the shareholders of the holding company this does not absolve the directors of the subsidiaries themselves from complying with their duty to maintain individual accounts.[19] In the event of the Ninth EC Harmonisation Directive being agreed and implemented the position on disclosure will be modified to improve acccess to information.

The state is entitled to treat the group as a single enterprise when exercising its power to investigate companies. Thus under section 433 of the Companies Act 1985 inspectors appointed to investigate the affairs of one company within a group can extend their enquiries to other group members. If a company is deemed to be in a group relationship with another company this can also have a variety of other potential consequences. Transactions between group members will be deemed to be between "connected persons" and time limits fixed for the invalidation of suspect transactions on insolvency will be extended.[20] Another rule, which is currently under review in English law,[21] is the prohibition in section 23 of the Companies Act 1985 on subsidiaries owning shares in their parent. English law is not unique in its efforts to discourage cross holdings, though this particular prohibition is directed more at supporting the capital maintenance rule than representing a serious attempt to get to grips with a potential problem associated with groups.[22] Notwithstanding these legal consequences it is clear from section 741(3) of the Companies Act 1985 that a parent is not automatically a shadow director of a subsidiary for the purposes of company law. Indeed it seems that the fact that a company's accounts are consolidated to include all group members dos not entitle the shareholders of the parent

---

[18]   On this problem see Hare and Archimandritou [1986] JBL 249.

[19]   *Dairy Containers* v. *NZI Bank Ltd* [1995] 2 NZLR 30 at 88, *per* Thomas J.

[20]   See e.g. Insolvency Act 1986, ss. 240 and 435(6).

[21]   This particular rule is under review as part of a general reconsideration of the capital maintenance concept in the run up to the introduction of EMU. This prohibition, which appears to have surfaced in CA 1947, s. 80, was modified by SI 1997/2306 to prevent it operating to frustrate the orderly conduct of stock market operations.

[22]   For a similar prohibition in other jurisdictions see Corporations Law, s. 185 (Australia), CA 1993, s. 82 (New Zealand). This prohibition is also found in Art. 24a of the Second EEC Company Law Harmonisation Dir. There is very little in the way of judicial discussion of this prohibition— for rare examples see *Stenhouse London Ltd* v. *Allwright*, 1972 SLT 255 and *Bond Corporation* v. *White Industries* (1980) 5 ACLC 88.

to a dividend based upon the profits of the subsidiaries.[23] At best, therefore, one is forced to conclude that the legal consequences of the existence of a group of companies are mixed.

Issues of Liability

The most controversial aspect of the law relating to groups concerns the issue of allocation of responsibility for liabilities undertaken by one group member. This issue becomes acute in situations of insolvency. This question has been considered by scholars in many a lively debate.[24] Generally speaking the strict legal approach has been in favour of disregarding the separate personality of group members. Thus members of a group are responsible for their own debts and, as Mason J stressed in the High Court of Australia in *Walker* v. *Wimborne*,[25] creditors of a group company do not have the right to go fishing for a solvent group member to settle their debt. Economists also favour retaining the present regime on the grounds that it is believed to be more economically efficient.[26]

It is clear that one member of a group cannot be held responsible for the liabilities of another member because on insolvency each group member is to be treated as a distinct company[27]. This position was described in lurid terms by Templeman J in *Re Southard & Co Ltd*[28]:

> "English company law possesses some curious features which may generate curious results. A parent company may spawn a number of subsidiary companies, all controlled directly or indirectly by the shareholders of the parent company. If one of the subsidiary companies, to change the metaphor, turns out to be the runt of the litter and declines into insolvency to the dismay of its creditors, the parent company and the other subsidiary companies may prosper to the joy of the shareholders without any liability for the debts of the insolvent subsidiary."

[23] See *Pennington's Company Law* (7th edn., 1995) at 982 where this point is supported by reference to US authority.

[24] The leading work on the issue of external liability is the excellent treatise by Muscat, *The Liability of the Holding Company for the Debts of its Insolvent Subsidiaries* (1996).

25 (1976) 137 CLR 1 at 7. The corollary of this is that the assets of individual group members should be respected for the protection of their creditors.

26 An illuminating rehearsal of the rival arguments is provided by Landers (1975) 42 *Univ. Chic. Law Rev.* 598 and Posner (1976) 43 *Univ. Chic. Law Rev.* 499. Landers argues for exposure of parents to liability for a wholly-owned subsidiary's debts, deferment of intra-group debts and pooling of assets on liquidation. Posner rejects these policy changes by outlining the alleged economic benefits flowing from the *status quo* and pointing out that interest rates can always reflect the degree of risk faced by creditors. In a convincing reply—(1976) 43 *Univ. Chic. Law Rev.* 527—Landers argues that trade creditors are not properly equipped to investigate risk and that interest rates are rarely individually tailored in the way that Posner suggests.

[27] A procedural chink in this wall occurred in *Re Wm. Pickles plc* [1996] BCC 408 where to save costs a single application was permitted in respect of a group which was in the process of being wound up.

[28] [1979] 1 WLR 1198. For criticism see Schmitthoff [1979] JBL 218.

This insulation of a parent from the obligations of a subsidiary has subsequently been reaffirmed by the Court of Appeal, in a somewhat different context, in *Adams* v. *Cape Industries*.[29] Resentment at this position often centres upon the fact that the collapsed subsidiary had a low capitalisation and secured credit solely because of its connection with the more substantial parent. By the liberal creation of undercapitalised subsidiaries a second level of limited liability protection is thus created for businesses wishing to insulate themselves from enterprise liabilities. This state of affairs has attracted criticism from a variety of sources, including leading members of the judiciary:

> "The creation or purchase of a subsidiary with minimal liability which will operate with the parent's funds and on the parent's directions but not expose the parent to liability may not seem to some the most honest way of trading."[30]

In spite of these indisputable points the orthodox approach is maintained in more cases than it is denied.

The position is exacerbated by allowing group members to prove in competition with outside creditors on the winding up of a fellow group member provided the credit transaction cannot be challenged.[31] Intra-group financing is a feature of the group economy[32] but to many observers to treat intra-group creditors as if they were independent is adding insult to injury. There are also potential problems of conflict of interest here for insolvency practitioners accepting appointment as liquidator where such cross-claims within a group exist; this matter has troubled the courts[33] but official guidelines do not prohibit an insolvency practitioner accepting multiple appointments in such circumstances.[34] In spite of these concerns the orthodox position permitting proof of debt between group members was most recently maintained in *Re Polly Peck International plc (No 3)*.[35]

As far as English law is concerned there are a number of recognised exceptions from this policy of denial of responsibility.

---

[29] [1990] 2 WLR 657.

[30] *Per* Staughton LJ in *Atlas Maritime Co* v. *Avalon Maritime Ltd (No 1)* [1991] 4 All ER 769 at 779.

[31] The repayment of a debt or the creation of a secured debt may fall foul of the rules on transactional avoidance in an insolvency situation. Note here ss. 239 and 245 of the Insolvency Act 1986 and *Re Shoe Lace Ltd* [1993] BCC 609. Generally speaking time limits relating to vulnerable transactions are extended where the beneficiary was a fellow group member, but apart from this variation the standard rule that a debtor can repay creditors in the order that he chooses applies in the group context: see *Re Sarflax Ltd* [1979] 2 WLR 202, *per* Oliver J at 217. It is of course open to companies within a group to agree to defer intra-group indebtedness to the claims of outside creditors; such voluntary subordination is acceptable. see *Banque Financière de la Cité* v. *Parc (Battersea) Ltd* [1998] 1 All ER 737 which is analysed by Bridge in [1998] *Journal of Business Law* 323.

[32] See Hadden (1984) 12 *Int. Jo. of Sociology of Law* 271 at 277.

[33] Compare here the comments of Harman J in *Re Corbenstoke Ltd (No 2)* (1989) 5 BCC 767 with those of Dillon LJ in *Re Esal Commodities Ltd* (1988) 4 BCC 475.

[34] *Katz* v. *McNally* [1997] BCC 784.

[35] [1996] 1 BCLC 428.

1. Guaranteed Liabilities

It may be lawful for a parent to agree by contract to guarantee the debts of a subsidiary (or vice versa). Cross-guarantees within groups are becoming the norm for group treasury arrangements.[36] Once questions relating to the proper exercise of corporate powers have been resolved,[37] the issue here is essentially one of construction of the relevant paperwork. Is the document in question a guarantee, and what is the extent of the responsibility that is being undertaken? On the first issue it is important to distinguish between a legally enforceable guarantee and the more nebulous letter of intent or comfort.[38] The true legal status of these documents depends essentially upon their precise wording. The use of such documents in a group environment was considered in *Re Augustus Barnett Ltd*.[39] A similar issue arose in *National Australia Bank Ltd* v. *Soden*[40] and Chadwick J held that the recipient of the letter of comfort, which had been issued to placate a creditor of a subsidiary, could not rely on that letter to assert creditor status with respect to the parent. Even where the document is indisputably a guarantee there may be questions about the extent of liabilities undertaken. The House of Lords addressed these issues in *Ford and Carter Ltd* v. *Midland Bank*.[41] Here a parent and a number of subsidiaries had entered into a mutual guarantee. The question was whether a subsidiary which had joined the group at a later date was a party to the mutual guarantee. Their Lordships refused to impose such a burden without clear evidence of voluntary assumption and rejected an argument that an officer within the group enjoyed continuing authority to bind all members of the group to such a commitment.

There is still an unresolved possibility that may be tested in the courts in future. If a parent allows a subsidiary to exploit the goodwill in its name and to undertake obligations could it not be argued on the basis of general agency principles that it is permitting the subsidiary to hold itself out as its agent and that any resulting obligations should be met by it as principal?

2. Judicially Approved Pooling Arrangements

As was explained above the general rule on corporate insolvency is that the assets and liabilities of the group members must be dealt with on the basis of strict separation. That rule however does permit of exceptions. Thus the court

[36] For discusion of the role of cross guarantees in Australia see Hill (1995) 24 *Can. Bus. Law Jo.* 321.

[37] A guarantee of a parent's debts given by a subsidiary was struck down in *ANZ* v. *Qintex* (1990) 2 ACSR 676 on the grounds that the subsidiary itself was insolvent and the guarantee could not possibly be of benefit to it.

[38] *Kleinwort Benson* v. *Malaysian Mining Corp. Bhd* [1989] 1 WLR 379.

[39] [1986] BCLC 170. Discussed by Prentice in (1987) 103 *LQR* 11 and Milman (1986) 7 *Co. Law* 245.

[40] [1995] BCC 696.

[41] (1979) 129 *NLJ* 543.

does have the power to approve of a scheme of arrangement under section 426 of the Companies Act 1985 that departs from that simplistic solution.[42] More importantly, it does appear that in wholly exceptional cases the court may support proposals from liquidators which in effect pool assets and liabilities, even though no formal scheme of arrangement is on the table. One such case presented itself in *Re BCCI SA*,[43] where a pooling arrangement entered into pursuant to a liquidator's statutory power to compromise was upheld. This case involved massive fraud and horrendous practical complications because of the multi-jurisdictional basis of the group enterprise. It was therefore hardly surprising that standard company law solutions would prove wanting and that professional and judiciary creativity would come to the fore.

This pragmatic issue has arisen recently in a number of Australian liquidation cases. In *Deans-Willcocks v. Soluble Solution Hydroponics Pty Ltd*[44] Young J supported a proposal (which was backed by creditors) under which the assets and liabilities of two companies in the same group were consolidated. Young J pointed out that in bankruptcy law there were precedents for such an equitable solution. Here the business affairs of the two companies were so inextricably mixed that any attempt to separate assets and liabilities would be unsound. Young J favoured a similar solution in *Re Charter Travel Co Ltd*.[45] Here there was a similar confusion of assets/liabilities and the learned judge had no difficulty in agreeing that a proposal should be put to creditors recommending consolidation. Young J made the point that with the increasing instances of complex multijurisdiction corporate group collapses this solution based upon consolidation was likely to become more necessary in the future. Although these cases were decided under the Australian jurisdiction it is submitted that they may also be said to represent an approach available in English law.[46]

---

[42] See here *Re Trix Ltd* [1970] 3 All ER 397 and *Re BCCI (No 3)* [1993] BCLC 1490 where the availablity of pooling through a scheme of arrangement was confirmed. In Australia formal statutory provision has now been made for schemes of arrangement involving groups: Corporations Law, s. 411(1A), (1B) and (1C).

[43] The key authorities in this legal maze are *Re BCCI SA (No 3)* [1993] BCLC 1490 (CA) and *Re BCCI (No 10)* [1997] 2 WLR 172 (Scott VC) . The view taken by Plowman J in *Re Trix Ltd*, n. 42 above, that pooling could not be effected under the liquidator's power of compromise must therefore be regarded as doubtful. In reaching that unhelpful conclusion Plowman J was mindful of the need for the final decision to be in the hands of creditors but that becomes more difficult to manage with large groups of creditors based in several jurisdictions.

[44] (1997) 24 ACSR 79.

[45] (1997) 25 ACSR 337. See also *Metha v. GE Capital* (1998) 27 ACSR 696 where Finkelstein J supported an argument that the power of the court to agree to a deed of company voluntary arrangement included a power to agree to group consolidation.

[46] The case of *Re Wm Pickles plc* [1996] BCC 408, albeit a case on procedure rather than substantive rights, is a good pointer of how judicial attitudes in this country are developing on the issue of consolidation.

3. Assumption of Management Responsibilities

Liability within a group may also be shared where the insolvent member company has been mismanaged and that mismanagement can be traced back to the parent. Under English law if the parent company controls the actions of the directors of a subsidiary and their conduct could be characterised as wrongful trading contrary to section 214 of the Insolvency Act 1986, the parent might be regarded as a "shadow director" and treated as equally responsible; automatic liability is replaced by a form of functional liability.[47] This issue was reviewed recently in *Re Hydrodam (Corby) Ltd.*[48] This conclusion is consistent with established authority which existing that it is too simplistic to assume that the board of the parent automatically controls the actions of the subsidiary.[49]

4. New Perspectives on the Problem

These exceptions to the rule of no liability do not undermine it to any significant extent. The fundamental problem of group responsibility for group debts has not been grasped in English law. The issue was for the most part dodged by the Cork Committee in its 1982 *Report on Insolvency Law and Practice.*[50] The Cork Committee acknowledged the existence of a problem here which it attributed to the late arrival of groups onto the commercial scene; the basic principles of corporate insolvency law had been determined long before the group phenomenon had surfaced. According to the Cork Committee there were two areas of difficulty. The more fundamental issue was the liability of parent companies for the external debts of subsidiaries. After consideration of the possibilities for reform here the Committee felt unable to propose a solution. There would be technical difficulties, arising in particular in the case of partly owned subsidiaries,[51] but there were more fundamental obstacles:

---

[47] In effect this is the approach adopted in Australia which has a modified provision (s. 588V–X of the Corporations Law) detailing the circumstances under which the parent may incur liability for insolvent trading by its subsidiaries. This provision, which is a variant on the general regulation with regard to insolvent trading, flowed from the recommendations of the Harmer Committee in 1988: Law Reform Commission Report No. 45, *General Insolvency Inquiry*, paras. 334 ff. The Australians apparently considered discrete provisions along the lines of the New Zealand model (q.v.) but shied away from these on the grounds that they may have generated too much uncertainty by vesting too much discretion in the courts: see Dabner [1995] *JBL* 282 and Stapledon (1995) 16 Co. *Law* 152 for general comment. For an economic analysis of the Australian provisions see Ramsay (1994) 17 *Univ. NSW Law Jo.* 520. The dangers facing parent companies in English law were reviewed by the Financial Law Panel in its 1994 paper, *Shadow Directors*.

[48] [1994] BCC 161. See also *Standard Chartered* v. *Antico* (1995) 18 ACSR 1.

[49] See here *Lonrho* v. *Shell Petroleum* [1980] 1 WLR 627. In New Zealand what is required to generate a duty on the part of the controlling parent is actual interference with the conduct of the subsidiary's business; the mere existence of control is not sufficient: *Dairy Containers* v. *NZI Bank Ltd* [1995] 2 NZLR 30.

[50] Cmnd. 8558, ch. 51.

[51] *Ibid.*, para. 1942. Partly-owned subsidiaries are less common in the UK than in other jurisdictions.

"It is impossible to divorce the position in insolvency from the position prior to insolvency, and we have reluctantly come to the conclusion that we should not recommend a fundamental change in company law by means of proposals to effect a change in insolvency law."[52]

In spite of the exhortation of the Cork Committee that such a general review be launched nothing was done. The Cork Committee did however feel able to be more constructive about coping with the problem of intra-group company indebtedness. It was recognised that to allow companies within a group to prove in equal competition with external creditors was perceived as an abuse. In spite of this the Committee rejected a suggestion for automatic deferred status for domestic creditors.[53] Instead it favoured a more sophisticated appproach under which only those loans to connected companies which may be characterised as being in the nature of capital contributions should be deferred.[54] In adopting this flexible solution the Cork Committee was heavily influenced by the position in the USA. Although this solution does offer the benefits of flexibility it does raise the spectre of complex and expensive litigation. It is hardly surprising therefore that it was not acted upon. As no action has followed in the wake of the Cork Report we need to look to other jurisdictions for possible solutions that might appeal to the legislature.

In New Zealand the 1980 Companies Amendment Act introduced (by section 30) two novel mechanisms.[55] First, it opened up the possibility for *contribution orders* by means of which one company within a group could be ordered to contribute towards the assets of another to improve the dividend prospects for creditors. This scenario, which is now governed by section 271 of the Companies Act 1993, enables a liquidator, creditor or member to apply to the court for such an order and the court will grant this request if it considers it to be just and equitable. In so deciding it will examine closely the conduct of the parent *vis-à-vis* the subsidiary, and in particular whether it was responsible for the collapse. Thus the prospect of a contribution order is heavily qualified by the exercise of judicial discretion. Unfortunately there have been very few cases before the New Zealand courts dealing with this innovation.[56]

New Zealand pioneered a second strategy, which might prove useful where the group as a whole had collapsed, which was to allow for the assets and liabilities of the group to be *pooled* and distributed on that basis (see now

---

[52] Para. 1952.

[53] Para. 1959.

[54] Para. 1963.

[55] These provisions seem to have originated in the recommendations of the McArthur Committee, discussed by Russell in [1981] *NZLJ* 71. For discussion of the position in New Zealand see Watson [1983] *JBL* 295. The New Zealand innovations were considered by the Cork Committee and did appeal to some of the Committee members: see paras. 1947–50.

[56] For a rare case where the issue of contribution orders was discussed see *Rea* v. *Barker* (1988) 4 NZCLC 6,312. It is arguable however that the existence of this statutory nudge might tempt judges in New Zealand to adopt innnovative approaches to group insolvency situations. See here *Rea* v. *Chix* (1986) 3 NZCLC 98,852 and *Bullen* v. *Tourcorp Developments Ltd* (1988) 4 NZCLC 64,661.

Companies Act 1993, section 272). Again this is not an automatic feature but rather dependent upon the exercise of judicial discretion. In *Re Dalhoff and King Holdings Ltd*,[57] a case that came before Gallen J in the High Court of New Zealand, a pooling order was made. Gallen J found that not merely had the directors of the various companies treated the group companies as a single enterprise but also there was a public perception to that effect. To deny the expectation that had thereby been created would be unjust.

The Irish adopted these constructive mechanisms in their reforms of 1990 as part of the Companies Act of that year.[58] As far as contribution orders are concerned (see section 140) the scheme is very similar, with the qualification that the exercise of judicial discretion appears to be further constrained by focusing attention on the impact of such an order on creditors of the parent and requiring the related company to have been responsible for the collapse of the liquidated company. Section 141 of the 1990 Act also provides for pooling orders, again subject to the exercise of judicial discretion. Unfortunately, there is no evidence of these provisions having been invoked in Ireland since their introduction and it is difficult to judge their impact.

Other jurisdictions adopt more subtle approaches to this conundrum. In the USA the courts have developed a flexible concept of equitable subordination[59] in order to disqualify group members from proving in competition with outside creditors. Under this concept (mysteriously characterised as the "Deep Rock"[60] doctrine), if a company has been allowed to operate undercapitalised the controlling shareholder who provides finance for its operations may not be allowed to enjoy the same priority as an external funder. There is no automatic rule of subordination here; merely the possibility that this consequence will attach. Thus there is an element of uncertainty; a trigger for expensive litigation. The American courts have also been adept in developing "substantive consolidation" to cover cases where group assets and liabilities may be dealt with as a single unit as part of a pooling arrangement.[61]

Turning away from the common law jurisdictions the problem of parental responsibility for the obligations of subsidiary undertakings has tested the juris-

---

[57] [1991] 2 NZLR 296. For further discussion of pooling orders see *Re Pacific Syndicates (NZ) Ltd* (1989) 4 NZCLC 64,757 and *Re Grazing and Export Meat Co Ltd* (1984) 2 NZCLC 99,226.

[58] The Irish position is reviewed by McCormack in (1992) 13 *Co. Law* 191.

[59] See Schulte (1997) 18 *Co. Law* 2; Blumberg (1996) 28 *Connecticut Law Review* 295; and Whincup (1981) 2 *Co. Law* 158. Good background material on the approach of the US courts may also be gleaned from Douglas and Shanks in (1939) 39 *YLJ* 198, the note in (1958) 71 *Harv. L Rev.* 1122 and the summary by Gallagher and Ziegel in [1990] *JBL* 292 at 300–2. A typical illustration of the width of the US judicial approach is afforded by *Abbott* v. *Anderson* (1943) 321 US 349 where the importance of not allowing a group structure to frustrate a legislative policy was stressed.

[60] The concept earns its name from a subsidiary company featuring in *Taylor* v. *Standard Gas and Electric Co* (1939) 306 US 307. For contemporary comment see Israels (1942) 42 *Colum. L Rev.* 376. For legislative expression see US Bankruptcy Code, s. 510(c). The concept has not found favour in Canada: *BG Preeco (Pacific Coast)* v. *Bon Street Developments* (1989) 60 DLR (4th) 30 at 37, *per* Seaton JA.

[61] For discussion see Borrowdale in Grantham and Rickett (eds.), n. 2 above, ch. 5.

dictions on the Continent.[62] Germany can claim to be the most experienced in dealing with this problem, having introduced dedicated legislation[63] to deal with public company groups in 1965. This legislation, which has no parallel in terms of its sophistication, is not without its critics who argue that it is unduly rigid. Essentially the 1965 legislation seeks to define the parameters of formal legal relations between group members. On the specific point of parental liability a holding company can be held liable where there is a formal control contract with the dependant company or where the enterprises are integrated. In France there appears to be a balance between the exercise of judicial discretion, which is typically found in common law jurisdictions, and the introduction of statutory provisions designed to address the issue of parental responsibility on specific questions. Certainly there is a real possibility of a parent company being found to be a shadow director and thereby at risk if mismanagement can be established.[64] At European Union level this issue has not generated harmonised action. In the Draft Ninth Directive[65] an attempt has been made to promote a co-ordinated approach relying heavily on the German group regime, but this draft directive appears, like so many others, to be becalmed.

5. *The Way Forward?*

Having reviewed this issue the question that must be addressed is not so much whether legislative action should be taken but what form should it take. A simple solution would be to provide that a parent should be automatically responsible for the liabilities of a subsidiary because at the moment the law permits a group business to externalise its costs by transferring risks to creditors of its insubstantial subsidiaries. Unfortunately, that radical reform is unlikely to find support in a cautious legislature. The flexible solution of making a parent liable in specified circumstances is more likely to appeal, and indeed we have already gone some way down that road with the potential combination of wrongful trading and shadow directors. The addition of contribution orders to the range of options might help. The disadvantage of discretion-based solutions is the fact that they are often dependant upon the pursuit of hazardous and expensive litigation in circumstances where there are always major financial constraints. The experience in a number of jurisdictions is that these partial remedies may appear to be cosmetically attractive but the actual success rate of these mechanisms is

---

[62] See Hofstetter (1990) 39 *ICLQ* 576.

[63] This is the celebated Konzern law, a highly formalised regime governing many aspects of group life for an AG. For discussion see Lutter [1973] *JBL* 278 and Hofstetter (1990) 39 *ICLQ* 576 at 579 ff. An illuminating account of the history of group regulation in Germany is to be found in Wooldridge (1995) 24 *Anglo-Am. L Rev.* 57. The 1965 law applies only in the context of the AG, or public company; nevertheless the courts have been adept at extending its principles to groups involving the GmbH, or private company: see Wooldridge [1997] *JBL* 627. See generally Wooldridge (1992) 3 *Eur. Bus. Law Rev.* 67.

[64] Again there is a perceptive analysis of the French position in Hofstetter, n. 63 above, at 583 ff. See also Omar (1997) 20 *Insolvency Lawyer* 15.

[65] See Wooldridge, n. 14 above, at 125 ff. See also Hofstetter, n. 63 above, at 588 ff.

poor. A significant improvement might be introduced if a rebuttable presumption was introduced to the effect that parents were to be held liabile for subsidiary obligations unless they could establish that there had been no interference with the business management of the subsidiary and that the subsidiary had not been able to obtain any credit by virtue of its relationship with the parent. By reversing the burden of proof in this way the policy of the law would be directed very much towards enterprise liability and would reflect the realities of the situation. On the other hand, by persisting with fudge and compromise we conspire to make the regulation of companies more complex, thereby introducing economic costs. There is thus a case to be made for radical change or adhering to the separate personality rule. This commentator favours the former option.

Less controversially, action could be implemented on the issue of subordination of intra group indebtedness. The choice here again seems to be between an automatic rule and one involving the exercise of discretion.[66] In this situation the automatic rule would seem less likely to appear objectionable to the legislature, in that it does not expose a parent to liability but rather denies it equality of treatment with other creditors. In its 1994 paper[67] on insolvency law reform, JUSTICE indicated that subordination for intra-group company loans could be seen as a prime candidate for legislative action to create an exception to the *pari passu* rule. We deny unsecured creditors equality of treatment *vis-à-vis* secured and preferential creditors and to introduce a further class of deferred creditors in the group situation is hardly revolutionary. Finally a dedicated procedural mechanism that would allow for the pooling of assets and liabilities of group companies in appropriate situations would be welcome if only because this might reduce realisation costs.

Powers and Duties of Directors

Questions relating the the duties of directors of a subsidiary frequently arise in cases where the subsidiary collapses but the remainder of the group is viable, or in cases where there is an independent minority shareholding in a partly-owned subsidiary. In the event of a legal challenge the starting propositions here are clear. Under English law a parent company is not in a fiduciary position with regards to its subsidiaries.[68] It is also trite law that a director of a company owes

---

[66] Both the Cork Committee (para. 1963) and Schulte (n. 59 above, at 13) favour flexible solutions to this problem centred upon the need to identify whether the loan was in the nature of a disguised capital contribution, in which case it should be deferred. But both suggestions would create uncertainty, generate litigation and increase the costs of management of the process of winding up. In my opinion those costs are not justified on the grounds of possible unfairness to related companies.

[67] *Insolvency Law: An Agenda for Reform* (London, JUSTICE, 1994), para. 5.16.

[68] *Dairy Containers* v. *NZI Bank Ltd* [1995] 2 NZLR 30. In the USA a more stringent view is taken of the parent's role and certain fiduciary duties are imposed: *Southern Pacific Co* v. *Bogert* (1919) 250 US 483; *Sinclair Oil Corp* v. *Levien* (1971) 290 A (2d) 717.

a duty to that company and must exercise the powers vested in him for the benefit of that particular company. How does this latter principle apply to the group situation?[69] Can a director of one member in a group of companies owe legally enforceable duties to other companies within the same group? The answer here is *prima facie* a negative one, as Harman LJ indicated in *Lindgren* v. *L & P Estates Ltd*:

> "To hold that Lindgren, a director of CCP, was bound to protect the interests of one of its subsidiaries which had an independent board is to stretch the principle altogether beyond reason."[70]

Orthodoxy was reasserted once again. More problemmatical however is whether corporate powers can be exercised for the benefit of the group rather than solely in the interests of individual members. This issue was considered in *Charterbridge Corporation* v. *Lloyds Bank*.[71] Again orthodoxy dictates that a director must first and foremost act to protect the interests of the particular company of which he is a director. Pennycuick J declared:

> "Each company in the group is a separate legal entity and the directors of a particular company are not entitled to sacrifice the interest of that company."[72]

There was an easy solution to this case as both the interests of the group as a whole and those of the particular company within the group coincided. A similar approach formed the basis of the judgment in *Facia Footwear* v. *Hinchcliffe*[73] where joint treasury/security arrangements existed within the group. In those circumstances Scott VC indicated that it may be justifiable for the directors of a subsidiary to allow its funds to be used for the benefit of other group members.

Irrespective of the position at common law the question of an abusive parent may generate petitions under the burgeoning Companies Act 1985, section 459, jurisdiction alleging that the affairs of the company (i.e. subsidiary) are being managed in an unfairly prejudicial manner. Indeed one such petition (under the statutory predecessor of section 459) is directly in point. In *SCWS* v. *Meyer*[74] we

---

[69] Readers should note the curious provision in s. 741(3) of the CA 1985 which appears to reduce the risk of parent companies being regarded as shadow directors for the purposes of a number of statutory duties normally imposed upon directors. For a review of the issue of directors liabilities in a group scenario see Wheeler and Wilson, *Directors Liabilities in the Context of Corporate Groups*, Insolvency Lawyers' Association Research Report (Oxford, GTI Specialist Publishers, 1998).

[70] [1968] Ch. 572 at 595. For the converse proposition that directors of a subsidiary normally owe no duty to the parent see *Bell* v. *Lever Bros. Ltd* [1932] AC 161 at 228, *per* Lord Atkin.

[71] [1970] 1 Ch 62. The Charterbridge test has been the subject of unfruitful discussion in the Australian courts: see e.g. *Equiticorp Finance* v. *Bank of New Zealand* (1993) 11 ACSR 642.

[72] *Ibid.*, at 74. See also *Walker* v. *Wimborne* (1976) 137 CLR 1 and *Linter Group Ltd* v. *Goldberg* (1992) 7 ACSR 580 at 620–2.

[73] [1998] 1 BCLC 218. It has been recognised for some time that banks can lend on the security of a group debenture which purports to create a charge over the entire group assets: see e.g. *Barclays Bank* v. *Willowbrook International*, *The Times*, 27 Jan. 1987. See also *H Timber Protection Ltd* v. *Hickson International plc* [1995] 2 NZLR 8 where the transfer of funds from a solvent subsidiary to its parent was found to be lawful.

[74] [1959] AC 524.

had the classic illustration of a holding company deliberately running its subsidiary down in order to promote its selfish commercial interests. It is hardly surprising that the court intervened and offered relief to the minority shareholders of the subsidiary. There is no doubt that a similar result would pertain under the unfair prejudice jurisdiction were the facts to be repeated.[75] A more marginal case arose in *Nicholas* v. *Soundcraft Electronics Ltd.*[76] Here the parent company, which exercised considerable financial control over the subsidiary, failed to make promised payments to the company. This failure was a direct result of the financial difficulties which the parent itself was experiencing. The Court of Appeal held that his policy of witholding cash from the subsidiary could be regarded as part of the conduct of the subsidiary's affairs because of the degree of control which the parent enjoyed over those affairs. Although prejudicial, it was not however "unfair" within the meaning of section 459 as Fox LJ explained:

> "But the attempt to keep the group afloat by recourse to the assets of both companies was a reasonable commercial judgment in the circumstances which existed, and was not unfair."[77]

The question of a director's duties in a group scenario was considered in a somewhat different context in *Re Dominion International Group plc (No 2)*.[78] The facts of the case were complex, but essentially we were faced with a group operating with subsidiaries incorporated in a number of jurisdictions. One issue that arose was whether a director who held that position in both parent and subsidiary could be said to owe a duty of care to the parent when dealing with the assets of the subsidiary. Knox J, rejecting the fragmentary perspective on groups, concluded that such a duty could arise:

> "Put baldly, the question is whether a director of a subsidiary company, who is also a director of its holding company, is in breach of his fiduciary duty to the holding company, if he improperly gets rid of an asset of significant value. It is clear that that conduct inflicts harm on the holding company because it reduces the value of its investment in the subsidiary. In my view a director in such a position is in breach of his duty to both the holding company and the subsidiary."[79]

This review of the authorities reveals a typical mass of contradictions. More than one commentator[80] has sympathised with the dilemmas facing directors in a group scenario in that their natural business inclinations often conflict with

---

[75] Similar issues have arisen in Australia under the counterpart of s. 459: see *Re Spargos Mining NL* (1990) 3 ACSR 1 where the court intervened an appointed an independent board of directors.

[76] [1993] BCLC 360.

[77] *Ibid.*, at 366.

[78] [1996] 1 BCLC 572.

[79] *Ibid.*, at 634.

[80] See Yeung [1997] *Lloyds Maritime and Commercial Law Quarterly* 208. Yeung's solution to this dilemma is to allow directors to take into account group economic interests whilst at the same time providing enhanced mechanisms for the protection of rights of creditors and shareholders in the event of abuse.

their strict legal responsibilities. The solution may well be to introduce mechanisms whereby the shareholders in group companies can agree that corporate powers be exercised for the collective good.

The Group and the Multinational Enterprise

Multinational companies will invariably adopt a group structure to conduct their business operations across a number of jurisdictions. The utility of such a strategy was illustrated in *Adams* v. *Cape Industries*[81] where the group was structured in such a way as to minimise the legal risks attendant upon the marketing of a dangerous product (asbestos) in a lucrative market based in a litigious jurisdiction (the USA). Again the use of the group device isolates risks and is seen as economically efficient. As one commentator has put it "the group-structured multinational enterprise symbolises the efficient modern business actor".[82]

A case of some political significance is *Lonrho* v. *Shell Petroleum*,[83] a case which was primarily concerned with alleged sanctions busting by the supply of prohibited goods to Rhodesia. On a technical level the question was whether a parent company could be said to be in control of documents in the possession of its foreign subsidiaries. The Court of Appeal answered this question in the negative, largely because of the degree of autonomy enjoyed by these local subsidiaries, but this conclusion was once again founded upon the separate personality approach.

Notwithstanding these authorities it is clear that the UK courts are increasingly alert to the dangers posed by cross border groups to the sovereignty of UK companies legislation. Thus in *Re Dominion International Group plc (No 2)*[84] the prime motivation for the decision that a director of a subsidiary can owe a duty to its parent when dealing with its assets was to protect the effectiveness of the director disqualification regime. As Knox J explained:

> "If it were otherwise, the Disqualification Act would not apply to a director of a non-trading UK holding company with only foreign subsidiaries, if he misappropriated the assets of the foreign subsidiaries of which he was also a director and thereby rendered the United Kingdom holding company insolvent."[85]

By way of contrast, in *Arab Bank* v. *Mercantile Holdings*[86] Millett J was prepared to accept that the prohibition on a subsidiary company providing

---

[81] [1990] 2 WLR 657. Discussed by Griffin in (1991) 12 *Co. Law* 16 and Wardman in (1994) 15 *Co. Law* 179. A similar approach was adopted by the Canadian courts in *Bow Valley Husky (Bermuda) Ltd* v. *St John Shipping Ltd* (1995) 126 DLR (4th) 1. An illustration of the potential liabilities that may be incurred in tort from the wrongful acts of a subsidiary is afforded by the Bhopal incident—for the background see Muchlinski (1987) 50 *MLR* 545.

[82] See Hofstetter (1990) 39 *ICLQ* 576 at 576.

[83] [1980] 1 WLR 627.

[84] [1996] 1 BCLC 572.

[85] *Ibid.*, at 634.

[86] [1993] BCC 816.

financial assistance towards the acquisition of shares in its parent could be circumvented in cases where the subsidiary was incorporated overseas, though a deliberate attempt to exploit this loophole might attract judicial opposition.

The fact that the device of the group is such a key player in the international business scene has undoubtedly been one factor behind the reluctance of national legislatures to regulate. If a jurisdiction were to introduce a regime that was hostile to groups (for example by making a parent company liable for the obligations of subsidiaries) that might deter multinationals from investing in certain jurisdictions.[87] The solution to this demotivating factor must lie in regulation beyond the purely national level so as to eliminate potential economic disadvantage.

How have the international organisations responsible for regulating trade at this level responded to this practice? In the early 1980s there were indications that both the UN and the OECD were beginning to make tentative steps in this direction.[88] However, these initiatives appear to have made little progress, with the result that group regulation still remains a largely national prerogative.

The Group Outside Company Law

When considering the legal regulation of groups in the UK it would be misleading to view this as solely a matter for company law. An interesting dichotomy opens up when one looks beyond the traditional boundaries of the subject. In terms of tax law the orthodox view has long been abandoned and the peculiar position of groups has been well recognised.[89] The related but crucial issue of transfer pricing[90] is currently under review by the UK authorities.

In more modern subjects, such as competition law, the economic perspective also holds sway. As this area of regulation is increasingly influenced by European theory it is instructive to note that the Commission adopts the view that a group is to be determined as a single undertaking.[91] Thus there cannot be an anti-competitive agreement between members of a group.[92] Moreover, the economic power/market share of the whole group is combined for the purposes of any economic assessment.

---

[87] The DTI Consultative Document, *Modern Company Law For a Competitive Economy* (March 1998) in ch. 4 recognises this problem in general.

[88] See Wedderburn (1984) 47 MLR 87, at 91.

[89] See Morse (op. cit. note 10 above).

[90] For the connection between transfer pricing and issues of company law see Fitzpatrick [1975] *JBL* 202. The problem of disclosure for intra group transactions has been noted above: see page 222 above.

[91] *Re The Joint Venture of Olivetti and Canon* [1989] 4 CMLR 940. This view informs other areas of Commission thinking: see Case C–389/92, *Ballast Nedam Groep NV v. Belgium, The Times*, 8 June 1994 and the related ruling in Case C–5/97, *Ballast Nedam Groep NV v. Belgium*, noted in ECJ Proceedings 35/97.

[92] *Centrafarm* v. *Sterling Drug* [1974] 2 CMLR 480.

In industrial law the potential for groups of companies to be used to frustrate employment rights has long been recognised, and much of the scope for abuse has been neutralised in English law to some extent via the concept of "associated employer".[93] Having said that, the courts are reluctant to add a gloss on that concept simply to deal with oddities thrown up by the group situation.[94] The existence of dedicated legislation may consequently be said to restrict judicial flexibility.

TOWARDS A RECOGNITION OF GROUPS AS DISTINCT BUSINESS ENTITIES

The approach of English law to the difficult questions of company law thrown up by the existence of groups has been inconsistent and unco-ordinated. There has been disagreement on the most basic issue of whether the principle of separate corporate personality should be allowed to operate without qualification in the group environment. Orthodoxy favours blind application of the basic rule.

Individual judges have been able to adapt the so-called exceptions to the *Salomon*[95] rule to the group context. Of these exceptions the "agency" mechanism has been floated in cases like *Smith Stone and Knight* v. *Birmingham Corporation*[96] as a suitable instrument of legal analysis, but it is clear that there is no automatic agency relationship arising between parent and subsidiary.[97]

The leading dissenter from the orthodox analysis has been Lord Denning. In *Littlewoods Mail Order* v. *McGregor*,[98] a tax avoidance case, he advocated lifting the veil in the group context as a matter of law, stating that the separate personality principle had to be watched carefully. Subsequently this approach matured in *DHN* v. *Tower Hamlets LBC*[99] where he was prepared to treat a

[93] See Employment Rights Act 1996, s. 231. For critique see Collins (1990) 53 *MLR* 731 at 739 ff. The test for control used in s. 231 is one of strict voting control rather than a more realistic test based upon *de facto* control.

[94] *Dimbleby* v. *NUJ* [1984] 1 WLR 427. It is interesting to compare here the BC Sup. Ct. ruling in *Canada Safeway Ltd* v. *Canadian Food and Allied Workers* (1974) 46 DLR (3d) 113, where the veil between parent and subsidiary was lifted in dealing with legal issues arising on an industrial dispute. See also *Nedco Ltd* v. *Clark* (1976) 43 DLR (3d) 714.

[95] [1897] AC 22.

[96] [1939] 4 All ER 116. For a contemporary case note emphasising the novelty of the decision see Kahn Freund (1940) 3 *MLR* 226.

[97] *Gramophone and Typewriter Ltd* v. *Stanley* [1908] 2 KB 89; *AG* v. *Equiticorp Industries Group Ltd* [1996] 1 NZLR 528 at 539, *per* McKay J. Compare *Apthorpe* v. *Peter Schoenhofen Brewery Co* (1899) 4 Tax Cas. 41.

[98] [1969] 1 WLR 1241.

[99] [1976] 1 WLR 852. For discussion see Hayton [1977] *CLJ* 12; Sugarman and Webb (1977) 93 *LQR* 170; Powles (1977) 40 *MLR* 339; and Rixon (1986) 102 *LQR* 415. It is interesting to note that a parallel approach was used by the NZCA in *JR McKenzie Ltd* v. *Gianoutsos* [1957] NZLR 309 to conclude that a parent was in occupation of business premises owned by its subsidiary, but whether this reflects contemporary atttitudes in that jurisdiction is to be questioned (see cases cited in n. below). Lord Denning took a similar view in *Amalgamated Property Co* v. *Texas Bank* [1982] QB 84. As is typical of CA decisions of that era his fellow appeal judges were able to come to the same conclusion without recourse to such controversial reasoning. See also *Revlon* v. *Cripps and Lee* [1980] FSR 85.

group as a single economic entity in order to maximise compensation payable to it on compulsory purchase of its business premises. Here we had a senior judge suggesting a revolutionary new strategy for the treatment of groups involving lifting the veil as the normal method of legal analysis. This radicalism did not find favour with most other members of the judiciary in a number of jurisdictions.[100] In *Woolfson v. Strathclyde Regional Council*,[101] a Scottish case that went to the House of Lords, their Lordships refused to depart from the strict separate personality rule on analogous facts. Subsequently the basic orthodox position was confirmed by the House of Lords in *Rayner v. DTI*[102] and the Court of Appeal in *Adams v. Cape Industries*.[103]

In the past few years, however, there have been signs that the realistic view of groups as single economic enterprises may be beginning to find favour once again. The availability of group economic resources to the subsidiary company was at the heart of its defeats in the *Atlas Maritime* litigation where a subsidiary unsuccessfully sought to secure a release from a Mareva injunction.[104] One interpretation of *Geo Fisher (UK) Ltd v. Multi Construction Ltd*,[105] a case involving loss of value of shareholding caused to a parent through alleged breach of contract inflicting direct loss on the subsidiary's business, is that the decision can be explained by reference to the fact that the contracting party (the parent company) and the direct victim of the breach of contract were part of the same group, and therefore the privity of contract rule did not operate to create a problem. There may also have been an element in this case of the court wishing to avoid a situation where an alleged wrong could not have been actionable merely by reason of technicality. However, this case has been followed subsequently in a situation where the subsidiary may have been able to sue on its own behalf. For in *Barings v. Coopers and Lybrand*,[106] a case which illustrated the vulnerability of groups in an international business environment, the issue to be resolved was whether auditors of a subsidiary company owed any duty of care to the parent. The Court of Appeal ruled that there was a serious issue to be

---

[100] The DHN-type approach was thus rejected by the Australian courts in *Industrial Equity Ltd v. Blackburn* (1977) 137 CLR 567 and *Pioneeer Concrete Services Ltd v. Yelnah Pty Ltd* (1986) 5 NSWLR 254. In New Zealand a similar negative response is attested by *Re Securitibank Ltd* [1978] 1 NZLR 97 and *AG v. Equiticorp Industries Group Ltd* [1996] 1 NZLR 528. In Ireland the radicalism of Lord Denning was embraced by Costello J in *Power Supermarkets v. Crumlin Investments* (unreported, High Court, 22 June 1981) but a more conservative analysis surfaced in *Allied Irish Coal v. Powell Duffryn International Fuels Ltd* [1997] 1 ILRM 306.

[101] (1979) 38 P & CR 521, 1978 SC 90.

[102] [1990] 2 AC 418.

[103] Above. See also *National Dock Labour Board v. Pinn and Wheeler* [1989] BCLC 647.

[104] *Atlas Maritime Co v. Avalon Maritime Ltd (The Coral Rose) (No 1)* [1991] 4 All ER 769. For a similar judicial approach adopted in later proceedings in this case see *Atlas Maritime Co v. Avalon Maritime Ltd (No 3), The Times*, 24 June 1991.

[105] [1995] BCC 310, discussed by Houston in (1997) 18 Co. Law 27. For a comparable Australian decision see *Qintex Australia Finance v. Scroeders Australia Ltd* (1991) 9 ACLC 109 noted by Baxt in (1991) 65 *Australian Law Journal* 352. But compare *Gregorio v. Intrans-Corp* [1994] 115 DLR (4th) 200.

[106] [1997] BCC 498.

tried. Matters progressed further in *BCCI (Overseas) Ltd* v. *Price Waterhouse*[107] where the Court of Appeal found that such a duty of care did indeed arise where the banking operations of various companies within the BCCI group were run as a single business. One observation worth putting forward is that the courts may be more inclined to treat a group as a single unit where, in so doing, they enable it to pursue a claim or otherwise seek to gain an advantage rather than expose it to an external claim.[108]

The real problem here, as always, remains one of inconsistency. The recent pronouncements of the judiciary in the cases noted immediately above are placed in a more qualified context by the Court of Appeal ruling in *Ord* v. *Belhaven Pubs. Ltd*[109] where a liberal use of the single economic entity approach by the trial judge was deplored, and an earlier case[110] suggesting a cavalier attitude towards the separate personality rule was expressly overruled.

In spite of creative attempts by certain judges to mitigate the injustices that can arise by application of general rules of company law to the group scenario it has to be recognised that this is an issue of such fundamental importance that only the legislature can address the issue directly and provide the necessary degree of predictability.[111] Failure to legislate has a cost here, as Rogers CJ pointed out in *Qintex Australia Finance Pty Ltd Finance* v. *Schroeders Australia Ltd*.[112] That cost is the social burden of expensive and unnecessary litigation in which the courts are asked to determine the indeterminable. Unpredictability means that the parties have the incentive to drag out the litigation to the bitter end as each side has a fair chance of winning in this legal lottery. Statute has of course progressively taken cognisance of the peculiar problems posed by the group in areas of tax law and employment law but is less noticeable in the critical area of companies regulation. Some commentators[113] have favoured this cherry-picking approach on the basis that a monolithic and one-dimensional strategy will not be possible to construct through legislation.

---

[107] *The Times*, 4 Mar. 1998.

[108] For a case which indirectly supports this perception of an "enabling" rather than an "imposing" approach in favour of groups see *Holdsworth & Co (Wakefield) Ltd* v. *Caddies* [1955] 1 WLR 352 where the HL treated a group as a single commercial entity in order to frustrate an action for breach of contract by an employee. As always there are cases which run counter to any general thesis in such an area of legal inconsistency, *Atlas Maritime Co* v. *Avalon Maritime Ltd (No 1)* [1991] 4 All ER 769 being just one such example.

[109] [1998] BCC 607. For discussion see Maughan and Copp (1998) 148 *New Law Journal* 938.

[110] *Creasey* v. *Breachwood Motors* [1992] BCC 638—this was not a parent/subsidiary scenario but rather involved two companies with common ownership.

[111] This fact of life was emphasised by Wedderburn in (1984) 47 *Modern Law Review* 87. See also the view of Berle set forth in (1947) 47 *Col. L Rev.* 343 that it was important to adopt an enterprise entity approach to groups to enable the law to reflect the new commercial reality of the conglomerate.

[112] (1990) 3 ACSR 267. Here the court had the task of identifying contracting parties in the case of a group operating as a single entity. See the comments of Rogers CJ at 269 especially. The same judge had earlier made pertinent observations on the uncertainty of the law in *Briggs* v. *Hardie & Co* (1989) 16 NSWLR 549 at 567 ff.

[113] See e.g. the paper by Prentice in ch. 19 of McCahery, Picciotto and Scott, n. 2 above.

A review of these developments illustrates that both the courts and the legislature are increasingly affording a formal recognition to the group. This is a welcome development as the group is such an important player in the conduct of commerce. There are encouraging signs that the regulation of groups is now seen as a key issue by policy-makers in many jurisdictions. We have already noted the efforts of the legislature in New Zealand and Ireland to tackle the problem of group liability. More radically, the legislature in Guernsey in 1997 introduced the concept of cell companies.[114] A cell company involves the creation of a single company within which internal divisions are found. Such a company may be created *de novo* or by acquisition. These cell company structures are not generally available, and only operate within the area of financial services, but the concept is still an intriguing one.

One useful development would be an international convention on the recognition of groups and on the availability of this structure to multinationals for business planning purposes. Unfortunately, as one commentator[115] has observed the prospects for action here are not good.

Looking at the three key areas identified in this essay it is possible to say that recent decades have witnessed the emergence of an effective body of regulation for groups. This is most readily apparent in the context of financial disclosure, but the general improvement in the rights of minority shareholders and the controls imposed upon directors is adequate to protect the interests of shareholders in partly-owned subsidiaries. The critical next stage will be to grasp the nettle of external liability. In the opinion of this commentator that development is likely to occur in the next few years.

Finally there is a presentational issue to consider. The current statutory provisions on groups are typically scattered around the Companies Act; a consolidation of the relevant provisions in a discrete Part of that Act would do much to promote clarity and to signify an appropriate recognition of the peculiar legal problems posed by the group enterprise.

---

[114] See Walters and Sarchet (1997) 18 *Co. Law* 219.
[115] See Muscat, n. 24 above, at 471.

11

Joint Ventures

MICHAEL LOWER[1]

1. INTRODUCTION

Joint ventures are by no means new arrangements, but they are probably destined to play an increasingly significant part on the commercial scene. One reason for this is that they are often used as a means of entering a new geographical market and trade is increasingly organised without regard to national boundaries. Another reason is that "strategic alliances" are expected to be common in significant and dynamic industries such as telecommunications. Schauss, the Director General for Competition in the EC Commission, speaks of a "wave of mega mergers and joint ventures" being formed in Europe.[2]

The term "joint venture" encompasses horizontal arrangements such as joint production and distribution, joint buying or joint selling or marketing agreements as well as research and development joint ventures. Some vertical arrangements, too, might be described as joint ventures.

This essay will look at the particular concerns which competition authorities often have with regard to joint ventures. Section 2 looks at the policy issues raised by joint ventures in general and at the institutional mechanisms which might be set up to evaluate joint ventures. Sections 3 and 4 will look at the relevant policies and mechanisms of the UK and EC respectively to see how they cope with joint ventures.

Joint ventures also raise interesting problems for company law. Section 5 looks at one such issue, the mis-match between the fiduciary duties of nominee directors and the commercial expectations to which they are subject. The problem is explained, together with its implications for nominee directors and the joint venturers who appointed them. Some reform proposals are then considered.

---

[1] Senior lecturer in law at Liverpool John Moores University.
[2] A. Schauss, "Competition Policy in the Telecoms Sector", EC Competition Policy Newsletter, Spring 1996, 1 at 2.

2. COMPETITION LAW AND JOINT VENTURES

What is a Joint Venture?

The EC Commission defines joint ventures as "undertakings which are jointly controlled by two or more other undertakings".[3] This implies that a new entity (the undertaking) is created. The joint venture need not create an entity in the legal sense of the word. Brodley has argued that a joint venture should exist, "as a business entity separate from its parents"[4] and this helps to convey what is meant by the term "undertaking". The second major element of the Commission's definition is that the new undertaking should be jointly controlled by other undertakings; the arrangements for joint control may arise out of a contract but could arise out of non-contractual methods for co-ordinating policy concerning the new entity.

One other feature of joint ventures is that they can be difficult to classify for competition law purposes. Typically, competition law authorities have separate regimes for the scrutiny of mergers, cartels and the abuse of a dominant position. Some joint ventures resemble mergers whilst others come closer to co-operation agreements between independent enterprises which need to be examined with anti-cartel legislation in mind. In the EC context, the Merger Regulation has, as will be seen, tried to make explicit provision for this fact.

The Aims Pursued by Competition Authorities

Competition agencies typically aim to prevent the formation of cartels, to scrutinise mergers where the merged firm would enjoy a dangerously high degree of market power and to prevent already dominant firms from exploiting their dominance. For some competition authorities, a broader range of policy factors might be taken into account; they may, for example have a commitment to fostering small and medium-sized enterprises.[5] In the European Union, competition policy is seen as having a part to play in breaking down internal barriers between Member States; this has a political rationale as well as an economic one.

Joint ventures raise concerns for several reasons. A "joint venture" might facilitate collusive behaviour by providing for the exchange of information. Restraints in joint venture agreements, such as non-competition clauses, might have no economic justification and simply be a means for dividing geographical

---

[3] Commission Notice on the concept of full-function joint ventures under Council Regulation 4064/89 on the control of concentrations between undertakings [1998] OJ C66/1. The concept of control is explained in the Notice on the concept of concentration [1998] OJ C66/5.

[4] J. Brodley, "Joint Ventures and Antitrust Policy" (1982) 95 *Harvard Law Review* 1523 at 1526.

[5] For an indication of the importance of this factor in European competition policy, see Karel van Miert, "Foreword" to the *27th Report on Competition Policy* (Brussels, EC Commission), 4.

markets between the parties or fixing prices. Then there is the fear of the "spill-over effect". Even where there is no concern about the effect on competition in the joint venture market, competition authorities may fear that the joint venturers will develop a taste for collaboration with the effect that it spills over into other markets where the joint venturers are competitors. For these and other reasons, joint ventures have to be scrutinised as potential cartels. Where the joint venture creates an essential facility then competition authorities will want to be assured that access to it is available on reasonable terms.

Joint ventures can lead to a more concentrated market structure; this fact entails the risk of inefficient allocation of resources. Thus, joint ventures may also need to be scrutinised under the rules applicable to mergers.

It is not only the formation of the joint venture that has to be considered. On occasions, individual terms of the joint venture may need to be assessed separately from the joint venture itself. Joint venture agreements commonly include terms which are potentially anti-competitive in their own right: an agreement by the joint venturers not to compete with the joint venture is a typical example.[6] If the joint venture is found to be pro-competitive, does that mean that all of its terms are necessarily acceptable to the competition authorities? The answer generally given to this question is that it depends on whether the term in question is reasonably necessary to the achievement of the joint venture's legitimate aims.[7] If it is then antitrust clearance of the joint venture will usually extend to the term. If not, then the term will be separately assessed.

Although joint ventures can be anti-competitive, they can also give rise to significant efficiencies.[8] One of the major benefits associated with joint ventures is that they can lead to economies of scale.[9] They can also reduce transaction costs[10] because, for example, of the fact that profit-sharing (a common feature of joint ventures) reduces the motivation for each joint venturer to behave opportunistically; to do so would harm the joint venture and reduce the value of all stakes in it. Another source of transaction cost savings comes from the use of a governance structure such as the limited company or the partnership, which reduces the need to cater for all contingencies in the joint venture contract.[11] Joint ventures can also overcome the appropriability problem: research and development, for example, can be extremely expensive and, at the same time, it may be that no one firm can make use of all of the know-how that it yields. If the research is funded by more than one firm then there is a better chance that

---

[6] For an explanation of the restrictions commonly found in research and development joint ventures, see S. Katsh, "Collateral Restraints in Joint Ventures" (1985) 54 *Antitrust Law Journal* 1003.

[7] *Ibid.*, 1005.

[8] For an explanation of the benefits of joint ventures, see E. Kitch, "The Antitrust Economics of Joint Ventures" (1985) 54 *Antitrust Law Journal* 957.

[9] See F. Fishwick, *Making Sense of Competition Policy* (London, Kogan Page, 1993), 35–7 for a brief explanation of the concept of economies of scale.

[10] For an explanation of transaction costs, see O. Williamson, "Transaction-cost Economics: The Governance of Contractual Relations" (1979) 22 *The Journal of Law and Economics* 233.

[11] G. Pisano, "Using Equity Participation to Support Exchange: Evidence from the Biotechnology Industry" (1989) 5 *Journal of Law, Economics and Organization* 109.

all of its fruits can be exploited.[12] In this way, joint ventures can help in the diffusion of innovation.[13]

As has already been mentioned, competition agencies may have regard to broader policy issues when carrying out the tasks assigned to them. The example that has already been given is the breaking down of barriers to trade between the Member States of the European Union. To take another example, competition authorities might seek to foster national product champions; these are firms or alliances able to compete on the world stage.

Should Joint Ventures be Subjected to a Rule of Reason Analysis?

One task of competition law and policy is to articulate the range of factors that agencies have to take into account when evaluating joint ventures. In addition, where a joint venture possesses both positive and negative features, guidance is needed on how to strike the balance. For example, a joint venture may pose a threat to competition, but the parties may claim that the joint venture is nevertheless justified on the grounds of the economies of scale to which it gives rise. How is the competition authority to react to these conflicting factors?

Save for obvious cartels, it will usually be appropriate to evaluate joint ventures according to a rule of reason.[14] A number of commentators have put forward approaches to evaluating joint ventures which would take account of their distinctive nature and purposes.[15] In general, it seems to be accepted that an initial evaluation should be carried out. Blatantly anti-competitive joint ventures can be filtered out at this stage, as well as joint ventures which raise no anti-competitive risk; the former are to be prohibited whilst the latter are to be allowed to proceed without further analysis. Where a joint venture merits further consideration, competition authorities should acknowledge the significant potential of joint ventures to yield efficiencies. Where possible, fears that the joint venture will be anti-competitive should be addressed by modifying rather than prohibiting it.

---

[12] G. Grossman and C. Shapiro, "Research Joint Ventures: An Antitrust Analysis" (1986) 2 *Journal of Law, Economics and Organization* 315 at 316.

[13] J. Langenfeld and D. Scheffman, "Innovation and US Competition Policy" (1989) 34 *The Antitrust Bulletin* 1 at 3.

[14] For a history of the evolution of the rule of reason/*per se* distinction, see T. Everett Peyton, "Unravelling the Current Rule for Applying the *per se* Rule: Explanations, Solutions and a Proposal" (1985) 10 *Journal of Corporation Law* 1051 at 1053–5. For a list of the perceived benefits of both tests see O. Black, "*Per se* Rules and Rules of Reason: What are They?" [1997] 3 *European Competition Law Review* 145 at 151–2.

[15] J. Brodley, n. 4 above; J.F. Weston and S. Ornstein, "Efficiency Considerations in Joint Ventures" (1984) 53 *Antitrust Law Journal* 85; R. Pitofsky, "A Framework for Antitrust Analysis of Joint Ventures" (1986) 74 *The Georgetown Law Journal* 1605; T. Piraino, "Beyond *per se*, Rule of Reason or Merger Analysis: A New Antitrust Standard for Joint Ventures" (1991) 76 *Minnesota Law Review* 1; and J. Brodley, "Proof of Efficiencies in Mergers and Joint Ventures" (1996) 64 *Antitrust Law Journal* 575.

3. JOINT VENTURES AND UK COMPETITION LAW

Introduction

Joint ventures in the United Kingdom may fall to be assessed under the merger control provisions of the Fair Trading Act 1973 ("the FTA"). Ancillary restraints, such as non-competition covenants, currently need to be scrutinised with the Restrictive Trade Practices Act 1976 ("the RTPA") and with the common law doctrine of restraint of trade in mind. The RTPA, along with other aspects of current UK competition law, is soon to be replaced by the provisions of the Competition Act 1998. The Competition Act 1998 received the Royal Assent on 9th November 1998 but many of its provisions only come into force on 1st March 2000. This essay was written before November 1998 and, accordingly, includes a discussion of the treatment of joint ventures under the RTPA. In any event, the RTPA retains some significance during the Interim and Transitional Periods provided for in the Competition Act. This section will outline the institutions and processes in UK competition law before considering the policies which they apply, or are likely to apply, to joint ventures.

The Merger Control Provisions of the Fair Trading Act 1973

Joint ventures might be caught by the merger control provisions of the Fair Trading Act 1973 ("FTA"). Section 64 of the FTA provides that there is a "merger situation qualifying for investigation" where: two or more enterprises (at least one of which must have been carried on in the United Kingdom or have been controlled by a United Kingdom company) have ceased to be distinct enterprises (this would cover joint ventures that involve the pooling of two existing businesses) and where either the value of the assets taken over exceeds £70 million ("the asset value test") or the merger will lead to an increased concentration of market power in the United Kingdom or a substantial part thereof ("the market share test").[16] No merger reference may take place once six months have elapsed since the date of the merger (provided it was notified to the DGFT or the Secretary of State or in the public domain[17]).

Assuming that there is a merger situation qualifying for investigation, it is for the Secretary of State to decide whether or not to refer it to the Monopolies and Mergers Commission ("the MMC").[18] The Secretary of State has an unfettered discretion in this matter but government policy is that the decision will be based primarily on competition grounds.[19] The DGFT has a responsibility to advise

---

[16] For the market share test to be satisfied the merger must lead to control of 25% of the relevant market or strengthen a market share which already exceeded 25%. S.64 envisages that the market share might be jointly held by the parties to the merger.

[17] FTA, s. 64(1) and (4).

[18] FTA, s.64(1).

[19] See the collection of ministerial statements affirming this doctrine in R. Finbow and N. Parr, *UK Merger Control: Law and Practice*, (London, Sweet & Maxwell, 1995), 98–102.

the Secretary of State[20] but this advice need not be taken. The OFT focuses primarily on competition issues in preparing its advice although the other public interest issues mentioned below are also considered.[21] In particular, the OFT recognises that a merger "might also offer the prospect of greater efficiency through economies achieved by large-scale production, or improvements in manning levels or other practices".[22] Currently-stated government policy, which places great emphasis on competition, is taken into account in addition to the provisions of the FTA.[23] The OFT does not go to great lengths to balance efficiency gains against adverse effects on competition since it believes that this level of analysis is best left to the MMC.[24]

If the Secretary of State decides to refer a joint venture to the MMC, the MMC will consider for itself whether a merger situation qualifying for investigation has been created.[25] Assuming that it has, it will then make an assessment as to whether or not the joint venture is in the public interest.[26] Section 84 of the FTA specifies the matters which the MMC is to consider when making its assessment. It should be noted, however, that section 69 allows the Secretary of State, when making a reference, to impose limitations on the matters to be considered by the MMC;[27] the reference may, for example, require the MMC to consider only specific consequences of the joint venture.[28]

The public interest criteria in section 84 are wide-ranging; some of them clearly relate to competition, but the MMC may also have regard to the effect of a joint venture on the "balanced distribution of industry and employment in the United Kingdom"[29] and on the ability of UK businesses to compete abroad.[30] In fact, section 84(1) allows the MMC to "take into account all matters which appear to them in the particular circumstances to be relevant".

Finbow and Parr preface their analysis of the criteria employed by the MMC by pointing out that they focus mainly on competition-related issues.[31] They have, however, been prepared to take other factors into account. The parties may, for example, argue that the merger gives rise to efficiencies, such as economies of scale and the other efficiencies mentioned earlier. Finbow and Parr report that the MMC have considered claims that a merger gives rise to efficiencies but that it is unlikely that an otherwise anti-competitive merger will be saved by the presence of efficiencies.[32]

[20] FTA, s.76(1)(b).
[21] See the OFT publication, *Mergers: A Guide to Procedures under the Fair Trading Act 1973*, at 7–8.
[22] *Ibid.*, at 12.
[23] *Ibid.*, at 13.
[24] *Ibid.*, at 17.
[25] FTA, s.69(1)(a).
[26] FTA, s.69(1)(b).
[27] FTA. s.69(2)–(4).
[28] FTA, s.69(4).
[29] FTA, s.84(1)(d).
[30] FTA, s.84(1)(e).
[31] Finbow and Parr, n. 19 above, 171.
[32] *Ibid.*, 246–52.

The MMC is under a duty to report on a merger reference made to it.[33] If it concludes that the joint venture does not threaten the public interest, the Secretary of State has no power to take any action with regard to it. Where, however, the MMC concludes that the joint venture does operate against the public interest, or may do so, then the Secretary of State has the powers referred to in section 73 of the FTA. The relevant powers are set out in Schedule 8 to the FTA; the Secretary of State can make a range of structural orders (prohibiting the merger or requiring the sale of particular areas of business or assets) and orders concerning the subsequent behaviour of the parties. The Secretary of State is not obliged to take the course of action recommended by the MMC, or any action at all. In this respect, the merger control provisions of the FTA are characterised by a high level of political discretion.

The Restrictive Trade Practices Act 1976

The RTPA is soon to be repealed by the Competition Act 1998. For that reason, it will only be briefly outlined here. The RTPA requires joint venturers to register (the RTPA actually speaks of a need to furnish particulars) their agreement if it falls within any of four very broadly defined categories[34] and restrictions are accepted by two or more parties and the agreement is between two or more parties carrying on business in the United Kingdom (the parties accepting the restrictions need not be the same as the parties carrying on business in the United Kingdom)[34b].

Once particulars of an agreement have been registered, the DGFT is under a duty to bring proceedings before the Restrictive Practices Court ("RPC").[35] The RPC has jurisdiction to declare whether or not restrictions are contrary to the public interest;[36] if it decides that they are, the agreement is void in respect of those restrictions.[37] If proceedings are brought before the RTPA, the RPC applies the public interest criteria contained in sections 10 and 19. Restrictions are deemed to be contrary to the public interest unless one of the circumstances listed in sections 10 and 19 can be shown to exist. These include: the need to protect the public against injury; securing for purchasers, consumers or users "specific and substantial benefits or advantages"; the need to overcome anti-competitive activity of others not party to the agreement; the need to help the parties to the agreement to bargain on fair terms with others who occupy a dominant position in a particular market; avoiding "a serious and persistent"

---

[33] FTA, ss. 70–72.

[34] Restrictive agreements as to goods (s.6) or services (s.11) and information agreements as to goods (s.7) or services (s.12).

[34b] The Competition Act 1998, Sch. 13, para. 5, drastically reduces the categories of new agreements which have to be notified for the purposes of the RTPA.

[35] RTPA, s.2(c). Note, however, that following the enactment of the Competition Act 1998, the DGFT is no longer under a duty to bring proceedings but has a discretion as to whether to do so or not.

[36] RTPA, s.1(3).

[37] RTPA, s.2(1).

adverse effect on the general level of unemployment in an area; the need to preserve and enhance British export trade and the fact that the restriction "does not directly or indirectly restrict or discourage competition to any material degree". There is a further need to show that the restriction is not unreasonable, having regard to the need to balance those circumstances and harm done to third parties. On the face of it, the public interest criteria involve the application of a rule of reason; the chances of an agreement being found to satisfy the public interest criteria are, however, remote; Whish points out that only 11 agreements were upheld by the RPC between 1956 and the end of 1991.[38] As a result, although the public interest criteria appear to allow for a rule of reason analysis, once proceedings have been brought the presumption is one of illegality.[39]

In fact, however, the picture is not so bleak when one considers the operation of the RTPA as a whole. Scattered throughout the RTPA, the Restrictive Trade Practices Act 1977 and secondary legislation are examples of types of agreement which are deemed not to be registrable agreements within the RTPA or which are excluded from registrability; there are also agreements which are excluded because they contain only restrictions which the legislation declares should be disregarded.[40]

Section 21(2) of the RTPA has great practical significance[40b]. Under it, the DGFT can ask the Secretary of State to give directions discharging the DGFT from the duty to bring proceedings before the RPC. The Secretary of State can give directions where it appears to him that the restrictions are not of such significance as to call for investigation by the RPC. Whish laments the lack of transparency which characterises the procedure; many agreements benefit from directions but little guidance is available to explain when they are likely to be given.[41] One result of this is that it is not possible to comment on the DGFT's approach to joint ventures, or even to say whether he has particular views on how joint ventures should be analysed.

The Competition Act

The RTPA will be repealed by the Competition Act 1998. The Competition Act will align UK competition law much more closely with Articles 81(85) and 82(86) of the EC Treaty. In the first place, it will do so because the key provisions of the Competition Act are two prohibitions which closely resemble Articles 81(85) and 82(86): one is directed at cartels and the other at the abuse of a dominant position. Secondly, section 60 of the Competition Act imposes an

---

[38] R. Whish, *Competition Law* (3rd edn.), (London, Butterworths, 1993), 161.

[39] For other criticisms of the RTPA, see D. Klein, "Cooperation and the *per se* Debate: Evidence from the United Kingdom" (1989) 34 *The Antitrust Bulletin* 517.

[40] For a convenient list, see the OFT booklet, *Restrictive Trade Practices* (OFT, London, Nov. 1995 edn.), 12–17.

[40b] Following the enactment of the Competition Act 1998, it is no longer possible for the Secretary of State to give direction under Section 21(2).

[41] Whish, n. 38 above, 158–61.

obligation on the courts to interpret the Competition Act with a view to ensuring that the principles which it applies are consistent with the principles laid down by, and the decisions of, the European Court. Further, section 10 provides for a system of parallel exemptions; agreements which have the benefit of an exemption under Article 81(85) will also be exempted for the purpose of the anti-cartel prohibition in the Competition Act. This should simplify matters for those joint ventures caught by both the Competition Act (as it will then be) and Article 81(85); a single exemption will provide clearance for both UK and EU purposes. As a result of all of these facts, the law and policy concerning the application of Articles 81(85) and 82(86) to joint ventures will also apply to joint venture agreements of purely domestic significance. The next section of this essay will examine, amongst other things, the application of Article 81(85) to joint venture agreements. The merger control provisions in the FTA will continue in force after the enactment of the Competition Act and merger situations qualifying for investigation will not fall under the jurisdiction of the DGFT under the Competition Act.[42]

Common Law Doctrine of Restraint of Trade

Joint venture agreements often contain covenants by the joint venturers not to compete with the joint venture and may contain other restrictive covenants. This can be reasonable; such a covenant, by removing the joint venturers as potential competitors of the joint venture, can improve the prospects for the joint venture to be profitable. At the same time, non-competition covenants can be caught by the common law doctrine of restraint of trade. It is not easy to say when, exactly, the doctrine will apply. Where a contract term is caught by it, however, its validity will depend on showing three things: that the covenant is necessary to protect some legitimate interest of the covenantee; that it is no wider than is reasonable to protect the covenantee's interest and, finally, the restriction is reasonable in the public interest. The application of the doctrine in the joint venture context was examined in *Dawnay, Day & Co Ltd* v. *Frederic de Braconier d'Alphen*.[43] Significantly, the judgment in this case recognises that, like business sale agreements, joint ventures deserve special recognition when applying the restraint of trade doctrine.

4. JOINT VENTURES AND EC COMPETITION LAW

Introduction

This section will provide a brief overview of the relevant European competition law regimes; specifically, it will look at the treatment of joint ventures under

---

[42] Competition Act 1998, Sched. 1.
[43] [1997] IRLR 442.

Article 81(85) and the Regulation on the control of concentrations between undertakings ("the Merger Regulation").[44] Some joint ventures must be analysed under both the Merger Regulation and Article 81(85), a point that will be discussed below.

Article 81(85)

Article 81(85) of the EC Treaty is the anti-cartel provision in EC competition law; agreements caught by the prohibition in article 81(1) (85(1)) are void and the Commission has power to impose fines not exceeding 10 per cent of the annual turnover of the parties.[45] Thus, one task facing the Commission in its enforcement of Article 81(85) is to decide whether or not an agreement is caught by Article 81(1) (85(1)). Joint ventures, or some of the terms of the joint venture agreement, may be caught by Article 81(85). Even then, the joint venture may be saved if the Commission is prepared to grant an individual exemption under Article 81(3) (85(3)) or the parties are able to bring the joint venture within the terms of one of the block exemptions.

Korah points out that the Commission has historically favoured the formation of joint ventures where these might be expected to help small and medium-sized enterprises to achieve economies of scale or other efficiencies that might otherwise not be available to them.[46] She also discusses recent decisions of the Commission suggesting that the Commission is prepared to clear joint ventures which are risky and involve massive investment.[47] It may well be that it is beyond any one firm, however large, to undertake this type of project alone, and a joint venture may well be crucial in these circumstances.

In granting clearances in the cases discussed by Korah, rather than exemptions, the Commission is departing from its normal practice. A clearance is a decision by the Commission that Article 81(1) (85(1)) is not infringed; an exemption involves a finding that the joint venture is *prima facie* caught by Article 81(1) (85(1)) but that it is, on balance, pro-competitive because of the presence of efficiencies and the fact that consumers obtain "a fair share of the resulting benefit".[48] The significance of the distinction for joint venturers is that exemptions can only be granted for a specified period; they cannot be granted for an indefinite period or on a permanent basis. What is more, the Commission may attach conditions and obligations to any exemption that it grants.[49] The fact that the joint venture agreement, as originally drafted, may need to be modified to comply with conditions imposed by the Commission is a source of uncer-

---

[44] Reg. 4064/89 [1989] OJ L395/1, as amended by Reg. 1310/97 [1997] OJ L180/1.

[45] Council Reg. 17/62, Art. 15(2).

[46] V. Korah, *An Introductory Guide to EC Competition Law and Practice* (6th edn., Oxford, Hart Publishing, 1997), 279.

[47] *Ibid.*, 292–4.

[48] EC Treaty, Art. 85(3).

[49] Council Reg. 17, Art. 8(1).

tainty for the parties; so is the fact that they cannot know the attitude that the Commission will take once the exemption expires. The fear is that desirable joint ventures may never be formed because of these sources of risk.

The Commission's concerns about the possible adverse consequences of joint ventures largely relate to the issues discussed earlier. That is to say, the Commission is concerned about the loss of actual or potential competition; the possible spillover of the habit of co-operation to areas of activity not envisaged by the joint venture agreement; foreclosure (where the joint venture relates to some scarce resource or essential facility) and the formation of networks of joint ventures where one or more joint venturers are members of several joint ventures which are, therefore, unlikely to compete with each other.[50] Clearly, these concerns will be more or less acute, depending upon the market share enjoyed by the parties.

As already mentioned, it is possible that the joint venture will benefit from an exemption or, more rarely, a clearance but that some of the restrictions or obligations that it contains are found to be anti-competitive. Joint venture agreements frequently contain non-competition clauses such as covenants by the joint venturers not to compete with the joint venture or with each other. On the face of it, these terms involve the creation of a cartel since they involve the allocation of markets between the parties. On the other hand, it may be, for example, that neither party would enter into the joint venture were it not for some assurance that the joint venture will have a clear run at the relevant market free from competition from the joint venturers themselves.[51] That is, the joint venturers will want to be assured that the return on their investment in the joint venture is not jeopardised by the actions of another joint venturer. The Commission could grant clearance or exemption to the joint venture but insist on the removal of some of the restrictions contained in the joint venture agreement. Its role, in this context, is to judge whether the restriction is required in order to make the basic transaction viable.[52]

Some joint ventures will be able to take advantage of the terms of one or more of the block exemptions; the block exemptions for specialisation agreements[53] and research and development agreements[54] are particularly relevant. Block exemptions are an effective way of encouraging particular types of arrangement: joint ventures covered by one or more block exemptions are virtually immune from challenge either by the Commission or third parties. Unless the opposition procedure is invoked, there is no need to notify the Commission, as is the case with clearances or individual exemptions.

---

[50] Korah, n. 46 above, 284–7.

[51] For an explanation of the legitimate role that ancillary restrictions might have to play in an R & D joint venture, see V. Korah, "Collaborative Joint Ventures for Research and Development where Markets are Concentrated: The Competition Rules of the Common Market and the Invalidity of Contracts" (1991–2) 15 *Fordham International Law Journal* 248 at 265–8.

[52] Korah, n. 46 above, 287–8.

[53] Council Reg. 417/85 as amended by Reg. 2236/97.

[54] Council Reg. 418/85 as amended by Reg. 2236/97.

The Merger Regulation

Introduction

The point has already been made that joint ventures lie somewhere on a spectrum between mergers on the one hand and agreements between firms that retain their capacity to act independently on the relevant market on the other hand. A significant feature of EC competition law is its approach to dealing with joint ventures which, whilst resembling mergers in some respects, also need to be considered as agreements betwen independent undertakings. The Merger Regulation applies to all concentrations with a community dimension.[55] Where it applies, it does so to the exclusion of all national legislation[56] and of other aspects of community competition law.[57] Joint ventures to which it does not apply potentially fall within Article 81(85) and national competition law.

This section will look at the criteria to be applied in deciding whether or not a joint venture is a concentration for the purposes of the Merger Regulation (this type of joint venture will be referred to, for reasons which will become clear, as a "full-function joint venture"). It will also explain how EC competition law deals with full-function joint ventures when considered, not from the merger point of view, but as potential cartels. The substantive tests to be applied when assessing full-function joint ventures will be examined. Finally, the treatment of ancillary restraints will be considered.

Full-function Joint Ventures

Article 3(2) of the Merger Regulation provides that a joint venture is a concentration[58] (and so is caught by the Merger Regulation) where it performs on a lasting basis all the functions of an autonomous economic entity; joint ventures which satisfy this definition are also known as "full-function" joint ventures.[59] Before the recent amendments to the Merger Regulation, not all full-function joint ventures were concentrations; even full-function joint ventures were termed "co-operative" (a residual category to which all non-concentrative joint ventures belonged) if they had the object or effect of co-ordinating the competitive behaviour of undertakings which remained independent.[60]

Before the 1997 amendments, the distinction between concentrative and co-operative joint ventures had significant practical consequences for the parties. The substantive criterion for the appraisal of concentrations (see below) is

---

[55] The Merger Reg., Art. 1(1).

[56] The Merger Reg., Art. 21(2).

[57] The Merger Reg., Art. 22(1).

[58] Joint ventures and the acquisition of joint control were the largest category of concentrations notified to the Commission in 1997, comprising 77 of the 172 notifications (*27th Report on Competition Policy*, n. 5 above, para. 145).

[59] The Merger Reg., recital 23. Guidance on the essential elements of a full-function joint venture is given in the Commission Notice on the concept of full-function joint ventures.

[60] The Merger Reg. (unamended version), Art. 3(2).

thought to be more favourable than the test applied under Article 81(1) (85(1)) and the parties to a concentration also benefit from the timetable for reaching a decision in the Merger Regulation context.[61] Commentators thought that this divergence of treatment was unfortunate, particularly so bearing in mind the difficulty inherent, under the unamended Merger Regulation, in making the distinction between concentrative and co-operative joint ventures. Hawk thought that the procedure was theoretically flawed[62] and he advocated a search for ways of reducing the practical significance of the distinction.[63]

The amendments to the Merger Regulation attempt to meet this criticism by altering the significance of the negative criterion contained in article 3(2) of the unamended Merger Regulation. Under the revised article 3(2), as we have seen, all full-function joint ventures are concentrations, even where the joint venture co-ordinates the competitive behaviour of independent undertakings. However, to the extent that a joint venture has this object or effect, it will be appraised in accordance with Article 81(1) (85(1)) and 81(3) (85(3)).[64] This is an improvement for joint venturers, though, because even if a full-function joint venture has to be appraised in accordance with Article 81(85), the Commission must comply with the time-scale and procedures of the Merger Regulation.

Procedure under the Merger Regulation

Brodley suggested a three-stage approach to the evaluation of joint ventures: an initial investigation would be followed by a more detailed scrutiny, where the initial investigation indicated antitrust risk. Where the parties failed to rebut the presumption of antitrust risk following a second-stage investigation, an appropriate corrective remedy would be imposed.[65] Where some form of remedy is required, Brodley favours incentive-modifying remedies over outright prohibitions.[66]

The procedure provided for in the Merger Regulation could be said to take this approach as its ideal. Full-function joint ventures are to be notified to the Commission within specified time limits.[67] They are then suspended until they have been cleared by a declaration of their compatibility with the Common Market.[68] Following notification, the Commission must make an initial decision within one month of notification.[69] At this stage, the Commission can clear the joint venture on the basis that there are no serious doubts about its compatibility with the Common Market[70] (it may also decide that the joint venture is

---

[61] Korah, n. 46 above, 299.

[62] B. Hawk, "Joint Ventures under EEC Law" (1991–2) 15 *Fordham International Law Journal* 303 at 323.

[63] *Ibid.*, 324.

[61] The Merger Reg., Art. 2(4).

[65] Brodley, n. 4 above, 1539.

[66] *Ibid.*, 1544.

[67] The Merger Reg., Art. 4(1).

[68] The Merger Reg., Art. 7(1).

[69] The Merger Reg., Art. 10(1).

[70] The Merger Reg., Art. 6(1)(b).

not caught by the Merger Regulation[71]). A finding that there are no serious doubts concerning the joint venture amounts to a decision that, in the Commission's view, it raises no presumption of an antitrust risk to be rebutted by the parties.

The Commission may initially decide, following notification, that there are serious doubts concerning the compatibility of the joint venture with the Common Market; that is to say, there might be a finding of antitrust risk. In this event, the Commission will initiate proceedings.[72] It then has four months from the date when proceedings are initiated to make a decision whether or not the joint venture is compatible with the Common Market.[73] Under Brodley's approach, the burden of proof falls on the parties seeking to uphold a joint venture if the initial investigation reveals some presumptive anti-trust risk; the Merger Regulation is silent on the question of the burden of proof.

The incentive-modifying approach advocated by Brodley is reflected in the ability of the Commission to attach conditions and obligations to its finding that there are no serious doubts about the joint venture's compatibility with the Common Market; they may be imposed either as part of its initial decision[74] or following proceedings.[75] It is also worth noticing that the parties can agree to modify the joint venture arrangements; if, by doing so, they deal with any objections that the Commission may have then it may declare the joint venture compatible with the Common Market.[76] Thus, the Merger Regulation seems to envisage that a dialogue may occur between the parties on the one hand and the Commission on the other following the initiation of proceedings.[77]

Compatibility with the Common Market

The test to be applied when evaluating joint ventures under the Merger Regulation is set out in Article 2; they are to be appraised with a view to establishing whether or not they are compatible with the Common Market. Article 2(1) lists the factors to be taken into account. Although they nearly all relate to the joint venture's effect on competition, there are some suggestions in the text that other factors may be taken into account. Article 2(1)(b), for example, includes a reference to "technical and economic progress". The thirteenth recital further muddies the waters when it requires the Commission to "place its appraisal within the general framework of the achievement of the fundamental objectives referred to in Article 2 of the Treaty, including that of strengthening

[71] The Merger Reg., Art. 6(1)(a).

[72] The Merger Reg., Art. 6(1)(c).

[73] Only one concentration (*Blokker/Toys "R" Us*) was declared incompatible with the Common Market in 1997 (*27th Report on Competition Policy*, n. 5 above, para. 146).

[74] The Merger Reg., Art. 6(1a).

[75] The Merger Reg., Art. 8(2).

[76] The Merger Reg., Art. 6(1a).

[77] In 1997, the Commission declared 8 concentrations to be compatible with the Common Market following in-depth investigations. Conditions were imposed in 7 of these cases (*27th Report on Competition Policy*, n. 5 above, para. 146).

the Community's economic and social cohesion, referred to in Article 130a". Does the reference in Article 2(1)(b) mean, for example, that a joint venture which facilitates the emergence of a European product champion should be deemed to be compatible with the Common Market even if it is anti-competitive? Does the thirteenth recital allow the Commission to consider aspects of industrial and commercial policy other than competition when appraising a joint venture?

The answer to both of the questions posed by the preceding paragraph is supplied by Article 2(2) and (3); this makes it plain that the Commission's appraisal is to be exclusively concerned with competition policy. The question to be posed by the Commission, as both clauses make clear, is whether the joint venture creates or strengthens a dominant position as a result of which effective competition would be significantly impeded in the Common Market or in a substantial part of it. Sir Leon Brittan, then the Commissioner responsible for competition, made it clear that he regarded competition as the dominant criterion.[78] This conclusion is borne out by a recent analysis of decisions under the Merger Regulation which finds that competition is the dominant criterion and that other Treaty objectives are only likely to be taken into account on a subsidiary basis.[79]

As already mentioned, full-function joint ventures with a Community dimension are also to be appraised in accordance with Article 81(85) to the extent that they co-ordinate the competitive behaviour of undertakings that remain independent. The Commission's concerns when evaluating joint ventures under Article 81(85) have already been discussed.

Ancillary Restraints

Where a joint venture is declared to be compatible with the Common Market, this declaration, "shall also cover restrictions directly related and necessary to the implementation of the concentration".[80] It is, therefore, important to know whether or not a restriction is "directly related and necessary" to the joint venture. If not, the restriction in question might be the subject of separate scrutiny under Article 81(85) or 82(86).[81]

The Commission notice regarding restrictions ancillary to restrictions[82] provides guidance on this issue. Paragraphs 4–6 set out a number of criteria which have to be met: the restriction must be subordinate in importance to the main object of the concentration; the restriction must be such that, without it, the

---

[78] Sir Leon Brittan, "The Law and Policy of Merger Control in the EEC" (1990) 15 *European Law Review* 351 at 352–4.

[79] D. Banks, "Non-competition Factors and their Future Relevance under European Merger Law" (1997) 18 *European Competition Law Review* 182 at 186.

[80] The Merger Reg., Arts. 6(1) and 8(3).

[81] Commission Notice on the concept of full-function joint ventures, para. 16. The Commission's decisions in this area are discussed in J. Modrall, "Ancillary Restrictions in the Commission's Decisions under the Merger Regulation: Non-competition Clauses" (1995) 16 *European Competition Law Review* 40.

[82] [1990] OJ C203/5.

joint venture would not be implemented or could only be implemented with greater cost or difficulty; and the scope of the restriction must not exceed what is necessary if the joint venture is to be implemented. Part V of the notice provides specific help in applying these general criteria to concentrative joint ventures. This part of the notice explains, for example, that the grant by one of the joint venturers of an exclusive licence to use technology needed by the joint venture is an acceptable substitute for the outright transfer of the relevant rights to the joint venture. Since the right to use this technology will be necessary if the joint venture is to function autonomously, the exclusive licence will be deemed ancillary to the joint venture.

5. COMPANY LAW AND JOINT VENTURES

Introduction

Joint ventures are usually under the joint control of the parties; this is one of the most distinctive characteristics of the joint venture relationship. Where the joint venture takes the form of a limited company, this usually means that each party is represented on the board of the joint venture company by nominee directors.[83] The problem is that there is a conflict or potential conflict between the commercial expectations which joint venturers may have concerning the role of their nominee and the fiduciary duties which directors, nominee or otherwise, owe to the joint venture company. This section will examine this conflict. It will also consider whether liability for breach of fiduciary duty attaches only to the nominee director or whether the appointors might also be liable.[84]

The Commercial Role of Nominee Directors

The intention is that the nominee directors should assume the task of managing the joint venture company; they will usually be responsible for setting policy and for overseeing its implementation. It is reasonable to assume, however, that the nominees are often also appointed in order to represent their respective appointors and to protect the latters' interests. This would involve seeking to give effect to the wishes of their appointors and acting as a conduit for the flow

---

[83] Nominee directors have been defined by the Australian Companies and Securities Law Review Committee as "persons who independently of the method of their appointment, but in relation to their office, are expected to act in accordance with some understanding or arrangement which creates an obligation or mutual expectation of loyalty to some person or persons other than the company as a whole": see *Nominee Directors and Alternate Directors*, Report No. 8, 2 Mar. 1989, at 7.

[84] For a full and interesting analysis of the issues dealt with in this section see K. Yeung, "Corporate Groups: Legal Aspects of the Management Dilemma" [1997] *Lloyd's Maritime and Commercial Law Quarterly* 208.

of information between the appointor and the representatives of the other venturers on the board of the joint venture company.

The Fiduciary Duties of Nominee Directors

There are a number of legal problems arising out of the ambivalent role of the nominee directors. They are responsible not just to their appointors but also, and in fact principally, to the joint venture company as a separate legal entity. They must keep a watchful eye on their fiduciary duties and duties of skill and care as directors of the joint venture company.

Nominee directors have a narrow path to tread between too zealous a pursuit of the interests of their appointors on the one hand and too scrupulous a disregard of those interests in favour of the interests of the company on the other.[85] There may be circumstances in which these interests conflict. Orthodox formulations of the fiduciary duties of directors do not reflect this ambivalence. Such formulations make it clear that directors, nominee or otherwise, owe fiduciary duties to the company and that once those duties have been "activated", so to speak, there is no room for loyalties or partiality to individual shareholders or groups of shareholders, and much less to third parties, which relate to the assets or sphere of operation of the company.

One problem lies in the duty to act in the best interests of the company. Lord Greene MR in *Re Smith & Fawcett Ltd*[86] expressed the duty as a requirement that directors must:

"exercise their discretion bona fide in what they consider—not what a court may consider—is in the interests of the company and not for any collateral purpose".[87]

On the face of it, for a nominee director consciously to aim to further the commercial goals of the appointor is for him to act for a collateral purpose even if there is no inconsistency between the best interests of the company and those of the appointor. The chief implication for nominee directors of the traditional understanding of their fiduciary duties is that they must not have any special regard for the interests of their appointors. In practice, the nominee may well believe that his or her primary duty is to the appointor.

In his judgment in *Scottish Cooperative Wholesale Society Ltd* v. *Meyer*,[88] Lord Denning referred expressly to the position of the nominee director.[89] He returned to the theme in *Boulting* v. *Association of Cinematograph Television*

---

[85] P. Crutchfield, "Nominee Directors: The Law and Commercial Reality" (1991) 12 *The Company Lawyer* 136.

[86] [1942] Ch. 304.

[87] [1942] Ch. 304 at 306.

[88] [1959] AC 324. This was an action, indeed the first, based on the unfair prejudice provision in s. 210 of the Companies Act (CA) 1948.

[89] [1959] AC 324 at 366–7.

and Allied Technicians.[90] These *dicta* make it plain that, when there is a conflict between the interests of the appointor and of the joint venture company, nominee directors must give preference to the interests of the joint venture company. Even this position seems somewhat lax in the light of the principle enunciated in *Aberdeen Railway Co* v. *Blaikie Bros.*[91] that directors must avoid placing themselves in a position where their interest and duty may conflict.

To conclude this part of the discussion, then, it seems clear that if the appointor company and the joint venture company are not competitors or, presumably, if their interests are not in conflict for some other reason then there is no question of breach of fiduciary duty by the appointor. The mere fact of the two companies being in competition is likewise not sufficient to put the director in breach of duty.[92] It is clearly possible, however, that this competition, or some other circumstance, may mean that the director cannot reconcile his or her duties to both companies

Liability of the Appointor for the Nominee Director's Breach

Introduction

Nominee directors run the risk that the commercial demands made upon them will result in their actions amounting to a breach of fiduciary duty. Where the joint venturers are substantial enterprises, a transferee of the interest of one of the joint venturers or a liquidator may prefer proceedings to be brought against the joint venturer rather than against the nominee director. This will not usually be possible because of the fact that the fiduciary duty was owed by the director and not by the appointor. There are, however, two possible grounds upon which a finding of liability might be made: under the shadow directorship provisions of the Companies Act 1985 and the Insolvency Act 1986 and under the doctrine in *Barnes* v. *Addy.*[93]

Liability as a Shadow Director

As a matter of commercial reality, the function of nominee directors is not only to manage the joint venture, but in doing so to further the goals of their appointor. We have seen how the conflict between these functions may expose the nominee to liability for breach of duty. At the same time, there are dangers for the appointor inherent in the fealty of the nominee director. One of the main reasons for using a company as the vehicle for the joint venture is the benefit of

[90] [1963] 2 QB 606.
[91] (1854) 1 Macq. 461.
[92] *London & Mashonaland Exploration Co.* v. *New Mashonaland Corporation Co* [1891] WN 165.
[93] (1874) 9 Ch. App. 244.

limited liability. This benefit might be lost to the joint venturer if it is found to be a shadow director of the joint venture company. Shadow directors can, for example, be made to contribute to the assets of an insolvent company under the wrongful trading provisions of the Insolvency Act 1986.[94] There are *dicta* in *Re Unisoft Group Ltd (No 2)*[95] to the effect that shadow directors might owe fiduciary duties to the company in the same way as properly appointed directors. It is to the shadow directorship provisions of the Companies Act 1985 and the Insolvency Act 1986 that we now turn our attention.

Section 741(2) of the Companies Act 1985 is as follows:

> "In relation to a company, 'shadow director' means a person in accordance with whose directions or instructions the directors of the company are accustomed to act. However, a person is not deemed a shadow director by reason only that the directors act on advice given by him in a professional capacity."

The definition in 251 of the Insolvency Act 1986 is virtually identical. There is, however, a major difference between the shadow directorship provisions in the Companies Act and in the Insolvency Act. Section 741(3) of the Companies Act provides that a body corporate is not to be treated as a shadow director of any of its subsidiary companies by reason only that the directors of the subsidiary are accustomed to act in accordance with its directions or instructions. It is not clear what additional factors must be present before a parent company can be a shadow director of its subsidiary. Clearly, however, the practical effect is that a joint venturer which is the parent company of the joint venture company will hardly ever be liable as a shadow director under the Companies Act. There is no such protection for parent companies in the Insolvency Act; thus, joint venturers might be liable as shadow directors for wrongful trading.[96]

The scope for the shadow directorship provisions to apply in the joint venture situation is obvious. The statutory definitions of a shadow director are, however, silent on some key points. For practical purposes, the appointors and the nominee need some guidance on the relationships and types of conduct likely to fall within the above definition.

The judgment of the Privy Council in *Kuwait Asia Bank* v. *National Mutual Life Nominees Ltd*[97] provides important guidance on the extent of the control that a shadow director must be able to exert: it will not be sufficient to be able to dicate policy to a minority of the board. In *Re Unisoft Group Ltd (No 2)*,[98] a section 459 case, Harman J, in comments which were *obiter*, thought that the influence of a shadow director should extend to at the very least, to a "governing

---

[94] Insolvency Act 1986, s. 214(7). A list of the provisions of the CA 1985 and the Insolvency Act 1986 which apply to shadow directors is to be found in R. Pennington, *Company Law* (7th edn., (London, Butterworth Law, 1995), 711.

[95] [1994] BCC 766.

[96] Insolvency Act 1986, s.214(7).

[97] [1990] 3 All ER 404.

[98] [1994] BCC 766.

majority" of the board of directors.[99] Writing in *The Insolvency Practitioner*, Millett J went further and suggested that the reference to "the directors" makes it clear that it must be possible to dictate policy to the whole board and not simply some members of it.[100]

It is not enough for an appointor to be able to exert control over a board of directors; it seems that that control must actually be exercised. In *Re Hydrodan (Corby) Ltd*,[101] Millett J, in effect, held that there was no automatic presumption that the board of a subsidiary is accustomed to act on the instructions of the directors of the parent. Millett J thought that the court needed to determine the degree of independence afforded to each subsidiary. The greater this is, the less likely it is that the directors of the parent company will be found to be shadow directors.

Occasional exercise of the power to control the board's decisions seems not to be sufficient; commenting on the phrase "accustomed to act" in the definitions of a shadow director, Harman J explained in *Re Unisoft Group Ltd (No 2)* that this must refer to acts "not on one individual occasion but over a period of time and as a regular course of conduct".[102]

In his article in *The Insolvency Practitioner*, Millett J suggested that not only must the shadow director's interventions have amounted to a course of conduct and have influenced the behaviour of the board, but the shadow director must also have had a conscious intention to control the decisions of the board.[103] If only in theory, this contemplates the possibility of a board of directors which complies with "suggestions" of the parent company because, having considered them and with utter freedom to accept or reject them, it decides that the advice they contain is sound and should be followed. If Millett J is right, in these circumstances, the nominee would not be a shadow director.

Finally, the decision of Judge Paul Baker QC in *Re PFTZM Ltd (in liquidation)*[104] gives rise to further difficulty. Here, a borrower had run into financial difficulty. It informed its lender. From then on, the lender exercised very tight control over payments made by the borrower. In addition, it exercised control over capital expenditure and staff changes.Nevertheless, Judge Paul Baker felt that the representatives of the lender were not shadow directors because they merely acted with a view to protecting the rights of the lender in its capacity as unsecured creditor.[105] It is difficult to see why the reason for dictating policy to the board is relevant, and the reasoning has been criticised[106] on the basis that

---

[99] [1994] BCC 766 at 775.

[100] P. Millett, " 'Shadow Directorship'—A Real or Imagined Threat to the Banks", *Insolvency Practitioner*, Jan. 1991.

[101] [1994] BCC 161.

[102] [1994] BCC 766 at 775.

[103] See also P. Fidler, "Banks as Shadow Directors" (1992) 3 *Journal of International Banking Law* 97 and L. Jones, "Distinguishing Shadow Directors" [1994] *Sol. Jo.* 440.

[104] [1995] 2 BCLC 354.

[105] [1995] 2 BCLC 354 at 367.

[106] D. Milman, "Shadow Directors: Further Guidance from the Courts" (1995) 15 *Insolvency Lawyer* 15.

it has already been accepted implicitly in *Kuwait Asia Bank* that shareholders who take steps to protect their economic interests can be shadow directors. There is no obvious reason why the same steps should not have the same effect simply because the person taking them is a lender rather than a shareholder.

Liability under the Doctrine in Barnes v. Addy

Under the doctrine in *Barnes* v. *Addy*,[107] where trust property has been misapplied, a stranger to a trust becomes liable as a constructive trustee where he "receives and becomes chargeable with some part of the trust property" or where he "assists with knowledge in a dishonest and fraudulent design on the part of the trustees". This doctrine can also be applied to render appointors liable for breach of fiduciary duty on the part of their nominees. The knowledge required before a finding of knowing assistance will be made was considered recently in *Royal Brunei Airlines Sdn Bhd* v. *Tan Kok Ming*.[108] The joint venture company is the beneficiary of the fiduciary duty and it is unlikely that it will bring an action against the parties to the joint venture; certainly this is true where the nominee in breach of duty represents a joint venturer with 50 per cent or more of the voting rights in the company. As a result, the doctrine is probably only significant, for present purposes, where the joint venture company is in liquidation.

Conclusion

There is a mismatch between the commercial role of nominee directors and their fiduciary duties. As a result, the nominee, though acting honestly and competently, faces the prospect of proceedings for breach of fiduciary duty; the appointor might also be liable, either as a shadow director or under the principles established in *Barnes* v. *Addy*. It is unlikely that proceedings will be brought against the nominee director by the appointor; it is conceivable, however, that a liquidator of the company might bring proceedings.

It is undesirable that this mismatch should occur. One possible response would be to amend the Companies Act 1985 with a view to bringing the nominee's fiduciary duties into line with the commercial expectations placed upon them.[109] This is the line taken by the New Zealand legislature; section 131(4) of the New Zealand Companies Act provides:

> "A director of a company incorporated to carry out a joint venture between the shareholders may, when exercising powers or performing duties as director in connection

---

[107] (1874) 9 Ch. App. 244.

[108] [1995] 2 AC 378.

[109] Thomas J advocates this approach in "The Role of Nominee Directors and the Liability of their Appointors" in MacMillan Patfield (ed.), *Perspectives on Company Law*: 2 (London, Kluwer Law International, 1997), 235 at 236.

with the carrying out of the joint venture, if expressly permitted to do so by the constitution of the company, act in a manner which he or she believes to be in the best interests of a shareholder or shareholders, even though it may not be in the best interests of the company."

This reconciles the conflict between the law and commercial reality. It has the benefit that joint venturers and their nominees can be certain of their legal position.

This certainty is, however, achieved at a price. The nominee is licensed to relegate the interests of all other "stakeholders" in a company to those of its present shareholders. It is possible that creditors of the joint venture company could be harmed by the New Zealand approach. This is odd, given the fact that it is quite clear that directors can come to owe their fiduciary duties primarily to a company's creditors rather than to its members.[110]

An alternative to the New Zealand approach would be to leave the law as it is, or to vary it only slightly. Efforts could be made to educate nominee directors and appointors concerning the effect of the nominee's fiduciary duties. It may be better to provide nominees with a defence to an action for breach of fiduciary duty where they acted in good faith and on the instructions of their appointor. Where this defence was made out, liability would be transferred to the appointor.[111] Appointors could take out insurance against the risk of an action for breach of duty.

6. CONCLUSION

This essay has looked at how EC and UK competition law treat joint ventures; there are signs that they are beginning to cater for the distinctive nature of the joint venture. In the UK, the decision in *Dawnay, Day & Co Ltd* v. *Frederic de Braconier d'Alphen*[112] is one such sign; it recognises that the joint venture merits special treatment under the common law doctrine of restraint of trade. Clearly, the process of developing specific institutions and policies for joint ventures has gone further in European competition law; this is particularly true of those aspects of the Merger Regulation which deal specifically with joint ventures.

UK company law, by contrast, fails joint ventures in some significant respects; one of these failings has been considered in this essay. It is not the only failing;

---

[110] See, *inter alia*, the *dicta* in *Liquidator of West Mercia Safetywear Ltd* v. *Dodd and another* (1988) 4 BCC 30; *Re Horsley & Weight Limited* [1982] 3 All ER 1045; and *Winkworth* v. *Edward Baron Development Co Ltd* [1987] 1 All ER 114.

[111] As well as suggesting that the fiduciary duties of nominee directors should be modified, Thomas J argues that the courts should be entitled to impose liability on appointors for the actions of their nominees under the law of agency (on the basis that the nominee is the agent of the principal) or that appointors should be vicariously liable for the actions of their nominees who are employed by them. See n. 109 above, 255.

[112] [1997] IRLR 442.

company law also fails to recognise the fiduciary relationship between the members of a joint venture company. It is to be hoped that these problems will be considered, at least, in the review of UK company law which is just beginning.

There is every reason to believe that the "wave of mega mergers and joint ventures" mentioned at the outset will come upon us. It is important that the law is ready for it.

12

Regulation of Overseas Companies

FRANCIS TANSINDA[1]

INTRODUCTION

This essay covers the rules that have been developed through the years by Parliament in the main, and by the English courts to a limited extent, to regulate the registration and carrying on of business in Great Britain by foreign companies. The essay briefly looks at the history of recognition of foreign companies, but the discussion focuses principally on the law regulating these companies as it is today as represented by the Companies Act 1985 and the amendments introduced by the Companies Act 1989, as well as the influence from European law.

It will be observed that some of the provisions are fairly settled, but in general the rules are constantly being modified to facilitate the regulation of overseas companies amidst the difficulties that arise in relation to their regulation. The section on insolvency proceedings in particular bears testimony to this assertion and has been given full coverage accordingly. Influence from European Community law on UK registration on oversea companies' provisions has also been discussed, as this constitutes the most recent source of change in this area.

RECOGNITION OF FOREIGN COMPANIES

The recognition of foreign companies in English law dates back to the eighteenth century in cases like *Dutch West Indies Co v. Moses*, and others.[2] The basis of recognition then was that the foreign company was legally recognised in its country of incorporation. This recognition by English courts has been reaffirmed in more recent times,[3] and it is now unquestionable as foreign companies are able to and in fact do have their shares quoted on the London Stock

---

[1] Senior Lecturer, The School of Law, Manchester Metropolitan University.
[2] (1723) 1 Stra. 613; *Henriques* v. *Dutch West India Co* (1728) 2 Ld. Raym. 1532 at 1535. See also *Bonanza Greek Gold Mining Co* v. *R.* [1916] 1 AC 566 (PC); *Lazard Bros* v. *Midland Bank* [1933] AC 287 at 297.
[3] *National Bank of Athens SA* v. *Metliss* [1958] AC 509.

Exchange. Furthermore, foreign companies can now come in and register to carry on business in the UK subject to the regulations which are currently in place.

Recognition of foreign companies seems to me to be based *prima facie* on the principle of comity among nations which is a trait of customary international law. Little wonder, therefore, that its incidence in the UK dates back to the eighteenth century. The need to facilitate the flow of business transactions among nations and the commercial activities of individuals from different countries seem to rationalise the principle of comity and, consequently, the acceptance of foreign companies to do business in the UK. Recognition is a reciprocal exercise among states and this has a firm customary background.

In the UK, however, this generally accepted custom of recognising foreign companies did not end in the courts, in subsequent years, it was to be embodied in the Statute Book through various Companies Acts, and most recently in the Foreign Corporations Act 1991. This Act sanctions the recognition of foreign corporations incorporated in accordance with the law of territories which the UK does not necessarily recognise as states. These foreign corporations, thanks to the Act, are therefore treated for the purposes of UK corporate law as having legal personality. This again is another clear indication of how recognition of foreign companies is a matter of comity among nations.[4] It follows therefore that foreign companies are recognised in two distinct situations in the UK, (1) where they remain outside the jurisdiction but have a cause of action in the courts here, and (2) where they actually carry on business here and are registered here. For the purpose of this essay, focus is mainly on the latter, which are legally labelled "overseas companies".

Statutory Recognition

The statutory recognition of foreign companies was discussed in 1905.[5] The Committee approved the recognition of foreign companies based on comity among states but thought it desirable to require foreign companies carrying on business in the UK to register or comply with any of the requirements of the Companies Act 1900 concerning prospectuses and/or to make deposits in this country, with a view to securing the protection of British creditors. The provisions on the issuing of any prospectus by foreign companies are still applicable today.[6]

The Committee suggested that foreign companies trading in England and applying for English capital, which used the distinctive word "limited" as the

---

[4] *The Arab Monetary Fund* v. *Hashim & Others (No 3)* [1991] 2 AC 114. See also Abla Mayss, "The Status of the Arab Monetary Fund in English Law" (1990) 7 *Co. Law* 140.

[5] The Loreburn Report, Cmd. 3052 (1906).

[6] See particulars of prospectuses of overseas companies in Companies Act (CA) 1985, s. 72(1), (2), (3).

last word of their name, should fulfil the following conditions: they should be required to file in England a verified copy (with a verified English translation) of their charter, statutes or memorandum and articles of association, with the names of all directors, as well as the name of some person or persons resident in the UK, authorised on behalf of such company to accept service of process or any notices required to be served on such company. The person so registered should be the only person entitled to commence or authorise proceedings on behalf of such company in any court in the UK. As a safeguard, these foreign companies using the word "limited" should in any prospectus inviting subscriptions in the UK, state the company's place of origin, and should, when carrying on business in the UK, be compelled under penalty to put up its name with the place of origin on its business premises.

Furthermore, the Committee recommended that foreign companies should file with the registrar a verified copy of their annual balance sheet with a substantial penalty for default. These demands on foreign companies were considered appropriate and in no way onerous because, in the words of Lord Faber:

> "These are particulars to which we think we are entitled and they are the sort required in foreign countries from English companies trading there. We think it is a fair demand to make and that general advantage will result."[7]

In the same vein, it was suggested that foreign companies which established a place of business here should in some respects satisfy conditions which domestic companies were subjected to. This was because, among other things, these companies would seek investment from shareholders here and it was only reasonable that prospective investors and shareholders be protected as such. To quote Lord Faber again, while reiterating the importance of the proposal on foreign companies:

> "The Bill proposes to enlarge the requirements of the Companies Act 1900 so as to provide that no material fact which would be calculated to influence the minds of intending investors should be omitted from the prospectus. We of the Committee thought that a man who was applying for shares in a limited company should know everything that it was material for him to know, otherwise he would be unable to form a true and accurate judgment of the company and its standing."[8]

These proposals were clearly intended to protect domestic investors and came as a small price to pay for recognition and acceptance. The next section will show how these ideas were incorporated in the statute book.

---

[7] Hansard (1907), vol.171, 170, 171.
[8] *Ibid.*, 172.

Pre-1985 Companies Acts

The introduction of statutory provisions to regulate overseas companies in the UK was triggered by the recommendations of the Loreburn Report.[9] The relevant provision was contained in section 35 of the Companies Act 1907.[10]

In 1925 the Greene Committee made public its recommendations which portrayed a sense of dissatisfaction at the amount of information which was not obtained from overseas companies. It was thought that this fact put overseas companies in a better position than domestic companies:

> "We see no reason why these companies should be in a better position than British companies with regard to the contents of prospectuses and we recommend that the relevant sections should be made applicable to them with any necessary modifications."[11]

The recommendations pointed to the need for the registrar of companies to be kept abreast of any changes that took place within the company.[12] This provision gave room for greater supervision of foreign companies registered under the Companies Act as oversea companies.

The Companies Act 1947, which was consolidated in the Companies Act 1948, followed the trend of the previous Acts by elaborating on the provisions on overseas companies. However in this Act, unlike the previous ones, the secretary of the company was given as much importance as the director. It seems to me that the imposition of strict registration requirements for directors and secretaries was to enable Parliament to have a greater grip on overseas companies in order to safeguard the interests of persons doing business with them.

It can be seen from the above overview of earlier Companies Acts that there was already a growing tendency to place overseas companies, in certain matters, on the same footing with domestic companies. One could suppose therefore that eventually, on many other aspects, overseas companies would be treated in similar fashion as their opposite numbers incorporated in the UK. However, the present law dispels to a great extent any such aspiration.

It will be observed that the provisions regulating overseas companies are now more elaborate. This is of course true of domestic companies.[13] This trend can

---

[9] *The Loreburn Report on Company Law Reform* Cd. 3052 (London, HMSO, 1906).

[10] That section dealt with the requirements which foreign companies had to satisfy in order to be registered as overseas companies.

[11] *The Greene Committee Report on Company Law Reform* Cmd. 2657 (London, HMSO, 1925) paras. 90–91.

[12] The CA of 1928 required overseas companies to deliver to the registrar specifications of altered documents such as:
  (i)   the charter, statutes or memorandum and articles of association of the company or any such instrument,
  (ii) the directors of the company or the particulars contained in the list of the directors,
  (iii) the names or addresses of the persons authorised to accept service on behalf of the company.

[13] See Len Sealy, *Company Law and Commercial Reality* (London, Sweet & Maxwell, 1984).

quite clearly be explained by the fact that there has been an increase in international financial trade and economic relations in the world in the past decades; a fact that has seen the creation of many more companies with far reaching activities of international dimensions.

However despite this trend, the law regulating overseas companies is far from satisfactory. It is recommended that laws regulating overseas companies should be written out in the most unambiguous fashion, so that when disputes arise between overseas companies and UK investors, contractors or authorities, it will be easy for judgments to be delivered with as little discretion in interpretation by the judges as possible. Having said this, one must make the point that the room given to the Secretary of State to qualify provisions for overseas companies in certain respects makes the law applicable to these companies far from being settled.

The Companies Act 1989 has not dispelled the proposition that the provisions on the regulation of overseas companies are far from concise, straightforward and ascertainable. Instead the Act has introduced some amendments to certain provisions on the regulation of overseas companies,[14] although some have not been brought into force since their enactment.[15] However, all the main provisions dealing with overseas companies in English company law are still to be found in the Companies Act 1985.[16] The Companies Act 1989 in fact preserves a cosmetic integrity of the Companies Act 1985 by substituting its provisions for those of the 1985 Companies Act. The next section considers in some detail the rules on the regulation of oversea companies.

SPECIFIC PROVISIONS ON OVERSEAS COMPANIES

The law on overseas companies is contained in Part XXIII of the Companies Act 1985, but it is unsafe and incorrect to suppose that this Part, which has three chapters, regulates all aspects of overseas companies. The first and longest chapter, with two schedules, deals with registration formalities; it has incorporated the provisions of the 11th EC Company Directive on Branch Registration;[17] the second, with two schedules attached, is concerned with issues of accounts; and the third deals with the registration of charges, but it must be stressed that the provisions on the registration of charges are not yet in force.

These schedules are the provisions of the EEC Directive and have considerably amended Part XXIII of the Companies Act 1985. It is clear that foreign

[14] Notably in the areas of investigation and registration of charges by overseas companies. The area on disclosure of interests in shares (which applies both to overseas companies and domestic companies) has also been amended.

[15] For instance, the section on registration of charges by overseas companies.

[16] E.g., in introducing the changes in the area of registration of charges s. 105 of the CA 1989 reads thus: "the following provisions are inserted in Part XXIII of the Companies Act 1985".

[17] 11th Company Law Dir., 89/666/EEC as enacted in Overseas Company Regs. 1992 (SI 1992, No 3179).

companies wishing to carry on business in the UK must address these new registration provisions. It is appropriate however, to consider the changes that have been introduced and what effects these may have on foreign companies wanting to carry on business in the UK. A look at the old regime before an examination of the new will be instructive, bearing in mind that at the moment both regimes are applicable to overseas companies.

REGISTRATION FORMALITIES: THE OLD REGIME

Under the Companies Act 1985, as indeed under the previous Companies Acts, overseas company status was obtained upon registration of certain documents with the registrar of companies and establishing a place of business in Great Britain. As a matter of importance, one of these documents is a list of names and addresses of one or more persons resident in Great Britain authorised on the company's behalf to accept service of process and any notices required to be served on the company. Any alterations of particulars in these documents must be notified within 21 days of the making of the alterations.[18] One of the vexed questions which was a source of dispute under the old regime was to determine when a foreign company had established a place of business in the UK. The decided cases have not answered the question satisfactorily, largely because of the differences of opinion of judges. An attempt at a concise definition seems pointless; the cases suggest that all the circumstances of each case have to be taken into account to determine whether or not a company has established a place of business in Great Britain. The authorities date back to the nineteenth century.[19] For more recent answers to the problem, some guidance is afforded by the criteria set out in *Palmer's Company Law*[20]:

> "a company has an established place of business in Great Britain if it has a specified or identifiable place at which it carries on business";[21] 'a local habitation of its own e.g. an office';[22] there must be some 'visible sign or physical indication' that the company has connection with particular premises.[23] The requirement of an established place of business is only satisfied if the specified or identifiable habitation of the company is intended to have more than fleeting character."[24]

[18] CA 1985, s. 692(1)(3)(a), (b).

[19] *Newby* v. *Van Oppen* (1872) LR 7 QB 293; *Haggin* v. *Comptoir d'Escompte de Paris* (1889) 23 QB 579; *Badcock* v. *Cumberland Gap Park Company* [1893] 1 Ch. 362; *La Bourgogue* [1899] AC 431.

[20] (25th edn., Sweet & Maxwell, London, 1991), 2,237 para. 2.1701.

[21] See Evershed MR in *Banque des Marchands de Moscou (Koupetscesky)* v. *Kindersley* [1951] Ch. 112, 126, 132.

[22] See Lord Dunedin in *Lord Advocate* v. *Huron and Erie Loan and Savings Co*, 1911 SC 612 at 616.

[23] See Jenkins LJ in *Deverall* v. *Grant Advertising Inc.* [1954] 3 All ER 389, 391.

[24] *Lord Advocate* v. *Huron and Erie Loan and Savings Co*, 1911 SC 612 at 616. See also *Adams and Others* v. *Cape Industries plc and Another* [1991] 1 All ER 929.

So far the decisions suggest that the foreign company must itself trade here, and it can do so by establishing a branch or having an agent representing the company and carrying on the company's business.[25] Further, the "base" of the company, which constitutes its established place of business, must be more than transitory. The relevance of providing an answer to this question was paramount under the old law because those foreign companies which had not established a place of business in the UK were not subject to the regulations on oversea companies.

Much ink will not be spilt on this point because, as a result of the new regulations, the dispute over whether a company has an established place of business is only academic. Henceforth all foreign companies have to register as overseas companies under one of two regimes: "branch" registration and "place of business" registration.

What is also very interesting is that companies which come under the old definition of place of business will now register under the "branch" registration rules, while those companies which were considered as not having established a place of business under the old definition will have to register under the new "place of business" registration rules. A look at the EC based registration system will therefore be instructive.

REGISTRATION FORMALITIES: THE NEW REGIME

This new registration system became operational in the UK in January 1993.[26] As mentioned above, all foreign companies wishing to do business in the UK must register either under the "branch" registration rules or the "place of business" registration regulations. The old "established place of business" now becomes a "branch", and "fleeting presence" now becomes a "place of business". It is necessary to examine in some detail what, if any, difference exists between the definition of the old place of business and a branch. This is so not least because the "branch" rules originate from Europe but also because, as will be observed later, the rules under the "branch" registration are more onerous than those under the old "place of business" and indeed the new "place of business" regulations.

Branch Registration Rules

The Eleventh Directive does not define a "branch", but some guidance is given from EC case law. The concept of a "branch" in the EC sense is:

---

[25] *Newby* v. *Van Oppen & Colts Patent Firearms Manufacturing Co.* (1872) LR 7 QB 293.
[26] This new registration system is implemented in the UK as a result of the EC 11th Company Law Dir., 89/666/EEC and the EC Bank Branches Dir., 89/117/EEC.

> "a place of business which has the appearance of permanency, such as the extension of a parent body, has a management and is materially equipped to negotiate business with third parties so that the latter, although knowing that there will if necessary be a legal link with the parent body, the head office of which is abroad, do not have to deal directly with such parent body but may transact business at the place of business constituting the extension."[27]

The term "branch" denotes a part of a company which is incorporated abroad but is organised here to conduct business on behalf of the foreign company. It does not denote the sense of a local bank branch for example.

To all intents and purposes, a "branch" under the new registration scheme has the connotation of a "place of business" under the old law. Clearly therefore the law relating to the "place of business" under the old law remains in some respects relevant in considering issues similar to issues relating to "branch" registration. This notwithstanding, there is one case which was decided under the old law which may be interesting to discuss in the light of the preceding statement. The case indicates that there may be situations were reliance on the authorities under the old law may not be advisable. In *South India Shipping Corporation Ltd* v. *Export-Import Bank of Korea*,[28] the Court of Appeal held that a bank had established a place of business in the UK, although the bank did not conclude any banking transactions at its office in the UK and the business carried out here was incidental to its main objects. Relying strictly on the definition of a "place of business" and a "branch" one would say this case was wrongly decided because the company had no "base" here. However the Court of Appeal's reasoning was that if what the company is doing within the jurisdiction is that which, objectively, furthers the company's objects and aims, and provided this is done in a more or less permanent location, then that company will be considered as having established a place of business in the UK. In this case the Court looked at the *fond* and not the *forme* of the bank's presence in the UK to determine that it had established a place of business here. The Court prided itself by saying that its decision had the great merit of certainty, having drawn some inspiration from a decision as far back as 1912.[29]

If this case were to come before the court today, the decision would be that the overseas company should register under the "place of business" mode of registration. It is doubtful that the overseas company would have qualified as a "branch", bearing in mind that it is clear that the concept of branch does not include a place of business carrying on solely ancillary or incidental operations. However, it is fair to say that this is debatable.

Be this as it may, one is inclined to suggest that *South India Shipping Corp. Ltd* was decided on its own peculiar facts and did not follow the previous decisions on what constitutes establishing a place of business.[30] Similarly in today's

---

[27] Case 33/78, *Etablissement Somafer SA* v. *Saar-Ferngas AG* [1978] ECR 2183 at 2193.
[28] [1985] 2 All ER 219.
[29] See Buckley LJ in *Hercules* [1912] 1 KB 222 at 227–8.
[30] See cases cited above in *Palmer's Company Law*, n. 20 above.

state of the law the case may be decided on its facts without recourse to labels or previous decisions.

Certain changes have been introduced as a result of the new registration system, the rationale of which is clearly to exact more control over overseas companies. Although one must add that, as in the old law, some companies are exempt from registering under the branch registration regime.[31] More information is requested from foreign companies upon one month's registration as overseas companies. The foreign company must forward to the registrar the following:

(a) its registration number and identity of the register in its country of incorporation, if registration is required there;
(b) its legal form whether it is a private or public company;
(c) the extent of the authority of the director(s) to represent the company in dealings with third parties and in legal proceedings, indicating whether they may act alone or must act jointly and, if jointly, the name of any other person concerned.

Another new provision is that which requires foreign companies registering under the "branch" regime to notify the Registrar of particulars relating to any insolvency proceedings involving the company in its place of incorporation.[32]

In a nutshell all these new provisions[33] and the old ones are geared towards affording greater protection to domestic investors and creditors. The effect of these many requests on foreign companies may, however, cause a reduction in the number of foreign companies coming to do business in the UK. There is no evidence to suggest that this is the case. But if that were to happen, it would not be welcome in the UK for the simple reason that these companies have been known to provide a considerable amount of capital in the UK in the past. A fine balance needs to be maintained between regulation against possible abuse and facilitating enterprise to enhance the rewards of businesses carried on in the UK by foreign companies.

One other noteworthy change to registration formalities introduced by the new regime is the dichotomy between EC and non-EC companies.[34] This is an

---

[31] (a) unlimited companies incorporated outside Great Britain;
   (b) companies incorporated in Northern Ireland or Gibraltar; and
   (c) limited companies incorporated outside the UK, that do not have a branch in Northern Ireland and whose presence in Great Britain is not sufficient to fall under the branch registration regime, but is sufficient to fall within the place of business regime.

[32] CA 1985, s. 693(4)(c).

[33] See also provisions on prospectus, *ibid.*, s. 693(1). These are equally important as their effect is greater regulation of overseas companies. There are also provisions on restrictions on names: s. 694.

[34] The following is required from non-EC foreign companies:
   (a) the law under which the company was incorporated;
   (b) the address of its principal place of business in its country of incorporation, the company's objects and the amount of its issued share capital; and
   (c) its accounting reference date (or equivalent) and the time allowed under its parent law for the preparation and public disclosure of accounts.

aspect of overseas company regulation which was unknown in the UK. The idea may sow the seeds of the introduction of an elaborate two-tier regulatory regime for oversea companies: EC foreign companies on the one hand, and non-EC foreign companies on the other. Again the rationale behind this additional demand on non-EC companies is arguably the need to have more safeguards for the benefit of domestic contractors, given that it may be more difficult to lay hands on these companies, if things go wrong, than it would be in the case of EC companies. Furthermore it is arguably that EC companies are more transparent, better regulated and it is far easier to commence proceedings against them even in their countries of incorporation than in the case of non-EC companies.[35] Also it is fair to say that there is a tacit belief that the regulators of, and laws regulating, EC companies are more effective than those for non-EC companies.

Place of Business Registration

The second form of registration under the new law is for foreign companies with a "place of business" in the UK. A place of business is established if the foreign company is carrying out business which is only ancillary or incidental to the company's business as a whole and has a transient presence here. It should be recalled that under the old law a foreign company which carried out business which was only ancillary to its main objects could argue that it was under no duty to register as an overseas company.[36] But it must be said that under the old law there is authority which shows that if the ancillary activity was conducted in a specified or identifiable place, the foreign company would fail in its claim that it had not established a place of business and consequently did not have to register with the Registrar of Companies.[37] This issue is now a thing of the past because under the new law any company with a transient presence is required to register under the "place of business" mode but not under the "branch" registration mode.

Foreign companies which are required to register under this regime are categorised in three groups:

(a)   unlimited companies incorporated outside Great Britain;

(b)   companies incorporated in Northern Ireland or Gibraltar; and

(c)   limited companies incorporated outside the United Kingdom that do not have a branch in Northern Ireland and whose presence in Great Britain is not sufficient to fall under the branch registration regime but is sufficient to fall within the place of business regime.

---

[35] See e.g. the difficulties of securing legal settlements in the BCCI collapse in 1988–9.

[36] *South India Shipping Corporation* v. *Bank of Korea* [1985] 1 WLR 585.

[37] *Ibid.*; also see *Cleveland Museum of Art* v. *Capricorn Art International SA and Anor* [1990] BCLC 546.

Foreign companies falling under (c) below will be those which carry on businesses involving warehousing facilities, administrative transactions for the parent and internal data processing facilities.

The requirements on companies that have to register under the "place of business" mode are, not surprisingly, less stringent than those applicable to companies which have to register under the "branch" mode. Foreign companies subject to a place of business regime are less likely to abuse the privilege of doing business in the UK, they are less likely to be involved in substantial transactions with UK investors and contractors and generally do not enjoy the range of benefits which are available to domestic companies. For these reasons the less strict regulatory regime is justified.

Effect of new registration regime

The introduction of a dual registration system means that every foreign limited company (apart from the exceptions listed above) that carries on some business and establishes some degree of permanence in the UK has to register in the UK as an oversea company under one form of registration or the other. The exact form of registration will depend on the extent of business carried on and the degree of permanency of the foreign company in the UK. Under the new law, every branch is a place of business, but not every place of business is a branch.

It is not very clear yet what impact this new regime will have on overseas companies which are currently in the UK, neither is one clear about the effect the system will have on the influx of foreign companies in the UK. In fact it is debatable whether the introduction of the new system will be beneficial to the regulatory authorities in their endeavour to regulate overseas companies. An authority on company law has noted, "this area, always somewhat obscure, has now become over-complicated as a result of the way the UK has chosen to implement the 11th Company Law Directive".[38] The same author opines that the regulation is now so complex that it is likely to give company administrators headaches which they do not need or deserve.[39]

In the absence of a concise definition for certain terms and phrases applied in the new regime, the regulators of overseas companies in the UK will still have to rely on the case law and provisions of the old law for guidance and clarification. This is especially so because the new law has not affected, nor was it intended to affect, all aspects of the regulation of overseas companies.

Other aspects of the regulation of overseas companies which have been affected by the new law which will be looked at later are service of process and delivery of accounts, but a look at the effects of non-compliance with registration formalities is instructive at this point.

[38] P.L. Davies, *Gower's Principles of Company Law* (6th edn., London, Sweet & Maxwell, 1997), 129.
[39] *Ibid.*, 130.

Non-compliance with Registration Requirements

Non-compliance with registration requirements by an overseas company is penalised by a fine on the company, and every officer or agent of the company who *knowingly* and *wilfully* authorises or permits the default and, in the case of a continuing offence, by a daily default fine for continued contravention.[40] Non-compliance does not render a contract made by an overseas company unenforceable or invalid. The provision is seen as satisfactory to overseas companies, in that a breach is established only where there is evidence of intention to default as opposed to negligence or forgetfulness on the part of the oversea company.

The real test for the effects of non-compliance came before the English courts in *Curragh Investment Ltd* v. *Cook*.[41] The issue was whether a contract for the sale of land between an overseas company and the defendant could be struck aside for illegality because the foreign company had failed to register as an overseas company.[42] The court dismissed the purchaser's argument that failure to comply with the statute tainted the whole transaction with illegality or perhaps unenforceability, Megarry J said:

> "with respect, that argument seems to me to be completely fallacious. I accept of course, that where a contract is made in contravention of some statutory provision, then in addition to any criminal sanctions, the courts may in some cases find that the contract itself is stricken with illegality. But for this to occur there must be a sufficient nexus between the statutory requirement and the contract."

In this case the statutory prohibition or requirement is not sufficiently linked to the contract for questions to arise of the illegality of any contract made in breach of the statutory requirement. In concluding, Megarry J said:

> "even if the vendor is in breach of sections 407 and 416, I can not see any justification for the purchaser's failure to comply with the vendor's notice to complete."[43]

Had this decision been in favour of the purchaser's claim, it would have been not only contrary to the relevant provision but it could also have been very bad for business and regulation in general. It would have made it possible for foreign companies to wriggle out of transactions on the ground that they have not satisfied a statutory obligation. The decision does instil confidence in domestic contractors and businesses to deal with oversea companies. It also makes it impossible for foreign companies to use their own breach of the law to repudiate contracts.

---

[40] CA 1985, s. 697(1).
[41] [1974] 1 WLR 1559.
[42] CA 1948, s. 407 (see now CA 1985, s. 691).
[43] [1974] 1 WLR 1559 at 1564.

SERVICE OF DOCUMENTS

There are now two sections[44] on the service of documents on overseas companies following the implementation of the Eleventh EC Company Law Directive. These sections are pivotal to the regulation of oversea companies as they ensure the means by which overseas companies can be sued in the UK.

For the purpose of service, overseas companies must deliver to the Registrar of Companies the name and address of a person resident in the UK, who is authorised to accept on behalf of the company service of process or notices. However, if at any time all such persons cannot be served because they are dead, or have ceased to reside in the UK, or refuse to accept service, a document may be served on the company by leaving it at, or sending it by post to, any place of business established by the company in the UK.[45]

The provision on service is wide because of its great importance. The UK does not stand alone in giving this aspect of the regulation of foreign companies this degree of importance; in fact in perusing the practice of one or two jurisdictions on the regulation of foreign companies, one quickly notices that a similar provision is given prominence in Hong Kong and Australia.[46] The provision stands out as one of the ways to protect domestic contractors and assuring them that there is a means of redress from the activities of overseas companies.

Disputes over service have arisen in different forms, some of which will be considered along with the ways in which the courts have dealt with them. In *Employers Liability Assurance Corp.* v. *Sedgwick, Collins & Co*,[47] the overseas company argued that service was not good because the person whose details were delivered to the Registrar had ceased to have the authority to accept service on behalf of the overseas company. The court held that, as the Registrar had not been told of this fact, service was good although his authority to accept service had ceased. It is worth noting, however, that this decision seems unfair because the person whose name was filed with the registrar as having authority to accept service of process on behalf of the company took steps to secure the removal of his name from the register and only failed because the Act contained no provision for removal of names. It seems to me that this decision was based on good business sense and certainty. That case was decided in 1927, and it is comforting to say that since then the law has been improved, for there is now a provision which enables an overseas company to remove and replace the name

---

[44] CA 1985, ss. 649A(2) and 695.

[45] *Ibid.*, s.695(2).

[46] In Hong Kong, under the Companies Ordinance 1984, s.332, overseas companies are required on registration to deliver to the registrar of companies, *inter alia*, "the name and address of at least one person resident in Hong Kong authorised to accept service served on the company". In Australia, s. 530 of the CA 1981 provides that "a memorandum of appointment or power of attorney . . . of the foreign company . . . stating the name and address, . . . of one or more persons resident in the territory . . . authorised to accept on its behalf service of process and any notices required to be served on the company".

[47] [1927] AC 95.

of a person previously submitted as one authorised to accept service on the company's behalf.[48] Where a person's name is removed, and the registrar is notified of the change, in the absence of a replacement, the writ will be served on the company instead, by leaving it at, or sending it by post to, any place of business established by the company in the UK.

Another source of dispute relating to service was dealt with in *Rome and Another* v. *Punjab National Bank*.[49] Here the foreign company argued that service on persons whose details had been delivered to the registrar was invalid because the company had ceased to carry on business in the UK. Sir John May held that, on a true construction of section 695(1) of the Companies Act 1985, a writ was sufficiently served on an oversea company if addressed to a person whose name and address had been delivered to the registrar of companies, notwithstanding that the company had ceased to carry on business in the UK. This was the case, the judge added, even if the persons so named were no longer resident here, and those facts had been notified to the registrar under section 696(4).

A somewhat illogical decision, one might say, but one which is in line with the object and purpose of the rule on service of writs on oversea companies as Lord Sumner stated way back in 1927[50] that the purpose and object of the rule was:

> "to protect the company's British creditors by obtaining for them *ab initio* the means of serving process in this country, free from the inconvenience of seeking out the foreign company in its country of incorporation."

A similar view was reiterated in the same case by Lord Parmoor.[51] This decision could again be seen as an indication of the courts' willingness to protect domestic litigants against foreign companies. Here again one sees an example of the court interpreting a statutory provision in a somewhat dubious manner, if only for the sake of certainty and to give it business sense.

This observation on the interpretation of the law is justified because of the views of Parker LJ, expressing the need to improve the law in this area. His words are instructive:

> "The issue on the construction of section 695(1) of the Companies Act 1985, will result, whichever way it is decided, in what may appear to be an absurdity. If the defendant is right, it will be open to an overseas company to carry on business here for a period and run up huge debts and then close down its business and remove itself, leaving its creditors to follow it home to seek leave to serve it out of the jurisdiction. This appears to be wholly contrary to the plain wording and clear intention of the provision. If, however, the plaintiffs are right, an overseas company will be exposed to

---

[48]   CA 1985, s. 695(2).
[49]   [1989] BCLC 328.
[50]   [1927] AC 95, at 108.
[51]   The main object of s. 274 is to take away any difficulty in the service of a writ on foreign corporations carrying on business in this country, and in effect to place a foreign corporation for this purpose on the same footing as an English company, and liable to the service of a writ under a similar form of procedure.

service under the provision notwithstanding (a) it may have ceased to carry on business and removed itself previously, and (b) that the cause of action arises out of matters which occurred after it had so ceased and removed itself. This does not appear to be likely to have been the legislative intention but it is not contrary to the plain wording."[52]

The view of Parker LJ is important, not least because it supported the court's decision, which was in favour of the plaintiff's contention, but it underscored the view that the law was unsatisfactory and needed an amendment. Such amendment will restrict resort to section 695(1) to proceedings arising out of matters which had their origin in the period before an overseas company ceased to carry on business in the UK.

The unsatisfactory nature of this part of the law could be tidied up if the approach implemented by Hong Kong[53] were adopted. In Hong Kong,[54] an overseas company has a continuing duty, like all domestic companies, to ensure that there is always an authorised representative available *until three years after it ceases to have a place of business* in Hong Kong. The obligation to have a representative is intended to facilitate the taking of legal action against the overseas company, even after the company has ceased to have a place of business in Hong Kong. If this provision is introduced in the UK, the problem that arose in *Rome and Another* v. *Punjab National Bank* would be resolved by statute. Furthermore, an adoption of the Australian style would solve this problem of interpretation. In Australia the problem does not arise because the court has the power to authorise a document to be served on a registered foreign company in a manner not provided for by the Companies Act.[55]

At the moment, the courts in this country tend to adopt a discretionary approach in interpreting section 695(2) of the Companies Act 1985. To guarantee certainty, the law in this area must be amended. That will quite obviously dispense with the pragmatic interpretation by the courts in favour of a statutory-based solution.

In *Boocock* v. *Hilton International Company*,[56] the dispute about service took on a different form. The issue here was that service must be ruled ineffective if addressed to the overseas company's place of business instead of to the person whose name has been delivered to the registrar of companies. The Court of Appeal reiterated the view that for service on an overseas company to be effective, it must be addressed to any person whose name has been delivered to the registrar under section 695(1) of the Companies Act 1985, and left at or sent by post to the address which has been so delivered. The defendants sought to rely on the exception to this rule in section 695(2), but in *Boocock*, it was stressed that this exception could only apply where the person whose name had

---

52 [1989] 1 WLR 1211 at 1220–1.
53 Companies Ordinance 1984, Cap. 32, s.332.
54 *Ibid.*, s.333.
55 Australian Companies Act 1981, s.530(5).
56 [1993] BCLC 1363.

been delivered was dead, had ceased to reside in the UK or refused to accept service or for any reason could not be served. Clearly therefore the service was defective when it was not addressed to the person whose name had been filed with the registrar, but instead sent to the overseas company's address.

This decision seems to me to go against the principle of sensible and simple interpretation of the Act; in fact it borders on pedanticism. It was clear that the person whose name had been delivered to the registrar would have seen the writ on the same day or shortly after it was sent to the address of the overseas company. This decision is strict considering what has been said about the whole purpose of the rules governing service, namely, to ensure that legal proceedings can be brought with the least hardship by domestic plaintiffs. Surely it would have been practical and pragmatic if the judge had overlooked the technical error of the plaintiffs in so far as the defendant still saw the writ, albeit not addressed to him personally. It is interesting to note that the court has held that service to an overseas company is not defective simply because it is addressed both to the company and to the person whose name is so delivered to the registrar of companies.[57] These decisions go further to highlight the unsatisfactory state of some of the rules on the regulation of overseas companies, and as a result it is apparent that amendments need to be made to make the provisions more user-friendly to judges, overseas companies and domestic contractors and businesses.

Most recently the issue of service has again surfaced, but this time it is a more intricate problem, as well as relating to the new law on "branch" registration. In *Saab & Anor* v. *Saudi American Bank*.[58] The overseas company argued that service was improper because the proceedings in question were not in respect of the carrying on of business of the branch in the UK. Tuckey J resolved the dispute by holding that for service of process on a branch to be good service the proceedings need not be exclusively in respect of the carrying on of business by the branch. In fact in this case there was some evidence that the contract which was the source of the proceedings was negotiated partly abroad and and partly at the branch in London. The defendants in this case argued that unless the proceedings related only to the carrying on of business by the branch, the service would be invalid. We now know that this stance is incorrect, and from the facts of the case, the proceedings were related, albeit to a small degree, to the carrying on of business of the branch. What the case did not address was whether service can be good where the proceedings were completely *unrelated* to the carrying on of business by the branch. It seems to me that in that case service on a branch would be improper. One must however add that the decision would depend on the facts of the case, and it may well be that such a case would never be brought to the court based on the principle of *forum non conveniens*.[59]

---

[57] *Foster Fothergill & Harting* v. *Russian Transport and Insurance Co* [1927] WN 27 (CA).

[58] [1998] 1 WLR 937.

[59] For a detail discussion of this case, see a forthcoming article on this case by the author in the *Company Lawyer*.

DELIVERY OF ACCOUNTS

This is an area with the potential to cause serious problems to the regulator and domestic investors and contractors. It is one aspect of regulation which requires as much disclosure as possible, for misrepresentation of accounts could provide a glossy picture of an overseas company so as to attract investors or contractors when in actual fact the company may be in debt.

The Eleventh Directive has had an impact on this area as well. However, these new regulations are in respect of overseas companies registering under the new law. Prior to the implementation of the Directive the law on delivery of reports and accounts was largely the prerogative of the Secretary of State, although there were provisions under Part 23 of the Companies Act 1985. It should also be said that the EC has a special Directive on the filing of accounts by foreign corporations, and this has been adopted by the UK.[60]However, this is not relevant to overseas companies and so will not be dealt with here.

The Companies Act 1985 gives greater prominence to the issue of accounts than the previous Companies Acts,[61] as the Act covers it in one separate chapter, spreading through three sections.[62] Overseas companies enjoy some privileges in respect of accounting rules. The Secretary of State may make an order which modifies or exempts an overseas company from the requirements on delivery of accounts.[63] The Secretary of State may make concessions to an overseas company in relation to its accounting reference and delivery periods. The object of this flexibility which the Secretary of State may exercise is probably to encourage foreign companies, which may have less rigorous accounting standards in their country of incorporation, to do business in the United Kingdom.

The new law[64] deals with matters of company accounts in two parts. The first relates to companies required to make disclosure under their parent law. The second part is to do with companies which are not required under their parent law to make disclosure. With regard to the former, these are required to comply with the accounting practice operating in their countries of incorporation, namely, to prepare, audit and disclose accounts. For the latter, recourse will be had to the solution provided in Part XXIII of the Companies Act 1985.[65] It is apparent therefore that Part XXIII remains the relevant law on the disclosure of accounts for overseas companies with no accounting practice in their country of incorporation. It is my guess that these sorts of overseas companies would be

---

[60] Company Accounting and Disclosure, (1978) Cmnd 7654.

[61] This topic was covered only in one section in the previous Acts: Companies (Consolidation) Act 1908, s.274(3); CA 1929, s.347; CA 1948, s.410(1)(2).

[62] CA 1985, ss.700–703.

[63] CA 1985, s.700(4). Note that no such order has been made yet, but by virtue of the Companies Consolidation (Consequential Provisions) Act 1985 s.31(2), the Oversea Companies (Accounts) Modification and Exemptions Order 1982, SI 1982/676, has effect as if made under the CA 1985, s.700(4).

[64] CA 1985, s. 699AA, Sched. 21D.

[65] CA 1985, s.700(4).

those from non-EC countries. This poses no problems because the old law is quite effective in this regard. Here once again one observes that the old law operates alongside the new law.

There are always going to be cases of non-compliance, especially because, as was noted at the beginning of this section, this is an area in which companies may not always be willing to provide the public with the true picture if that picture is not a very good one. The legislator has made provision for non-compliance. If an overseas company fails to comply with the accounting requirements, the company and each director commits an offence and is liable to a fine, and, if the default continues, to a daily fine.

Under this section it is not a defence to prove that the document in question was not prepared as required by the provisions relating to the preparation and delivery of accounts by overseas companies.[66] However, it has been suggested that it is a defence to show that an accused person took all reasonable steps to procure that the requirements would be complied with and that non-compliance was caused by some independent or extraneous cause.[67] It must be said that in the main the provisions on delivery of accounts are less onerous on overseas companies than on domestic companies; small wonder that non-compliance may be excused if the person responsible failed to prepare and deliver due to no fault of his. It seems to me that despite the importance of this subject, a softly softly approach has been adopted by the regulator.

INVESTIGATION

Provisions dealing with the investigation of oversea companies were first introduced in the Companies Act 1967,[68] as a result of the recommendation made by the Jenkins Report of the Company Law Committee of 1962.[69] In introducing the power to investigate overseas companies, the legislature simply extended the provisions for investigation of domestic companies to oversea companies.[70]

There have been some developments on the rules on the investigation of oversea companies, these have culminated in section 70 of the Companies Act 1989, which reiterates section 431 of Part XIV of the Companies Act 1985.[71] These rules are applicable with the possibility of exceptions, adaptations and modifications, and this is not surprising. Similar to other rules on overseas companies these exceptions are necessary for practical reasons. First, it is essential

---

[66] CA 1985, s.703(2).

[67] Colin Mercer, "Oversea Companies: Preparation and Delivery of Accounts in the UK" (1991) 12 *Business Law Review* 304.

[68] CA 1967, ss.42, 109.

[69] Cmnd. 1749 (1962), para. 213.

[70] *R. v. Secretary of State for Trade and Others, ex p. Perestrello & Anor.* [1981] QB 19.

[71] The provisions of Part XIV dealing with investigation of companies incorporated in Great Britain apply also to bodies corporate incorporated outside Great Britain, or have at any time carried on business in Great Britain, but subject to certain exceptions, adaptations and modifications.

to make the jurisdiction user-friendly to foreign companies, therefore onerous regulations are not worthwhile. Furthermore, practical problems may affect the investigation of an overseas company in the UK such as the acquisition of relevant information from abroad. However, the surge for increased co-operation between jurisdictions has brought with it an understanding among UK judges that English courts can make requests to foreign courts for assistance in ordering the production of specific documents in the possession of companies registered in those foreign jurisdictions. Sir Donald Nicholls V-C has opined that this jurisdiction does not derive from statute nor from the Rules of the Supreme Court but from the inherent powers of the High Court.[72] This is one way of getting around the difficulties which may ensue in attempting to institute formal investigations on an overseas company. This inherent jurisdiction is, I believe, explained better as deriving from comity and inter-state co-operation rather than some dubious notion of so called inherent powers of the High Court. The willingness of foreign courts to co-operate is surely based on comity among jurisdictions!

Despite the possibility of co-operation from abroad, investigating an oversea company on the strength of statutory provisions could be quite difficult; only increased international co-operation can guarantee effective investigation here. Investigation here is bound to be expensive. This is why exceptions, adaptations and modifications are necessary.

Only one case of investigation of the affairs of an overseas company by inspectors appointed by the Secretary of State has been reported so far. This is a good sign, although one must add that this is probably because an overseas company can only be investigated if, on the strength of the findings of the inspectors appointed by the Secretary of State, it is clear that the company's affairs are being conducted in a way that calls for an investigation.[73] There can be no investigation of an overseas company upon the strength of an application from the company or its members.

These difficulties make the need for co-operation between regulators essential. In this respect, it should be said that there is a surge for more co-operation and collaboration between international regulators in many other fields of corporate activity, including banking, insider dealing, mergers and acquisitions, to name but a few. This is encouraged because if companies engage in corporate malpractice, the ill-effects usually have international ramifications.

In the context of co-operation, there is some evidence of this to note in the law relating to insolvency of overseas companies,[74] and this example should be emulated in other areas of the law regulating overseas companies.

The next and last section is on insolvency proceedings. The section is divided into three headings for purposes of clarity and because the rules relevant to each

---

[72] *Panayiotou v. Sony Music Entertainment UK* [1993] 2 WLR 241.

[73] CA 1985, s.432(2)(a)–(d). See also *R. v. Secretary of State For Trade, ex p. Perestrello*, n. 70 above.

[74] Insolvency Act 1986, s.426(4), (5).

differ as well. Thus administration orders, administrative receiverships and winding up orders are dealt with in that order. The question is, do these apply to overseas companies?

INSOLVENCY PROCEEDINGS

Insolvency proceedings are applied to a company whose indebtedness threatens its continued existence, so as to salvage it (or bits of its business) or to guide it towards a less wasteful end of its corporate life so that creditors can equitably realise some, if not all, of their debts.

Administration Orders

The court has the power to make an order if it is satisfied that a *company* is unlikely to be able to pay its debts and that the order will achieve one or more of the purposes outlined in section 8(3).[75] The purpose of an administration order is primarily to facilitate the rescue and rehabilitation of an insolvent, but potentially viable, business.[76] However, the general rule is that a company incorporated in a foreign country cannot be put into administration in the UK under Part II of the Insolvency Act 1986.[77] This, it is argued, is because Part II of the Act deals with the administration of a "company" and company here does not include a foreign company.[78] A company is defined[79] as one formed and registered under the 1985 Act or former Acts. It therefore excludes a company incorporated abroad.

This interpretation of the law has come under enormous criticism in recent years, decided cases and the criticisms suggest that that interpretation of the law unsatisfactory. In *Re Dallhold Estates Property Ltd*[80] it was held that an English court can make an administration order in relation to a *foreign company* for the purpose of achieving a more advantageous realisation of the company's assets than would be effected on a winding up. This is the case where the English court

---

[75] *Ibid.*, Part II, s.8(3), which states:
    (a) the survival of the company, and the whole or any part of its undertaking, as a going concern;
    (b) the approval of a voluntary arrangement under Part I;
    (c) the sanctioning under s.425 of the Companies Act of a compromise or arrangement between the company and any such persons as are mentioned in that section; and
    (d) a more advantageous realisation of the company's assets than would be effected on a winding up.
[76] Practice Note [1994] 1 All ER 324, *per* Sir Donald Nicholls V-C.
[77] Hubert Picarda, *The Law Relating to Receivers, Managers and Administrators* (Butterworth Law, 1990) 501.
[78] See *Felixstowe Dock & Railway Co v. US Lines Inc.* [1989] QB 360.
[79] See s.251 of the Insolvency Act 1986 and s.735(1) of the CA 1985.
[80] [1992] BCC 394.

is called upon to assist the foreign courts with the corresponding jurisdiction. It is also important to add that where that assistance is requested, UK substantive law can be applicable to an overseas company[81].

The criticism of the rule that a foreign company cannot be the subject of an administration order is based on the fact that, since one of the purposes of making an administration order is for the company to achieve greater benefit from its assets, one fails to see why an English court should be barred from making orders to overseas companies simply because of a frivolous technicality based on the interpretation of the relevant statute, which seeks to restrict the application of the power of the court to a "company" as interpreted by the statute.[82]

It is also noteworthy that the Insolvency Act 1986 expressly empowers the court to wind up foreign companies.[83] It appears to me that there is no justification behind permitting a winding up and disallowing an administration order which will obtain a better realisation of the company's assets than would be effected on a winding up, simply because the definition given to "company" does not include an overseas company. This hard rule which is seen as irrational has ceased to be upheld in several cases that have come before the courts. The practice of the English courts suggests that judges are quite prepared to ignore the strict letter of the law in favour of closer co-operation with foreign courts.[84]

The difficulties pertaining to administration orders do not exist when dealing with schemes envisaged by section 8(3)(c) of the Insolvency Act 1986.[85] This is because section 425(6) defines "company" as *any company liable to be wound up under this Act*. This does of course include unregistered companies, and the Companies Act 1985 provides that an overseas company could be wound up in this country as an unregistered company.[86]

It seems to me that, given that the underlying purpose of the various insolvency procedures is more or less to salvage the company and more especially to benefit the creditors, it makes no sense for the legislature to deprive creditors of a better deal than would be achieved in a winding up, simply because they happen to be creditors of a company incorporated abroad which is doing business in the UK. The protection afforded by the insolvency procedures should apply to all companies carrying on business in the UK so long as that is practicable, because in so doing not only is the company advantaged but the investors are protected as well. It could, however, be argued that because an administration order may result in the company being placed under the control of an adminis-

[81] *Re Bank of Credit and Commerce International SA & Anor.* [1993] BCC 787.

[82] I.e. the meaning of "company" in the CA 1985.

[83] Part V (ss. 220–229), of course subject to certain conditions. See the section on winding up of overseas companies, below.

[84] In one recent decision, *Re R M C A Reinsurance Ltd* [1994] BCC 378, Morritt J held that a foreign company can benefit from an arrangement scheme pursuant to s.425 of the Companies Act 1985, which included the organisation of meetings abroad.

[85] This para. empowers the court to make an administration order if it is likely that an arrangement or compromise between the company and others under s. 425 of the CA 1985 could be achieved.

[86] Insolvency Act 1986, s.225. This topic will be treated in more detail later in this essay.

trator, to the exclusion of the directors of the foreign company, this may be difficult where the company is not managed here. That argument is weakened by the fact that not only is co-operation between the authorities of the foreign company's place of incorporation and the courts in this country very feasible and fast becoming a common occurrence, but an overseas company would generally be managed at a local level here.

Furthermore, the various references to "company" in section 8 of the Insolvency Act 1986 do not conclusively restrict "company" to mean those incorporated in the UK only. To the contrary, references to "company" in that section require that the word be construed in relation to other provisions of the Insolvency Act in which "company" has an extended meaning. There clearly are problems with making administrative orders on oversea companies, what about appointing administrative revivers?

Administrative Receivers

Administrative receivers are appointed for the benefit of creditors, to carry on the company's business and manage its undertaking when it becomes apparent that the company is unlikely to repay its loan. It seems to me therefore that since overseas companies are able to raise loans in the UK against charges over their assets here, it should be a matter of course that the appointment of administrative receivers should extend to them as well.[87]

Furthermore, there should be no discrimination between types of company because, as Mummery J pointed out, the protection of the company, its creditors, the contributories and the public is just as appropriate in the case of an unregistered company as it is for a registered one.[88] In practice there is no dispute about the appointment of administrative receivers on overseas companies, but on a strict interpretation of the relevant statutes, the word "company" does exclude overseas companies since they are not registered under the Companies Act 1985.

The way round this hurdle, if there is need for one, is to view the appointment of an administrative receiver in the context of the whole range of remedies available in situations where a company is, or is likely to become, unable to pay its debts. Bearing in mind the fact that these remedies are intended to provide greater flexibility and increased protection to those affected by actual or potential insolvency situations, it will be an anomaly to deny creditors the benefit of the remedy of appointing an administrative receiver simply because the company involved is an overseas company. The foreign element should be of no particular relevance, argued Mummery J, where the company in question has granted a debenture secured by a floating charge in the English form.[89]

---

[87] *In re International Bulk Commodities Ltd* [1992] 3 WLR 238 at 241.
[88] *Ibid.*, 241.
[89] *Ibid.*, 242.

A pragmatic approach should be adopted in dealing with these issues, and the *mischief rule* should be used in interpreting the statutory provisions. Furthermore, since the court has power to make an administration order in relation to an unregistered company under section 426,[90] that strengthens the case for arguing that the provisions relating to administrative receivers should also apply to unregistered companies. If overseas companies are classified as unregistered companies for the purposes of a winding up order, they should also be considered as such for the purposes of the making of an administration order and the appointment of administrative receivers. The general rationale behind insolvency proceedings is to protect creditors. There is good reason to extend all the stages of insolvency proceedings to any company which does business in the UK so long as the company has assets in this country and there are creditors here who are likely to benefit from the granting of the particular application.

However, the controversies that exist in relation to the making of administration orders and the appointment of administrative receivers are absent in the case of the winding up of overseas companies. The law pertaining to the winding up of overseas companies is very settled and has some of its roots in case law dating back to the nineteenth century.[91]

Winding Up

Where a company incorporated outside Great Britain which has been carrying on business in Great Britain ceases so to do, it may be wound up as an unregistered company under the Companies Act 1985.[92] This will be so even though the company has been dissolved, or otherwise ceased to exist, as a company under or by virtue of the laws of the country under which it was incorporated.[93]

As a general rule, a foreign company may be wound up as an unregistered company if it has assets in England, even though it never in fact had a place of business nor carried on business in England except through agents.[94] Furthermore, a foreign company will be wound up if it has sufficient connection with England and there is a reasonable chance that some benefit will accrue to the company's creditors from the winding up. If this analogy is taken to its logical conclusion, there should be no difficulty in winding up an oversea company, more so because such a company will of necessity have an established place of business or a branch in Great Britain and will most likely have creditors with a reasonable chance of benefiting from the winding up order.

In *International Westminster Bank* v. *Okeanos Maritime Corp.*,[95] where a

---

[90] *Re Dallhold Estates (UK) Pty Ltd* [1992] BCC 394.
[91] *Re English, Scottish and Australian Chartered Bank* [1893] 3 Ch. 385.
[92] For the definition of unregistered company see CA 1985, s.665; Insolvency Act 1986 Part V (ss.220–229). For the winding up of unregistered companies, see Insolvency Act 1986, s.221.
[93] Insolvency Act 1986, s. 225.
[94] *Banque des Marchands de Moscou (Koupetscesky)* v. *Kindersley* [1950] 2 All ER 549.
[95] [1987] 3 All ER 137.

winding up order was made, the company was carrying on business within the jurisdiction and there was a reasonable possibility that a winding up would benefit creditors, since it was possible for the liquidator to recover contributions to the assets of the company under the Insolvency Act 1986.[96] Relying for his judgment on the conditions set out by Megarry J,[97] Gibson J stated that English courts have no jurisdiction to make an order on a foreign company if there is no likelihood that some advantage would be achieved by the petitioning creditor. This will be the case where there are no assets within the jurisdiction.[98] But in the *Eloc Electro* case,[99] though there were no assets in the jurisdiction, it was held that there was a reasonable possibility that the petitioners would benefit if, and only if, the winding up order was made by the payment from the redundancy fund in accordance with the provisions of section 122 of the Employment Protection (Consolidation) Act 1978. It was further explained that, in order to satisfy the requirement that assets are in the jurisdiction, the assets could be of any nature and the consequential benefit accruing to a creditor need not be channelled through the hands of the liquidator. Therefore the ownership of the assets by the company is not a matter of crucial importance.

Recently in *Re Real Estate Development Co*[100] the court reiterated that for the English courts to have jurisdiction to wind up a foreign company, *three* requirements had to be satisfied:

(a)   there had to be sufficient connection with the UK;
(b)   there must be a reasonable possibility that the winding up will benefit those applying for it; and
(c)   the court must be able to exercise jurisdiction over one or more persons interested in the distribution of the assets.

English courts will almost invariably have the jurisdiction to wind up an oversea company, since most, if not all, of the three requirements will be satisfied. One fact to note is that the court's jurisdiction to make a winding up order is unaffected by the fact that a liquidation has already commenced in the country of incorporation. In these cases the winding up in England will usually be conducted as ancillary to the liquidation in the country of incorporation but in accordance with both English substantive and procedural law.[101]

While assisting the foreign court, the UK courts should use the forensic rules that govern the conduct of their own liquidation.[102] Failure to do this will result in the utmost possible confusion. Again one gets a sense of the court's desire to

---

[96]   S. 213: Fraudulent Trading.
[97]   *Re Compania Merabello San Nicholas SA* [1973] Ch.75, at 91–2.
[98]   In re *Eloc Electro-Optieck and Communicatie BV* [1982] Ch. 43.
[99]   *Ibid.*, 48.
[100]   [1991] BCLC 210.
[101]   *Per* Vaughan Williams J in *Re English, Scottish and Australian Chartered Bank* [1893] 3 Ch. 385.
[102]   Wynn Parry J in *Suidair International Airways Ltd* [1951] 1 Ch. 165.

regulate oversea companies with as much pragmatism as possible, especially where there are no specific rules set aside for the relevant problem.

CONCLUSION

Changes to the rules regulating overseas companies indicate some continuous interest in the activities of foreign commercial entities in the UK.[103] For the past 80-odd years, existing rules have been elaborated, new rules have been promulgated, but certain rules still have to be developed.[104] All these changes suggest some conscious effort by the legislature to facilitate the carrying on of business in this country by foreign companies. The Foreign Companies (Execution of Documents) Regulations 1994 is conclusive evidence that the recognition of foreign companies in the UK is here to stay. These Regulations have introduced two changes of particular importance. First, the Regulations stipulate that any documents of a foreign company which are signed and sealed abroad in accordance with the laws of the territory in which the company was incorporated and by the respective authority of that company will be treated as validly executed in the UK.[105] Secondly, these regulations have solved the problem of pre-incorporation contracts entered into on behalf of foreign companies. Prior to the making of these Regulations, a foreign company could not be held liable for a contract which was made before its incorporation by someone who claimed to have authority to bind the company.[106] Henceforth, any pre-incorporation contracts made by a foreign company will be enforceable so long as the person who signed the contract on behalf of the foreign company had the due authority so to sign.[107] Comity and business sense seem to me to be behind these welcome changes.

By this process of change, the English legal system enhances its credibility amongst foreign investors and thereby wins the confidence of these companies to operate in this jurisdiction. However, on a more general note it could be suggested that this is a manifestation of comity by the UK towards other countries. But, more realistically, it must not be forgotten that the United Kingdom stands to benefit financially from the business transactions being carried on within its borders by overseas companies.

The rules on overseas companies indicate that an account is taken of the increasingly international nature of business. The interpretation given to some of the provisions like those governing insolvency shows that in some of these matters the courts do take a practical approach to avoid unsatisfactory results.

---

[103] See for the latest, SI (1994) No 950: The Foreign Companies (Execution of Documents) Regulations 1994.
[104] The provisions on charges introduced in the CA 1989 have still not come into force.
[105] *Ibid.*, ss.4 and 5.
[106] *Rover International Ltd & Ors.* v. *Cannon Films Sales Ltd* [1987] 3 BCC 369.
[107] SI (1994) No 950, ss.5 and 6.

The problems of interpretation and sometimes inadequacy of the law on overseas companies, begs the question whether it is necessary to have a separate set of rules for overseas companies. That question is particularly pertinent if the purpose of the rules is to place, as much as is possible, overseas companies on an even playing field with companies incorporated in the UK. Would it be more convenient to the regulator if all companies doing business in the UK were subject to the same rules? The reality is that such a state of affairs would reduce the number of foreign companies that will be prepared to carry on business as overseas companies. There are far too many regulations on domestic companies which foreign companies would rather not have to deal with. That is precisely why they have opted for overseas company status.

The rules on overseas companies are far from satisfactory; the influence of EU law has not always helped. A thorough rethink of a comprehensive method to regulate overseas companies is beckoning. It may become necessary for the legislature to enact a short user-friendly statute for all foreign corporate bodies which will contain all aspects of the relevant law (and a provision for the inclusion of EU legislation) which will facilitate the operation, but also the regulation, of these foreign corporate bodies.

The implementation of EU rules in an *ad hoc* manner makes regulation more difficult, as evidenced by the provisions of the new registration system for oversea companies. There is, however, clear evidence of the efforts of the courts to balance the need for regulation against the desire to facilitate business enterprise by overseas companies.

13

Companies and Regulations: Theories, Justifications and Policing

JANET DINE

The Company Law Committee of the Law Society in its response to the government's paper, *Modern Company Law for a Competitive Economy*[1] quotes from *Hutton* v. *West Cork Railway Co*[2]:

> "the law does not say there are to be no cakes and ale, but there are to be no cakes and ale except such as are required for the benefit of the company",

using this to illustrate the accepted doctrine that interests of interest groups other than shareholders may be taken into account where it is for the benefit of companies to do so. What is for "the benefit of a company" is rooted in society's conception of what a company is, and how and by whom its operations may be controlled. It is therefore necessary to consider companies in the light of their historical and sociological context in order to invest the mantra "the interests of the company" with some useful content. Formulating a regulatory structure without such an enquiry invites incoherence Thus Bottomley[3]:

> "The broad and basic purpose of examining corporate theory is to develop a framework within which we can assess the values and assumptions that either unite or divide the plethora of cases, reform proposals, legislative amendments, and practices that constitute modern corporation law. This law has not sprung up overnight. We need some way of disentangling the different philosophical and political perspectives from which it has been constructed."

WHAT IS "THE BENEFIT OF THE COMPANY"?

Different theories concerning the origin and purpose of corporations influence the model of company adopted, and thus shape the relationship which companies have with all the participants in their economic activity and with their regulators. What is for the "benefit of the company" can only be discerned by

---

[1] Memorandum no 360, June 1998.
[2] (1883) 23 Ch.D 654.
[3] "Taking Corporations Seriously: Some Considerations For Corporate Regulation" (1990) 19 *Federal Law Review* 203 at 204.

understanding the role which society expects a company to play. If, for example, the company is solely a wealth-maximising mechanism for its investors, the only matters which will benefit the company are those which increase its profits. If the company is an instrument of social policy the benefit of the community will be co-extensive with the benefit of the company.

Although theories overlap and interweave it is suggested that a convenient structure can be imposed by taking as a starting point three theories that have been influential in shaping models of companies. These are the contractual, the communautaire and the concessionary theories. The contractual and communautaire theories represent two extremes, since they reflect notions of the company as a product of *laissez faire* individualism and as an instrument of the state respectively.

LEGAL CONTRACTUALISM

According to this contractual theory[4] two or more parties come together[5] to make a pact to carry on commercial activity, and it is from this pact that the company is born.[6] Bottomley labels this as the "aggregate" theory,[7] explaining various versions thus:

> "contract supplies the explanatory framework for both the judicial and the political status of the corporation. Internally the corporation is regarded as an association or aggregation of individuals; it comprises contractual relations between members *inter se*, and between members and management."[8]

The logical outcome of the theoretical contractual base is to limit the social responsibility of the company, and to create an entity remote from regulatory interference because any denial of the right to use the free enterprise tool which is available tends to interfere with this concept of the company.[9] The theory is reflected in UK rules like the rule in *Foss* v. *Harbottle*[10] which accepts that in most cases the majority decision of the contractors, taken according to the constitutional (contractual) rights of the shareholders, represents the will of the

---

[4] Different from the economic nexus of contracts theory: see J. Parkinson, *Corporate Power and Responsibility* (Clarendon, Oxford, 1995), 75–6; see discussion of economic theories below.

[5] It is unclear exactly how this theory adapts to one-person companies.

[6] N. 3 above.

[7] *Ibid.*, 208. He attributes the label to J. C. Coates, "State Takeover Statutes and Corporate Theory: The Revival of an Old Debate" (1989) 64 *New York U L Rev.* 806.

[8] See D. Sullivan and D. Conlon, "Crisis and Transition in Corporate Governance Paradigms: The Role of the Chancery Court of Delaware" [1997] *Law and Society Review* 713.

[9] D. Sugarman and G. Rubin (eds.), *Law, Economy and Society, 1750– 1914* (Professional Books, Abingdon, 1984) note "The ideology of freedom of contract was an important element in the liberalisation of English company law in the 19th century . . . However, as in other areas of private law, the power of freedom of contract, the rise of legal formalism and perhaps, on occasions, a sympathy for these agencies of economic growth, encouraged the courts frequently to adopt the mantle of legal abstentionism rather than the watchdog (12–13).

[10] (1843) 2 Hare 461.

corporation. This approach has roots in realist[11] theory "according to which groups have natural moral and legal personality".[12] The theory sees companies as made up of natural persons, the majority of members representing the will of the corporation. The corporation is thus entitled to autonomy from the state as being "the natural expression of desires of the corporators".[13] Consequently, corporations obtained their political, and thus legal, status independently of the state.[14]

Legal contractualism differs substantially from economic contractualism although each is arguing from a similar foundation, in that the essence of the company is seen as residing in the contractual relationships between the actors.

ECONOMIC CONTRACTUALISM

The economic analysis starts from the perspective that "the company has traditionally been thought of more as a voluntary association between shareholders than as a creation of the state". Cheffins[15] argues that "companies legislation has had in and of itself only a modest impact on the bargaining dynamics which account for the nature and form of business enterprises. Thus, analytically an incorporated company is, like other types of firms, fundamentally, a nexus of contracts". For the purposes of economic analysis individuals, rather than the state, are the legitimation for the operation of the commercial venture. Denial of personality to the group of actors[16] is a necessary foundation[17] for the application of market theories, since the underlying assumption is the creation of maximum efficiency by individual market players bargaining with full information[18]. Taking the view that free markets are the most effective wealth-creation

[11] See in particular P. Ewick, " 'In the Belly of the Beast': Rethinking Rights, Persons and Organisations" (1988) 13 *Law and Social Inquiry* 175 at 179: "Individuals can no more be separated or detached from their organisational affiliations than the organisation can be abstracted from its membership". See also Bottomley (1997) 19 *Sydney Law Review* 277 at 288. For a study of the way in which association means sacrificing selfish "ends" see S. Leader, *Freedom of Association* (Yale University, 1992), especially ch. 7.

[12] Leader, n. 11 above, 41.

[13] *Ibid.*

[14] G. Mark, "The Personification of the Business Corporation in American Law" (1987) 45 *University of Chicago Law Rev.* 1441 at 1470.

[15] *Company Law: Theory, Structure and Operation* (Oxford, OUP, 1997), 41. Gower disagrees: "it is clear that without the legislative intervention, limited liability could never have been achieved in a satisfactory and clear-cut fashion, and that it was this intervention which finally established companies as the major instrument in economic development. Of this the immediate and startling increase in promotions is sufficient proof": Gower, Company Law (6th edn. by Paul Davies, Sweet and Maxwell, London, 1997).

[16] S.J. Stoljar, *Groups and Entities: An Enquiry into Corporate Theory* (Canberra, ANU Press, 1973), 40 and G. Teubner, "Enterprise Corporatism: New Industrial Policy and the 'Essence of the Legal Person' " (1988) 36 *American Jnl. of Comparative Law* 130.

[17] But Bottomley sees it as a way to "submerge the tension that exists in making choices between individual and group values": see n. 3 above, 211.

[18] Cheffins, n. 15 above, 6.

system,[19] neo-classical economists including Coase have analysed companies[20] as a method of reducing the costs of a complex market consisting of a series of bargains among parties.[21] Transaction costs are reduced by the organisational design of the company.[22]

The theories rest on notions of rationality, efficiency and information. The economists posit that a person acting rationally will enter into a bargain which will be to his benefit. In a sale transaction both parties acting rationally will benefit themselves, and therefore society.[23] However, notions of the measurement of efficiency vary. Pareto efficiency requires that someone gains and no-one loses. However, the Kaldor-Hicks test accepts as efficient "a policy which results in sufficient benefits for those who gain such that *potentially* they can compensate fully all the losers and still remain better off".[24]

The explanation of what is "rational" also varies widely, from simple wealth maximisation to complex motives including altruism leading to the somewhat exasperated criticism that "[f]rom the point of view of understanding motivation in terms of rational self interest . . . if we expand backward with self-interest as an explanation until it absorbs everything, including altruism, then it signifies nothing—it lacks explanatory specificity or power".[25]

The third pillar for the economic analysis is information flows. The rational actor is seen as making rational choices with full and perfect information at his command.

Rational actors utilising perfect information will produce maximum allocative efficiency by making choices which exploit competition in the market. However, allocative efficiency will not occur unless all the costs incurred in the transaction are internalised. Thus, if a company pollutes a river, causing damage to other river users but incurring no penalty, the goods produced by that company will be underpriced. That this type of behaviour causes real problems for those who would impose minimal regulation and rely instead on market behaviour and private law instruments is evident.

---

[19] After A. Smith, *The Wealth of Nations* (London, Everyman, 1982).

[20] And firms which are not always companies.

[21] Alice Belcher, "The Boundaries of the Firm: The Theories of Coase, Knight and Weitzman" (1997) 17 *Legal Studies* 22.

[22] O. E. Williamson, "Contract Analysis: The Transaction Cost Approach" in P. Burrows and C. G. Velanovski (eds.), *The Economic Approach to Law* (Butterworths, London, 1981); E. Williamson, "Transaction-Cost Economics: The Governance of Contractual Relations" 21 *Journal of Law and Society* 168.

[23] Ogus gives the following example: "Bill agrees to sell a car to Ben for 5,000 pounds. In normal circumstances it is appropriate to infer that Bill values the car at less than 5,000 pounds (say 4,500) and Ben values it at more than 5,000 (say 5,500). If the contract is performed, both parties will gain 500 pounds and therefore there is a gain to society—the car has moved to a more valuable use in the hands of Ben . . . this is said to be an allocatively 'efficient' consequence". See A. Ogus, *Regulation: Legal Form and Economic Theory* (Oxford, Clarendon Press, 1994).

[24] Explanation given by Ogus, see n. 23 above, 24, who immediately points out that there is no requirement for the gainers to compensate the losers; see below in the criticism section.

[25] I. Ayres and J. Braithwaite, *Responsive Regulation* (Oxford, OUP, 1992), 23.

Applying market economics to company law involves seeing the company not as a free-standing institution but as a network of bargains between all involved, all acting rationally with perfect information. The utility of company law is to prevent the high costs of reaching individual bargains with every involved person. Company law thus reduces transaction costs.

CRITICISM OF CONTRACTUAL THEORIES

The economic contractualist attracts criticism both at the level of the conception of companies and company law and on the basis of the perceived political results of the analysis. The former are criticisms which go to the utility and accuracy of the analysis itself. Further problems may arise when the economists view the company in action and designate the interaction between the company and the state (the justifications for regulation) and the relationships between individuals concerned with the working of the corporate constitution.

On the first level we have seen that the conception of rationality is variously perceived, and that the further away from pure wealth maximisation as motivation it is the less valuable it is as an analytical tool. Further, rationality is bound up with the amount of information possessed by the rational actor. Accepting that "perfect information" is a myth, most economists accept the notion of "bounded rationality" or "satisficing". Bounded rationality accepts that the capacity of individuals to "receive, store and process information is limited".[26] Satisficing is "searching until the most satisfactory solution is found from among the limited perceived alternatives".[27] Thus, the "pure" concept of rationality suffers from the twin problems of simplistic motivation and a defect in the theory of perfect information.

THE COMMUNITAIRE THEORIES

The second theory to consider is the communitaire theory, which sees the grant of company status not only as a concession by the state but as creating an instrument for the state to utilise. This theory starts from a position diametrically opposed to the individualist contractual theories. This model was familiar in the former communist countries and in Fascist Italy.[28] "The standard of a corporation's usefulness is not whether it creates individual wealth but whether it helps society gain a greater sense of the meaning of community by honouring individual dignity and promoting overall welfare."[29] It has two consequences. The

[26] Ogus, see n. 23 above, 41.

[27] *Ibid.*

[28] P. J. Williamson, *Corporatism in Perspective: An Introductory Guide to Corporatist Theory* (Sage, London, 1909).

[29] D. Sullivan and D. Conlon, n. 8 above, and see Jackson and Carter, "Organizational Chiaroscuro: Throwing Light on the Concept of Corporate Governance" (1995) 48 *Human Relations* 875.

company has no strong commercial identity, as it has become a political tool with diffused goals. Although the diffused goals will give it considerable social responsibility,[30] it will remove its commercial focus. The state merely uses the corporate tool to further its ends. The emphasis is on identification of the aims of the company with those of society. As explained below, this is in contrast to the concession approach which emphasises the right of the state to ensure that a corporation is properly run according to its standards of fairness and democracy.

Those who argue that a company should have a social conscience[31] are thus running the risk, discussed at length by Dodd and Berle in the 1930s, that once profit maximisation by stockholders has ceased to be the narrow focus of the company businessmen will not know what interests to serve.[32] However, a modern version of this theory, known as "liberal corporatism", may have value in determining governance structures. The basis of this theory is still a blurring of the line between the public role of the state and private market domains, but emphasis is placed on creating a role within corporate governance for special interest groups within society which represent particular sectors (for example labour represented by Trade Unions). This model relies on dialogue between different interest groups, whereas some theorists lay emphasis on collective goals. Thus Stokes views the company through corporatist lenses as "an organic body which unifies the interests of the participants into a harmonious and common purpose under the direction of its leaders".[33] The theory seems to point in two directions simultaneously,[34] both putting forward a role for companies which emphasises their importance in fulfilling aspirational norms of the state and stresses the importance of good balancing between interest groups as the secret of internal regulation. This is an apparent conflict if viewed from the perspective of individualist contractarians as the public role is anathema to those theorists. However, the nature of the public role of companies needs to be carefully scrutinised, particularly in view of the identification of this group of theories with authoritarian regimes.

---

[30] As K. Wedderburn notes in The Social Responsibility of Companies (1985) Melbourne *ULR* 4, 14–15): "It may be said that this theory adopts a 'strong' fiction stance, although this may have been modified by recent developments. A limited 'social' expenditure may be justified by profit maximisation.: "The "social" expenditure so explained becomes no more than "seed corn", sown in the surrounding ground with a long-term view of profit, scattered because; "The best place to do business is in a happy, healthy community". He dismisses this view as giving support only to a very narrow range of corporate social activity. So narrow a view, he believes cannot explain the full picture but a way to conceptualise the ambit of social responsibility is not readily forthcoming.

[31] Including G. Teubner: see (1988) 36 *American Journal of Comparative Law* 130 at 131.

[32] A. Berle, Corporate Powers as Powers in Trust (1931) 44 *Harv LR* 1049; E. Dodd, For whom are Corporate Managers Trustees (1932) 45 *Harv LR* 1145.

[33] M. Stokes, "Company Law and Legal Theory" in W. Twining (ed.), *Legal Theory and Common Law* (Oxford, Blackwell, 1986), 155, 177.

[34] Though Bottomley sees no conflict: n. 3 above, 220–2.

Concession theory[35] in its simplest form views the existence and operation of the company as a concession by the state which grants the ability to trade using the corporate tool,[36] particularly where it operates with limited liability.[37] The contrast between this theory and communitarian notions is that concession theorists accept only that the state has a role to play in ensuring that corporate governance structures are fair and democratic. They would oppose the notion that the company should realign its aims to reflect social aspirations of the state. Hobbes[38] classified as "bodies politic" those organisations which have been granted corporate personality by "writ or letters from the sovereign". Private bodies are "those which are constituted by subjects among themselves". Now, clearly, we have just been examining the company's claim to figure among private bodies. What is to be said for the contrary claim that it is a Body politic? And what follows such a classification? Clearly the historic charter companies fell squarely into the category of companies that owed their powers and privileges to delegation by the Crown. Thus the Charter of the Newfoundland Company states[39]:

> "thinking it a matter and action well becoming a Christian King to make true use of that which God from the beginning created for mankind . . . therefore do of our special grace certain knowledge and mere motion . . . give grant and confirm by these presents unto [various persons] their heirs and assigns, and to such and so many as they do or shall hereafter admit to be joined with them in form hereafter. . . . That they shall be one body or communalty perpetual, and shall have perpetual succession, and one common seal to serve for the said body. . . . And that they and their successors shall be likewise enabled . . . to plead and be impleaded before any of our Judges or Justices in any of our Courts and in any actions or suits whatsoever."

This Charter was signed by King James and is a clear delegation of not only state right but delegation by virtue of divine right.[40] The idea of a state concession is closely linked to the concept of the company as a legal fiction. The attributes granted to the Newfoundland Charter Company in particular perpetual succession and the ability to be sued as a body, flow from state delegated powers.[41] The

---

[35] For a good analysis see *ibid.*, 207 ff.

[36] See Mark, "The Personification of the Business Corporation in American Law" (1987) *U of Chicago Law Rev.* 1441, examining the *Dartmouth College* decision (*Dartmouth College v. Woodward*, 17 US 518 (1819)).

[37] Bratton identifies "A strong version [which] attributes the corporation's very existence to state sponsorship. A weaker version sets up state permission as a regulatory prerequisite to doing business": W. Bratton Jr., "The New Economic Theory of the Firm: Critical Perspectives from History" (1989) 41 *Stanford L Rev.* 1471, 1475.

[38] Thomas Hobbes, *Leviathan* (Blackwell, Oxford, 1960), ch. 22, 146.

[39] Taken from H. Rajak, *Sourcebook of Company Law* (2nd edn., Jordans, 1995), 20.

[40] Clearly the very strongest version of the concessionary theory.

[41] M. Wolff, "On the Nature of Legal Persons" (1938) 54 *LQR* 494.

personality of the company is a fiction.[42] State regulation to interfere with the company is clearly easily legitimised[43] and the *ultra vires* doctrine is necessary since the body which has delegated powers may not go beyond those powers. Some of the immense confusion which has arisen concerning the *ultra vires* doctrine may thus be seen as flowing from a confusion of its original concession basis and the later justification that it served as a protection for the group of contractors which were involved in the commercial enterprise.

State concession as a source of regulatory justification was encapsulated in *Re Rolus Properties Ltd & Another*[44]:

> "The privilege of limited liability is a valuable incentive to encourage entrepreneurs to take on risky ventures without inevitable personal total financial disaster. It is, however, a privilege which must be accorded upon terms and some of the most important terms that Parliament has imposed are that accounts be kept and returns made so that the world can, by referring to those, see what is happening. Thus, a total failure to keep statutory books and to make statutory returns is significant for the public at large and a matter which amounts to misconduct if not complied with and is a matter of which the court should take account in considering whether a man can properly be allowed to continue to operate as a director[45] of companies, or whether the public at large is to be protected against him on the grounds that he is unfit, not because he is fraudulent but because he is incompetent and unable to comply with the statutory obligations attached to limited liability. In my view that is a correct approach and the jurisdiction does extend and should be exercised in cases where a man has by his conduct revealed that he is wholly unable to comply with the obligations that go with the privilege of limited liability."

The 'constitutionalism' approach[46] may be seen as flowing from the acceptance that the state has a legitimate role to play in regulating corporate governance. Bottomley calls for a 'reconceptualisation of the corporate legal structure in political terms',[47] arguing for the importation of values and ideas in public political life which "should be considered in the legal regulation of corporate governance".[48] Thus corporate constitutionalism has 'three key features: the idea of *dual decision making,* which recognises the different roles of the board of directors and the general meeting of shareholders in corporate life; the idea of *deliberative decision making,* which seeks to ensure that corporate decisions are made on the basis of an open and genuine consideration of all relevant issues; and the idea of a *separation of powers,* which aims to make corporate decision making power diffuse and accountable."[49]

---

[42] The theory relied on the idea that only human beings can be persons and thus naturally the subjects of rights: *ibid.*, 496.

[43] Wolff points out that it was used to confiscate Church property during the French revolution: *ibid.*, 508.

[44] (1988) 4 BCC 446, 447.

[45] The case concerned disqualification under the Company Directors (Disqualification) Act 1986.

[46] P. Bottomley, (1977) 19 *Sydney Law Review* 277.

[47] *Ibid.*, 278.

[48] *Ibid.*

[49] *Ibid.*, 278–9.

CONSEQUENCES OF THEORIES FOR JUSTIFICATIONS FOR REGULATION: FOUNDATIONAL AND OPERATIONAL THEORIES

Legal and economic contractualism have the effect of putting the corporation into the sphere of private law, of viewing the legitimation of the power it wields as coming from the entrepreneurial activities of the members and lessening the state's justification for regulatory interference.[50] Communitaire theories lead to an acceptance of state regulation to achieve public interest goals; concession theorists accept that the state has a legitimate role to play in setting the standards of corporate governance.[51] However, it may be argued that the rejection of public interest goals by contractualist theories is only a logical consequence if no distinction is made between *foundational* theories and *operational* theories of corporate existence. Both of the contractual theories rely on the concept of the bargain makers or contractors being of paramount importance, because they are the founders of the company. However, it is a central concept of company law that, once formed, a company becomes a separate personality. This legal technicality sometimes masks the practical reality which is that, in nearly all companies, after formation, parties other than the founders are involved. Most companies operate with employees, creditors, customers, etc. One key difficulty with both contractual approaches is the explanation of the rights and duties which arise when the constitution of the company is up and running. Legal contractualism struggles to explain the failure to enforce the contract in the articles and the regulation of the power of majorities over minorities. Economic contractualism has an exactly similar problem. It relies on an explanation of incomplete contracts. "Only in a world where some contracts contingent on future observable variables are costly (or impossible) to write ex-ante, is there room for governance ex-post".[52] Neither accepts the legitimacy of state regulation of corporate constitutional power. Most obviously the tension between foundational and operational theories and the consequent tension between contractualism and public interest regulation doctrine is reflected in section 14 of the Companies Act 1985,[53] which reads: "[s]ubject to the provisions of this Act, the memorandum and articles, when registered, bind the company and its members to the same extent as if they respectively had been signed and sealed by each member, and contained covenants on the part of each member to observe all the provisions of the memorandum and articles". Although

---

[50] *Ibid.*, 209.

[51] "Companies are political institutions not simply because they are players in social power relations, but also because they themselves are systems in which power and authority, rights and obligations, duties and expectations, benefits and disadvantages, are allocated and exercised, whether actively or passively, collectively or individually. Each company is a body politic, a governance system":Bottomley, n. 46 above, 291.

[52] Zingales, *The New Palgrave Dictionary of Economics and Law* (Basingstoke, Macmillan, 1998).

[53] And its equivalent, s.180(1) of the Corporations Law in Australia: Bottomley, n. 46 above, 281.

this expresses the contractual view well,[54] the difficulties which the court has had in its interpretation also flag the limits of the doctrine,[55] for example the "contract" is unenforceable if the plaintiff is suing in a capacity other than as shareholder.[56] The courts have categorised those given a "special" right by the articles as "outsiders" in order to exclude them from the right to enforce the section 14 contract.[57] *Eley* v. *Positive Government Security Life Assurance Co Ltd*[58] is a case which illustrates the court's dilemma well. In that case article 118 of the company's articles provided for Eley's indefinite employment by the company. The article provided that he could be removed only for misconduct. Eley had drafted the articles. Despite the fact that Eley was a shareholder and therefore a "party to the contract in the articles", the court refused to allow him to enforce the article. It can be suggested that this refusal can best be explained by understanding that the vision of the articles as a contract is false and that it is in fact a constitutional document which requires some public law principles to be applied for its proper interpretation.[59] These might well include preventing a solicitor from entrenching his employment position by using his privileged position as draughtsman of the constitution.

A further demonstration of the strain encountered by excessive reliance on foundational theories rests on the way in which the courts have sought to use the contract to designate insiders and outsiders in order to determine whether or not a right under the articles can be enforced.[60] As we have seen above, the courts' treatment of this issue gives powerful force to the argument that the company has a constitution rather than a contract, but there is a further dimension to this difficulty in that the focus on the contract between members and the company has the inevitable effect of excluding other participants in the economic enterprise from the governance structure, thus giving us a limited model serving the shareholders alone and emphasising the tendency of the foundational theories to limit the "interests of the company" to the interests of those contractors[61] and their free enterprise rights.[62]

---

[54] See also *Automatic Self-Cleansing Filter Syndicate Co* v. *Cunninghame* [1906] 2 Ch. 34.

[55] For a fuller discussion see J. Dine in I. Patfield (ed.), *Perspectives on Company Law* (Kluwer, 1995); and see Bottomley n. 46 above, 281.

[56] *Eley* v. *Positive Life Assurance* (1876) 1 Ex.D 88 (CA); see discussion below.

[57] See also *Hickman* v. *Kent or Romney Marsh Sheepbreeders' Association* [1915] 1 Ch. 881; *Beattie* v. *Beattie Ltd* [1938] Ch. 708; but management rights appear to have been enforced in *Quin & Axtens* v. *Salmon* [1909] AC 442; *Pulbrook* v. *Richmond Consolidated Mining Co* (1878) 9 Ch. D 610; and *Imperial Hydropathic Hotel Co, Blackpool* v. *Hampson* (1882) 23 Ch. D 1.

[58] (1876) 1 Ex.D 88 (CA).

[59] *Contra* see K.W. Wedderburn [1957] *CLJ* 194, arguing that a shareholder may enforce *any* right even if by chance they stand to gain in an "outsider" capacity; but see Goldberg (1972) 35 *MLR* 362 and Prentice [1980] 1 *Co. Law* 179, arguing along constitutional lines.

[60] See *Hickman* v. *Kent or Romney Marsh Sheepbreeders' Association* [1915] 1 Ch. 881, *Eley* v. *Positive Life Assurance* (1876) 1 Ex.D 88 (CA); *Rayfield* v. *Hands* [1960] Ch. 1; Gower, n. 15 above, 119.

[61] P. Bottomley, "From Contractualism to Constitutionalism: A Framework for Corporate Governance" (1997) 19 *Sydney Law Review* 278 at 287: "[economic] contractualism promises a framework that either eschews or plays down consideration of the company as an analytical construct, focusing instead on the roles of managers and shareholders."

[62] And the ownership of the founders. It is criticised by Wolff, n. 41 above, 497, citing the

Because legal contractual notions are "strained" in explaining the effects of this "contract", Bottomley suggests two explanations.[63] The first is the historical development of unincorporated joint stock companies from an amalgam of partnership and trust concepts, the second "allows us to define the boundaries of the company by circumscribing the rights of membership".[64] The first explanation he dismisses as conservative, requiring us to accept that time has stood still since the mid-nineteenth century. While this is a valid criticism, there is more. It can be seen that the climate for companies changed radically between the time when the state conceded both trading and political powers to trading organisations[65] to the situation where several persons could come together and, providing the formalities were in order, were entitled to form their own company. It is therefore not surprising that the focus for the courts and analysts changed from the paramountcy of public interest concepts such as *ultra vires* to ideas of bargains and contracts between individuals.

Bottomley's second explanation is a pragmatic acceptance of the fact that, if shareholder's interests are not the only interests to be served, we have to work much harder to define the interests of the company. This is a real difficulty[66] but is a conceptual laziness which has caused considerable confusion. Both explanations demonstrate the shortcomings of allowing foundational theories to dictate our view of how companies work. However, this difficulty can be lessened by firmly separating the communitarian approach which seeks to subvert the commercial aims of the company by realigning its purpose with social aspirations of the state, from the concession theorists who accept only that the state has a significant role to play in the proper equitable and democratic governance of companies. The latter theories accept that the state should play a significant role in the governance of modern companies, the essence of which is their

transfer of the property of 5 promoters to a company. "If we are to assume . . . that the five members still remain owners of the estate, we are obliged to add the proviso: But they are treated in every respect as if they were no longer owners and as if a new, a sixth, person had become the owner." He accepts that it has some justification where "economic" ownership is the issue rather than "juristic" ownership but feels that even here it is "not completely sound; not all the members of a corporation are (from the economic standpoint) masters of the undertaking and owners of the corporation's property. If one member has 95% of all the shares, he alone determines the fate of the enterprise." Stokes argues that the contractual model legitimises the power of the board of directors because they are the appointees of the owners: "Thus, by invoking the idea of the freedom of a property owner to make any contract with respect to his property the power accorded to corporate managers appears legitimate, being the outcome of ordinary principles of freedom of contract": Stokes, n. 33 above, 162.

[63] N. 61 above, 282.

[64] *Ibid.*, 283.

[65] See the above discussion of concession theory.

[66] S. Deakin and A. Hughes in "Enterprise and Community: New Directions in Corporate Governance", in Deakin and Hughes (eds.), *Comparative Corporate Governance: An Interdisciplinary Agenda* (Oxford, Blackwell 1997), 4, argue that "A major difficulty with stakeholder theory, at least as it has been applied in Britain, is that the term 'stakeholding' has been used to refer to a very wide range of interests which are loosely related at best. . . . If the category of stakeholding interests is widened to include those of all potential consumers of the company's products, for example, or to refer to the *general* interest of society in the sustainability of the environment, there is a danger that the idea of stakeholding will cease to be relevant.

limited liability. Trading with limited liability removes our modern companies to a momentous distance from unincorporated joint stock companies.

The change of focus occurred with the advent of incorporation by registration in 1844[67] and the grant of limited liability in 1855.[68] Despite the possibility that some form of limited liability could have been achieved by private law devices,[69] "it is clear that without the legislative intervention, limited liability could never have been achieved in a satisfactory and clear cut fashion, and it was this intervention which finally established companies as the major instrument in economic development. Of this the immediate and startling increase in promotions is sufficient proof".[70]

One interesting facet of the neo-classical economic models is the lowly place occupied by the doctrine of limited liability. It is seen as an incentive to investment,[71] but the role of the state in providing this potentially "market rigging" mechanism is generally played down,[72] and the argument is made that, if limited liability were not provided by the state as an available attribute of a company, participants would incorporate it into individual bargaining arrangements.[73] The importance of the enabling legislation is not underestimated by Gower,[74] and it seems to have the element of a self-serving argument to say that a mechanism which made a fundamental alteration to the structure of the market was merely a mechanism for removing transaction costs and recreating a more perfect market.[75]

The reluctance to accept a significant state role in the foundation and operation of companies, coupled with the perception that the free market is the optimal wealth creation system, leads to the conceptualisation of the state's role as solely an "enabling" one. As far as possible the market should be left to its own devices and regulation should only "correct market failure".[76] The contrary

---

[67]   Joint Stock Companies Act 1844.

[68]   Limited Liability Act 1855.

[69]   F. Maitland, *Trust and Corporation, in Collected Papers*, H. Fischer (ed.), iii (Cambridge, Cambridge U. Press, 1911) 321, 392.

[70]   Gower, n. 15 above, 46 citing Shannon [1931–2] II *Econ. Hist.* 290. Figures given by Shannon indicate that 956 companies were registered between 1844 and 1856. In the following 6 years, 2,479 were registered. In 1864 their paid-up capital was £31 million.

[71]   R. Posner, *Economic Analysis of Law* (4th edn., Little Brown & Co, Boston, Mass., 1992), 392.

[72]   See F. Easterbrook and D. Fischel, "Limited Liability and the Corporation" (1985) 52 *U of Chicago L Rev.* 89, sidestepping the argument by A. Manne in "Our Two Corporation Systems: Law and Economics" (1967) 53 *Va. L Rev.* 259 that the modern public corporation with many small investors could not exist without limited liability by arguing that limited liability shifts responsibility to creditors. This may be true but does not explain away the need to raise capital from shareholders.

[73]   See Cheffins, n. 15 above, 41 and 502, but apparently differing at 250, pointing out the importance of the 19th century enabling legislation See also Gower, n. 15 above, chs. 2 and 3.

[74]   See n. 70 above.

[75]   But for a contrary argument see Maitland, "Trusts and Corporations", arguing that limited liability would have come about by contract if not introduced by law. See also Farrah, *Company Law* (3rd edn., London, Butterworths, 1991), 21.

[76]   A further legitimate criticism of the economic view of the company in action is that it may foster a short-term view of the company's best course of action. It relies on the rationality of the actors involved in the company at any one time. The logical result of this is to exclude considerations of

view that power has been delegated or conceded by the state invites the imposition of public interest norms on the operation of companies.[77]

It is suggested that if we move away from simple foundational theories and into the sphere of examining the company as a living organism it can be viewed as neither wholly public nor private, but rather partly a creature of state creation with the state granting concessions such as limited liability and perpetual succession and partly as a private instrument of economic free enterprise. It follows that both public and private regulatory constraints should apply.

A good example of the convergence of economic theory and the concept of imposition of public interest norms in the governance structure can be seen in Lindley MR's statement in *Allen* v. *Gold Reefs of West Africa Ltd*.[78] In construing the section of the Companies Act which concerned the power of a company to alter its articles, he said:

> "the company is empowered by the statute to alter the regulations contained in its articles from time to time by special resolutions [s50]; and any regulation or article purporting to deprive the company of this power is invalid on the ground that it is contrary to the statute . . . Wide, however, as the language of s50 is, the power conferred by it must, like all other powers, be subject to those general principles of law and equity which are applicable to all powers conferred on majorities and enabling them to bind minorities. . . . These conditions are always implied, and are seldom, if ever, expressed."

The contractualist implied term analysis gains support from the latter phrase, but the passage could equally be read as the imposition of public interest general principles to the constitution of the company. The emphasis laid by the economists on the freedom of the *parties* to contract diverts attention from the fact that general principles of justice are being imposed by the courts. If the implied term analysis is to hold water it must be expanded to include the legitimate expectations of parties living in a state which imposes principles other than market forces to govern relationships even in the market-place. This brings back into play public interest justifications for regulation of corporate governance

"future generations". This point is well made by Ogus in an environmental context, but in the context of corporate governance the point is stronger as the actors may have only an ephemeral contact with the company. In effect, this is one facet of the acknowledged problem of "negative externalities". This is the term used to indicate transaction costs which may be unfairly allocated by a private bargaining system. This may be because small losses incurred by individual right-holders will not be corrected so as to incur the expense of court proceedings, for a small amount will not be worth while. Ogus describes this as "market failure" accompanied by "private law failure" and as a justification for public interest regulation.

[77] The enabling viewpoint was well put by Prof. Ballantine, who drafted new legislation for California in the 1930s. He wrote: "The primary purpose of corporation law is not regulatory. They are enabling Acts, to authorise businessmen to organise and operate their business, large or small, with the advantage of the corporate mechanism. They are drawn with a view to facilitate efficient management of business and adjustment to the needs of change."

[78] [1900] 1 Ch. 656. For an analysis which leads to the conclusion that the public and private interests are blurred see Jennifer Hill in R. Grantham and C. Rickett (eds.), *Corporate Personality in the 20th Century* (Oxford, Hart Publishing, 1998). She does not attribute the blurring to the concession theory which she regards as "defunct" (189).

which run counter to the view that regulation can only be justified to correct imperfect markets.

THE PUBLIC INTEREST: THE RIGHT TO ENSURE THAT A COMPANY IS PROPERLY RUN

If it can therefore be accepted that a state has the right to impose on companies some regulations reflecting public interest norms, the task is to understand what the aims of these regulations will be. Here it is suggested that the first step in understanding the role of state regulation is to understand the role of shareholders within a company. Leader[79] has shown that a shareholder has two distinct rights as a result of share ownership. The first is a *personal* right which entitles the shareholder to ensure that the value of the share is preserved so far as possible, using the relevant constitutional mechanisms such as the right to vote and the personal action under section 14 to achieve this. The second right is a *derivative* right which is the right to see that the company is properly run. This right is enforced via the derivative action and its overlap with section 459.[80] Of course derivative rights are derived from the company's own right to be managed in its own interests so that the shareholders' right to see that the company is run is a right to see that the company's interests are served. The enquiry into the ambit of *derivative* rights is a matter for determining what standards of morals and ethics society believes it is right to impose on corporate governance. Note that the warnings concerning diffused goals engendered by communitarian models have no resonance here as the public interest is in ensuring proper governance of a company so that it may best pursue its commercial aims rather than a re-alignment of those aims to serve state purposes. The focus here is on standards of *constitutional conduct or governance*. Thus the aim is to ensure that the company is run in a way that democratically and equitably takes account of those constituencies most nearly connected with its commercial function, not to impose general aims of social engineering as the communautaire approach would seek to do. The approach thus avoids imposing aims which may in any event be contradictory, such as an aim to provide the quickest possible road transport distribution system while at the same time preserving the environment. The company should not be viewed as an instrument of social policy, the separate personality of the company should continue to be afforded recognition and *corporate governance* should remain focused on the interests of the corporation, recognising that these interests diverge both from the interests of society and the interests of shareholders.

---

[79] "Private Property and Corporate Governance" Defining the Issues", in F. Patfield, n. 55 above.
[80] It is interesting to note that the nearly complete overlap was confirmed by the 1989 amendment of s.459 which enabled an action to be brought where all the shareholders were unfairly prejudiced, there was no need to show personal or class special damage.

WHO ARE THE GUARDIANS OF THE PUBLIC INTEREST?

It is arguable that excessive reliance on the contractual theories has left us with sharcholders as the only guardians of the public interest in corporate governance. An example illustrates this. Section 309(1) of the Companies Act 1985 provides that "the matters to which the directors of a company are to have regard in the performance of their functions include the interests of the company's employees in general, as well as the interests of its members". But the only possible mechanism for enforcing this duty to take account of such interests is the shareholders whose interests may be diametrically opposed to those of employees in certain circumstances.[81] The logic of the situation appears to be not only that the shareholders have a *right* to see that the company is properly run in its own interests, but that society has delegated a *duty* to them to achieve this.

The danger of adopting a model of company which relies on sharcholder control is that in many jurisdictions it has been less than useful in controlling management. The whole purpose of providing a company with separate personality is to enable a separation of ownership and control. This enables the directors to use their energies for the benefit of the company, not act as agents of the ownership pressure group. However, the separation has become extreme in many cases so that shareholders are no longer an effective governance mechanism, even where guardianship of their *own* interests is the issue. Effectiveness in guardianship of the *company's interest* is manifestly even more unlikely. Ineffectiveness has occurred for many well-known reasons.[82] In large companies small investors are apathetic, caring only for the return on investment. Institutional investors see their primary duty to their investors as best served by leaving a company where management difficulties are experienced, rather that becoming involved. Further, the supply of information is in the hands of management, as may be a significant quantity of "active" shares and proxies. To rely on shareholders as a governance mechanism is therefore to allow directors almost complete discretion, subject to the unpredictable whims of the market for corporate control. For that reason among others, some jurisdictions have adopted a governance mechanism which relies on a two-tier management structure, allowing a supervisory board a greater or lesser degree of control over the executive directors.

---

[81] It is interesting that the Law Society calls for 'clear expression of the purposes behind particular provisions of this type": Memorandum No 360, "Modern Company Law for a Competitive Economy", para. 2.4.

[82] For a full analysis see J. Parkinson, n. 4 above, and for an extensive analysis of the changing role of shareholders see Jennifer Hill "Changes in the role of the shareholder", in Grantham and Rickett (eds.), n. 78 above.

THE MOVE TO CONSTITUENCY/MULTIFIDUCIARY MODELS MAKES THINGS WORSE

Where, as in the UK and USA, single boards are still the rule it may be argued that the task of shareholders is becoming increasingly difficult as courts take on board the argument that there is not absolute congruence between the interests of shareholders and the interests of the company.[83] In attempting to guard the interests of the company the shareholders must thus attempt to second-guess the perspectives of other (as yet undefined) constituencies. The rejection of contractualism and the acceptance of the distinction between the interests of the shareholders and the interests of the company can be traced in both jurisdictions. Sullivan and Conlon[84] note that the high point of contractualism came with the court's endorsement of the takeover market as a corporate governance mechanism: "the discipline of capital markets pushed executives to maximise shareholder wealth so as not to attract the attention of unsolicited suitors".[85] The vote of shareholders to accept or reject a takeover bid was seen as the ultimate arbiter not only of the shareholders' personal right to maximise the price of their shares but of the company's interest. However "the relaxation of the fiduciary strictures inspired a variety of nefarious behaviours. Managers and raiders alike subverted shareholder democracy through such esoteric means as supervoting stock, poison pills, classified boards, lock-ups, leg-ups, creeping takeovers, bear hugs, white knights, white squires, black knights, preclusive defences, selective stock buyouts, stock options, greenmail, crown jewel sales, auctions and self-tenders".[86] Clearly the shareholders were not very effective in safeguarding even their own interests. However, in the move by the Delaware courts away from contractualism, Sullivan and Conlon detect a move towards a "multifiduciary" model of company. This is described by reference to the demise of the shareholder as a single fiduciary: "[p]roponents reason that the notion of a single fiduciary in the form of the shareholder is misleading and anachronistic and often destructive. Rather, the multifiduciary model . . . extends fiduciary duty to constituencies such as lenders, suppliers, employees,

---

[83] *Pender* v. *Lushington* (1877) 6 Ch.D 70 per Jessel MR: "In all cases of this kind, where men exercise their rights of property, they exercise their rights from some motive adequate or inadequate, and I have always considered the law to be that those who have rights of property are entitled to exercise them, whatever their motives might be for such exercise". Clear enough it would seem but strangely support is drawn in this view by the case of *Menier* v. *Hooper's Telegraph Works* (1874) LR 9Ch. 250, where Lord Justice Mellish observes: "I am of the opinion that, although it may be quite true that the shareholders of a company may vote as they please, and for the purpose of their own interests, yet the majority of shareholders cannot sell the assets of the company and keep the consideration." Why support was to be had for his proposition in a statement which set limitations on the selfish exercise of rights is unclear. For arguments rejecting the congruence see Dine, n. 55 above.

[84] "Crisis and Transition in Corporate Governance: The Role of The Chancery Court of Delaware", (1997) 31 *Law and Society Review* 713 at 732 ff.

[85] N. 8 above, 734.

[86] *Ibid.*

managers, consumers, bondholders *and* shareholders. As such, the multi-fiduciary model holds that the rights of the shareholders no longer supercede those of nonshareholders".[87] The move towards this model is perceives as pivotal to the decision in *Paramount Communications* v. *Time Inc*[88] where the Delaware Chancery Court held that Time's directors were able to decide to reject a takeover offer by Paramount even though it was an offer at a premium price. Chancellor Allen said:

> "corporation law does not operate on the theory that directors, in exercising their powers to manage the firm, are obligated to follow the wishes of a majority of shares. . . a board of directors, while always required to act in an informed manner, is not under any per se duty to maximise shareholder value in the short term, even in the context of a takeover."

The directors had successfully argued that their long-term plan for the company was a better strategy than a sale of the company to Paramount. An appeal to the Delaware Supreme Court was refused. "*Time* and its progeny hold that shareholder's rights are important but not supreme when management can enunciate a long term strategy that offers superior benefits to shareholders and 'the community of interests the corporation represents' ".[89]

A similar move from contractualism to a multifiduciary or constituency model can be detected in the UK. It is clear that the United Kingdom courts are moving away from the narrow contractual view of companies. A number of cases involve the extension of the "umbrella" of the company to cover interests other than the shareholders' interests.

The courts seem to be increasingly accepting that once the company is formed not only is it a creature separate from its members,[90] but that in exercising their voting rights members must take account of interests other than their own selfish concerns. This trend may be seen in four types of cases: (i) where increasing weight is given to the interests of creditors, (ii) where ratification of a decision by a majority is annulled by the court, (iii) where alteration of the articles of association by a special majority is declared invalid, and (iv) in decisions which have determined the balance of powers between the organs of the company.

(i) Creditors

In *Lonhro* v. *Shell Petroleum*[91] the interests of the creditors were acknowledged by Lord Diplock who said, "it is the duty of the board to consider . . . the best

[87] *Ibid.*, /16.

[88] 571 A 2d 1140 (1989), 571 A2d 1145(Del. 1990).

[89] Sullivan and Conlon, n. 8 above, 745, quote from the Opinion of Chancellor Allen in *Paramount Communications* v. *Time*, n. 88 above.

[90] *Salomon* v. *Salomon* [1897] AC 22; *Lee* v. *Lee's Air Farming* [1961] AC 12; *Macaura* v. *Northern Insurance Co* [1925] AC 619.

[91] [1980] 1 WLR 627.

interests of the company. These are not exclusively those of its shareholders but may include those of its creditors".[92] The Court of Appeal confirmed this view in *Liquidator of West Mercia Safetywear Ltd* v. *Dodd and Another*.[93] However, in that case the interests of the company were said to include the interests of the creditors because the company was insolvent at the time. In *Lonhro* insolvency was not an issue. Nor was insolvency an issue in *Winkworth* v. *Edward Baron*,[94] where Lord Templeman referred to a duty owed directly to creditors. In *Brady* v. *Brady*,[95] Nourse LJ regarded the interests of the company as synonymous with the interests of the creditors where the company was insolvent or "doubtfully solvent". In *Standard Chartered Bank* v. *Walker*[96] the wishes of creditors were held to be paramount and overrode the wishes of the majority of shareholders.

(ii) Ratification

Shareholders are not permitted to use their majority voting power in their own selfish interests to permit directors to act contrary to a duty owed to the company.[97] The courts have accepted that the majority of shareholders cannot prevail even when their decision is constitutionally correct. Some decisions of directors cannot be ratified even by 100 per cent of the shareholders.[98]

It may thus be argued that UK company law is moving towards a model of a company in which shareholders must take account of more than their own immediate interests when determining policy. There is increasing recognition of the company as an entity quite separate from its owners, which is not only evident from the overt recognition of other interests which must be taken account of when decisions are made by management but also by the inability of majorities to drive the company in whichever direction they wish. The point is reinforced by the attitude of the courts to the question of alteration of the articles of association.

(iii) Alteration of Articles

The courts have reserved the right to prevent any alteration of the articles of association of a company where the alteration is not "*bona fide* for the benefit

---

[92] At 634.

[93] [1988] BCLC 250.

[94] [1987] BCLC 193.

[95] [1988] BCLC 20.

[96] [1992] 1 WLR 561; and see J. Dine, "Shareholders Denied Voting Rights" [1992] *Insolvency Law and Practice* 150.

[97] *Prudential Assurance Co Ltd* v. *Newman Industries (No 2)* [1981] Ch. 257; *Alexander* v. *Automatic Telephone Co* [1900] 2 Ch. 56; *Estmanco (Kilner House) Ltd* v. *GLC* [1982] 1 WLR 2; and see further discussion of ratification below.

[98] *R.* v. *Gomez* [1992] 3 WLR 1067.

of the company". To prevent such an alteration means that the court will upset a resolution which has been passed by at least 75 per cent of the shareholders. While struggling greatly to define "the interests of the company" the court makes it plain that it cannot be equated with the selfish interests of even a very substantial majority of shareholders.[99]

(iv) Division of Powers

Further light is thrown on the separation of the identity of shareholder interests and company interests by the way in which the division of powers among company organs has evolved.

Historically it was accepted that the powers of directors derived from authority bestowed on them by the shareholders. This meant that powers so delegated could be retrieved and exercised by the company's shareholders voting in a general meeting. The modern view is that the directors' powers derive from the company itself, that some of the company's powers are devolved to the shareholders acting in general meeting; other powers are devolved directly to the management. This means that there is a division of powers. No longer can the general meeting interfere in the conduct of management.[100] The circle is complete when it is appreciated that the shareholders may interfere by altering the articles (but only "in the interests of the company" or by ratification (but the court may invalidate the ratification where there has been what Sealy suggests should properly be called a "fraud on the company").[101]

The vision of the company as separate from and involving interests apart from the selfish interests of its shareholders is gaining ground. The United Kingdom is beginning to see the company not as a contract made between owners for their own profit but as a commercial enterprise with purposes of its own which must be furthered by decisions taken with its interests in mind rather than the immediate and narrow property interests of its shareholders.

THE CRISIS IN CORPORATE GOVERNANCE

As Sullivan and Conlon have argued[102] this move from contract to constituency models has created a crisis in corporate governance. Shareholders, directors and the courts have lost the convenient yardstick of the majority decision of the

---

[99] See *Allen* v. *Gold Reefs of West Africa* [1900] 1 Ch. 656; *Dafen Tinplate* v. *Llanelly Steel Co Ltd* [1920] 2 Ch. 124; *Greenhalgh* v. *Arderne Cinemas* [1951] Ch. 286.

[100] *Automatic Self-Cleansing Filter Syndicate Co Ltd* v. *Cuninghame* [1906] 2 Ch. 34; *Quinn & Axtens* v. *Salmon* [1909] AC 442; *Breckland Group Holdings Ltd* v. *London and Suffolk Properties Ltd* [1989] BCLC 100.

[101] L. Sealy, *Cases and Materials in Company Law* (London, Butterworths, 5th edn.) 476.

[102] N. 8 above; note that the title is "Crisis and Transition in Corporate Governance Paradigms: The Role of the Chancery Court of Delaware".

shareholders. Shareholders are ineffective in safeguarding their own interests, how much less likely is it that they can effectively safeguard the public interest in proper governance. However, both legislation and codes seem to depend only on them as providing protection against poor or fraudulent management.[103] Some other system of regulation is clearly required.

Such a system would have two major aspects: a proper understanding of the nature of directors' duties and proper mechanisms for enforcing them. A proper understanding of directors' duties is increasingly necessary as a precursor to the identification of regulatory enforcement mechanisms. This is particularly true in the light of the identified modern tendency to include considerations other than the personal benefit of shareholders in the equation which identifies "the benefit of the company", a trend which will surely increase in the light of EU initiatives which seek to emphasise the partnership between managers and workers.[104] The duties of directors will expand in order to ensure that the proper mechanisms for consultation, provision of information and (if ever it happens) participation in the case of a European Company (SE). it seems arguable that failure properly to interpret the duties to employees through works councils would amount to a breach of fiduciary duty, either because it was contrary to section 309(1) of the Companies Act 1985 or in the light of *Bishopsgate Investment Management Ltd (in liquidation)* v. *Maxwell (No 2)*,[105] where failure to follow the correct stock transfer procedures led to a finding that the director was in breach of fiduciary duties. What is vital is to recognise the paramountcy of the duty of directors to act in the interests of the company and to acknowledge that this does not mean in the interests of shareholders. The consequence of this is that a shareholder vote to ratify a breach of director's duties only provides evidence rather than certainty that the actions were in the company's interest.[106] An excellent example of the current confusion can be found by examining the messages sent to directors over self-dealing. The present position is that section 310 reads:

> "(1) This section applies to any provision, whether contained in a company's articles or in any contract with the company or otherwise, for exempting any officer of the company or any person . . . employed by the company as auditor from, or indemnifying him against, any liability which by virtue of any rule of law would otherwise attach

---

[103] See the Cadbury emphasis on institutional shareholders as a control mechanism and the legislative penchant for demanding ever increasing disclosure, presumably with a view to the power of shareholders to remove directors, although there may also be an eye to public reaction, particularly where disclosure of salaries is required.

[104] Council Dir. 94/95/EC (European Works Councils). See B. Bercusson, *European Labour Law* (Butterworths, London, 1996), 248 ff. The Dir. now applies to the UK. The Collective Dismissals Dir. 75/129/EEC the proposals for a European Company Statute see J. Dine and P. Hughes, *EC Company Law* (Jordans, looseleaf).

[105] [1993] BCLC 814 where failure to follow procedures for stock transfers set out in accordance with procedures set out in the company's articles were held to be a breach of fiduciary duty, either because of the failure to follow the correct procedure or because that failure was evidence of a failure to act for the benefit of the company.

[106] For an expanded version of this argument see Dine, n. 55 above.

to him in respect of any negligence, default, breach of duty or breach of trust of which he may be guilty in relation to the company.

(2) Except as provided by the following subsection, any such provision is void."

The traditional view of the law is that directors of a company are under a fiduciary duty not to let their interests conflict with their duties.[107] The logic of the situation is therefore that any article which sought to permit "self-dealing" is void. However, for a number of years the Companies Acts have included in the model articles set out in Table A provisions which would permit "self-dealing" contracts in certain situations.[108]

The apparent conflict was judicially considered in *Movitex Ltd* v. *Bulfield*,[109] where Vinelott J held that the rule against self-dealing was a disability and not a fiduciary duty. It therefore fell outside the ambit of section 310. We have, then, reached a position where shareholders may define in advance situations where directors may put themselves in situations where they are in danger of breaching a fundamental duty and they may forgive them in retrospect (by ratification) if they put themselves in such a situation. However, section 310 and the restrictions on ratification make it plain that there is a duty which directors owe to the company which cannot be excluded by the articles, nor can a breach of it be forgiven after the event. The directors owe a fundamental duty to the company to act *bona fide* and in good faith, and this duty cannot be altered even by all the shareholders acting together.[110]

CONCLUSION: FILLING THE VACUUM WITH SELF-REGULATION

This author has argued elsewhere[111] that in the financial services sector the traditional external penal model of regulation has comprehensively failed. It should be and is being replaced by a model of regulation which looks to the regulated institution to design its own rules, leaving the regulator to assess the quality of those rules. In the commercial sector the difficulty is to design a regulator to oversee the whole sector and to ensure that the diversity of the sector is protected. This essay does not venture to construct a definitive model to replace shareholders as regulators, but suggests that an approach which could be pursued more vigorously exists in the growing interest in a movement in legal philosophy; '*la procéduralisation du droit*" led by the Centre de Philosophie du Droit at the Université Catholique de Louvain. In one form this approach involves the law stepping back from creating formal substantive norms and concentrating

---

[107] *Scottish Co-operative Society* v. *Meyer* [1959] AC 324.

[108] See now Art. 85 of Table A.

[109] [1988] BCLC 104.

[110] Thus, where sole shareholders and directors took money from a company this was theft, despite the consent of all the shareholders: *R.* v. *Phillipou* [1989] Crim. LR 559, affirmed in *R.* v. *Gomez* [1993] 3 WLR 1067.

[111] W.G. Hart, *Workshop Papers 1998* (Kluwer, forthcoming).

instead on providing the framework for decision making by ensuring that the best possible forum of interested parties can be convened to arrive at the eventual substantive norm. if applied more generally in approaches to regulation this approach should free regulators from the impossible task of formulating the best substantive rules and allow them instead to concentrate on providing the best possible decision making forum to achieve probity in the market place.

This approach has echoes in the recent outbreak of Codes including Cadbury,[112] Greenbury[113]and Hampel,[114] in that much of the thrust of the Cadbury, Greenbury and Hampel reports was to ensure that the proper *persons* were in the right positions within the company.[115] The enforcement approach which requires compliance or explanation of non-compliance has the effect of permitting diversity and encouraging flexibility. The Davignon report on the European Company Statute worker participation provisions[116] followed a similar approach, suggesting that the management and workforce should negotiate individual models of involvement in workplace decision-making, The proposals are characterised by a framework for negotiation between the company and employees.[117] The retreat from a compulsory minimum standard of worker involvement, together with the clear statements concerning the expected agenda and timetable for negotiations, sends a strong signal that the diversity of models of companies within Member States is recognised and acknowledged without a wholesale retreat from the previous position that the role of the employee is central to the commercial success of companies. This approach seeks to harmonise rules from a realistic understanding of diversity. The suggested legislation should provide only the timetable and agenda for negotiations. It is to be hoped that the UK takes the opportunity to fill the regulatory vacuum created by shareholder apathy using similar radical approaches.

---

[112] *The Report on the Financial Aspects of Corporate Governance* (London, Gee, 1992).

[113] *Directors' Remuneration: Report of a Study Group Chaired by Sir Richard Greenbury* (Gee, London, 1995).

[114] *Committee on Corporate Governance Final Report* (London, Gee, Jan. 1998).

[115] See the emphasis on the board composition (separation of CEO and chairman and non-executive directors (Hampel, *ibid.*, 2.2–2.5, following Cadbury), remuneration committees (Hampel 2.11, following Cadbury and Greenbury), the role of directors and composition and appointment of directors, Hampel 3.14 and 3.19).

[116] Final Report, May 1997, See Dine and Hughes, n. 104 above, ch. 3 and app. A3, 77.

[117] See Proposal for a Compromise on the proposal for a Council Dir. supplementing the European Company Statute with Regard to the Involvement of Employees: Dine and Hughes n. 104 above, A3–52.

Index